45.00

DISCARDED
Angus L. Macdonald Library

Ex Uno Plures

Ex Uno Plures

Federal-Provincial Relations in Canada, 1867–1896

GARTH STEVENSON

THE ANGUS L. MacDONALD LIBRARY
ST. FRANCIS XAVIER UNIVERSITY
ANTIGONISH, N. S.

McGill-Queen's University Press
Montreal & Kingston • London • Buffalo

JL
27
S7

© McGill-Queen's University Press 1993
ISBN 0-7735-0986-0

Legal deposit third quarter 1993
Bibliothèque nationale du Québec

Printed in Canada on acid-free paper

This book has been published with the help of a grant
from the Social Science Federation of Canada,
using funds provided by the Social Sciences and
Humanities Research Council of Canada.
Publication has also been supported by the Canada
Council through its block grant program.

Canadian Cataloguing in Publication Data

Stevenson, Garth, 1943–
     Ex uno plures: federal provincial relations in Canada,
     1867–1896
     Includes index.
     ISBN 0-7735-0986-0
     1. Federal government – Canada – History –
     19th century. 2. Federal-provincial relations –
     Canada – History – 19th century. 3. Canada – Politics
     and government – 1867–1896. I. Title.
     JL27.S719 1993   320.471   C93-090267-X

This book was typeset by Typo Litho composition inc.
in 10/12 Baskerville.

Contents

Tables

Preface

This book is in part at least a response to the crisis of Canadian federalism that has now lasted for three decades – ever since Quebec's Quiet Revolution in the 1960s – with no end in sight at the time of writing. Having read and written about and taught Canadian federalism for many years, it occurred to me some time ago that an analysis of the past might cast some light on the present and the future. My research for an earlier book on Canadian federalism, *Unfulfilled Union*, whetted my curiosity about the generation that followed the formation of the Canadian federal state. Over the next several years I read most of the Canadian histories and biographies dealing with that period, in both official languages, as well as the few scraps of information about nineteenth-century Canadian government that I could find in the political science literature. As the idea for this book was beginning to take shape I crossed paths with Daniel Elazar, whose own work has brilliantly illuminated the early years of intergovernmental relations in the United States. I discussed the project with him and he encouraged me to go ahead.

As I continued to read the secondary literature on the late nineteenth century I began to form several conclusions. Much of the literature was highly partisan, suggesting that the controversies of the nineteenth century still inspired strong emotions in the twentieth. The historical literature, while it cast light on many of the conflicts between the dominion and particular provinces, failed to consider in a satisfactory way the mutual impact of issues and institutions, or the ways in which conflicts were dealt with and resolved. As for the political science literature, it appeared so firmly committed to the notion that "real" federalism had emerged only after the passing of John A. Macdonald that it rarely bothered to explore intergovernmental relations prior to the Laurier era in any detail. For example, Donald V. Smiley's pioneering work, *The Canadian Political Nationality*, dismissed the whole period from 1867 to 1896 in six pages.

In the several years I have been working on this book, however, a new literature has begun to emerge on Confederation and its aftermath. Consciously inspired by the work of American scholars on the eighteenth-century origins of the United States, Canadianists like Janet Ajzenstat, Rod Preece, Paul Romney, Jennifer Smith, Peter J. Smith, Gordon Stewart, and Robert Vipond have begun to explore Canadian political thought in the nineteenth century and its influence on the design and operation of the federal constitution. Although it is fair to say that they have discovered no Canadian political thinker who deserves to rank with Hamilton, Jefferson, or Madison, their work has at least undermined the once fashionable belief that Canadians were as incapable of systematic political thought as the wildlife in our boreal forests.

The present work, however, has a somewhat different purpose from that of the scholars mentioned in the preceding paragraph, which explains why their work is cited only rarely in the pages that follow. Rather than political ideas, it concentrates on political practices and especially on political disputes, most of which, although not all, dealt with mundane questions of money, land, patronage, or electoral advantage. In doing so it complements, rather than challenges or competes with, the work of scholars more concerned with political thought and less with political practice. Both perspectives, I would argue, are needed to provide a complete view of Canadian political and constitutional development in the age of John A. Macdonald.

The essential raw materials for this study were the official government records of the time and the correspondence and other papers of influential political actors, particularly those who held the offices of minister of justice, prime minister, or governor general. The National Archives of Canada contains an impressive storehouse of such material and, like many other scholars, I am indebted to the capable and helpful staff of the archives for their invaluable assistance in tracking it down. To a lesser extent I also used the facilities of the archives of Queen's University, the Public Archives of Nova Scotia, and the Archives of Ontario. I would also like to thank the eighth marquess of Lansdowne for permission to quote from the papers of the fifth marquess, who was governor general from 1883 to 1888.

The three years of primary research that went into this book were supported by the Social Sciences and Humanities Research Council of Canada. I am grateful to the council and its three anonymous referees for making the project possible. I should also thank Broadview Press for permitting the republication of chapter 12, an earlier draft of which was published as chapter 1 of their volume, *Federalism and Political Community: Essays in Honour of Donald Smiley.*

A number of student research assistants contributed significantly to the project, including Tom Enders at the University of Alberta and Joe Mazzei, Ernst Bueckert, Denise Elliott, and Franca Mandarino at Brock University. My colleagues in the Department of Politics at Brock, to which I moved when the project was already underway, provided a congenial and stimulating environment, although some of them may be grateful that "the historical stuff," as they have been known to describe this work, is at last completed. My friend and former dean of social sciences, Lewis A. Soroka, was particularly supportive during his term of office. The manuscript was efficiently typed by the personnel of the Clerical Services Department at Brock, particularly Janet Hastie and Arlene Longo. Philip Cercone of McGill-Queen's University Press was a helpful and sympathetic editor.

Immersing myself for several years in the Canadian federalism of the nineteenth century, while the interminable constitutional and political crisis of the late twentieth century continued to unfold, has been a strange experience. The Canada I studied was an underdeveloped and predominantly agricultural country of only a few million people, where the state had little direct impact on everyday life. Nonetheless, I was constantly reminded of the continuity between past and present, and the impact of one upon the other. Like Housman's Shropshire lad watching the storm on Wenlock Edge, I came to realize that we are but transients in a physical setting where other persons, now dead and largely forgotten, have struggled with some of the same difficulties we confront today.

Today Canadians face the task of redesigning the political order created in the latter part of the nineteenth century to deal with radically different circumstances, both domestic and external. In many other parts of the world the interdependence of neighbouring peoples must somehow be reconciled with ethnic and religious conflicts far more severe than those Canadians experienced in the days of Macdonald, Mowat, and Mercier. The operation of a federal constitution in conditions of social diversity has never been a more important object of study than it is today. It is hoped that the present work will contribute, however modestly, to our understanding of that phenomenon.

Ex Uno Plures

The federal Union of Canada, unlike that of the American Republic, has had for its principle and basis the distribution of certain defined powers given to the provinces and not a voluntary cession of a portion of their powers by the provinces to a central authority and government. To use Sir George Cartier's words, our motto is not "E Pluribus Unum" but "Ex Uno Plures."

Joseph Adolphe Chapleau, in a letter to John Thompson, 5 March 1888

1 Confederation and the British North America Act

Few aspects of Canadian history have been as extensively or effectively described by professional historians as the process culminating in the formation of the federal state in 1867. The broad outlines of the story are familiar to most educated Canadians, or at least were so in the not too distant past when Canadian history was a compulsory subject in high school. The details, insofar as they can be reconstructed from surviving documents, have been ably filled in by Creighton, Morton, Waite, and a score of other specialists, most of whose work is easily accessible.[1] There is no need to repeat their research in the present work, which is essentially devoted to the period after Confederation.

Yet what happened after 1867 cannot be fully understood without some knowledge of what happened before. Confederation established the institutional context within which political discussion would be conducted, decisions made, and resources allocated after 1867. The British North America Act, to which reference will constantly be made in the pages that follow, was the embodiment of the understanding that the founding elites, conventionally termed the Fathers of Confederation, had of their country's needs and of the system of government that best suited those needs. It also embodied complex bargains and compromises among the different provinces, cultural groups, religious denominations, and economic interests they represented. Characteristics of the document that have often been criticized – its lack of eloquent or inspiring language, its excessive number of mundane details, and its failure to explain some matters of really fundamental importance – can only be understood, if not necessarily excused, by reviewing the process through which it was drafted and the purposes it was intended to serve.

The terms of the BNA Act thus embody in a congealed form the events and issues of the three-year period from the Charlottetown Conference to the formal commencement of the new dominion's existence, as well as, to some extent, events and issues of an even earlier time. In turn, that background helps us to understand what happened after Confederation for at least three reasons. First, the formal structures and rules created by the act or, as it soon came to be known, by Canada's "constitution," became the framework within which subsequent political activities took place, and this framework significantly shaped the form and the content of those activities. Second, the geographical, cultural, and economic cleavages to which the terms of the act were a response continued to characterize British North America (or "Canada" in the post-Confederation sense of the word) after 1867 as they had done before.[2] Third, many of the political actors who occupied significant roles after 1867 were the same individuals who had participated in the process of founding the dominion and drafting the terms of its constitutional document. To put it another way, the Fathers of Confederation were the core of a political elite that largely governed the country for about a generation afterwards. As nearly as one can fix the date at which they ceased to do so that date is 1896, when the election of Wilfrid Laurier's Liberals effectively passed the torch to a new generation. Hence 1867 and 1896 are the chronological boundaries for the study of federal-provincial relations in the chapters that follow.

The present chapter discusses the origins of Canadian federalism, with the aim of casting some light on its evolution in the first three decades after it was established. In contrast to other chapters in the book, this one is mainly based on a reading of the secondary sources rather than on original archival research. The parliamentary debates in the Province of Canada on the Quebec Resolutions (usually referred to as the Confederation Debates) have also been consulted, as have the Confederation documents published some thirty years after the event by Joseph Pope, who had been Sir John A. Macdonald's last private secretary.

The question that must pose itself at the outset is why Confederation took place at all, and particularly why it took place in 1867. The formation of a new state is hardly a routine event, and in normal circumstances the odds are long against any such project being attempted, let alone achieved. The idea of uniting the British North American colonies had occasionally been discussed or considered at least since the days of Lord Durham, but without any serious prospects of success. Yet quite suddenly between 1864 and 1867 the right circumstances fell into place and the task was accomplished. The reasons for this dramatic event may be explained by examining in turn the situation of the Province of Canada, the Maritime provinces, and the United Kingdom.

Many Canadians have consciously or unconsciously adopted a teleological interpretation that explains the event of Confederation in the light of what happened subsequently. This approach is perhaps best exemplified by the work of Donald Creighton, and especially by his brilliant and justly celebrated biography of John A. Macdonald. Creighton himself described the two volumes of the biography as the second and third volumes of a trilogy that began in 1937 with his first published book, *The Commercial Empire of the St Lawrence*.[3] The St Lawrence appears in the first sentence of the biography, referring to the immigrant Macdonalds. "In those days they came usually by boat."[4] More than a thousand pages later, after the moving account of Macdonald's last illness, death, and burial, a reference to the river concludes the story: "Beyond the dock lay the harbour and the islands which marked the end of the lowest of the Great Lakes; and beyond the islands the St Lawrence River began its long journey to the sea."[5] Mortal humans are born, live, and die, but the river flows on forever.

Creighton, in short, saw the meaning of Macdonald's life as the revival and perpetuation, in a much grander form, of the commercial empire that the Montreal merchants had lost, through American competition and British indifference, in the middle of the nineteenth century. By implication this was also the meaning of Confederation, Macdonald's greatest achievement and the watershed in his life that concludes the first volume of the biography. The purpose of Confederation, in other words, was to industrialize the St Lawrence–Great Lakes corridor behind the protective tariff wall of the National Policy, to build the Canadian Pacific Railway, and to populate the western provinces as Montreal's new hinterland.

By no means unique to Creighton, this approach reflects the fashionable economic determinism that dominated historical research in the first half of the twentieth century. It attributes to the politicians of the 1860s a superhuman foresight that was not apparent at the time, and ignores or underemphasizes much of the complex political and strategic environment that influenced the thinking and the behaviour of Macdonald and his contemporaries. Particularly it underestimates the importance of the central fact of Canadian history, and one for which Creighton had no great sympathy: the sometimes difficult relationship between English-speaking and French-speaking communities that shared the same territory in the northern half of North America.

The interpretation of Confederation that finds such eloquent expression in Creighton's work is presented much more explicitly and mundanely in the writings of some of his influential contemporaries. Frank H. Underhill, a man of whom Creighton had a low opinion, described the meaning of Confederation as follows, at a time when Underhill still considered himself to be a socialist:

The essential work of the Fathers of Confederation was to weld the scattered British possessions in North America into a unity within which Canadian capitalism could expand and consolidate its power, to provide for the capitalist *entrepreneurs* of Montreal and Toronto a half-continent in which they could realize their dreams and ambitions. The dynamic drive which brought Confederation about had its centre in Montreal among the railway and banking magnates who were dreaming of new fields to conquer. It was for this purpose, and not merely to illustrate the abstract beauties of brotherly love, that Macdonald and Cartier built up their Anglo-French *entente*; it was for this purpose that Galt and Head and Monck drafted their paper schemes of British-American union and carried on their obscure negotiations behind the scenes. Federalism was only an accident imposed by the circumstances of the time; union was the essential achievement.[6]

Canada's leading Marxist historian, Stanley Ryerson, made the same point, although in contrast to Underhill he correctly noted the essential British role in Canada's expansion:

Confederation of the British North American colonial provinces took place when it did because of two main pressures. One came from the growth of a native capitalist industry, with railway transport as its backbone, and expansion of the home market as the prime motive for creating a unified and autonomous state. The other sprang from an imperial strategy that required unification not only in order to preserve the colonies from United States absorption, but also to strengthen a link of Empire reaching to the Pacific and hence to the approaches to Asia.[7]

These teleological-materialist explanations, which at least have the merit of seeing Confederation as a noteworthy and commendable achievement, were subsequently countered by the even more misleading view of R.T. Naylor and other exemplars of the new political economy, who viewed Confederation and the National Policy as the reactionary and sterile work of a mercantile elite who deflected

Canada from the path of development and progress. They too saw Confederation as merely the prelude to the National Policy, but, unlike their opponents, they viewed both with disdain and contempt. According to them, the economic elites whose machinations allegedly brought about the union of the British North American colonies were not seeking to promote industrialization and nation building, as Underhill and Ryerson believed, but to prevent them.[8]

This debate over the National Policy has tended to dominate the historiography of Confederation, but there is reason to doubt whether the debate is really relevant. In their lengthy speeches defending the Quebec Resolutions, neither John A. Macdonald nor George-Étienne Cartier, the supposed representatives of the good industrialists or bad merchants (depending on which version one prefers), devoted much attention to economic matters. Neither even mentioned the prospect of expansion to the West.[9] Admittedly the speeches of George Brown and Alexander Galt provide more grist for the materialist mill, but Brown's ties to economic elites were in Toronto, not in the far more important city of Montreal. Galt was a relatively unimportant political figure who soon faded from the scene. It is surely Macdonald and Cartier, the leaders of the Conservative party and the most powerful politicians in the new dominion after 1867, whose views must be taken more seriously.

Macdonald in fact explained the real purpose of Confederation, as far as central Canada was concerned, in a private letter to another Father of Confederation written a few years after the event. Writing in 1870 to W.P. Howland, who was then lieutenant-governor of Ontario, Macdonald reminded his former cabinet colleague and fellow delegate to the London Conference that "Confederation was adopted for the purpose of putting an end to the unhappy sectionalism that existed between Upper and Lower Canada before the Union."[10] The context of the letter indicated that it had not fully succeeded in doing so, for the prime minister was defending himself against the accusation that Ontario, and specifically the Reform party, lacked sufficient representation in his government. However, that is another story.

Accommodation between the conquered French Canadians and the growing number of anglophone settlers was a problem that had preoccupied the colonial authorities, and the imperial government in London, a century before Macdonald wrote. The precarious *modus vivendi*, established by the Quebec Act of 1774 and maintained by the hasty partition of Canada seventeen years later in response to the Loyalist influx around Lake Ontario, had broken down completely in 1837, just as Macdonald was establishing his law practice and beginning to contemplate a political career. On Lord Durham's recommendation the partition was then reversed, in the probably unrealistic expectation that the French Canadians could be assimilated. By 1848 the effort at assimilation, such as it was, had been abandoned, although the union of the two provinces continued. Canada under Lord Elgin then developed a unique political system whose temporary success and ultimate failure paved the way for Confederation almost two decades later.

In his study of Dutch politics, Arend Lijphart introduced the concept of consociational democracy, meaning a regime in which elite accommodation maintains democratic stability in spite of deep ideological, cultural or religious divisions and the absence of shared values and symbols. From 1848 until 1867 the United Province of Canada had a consociational regime: the first to be established anywhere in the world.[11] The suffrage, although not universal, was the most extensive of any country at that time, apart from the United States. Although the governor general still presided, government was effectively in the hands of a cabinet of politicians responsible to the legislature. Since the two sections of the province, now known as Canada East and Canada West, were equally represented in the legislature, and since two political parties quickly emerged in each section, every government was by necessity a coalition including one party from Canada East and one from Canada West. Thus each government was jointly headed by two party leaders, who normally assumed the titles of attorney general for Canada East and attorney general for Canada West. Both English and French were official languages. The distinctive legal systems of the two sections, civil law in Canada East and common law in Canada West, were maintained. Political patronage ensured that a rough proportionality between the two linguistic communities existed in the public service. Even the location of the capital was alternated periodically between the two sections. Public policy was the result of compromises between the leading members of the two parties that made up each government, and thus between the interests of the two sections they represented. Patronage enabled the cabinet to dominate the legislature, and also enabled the members of parliament to dominate the emerging party organizations in their constituencies. Although the regime was unitary rather than federal, at least in form, the *de facto* autonomy and distinctiveness of the two sections, with their contrasting religious and legal traditions, was respected by mainstream politicians on both sides of the cultural divide. Subcultural segmentation at the mass level was reinforced by geography, although in a few places, particularly in Montreal, the coexistence of the two linguistic groups in immediate proximity to one another led to occasional friction.

In his study of consociational democracy in the Netherlands, Lijphart identified seven "rules of the game" that facilitate elite accommodation: be pragmatic and businesslike, don't try to change the fundamental convictions of other groups, practise proportionality rather than majoritarianism, make decisions through summit diplomacy, make decisions in secret, depoliticize issues whenever possible, and allow the executive to govern with minimal interference from the legislature or the voters.[12] Generally speaking, all of these rules were adhered to in Canada between 1848 and 1867.

In a recent and brilliant book on the political traditions of Ontario, S.J.R. Noel has argued that this regime was the best government in the entire world during the brief period in which it existed.[13] Yet it failed to survive. It failed because the politics of elite accommodation were increasingly rejected by anglophone Canadians. Democratic and populist ideas gained strength among the farmers of Canada West, which caught up with Canada East in population by about 1849 and rapidly outpaced it thereafter. The future Ontarians resented the fact that they were held to parity in legislative representation with Canada East, despite their larger population. Many of them were recent arrivals from the British Isles, particularly from Scotland and Northern Ireland, and were hostile to Catholicism. Many also resented the influence of Montreal merchants and bankers over their hinterland economy. The last straw came when a bill providing public funding of Catholic schools in Canada West was imposed by a legislative majority drawn mainly from Canada East. This seemed to violate some of the unwritten rules of consociational politics. (Some Ontarians still think so more than a century later, although the measure is now entrenched in Canada's constitution.)

The Conservative party of Macdonald and Cartier had resisted "rep by pop" for as long as possible, but by 1864 it was apparent they could not do so for much longer. At the same time, Canada East could never accept a unitary state in which majority rule prevailed. A repartition of the province, restoring the Upper and Lower Canada of 1791, would disrupt the economy, threaten the anglophones of Canada East, and place Canada West permanently in the hands of the Reform party. The only solution was federalism, but a federation with only two component parts would be unworkable; the rivalry between the two sections would continue, and the central government would probably be overshadowed by the two provincial governments. Bringing in other British colonies, however, would make a viable federation possible. The circle could thus be squared; majority rule could prevail at the centre while Canada East would be free, within limits, to control its internal affairs.

A secondary but still important motive for Confederation was military defence. Relations between the British Empire and the United States had been tense throughout the American Civil War. The British governing class, the anglophone elite of Montreal, and John A. Macdonald had all supported the southern rebels, although most Canadians had the good sense not to do so. By 1864 the southern cause was obviously hopeless. Sherman was within sight of Atlanta and Grant was already south of Richmond when George Brown joined the Macdonald-Cartier government in June of that year. Some northern Americans, viewing their civil war as a second American revolution, thought that the time might be ripe to remove the Union Jack from North America once and for all, a goal that had eluded their ancestors in 1776 and 1812. Macdonald and Cartier, who had both carried arms (on opposite sides) in 1837, shared a lifelong concern with Canada's military defence. A larger Canada with access to the Atlantic by railway, and with the important British military and naval base at Halifax on its territory, would be easier to defend than the existing Province of Canada. It would also be far less likely to be written off as indefensible by the British authorities, as Upper Canada nearly had been in 1812.

Confederation, it must be remembered, extended Canada's boundaries to the east, not to the west. A railway to the Pacific was not a high priority for Canadians at the time. Protective tariffs were also not a major concern. Canada actually reduced its tariffs in 1866, to accommodate anti-tariff sentiment in the Maritimes. Macdonald told Joseph Howe in 1868 that he still hoped for a new reciprocity agreement with the United States.[14] Even ten years later he did not consider tariff protection a major priority, although he was preparing to fight an election on the issue. In a private letter a few months before he formed his second government in 1878 he defined his major goals as construction of the Canadian Pacific Railway, establishment of an effective Canadian army, and the annexation of Newfoundland. Tariffs were not mentioned.[15] Like most lawyer-politicians, Macdonald had little interest in the economy. Tariff policies for him were not a matter of dogma or settled conviction, but merely means to his political ends.

The motives for Confederation in New Brunswick and Nova Scotia are more difficult to discern than those in central Canada. In fact, and quite understandably, Confederation was distinctly less popular, and faced more widespread opposition, in those two provinces than it did in Canada. The reasons for it were simply less compelling. New Brunswick, which had a long land boundary with the United States, shared to some extent Canada's sense of military insecurity. Nova Scotia, with its almost insular situation and its British garrison and naval base, shared it hardly at all. This fact doubtless explains why opposition to Confederation was so much greater and more formidable in Nova Scotia than in New Brunswick. By the same logic, it is understandable that Prince Edward Island waited six years, and Newfoundland more than eighty years, to enter Confederation. The farther a province was from the United States, the less reason it saw to surrender its quasi-independence.

Apart from military defence, another incentive for supporters of Confederation in the Maritimes was the promise of an intercolonial railway that would connect Halifax with central Canada. The motivation for this project was more strategic than economic, but some economic benefits were expected both from the construction of the railway and from its subsequent availability as a means of transportation. This motive was particularly significant in New Brunswick, where most of the construction would take place. The Intercolonial was expected to – and eventually did – encourage the development of the underpopulated northern and eastern sections of the province. Peter Mitchell, who represented that part of New Brunswick at the Quebec and London conferences, explained to John A. Macdonald in May 1867 that "the question of Confederation was one entirely subordinate to the question of *Railroad* in our Province."[16] With almost four hundred miles of its main line in New Brunswick, the Intercolonial would be the largest construction project in the province's history.

In both provinces the leaders of the pro-Confederation forces, Leonard Tilley of New Brunswick and Charles Tupper of Nova Scotia, seem to have craved a larger political stage on which to display their talents. Tilley, according to one account, thought that the Intercolonial Railway made Confederation economically feasible, while the condition of New Brunswick politics made it politically desirable.[17] Understandably, he did not use the latter argument in public, but there were probably others who shared his sentiments. Tupper probably found Nova Scotia too small for his ambitions; certainly he spent little time there once Confederation was achieved, although he lived another forty-eight years. In his case, another reason for taking up the cause of Confederation was to distract attention from the expensive and unpopular educational reforms his government introduced in 1864.[18] Continuing resentment over this issue may have contributed as much as Confederation itself to the Tupper government's electoral defeat in 1867.

It is probably safe to say that neither Maritime province would have agreed to confederation with Canada had the decision been entirely in its hands. At most each might have agreed to Maritime union, the project the Charlottetown Conference of 1864 was originally intended to discuss. In securing Confederation, therefore, the role of the Colonial Office in London, and of the colonial governors in Fredericton and Halifax, was probably decisive.

In the middle decades of the nineteenth century, interest in colonial problems was not great among the British governing class, let alone the general population. Many believed that free trade had made colonialism irrelevant and obsolete. The North American colonies in particular provided few economic benefits, imposed costly military commitments, and complicated relations with the United States. Various schemes to unite them into a larger entity attracted little or no interest, in the Colonial Office and elsewhere, until 1864.

In 1864, however, this indifference suddenly ended, and from that time onwards the imperial government was solidly committed to the cause of Confederation.[19] This sudden change cannot be attributed to domestic British politics, for it began under the Liberal government of Lord Palmerston and continued under Lord Russell after Palmerston's death in 1865, and under Lord Derby after the Conservatives took office (without an election) in 1866. Confederation after 1864 had bipartisan support in the United Kingdom, which was just as well given the roughly equal strength of the two parties and the frequent changes of government.

The real cause of the change was the imperial government's response to developments in the United States. From the outset of the civil war the Palmerston government had pursued a pro-southern policy, motivated in part by aristocratic disdain for American democracy and in part by the need of Lancashire textile mills for southern cotton. A southern victory was not only hoped for but expected. Had this occurred, the southern Confederacy would have become Britain's ally and economic partner in North America, while Canada would probably have sooner or later joined the United States. Goldwin Smith has suggested that Gladstone, whom he knew personally and who was then chancellor of the Exchequer, actually favoured this realignment.[20]

All such calculations, if they existed, were made useless by the obvious fact, in early 1864, that the South was losing the war. Having antagonized the United States through its ill-considered policies, the British government now faced a difficult situation. Supporting the confederation of the British North American colonies appeared as the best solution. As a united entity, the colonies would be less likely to run the risk of American attack, and would be easier to defend if the worst happened. In a more general sense, a Canadian confederation would replace the vanquished southern Confederacy as a counterweight to the United States. It could also be expected to relieve the imperial government of some difficult and embarrassing responsibilities in North America, particularly the derelict fur-trading empire of the Hudson's Bay Company in the northwest and the even more isolated Pacific colonies of British Columbia and Vancouver Island, which were united with each other in 1866.

For these reasons the imperial government after 1864 gave consistent support to Confederation. It did so by exercising discreet and effective pressure on the reluctant Maritime colonies to join with Canada, by assisting in the drafting of the British North America Act, and by securing the passage of the act through the British Parliament. The British government and Parliament also agreed to assist in the financing of the Intercolonial Railway, without which Confederation would have been impossible. Subsequent to Confederation the imperial government discouraged the separatist movement in Nova Scotia, brought about the transfer of the Hudson's Bay Company territories to the new dominion, and facilitated the adherence of British Columbia and Prince Edward Island.

The actual process that led to Confederation went through several stages involving successively the central Canadians, the Maritime provinces, and the imperial government. The first stage was the agreement between Macdonald and Cartier to make Confederation their first priority. The second stage was the adherence of George Brown and his followers to the Canadian government in June 1864, a liaison that transformed that government into a coalition and made Confederation a bipartisan movement, at least in Canada West. The third stage was the negotiations with the Maritime colonies, first at the Charlottetown Conference and then at the more important Quebec Conference later in the year. In February 1865 the Quebec Resolutions were approved by the Canadian Parliament, but shortly afterwards the timetable was set back by the electoral defeat of Tilley's government in New Brunswick. A year later the Fenian raid against New Brunswick increased support for Confederation and probably brought about Tilley's return to office. It was followed by Fenian attacks on both Canada East and Canada West. In December 1866 the London Conference further refined the constitutional design drafted at Quebec two years earlier. Subsequently the British North America Act, based on the Quebec and London resolutions, was drafted by the Colonial Office, and finally, in March 1867, the act was adopted by the imperial Parliament.

The terms of the British North America Act reflected the influence of these successive stages and the broadening at each stage of the circle of interests that had to be accommodated. At the very outset, Macdonald's Conservatives in Canada West and Cartier's Bleus in Canada East had different interests and perspectives; the Bleus, as is well known, insisted on a significant degree of autonomy for the province of Quebec that would replace the old section of Canada East. Thus, at this stage, the federal character of what would be Canada's constitution was established, despite Macdonald's misgivings about federalism as a system of government. Then Brown and his Reformers, with their interest in expansion to the west and their hostility to French and Catholic influences, added their input to the scheme. The details of the discussions among these three coalition partners, by which the common position of the Province of Canada was established, can unfortunately not be known with certainty. The negotiations with the other colonies, being mainly through formal conferences, are somewhat better documented. Prince Edward Island and Newfoundland dropped out of the discussions after the Quebec Conference, indicating that the accommodation of divergent interests was not entirely successful. Finally, the input of the Colonial Office, although it did not alter the essentials of the scheme, contributed some significant details.

Federalism, in the Canadian sense of the term, emerged as the product of all these conflicting influences and pressures rather than as a conscious design. William Ormsby has argued that a federal concept had emerged in Canada in the 1840s from the practices and conventions by which the interests of two nationalities were harmonized in a formally unitary state.[21] Certainly Macdonald and Cartier, and the political ideas they held, were in part the product of this experience.

The reputation of the federal idea had suffered severely from the American Civil War. The United States was the leading example of federalism, and the only one of which the Fathers of Confederation had any knowledge. Macdonald's view that the breakdown of the American experiment had been caused by an excessively decentralized constitution, and especially by the error of giving residual powers to the states, is well known. While he regarded the actual United States Constitution as a poor model for Canada, he was impressed by the more centralist constitutional notions of some of the American founding fathers, especially Alexander Hamilton.[22] Hamilton, like Macdonald, was a poor immigrant of Scottish ancestry who rose to fame and power in North America on the basis of his own ability and intiative. Both men even shared the same birthday, the eleventh of January. In many respects the British North America Act resembles the constitution that Hamilton would have preferred for the United States.

Another influence on Macdonald's thinking was the New Zealand Constitution of 1852, a copy of which is in the Macdonald Papers. The New Zealand Constitution was an example of what would now be called devolution, creating six provinces with elected legislatures in what had previously been a single colony. From a central Canadian perspective, Confederation was also an example of devolution, creating two provinces of Ontario and Quebec in what had previously been a single colony. The New Zealand provinces were subordinate to the central government since their acts could be disallowed by the governor of New Zealand, who could also remove the leaders of provincial governments from office. The list of subjects on which only the central government could legislate included customs duties, coinage and currency, weights and measures, the post office, bankruptcy and insolvency, beacons and lighthouses, the aboriginal peoples and lands reserved for them, and criminal law. Despite the last of these exclusions, the provinces could impose fines or short sentences of imprisonment for violations of their own laws. All other subjects were effectively concurrent, with statutes of the New Zealand Parliament paramount over those of the provinces. As it turned out, the provincial governments in New Zealand did not demonstrate much usefulness or acquire much popular support, and they were abolished in 1876.[23] Macdonald for a time hoped that provincial goverments in Canada would also be no more than a temporary expedient.

One must attribute to Cartier and his followers the fact that Canadian provinces, although excluded from most of the same fields as their New Zealand counterparts, were also given exclusive and substantial powers of their own, including jurisdiction over public lands and timber, hospitals, asylums, charities and eleemosynary institutions, municipal institutions, the solemnization of marriage, property and civil rights, and education. These provisions protected Quebec's distinctive characteristics, the Catholic faith, the civil law, and the French language, whose preservation had been accepted as a goal of British policy since the Quebec Act of 1774.

The Quebec Conference, the most important of the three that led to Confederation, opened in the old Canadian legislative building on 10 October 1864 and closed in St Lawrence Hall in Montreal on the 29th.[24] Apart from the last day, all the sessions took place in Quebec City, and there were sixteen sitting days in all. Canada East and Canada West were each represented by six delegates, with

those from Canada East including two anglophones, the Protestant
Alexander Galt and the Catholic Thomas d'Arcy McGee. The delegates from Canada West included three Conservatives, John A.
Macdonald, Alexander Campbell, and James Cockburn, along with
three Reformers: George Brown, Oliver Mowat, and William Mc-
Dougall. Nova Scotia sent five representatives, and New Brunswick
and Prince Edward Island each sent seven. Two Newfoundlanders,
who acted more as observers than as participants, completed the list
of thirty-three delegates. Sir Étienne Taché, who died a few months
later, was the nominal chairman of the Canadian delegation, but its
real leaders were Macdonald and Cartier. Macdonald, who had
probably read more widely in history and political philosophy than
anyone else present, was the dominant personality and introduced
more than half the resolutions adopted. Macdonald's private secretary, Hewitt Bernard, who later became his brother-in-law, acted as
the executive secretary to the conference.

The delegations from Nova Scotia and New Brunswick were
headed, respectively, by Charles Tupper and Leonard Tilley, the
premiers of those two provinces. Tupper was a medical doctor by
profession and Tilley a pharmacist, but whether the medicine they
prescribed for the Maritimes was appropriate is still considered a
moot point by some residents of the provinces concerned. Both were
strong and effective leaders, although not universally popular. Both
gravitated towards federal politics after 1867 and served for long
periods in cabinets headed by John A. Macdonald. Tupper was
briefly prime minister in 1896, at the very end of the period covered
by this book.

The essential design of what would become the distribution of legislative powers was apparently worked out among the central Canadians prior to the Quebec Conference and was modified only slightly
at that conference and afterwards. The records of the conference indicate that the Canadians arrived with a definite plan and that the
delegates of the small colonies merely responded to what the Canadians proposed. The records also indicate the surprising fact that
only three days at Quebec were devoted to discussing the distribution of powers. The financial provisions of the proposed constitution
occupied the conference for nearly two days, miscellaneous provisions for one day, and the design of central institutions, particularly
the Senate, for no less than eight days. Apparently the Maritimers
were more concerned with what is now called "intrastate federalism," or the representation of their relatively small populations in
the central government, than they were in the legislative powers
of the provinces.[25] Among Maritime supporters of Confederation

there was actually some sentiment in favour of a unitary state, on the grounds that two distinct levels of government would be costly, inefficient, and wasteful.[26] Tilley did succeed in deleting roads and bridges (an extremely important source of local patronage and electoral support) from the list of federal responsibilities, while Jonathan McCully of Nova Scotia tried unsuccessfully to do the same with agriculture, which the Canadians intended to be a concurrent jurisdiction.[27] In general, however, the Maritime delegates did not press for a more decentralized federalism than the version presented by the Canadians. The important elements of "interstate," as opposed to intrastate, federalism in the British North America Act must be attributed to the four French-Canadian Fathers of Confederation – George-Étienne Cartier, Étienne Taché, Hector Langevin, and J.-C. Chapais – and their desire for a strong province of Quebec. Their achievement is the more remarkable since they were a minority even within the Canadian delegation of twelve, and a very small minority among the thirty-three politicians assembled at the Quebec Conference.

Nonetheless, the celebrated "compact theory of Confederation" was first invented with reference to the agreement between the Maritimers and the Canadians at the Quebec Conference, not with reference to the earlier, and perhaps more significant but less formal agreement among the Canadians themselves. Macdonald inadvertently paved the way for the compact theory, which would become an important ideological weapon for his opponents, by suggesting during the Confederation debates that the Quebec Resolutions could not be amended by the Canadian Parliament because they had been agreed upon between Canada and the other provinces.[28] The use to which this apparently harmless observation might be put was foreshadowed as early as 1870, when the New Brunswick House of Assembly objected to certain provisions of the Macdonald government's Supreme Court Bill on the grounds that they were "a violation of the compact entered into at the time of the Union." The assembly went on to lecture the federal government as follows: "we humbly submit that if in any one particular that compact can be broken, without the consent of all the parties thereto, then the whole of the rights secured by said act to the separate provinces may be taken away, and the compact virtually destroyed."[29]

It was not until more than a decade later that Judge T.J.J. Loranger's *Letters on the British North America Act* popularized the idea of the "compact" in Quebec. Still later, some Quebec nationalists redefined the "compact" to be one between two nations, anglophone Canada and Quebec, suggesting by implication that the compact must have been negotiated not at the Quebec Conference, but in the private discussions between Cartier and Macdonald, or between Cartier, Macdonald, and Brown, in the early months of 1864.[30]

Although only three days were devoted at Quebec to the distribution of powers, the debate on the complex financial terms of Confederation was even briefer. These provisions included the distribution of public property between the federal government and the provinces, the assumption by the federal government of provincial debts, the "debt allowances" by which the Maritime provinces were rewarded for the relatively modest size of the debts with which they entered the federation, annual subsidies to the provinces based on the size of their populations as of 1861, and a clause guaranteeing the provincial ownership of public lands and natural resources. Alexander Galt, who represented the then-anglophone city of Sherbrooke in the Canadian Parliament, was largely responsible for drafting these portions of the Quebec Resolutions. Apart from the Prince Edward Islanders, who found them unacceptable, the delegates were not very critical of these provisions, and historians have also treated them kindly. Nonetheless, they proved to be a source of almost continuous disputation and conflict over the next forty years, much of which is described in the chapters that follow. Galt was appointed minister of finance in the first federal government in 1867, having earlier held the same office in the Province of Canada, but he resigned after only four months and never held cabinet office again. The task of deciphering the financial terms of the British North America Act was left to his successors.

Although the provincial ownership of public lands and natural resources was not controversial, an interesting discussion that foreshadowed some twentieth-century developments took place at the Quebec Conference regarding export duties. The Canadians proposed that the federal government be given an explicit power to impose duties on exports as well as on imports, but the Nova Scotians objected to the possibility of an export duty on coal, which would limit the province's ability to impose royalties on that resource. Galt argued that the intent was not to have the federal government impose export duties on coal, but merely to prevent the provinces from doing so. The Nova Scotians responded that their royalties were not export duties since they were imposed on all coal regardless of its destination.[31] The Quebec Resolutions as finally adopted embodied a compromise whereby the provinces could impose export duties on timber, coal, and other minerals while the federal government could impose them on other commodities. In the end the explicit references to export duties were omitted from the British North America

Act, apart from the special privilege, given only to New Brunswick, of continuing to impose export duties on timber.

Neither the New Brunswick nor the Nova Scotia legislatures ever adopted the Quebec Resolutions, although it is arguable that both signified assent in principle by empowering delegates to attend the London Conference two years later. The Canadian legislature did adopt the Quebec Resolutions early in 1865, with an overwhelming majority from Canada West and a narrow majority from Canada East voting in favour. The Rouge, or Liberal party in Canada East voted solidly against the resolutions. It, and a few radical Reformers from Canada West, favoured a loose confederation of the two Canadian sections but saw no reason to include the Maritimes. The Rouges also argued that the federation envisaged by the Quebec Resolutions would be too centralized. A few Conservative opponents, like Christopher Dunkin from Brome County and Matthew Cameron from Ontario County, did not oppose union with the Maritimes in principle but adhered to John A. Macdonald's original view that a legislative union would be more workable, and more compatible with the British system of government, than a federation.

Whatever their other differences, most opponents were sceptical about the claim that uniting the British North American provinces would facilitate their military defence. Sandfield Macdonald and Henri Joly, future premiers of Ontario and Quebec, respectively, pointed out that an intercolonial railway could be built without the necessity of creating new political structures. While correct, this observation inconveniently demolished the argument of their fellow opponent, A.-A. Dorion, who alleged that the whole purpose of the proposed federation was to build the Intercolonial so as to provide connecting traffic for Canada's largest existing railway, the Grand Trunk.[32] Both Joly and Dunkin also drew attention to the fact that the barriers to trade between Canada and the Maritimes could be removed without political unification.

Dunkin's speech, which extended over two days and fills sixty-two pages in the printed record of the debate, was the most interesting contribution to the argument on either side, as well as the longest. Dunkin was an Eastern Townships anglophone who subsequently became the first provincial treasurer of Quebec in 1867 and then the federal minister of agriculture in 1869. With remarkable foresight, he identified the features of the Quebec Resolutions that would cause the most conflict and controversy following their incorporation into the British North America Act, and that in some cases continue to do so more than a century later. These features included the appointed upper house of Parliament, the anomalous power of disallowance, the ambiguous position of the lieutenant-governor as both a federal and a provincial officer, the inconsistency between responsible government and federalism, the overlapping distribution of legislative powers, the location of the federal capital within one of the provinces rather than in a special district, the appointment of provincial court judges by the federal government, and the excessively complex financial provisions. Dunkin also predicted accurately that ethnic tensions between anglophones and francophones in Canada East would increase when it became the Province of Quebec, that the protective tariff would be a divisive issue between central Canada and the peripheries of the federation, and that the provinces would find it politically easier to blame the federal government for their financial problems than to impose taxation.[33]

One issue not resolved at the Quebec Conference was the one that had contributed more than any other to the deteriorating political climate in the Province of Canada: denominational schools. The Quebec Resolutions included a provision drafted by the Irish Catholic member of parliament for Montreal West, Thomas D'Arcy McGee, that would prevent either of the central provinces from interfering with "the rights or privileges which the Protestant or Catholic minority in both Canadas may possess as to their Denominational Schools, at the time when the Union goes into operation." This clause inspired efforts by both minorities to ensure that their privileges would be given the clearest and broadest possible definition in law before the federal union took place. It also encouraged the Catholic clergy in the Maritimes to lobby for entrenchment of the same minority rights in their provinces that would be enjoyed by Catholics in Canada West.[34]

The clause dealing with denominational schools in the revised resolutions that came out of the London Conference referred to rights and privileges existing "by law" in "any province." This was less of a change than it appeared to be, because the denominational rights enjoyed by Catholics in Canada West were not quite as extensive as those enjoyed by Protestants in Canada East, an effort to make them so having failed in the Canadian Parliament a few months before the London Conference. The Maritime Catholics were even worse off, since their rights to denominational schools actually existed only by custom, and not by law, a difference that would soon prove to be of decisive importance. At the suggestion of Galt, the spokesman for the Protestants of Canada East, the London Conference also added a provision whereby the minorities could appeal to the federal government for support if their rights were interfered with, and whereby Parliament could even legislate on their behalf "in the last resort." These provisions, in a slightly modified form, eventually became Section 93 of the British North America Act.

Apart from this clause, the changes made at the London Conference were relatively minor. In contrast to the Quebec Conference two years earlier, Canada sent only six delegates to London, and Nova Scotia and New Brunswick sent five each. The island provinces, having lost interest in federation at least for the time being, were not represented. All but three of the sixteen delegates at London had been at Quebec, and they included Macdonald, Cartier, Galt, Tupper, and Tilley. Among the absentees, however, were George Brown, who had resigned from the Canadian government; Oliver Mowat, who had been appointed to the bench; and Thomas D'Arcy McGee.

One interesting difference between the Quebec and London resolutions was that in the London version the proposed union of the provinces was described as a confederation rather than as a federation. Although there is no etymological reason to attribute different meanings to the two words, the parliamentary debate on the Quebec Resolutions suggested that many Canadians accepted the American usage according to which a "confederation" is less centralized than a "federation." The change in terminology was probably designed to reassure opponents of the union who feared that provincial autonomy would be reduced to the vanishing point.

The London Conference ended on Christmas Eve 1866 with the adoption of the resolutions. Early in the new year, the actual text of what became the British North America Act was drafted by officials in the Colonial Office. Although the document adhered closely to the spirit and content of the London Resolutions, two apparently slight changes that were made have a particular interest for students of the Canadian Constitution. Both the Quebec and London resolutions had provided that the Parliament of Canada could make laws for the "peace, welfare, and good government" of the country, an expression probably suggested by the "common defense and general welfare" clause in the constitution of the United States. The Colonial Office unfortunately changed this to "peace, order, and good government," the standard phrase used in the constitutional documents of British colonies. Thus this now-familiar phrase, which has been used as the basis for invidious comparisons between the political culture of Canada and that of the United States, was not even of Canadian origin, and was probably inserted by an official who had never set foot on Canadian soil and would never do so.

The second change was of even greater practical importance. Both the Quebec and London resolutions, while giving the provincial legislatures jurisdiction over "property and civil rights," had qualified this grant of authority with the phrase "excepting those portions thereof assigned to the General Parliament." The Colonial Office removed the qualification, perhaps deeming it superfluous. This change facilitated the process by which subsequently the Judicial Committee of the Privy Council, in F.R. Scott's words, would make "property and civil rights" in effect the residual power in Canada's constitution.[35]

Finally, the British North America Bill was introduced, debated, and adopted in both houses of the British Parliament, where its importance was unfortunately overshadowed by a far more controversial measure: Disraeli's bill to extend the parliamentary franchise in the United Kingdom. On the second reading of the British North America Bill in the House of Lords, the measure was defended by both Lord Carnarvon, the secretary of state for the colonies, and Lord Monck, the governor general of Canada both before and after Confederation. Carnarvon, according to *The Times*, was "imperfectly heard in the gallery,"[36] but his remarks have often been quoted, and deservedly so:

In geographical area this Confederation of the British North American Provinces is even now large – it may become one day second only in extent to the vast territories of Russia – and in population, in revenue, in trade, in shipping, it is superior to the Thirteen Colonies when, not a century ago, in the Declaration of Independence, they became the United States of America. We are laying the foundation of a great state – perhaps one which at a future day may even overshadow this country. But, come what may, we shall rejoice that we have shown neither indifference to their wishes nor jealousy of their aspirations, but that we honestly and sincerely, to the utmost of our power and knowledge, fostered their growth, recognizing in it the conditions of our own greatness.[37]

2 The Economic, Social, and Political Environment

A formal constitution depicts only a part of the reality of politics and government, and the economic and social environment within which a formal constitution operates should be accorded its due share of attention. What kind of country was Canada in 1867, and how did it evolve economically, socially, and politically over the next three decades? In some respects the Canada of a century ago was essentially similar to the Canada of today, but in other respects it was profoundly different. Stereotypical assumptions about the positions of particular classes, regions, and ethnic groups in nineteenth-century Canada may be used, consciously or unconsciously, to reinforce ideological prejudices. Efforts to demonstrate, for example, that "merchants" impeded industrialization, that the working class was in the vanguard of political and social progress, that Maritimers or French Canadians suffered from Confederation, or that "regionalism" was always the primordial fact of Canadian life are often based on just such stereotypes, rather than on an impartial reading of the facts.

The prevailing stereotype regarding the period from Confederation to 1896 is that it was a period of economic stagnation, an unhappy and protracted prelude to the contrastingly glorious period of expansion and growth that followed in the age of Laurier.[1] This view has been fostered by political propaganda, such as the interesting but unreliable *Reminiscences* of Sir Richard Cartwright, and also by economic historians schooled in the influential staples theory of Harold A. Innis and his disciples. Assuming the production and export of a staple commodity to be the necessary engine of economic growth, the staples theorists can find no dominant commodity in the Macdonald era such as timber was before Confederation and wheat was in the early part of the twentieth century. They are therefore inclined to assume that the period must have been one of stagnation.

In one sense, which happens to be the most obvious, growth was indeed slow and disappointing. The dominion of Canada began in 1867 with a population of about three-and-a-half million, which by coincidence was almost identical with the size of population possessed by the new American republic in 1787, or by the Commonwealth of Australia in 1901. Thirty years after Confederation the population of Canada had increased only to five million, despite a respectable level of immigration, a healthy excess of births over deaths, and a vast and painless territorial expansion that Alexander, Caesar, or Bonaparte might have envied. In contrast, the United States had attained a population of about nine million within thirty years of adopting its federal constitution. Even Australia, without benefit of territorial expansion, had about seven million inhabitants by 1931. Clearly the ease of out-migration to the United States, which imposed no restrictions whatever on entry by persons of European ancestry, inhibited the growth of Canada's population. By the 1890s more than a million Canadian-born persons were living in the United States.[2]

In another sense the picture is much brighter. Although reliable data were not collected at the time, it has been calculated retrospectively that Canada's gross national product (GNP) grew much faster than its population. From $319 million in 1860 it increased to $459 million in 1870, $581 million in 1880, $803 million in 1890, and $1057 million in 1900.[3] Since there was practically no inflation (indeed price indices actually fell during portions of the time under consideration), Canadians clearly enjoyed a much higher standard of living in 1896 than they had done in 1867. The total volume of goods and services produced must have almost doubled in the thirty-year period. Comparing the GNP estimates with the population counts for the year immediately following each (since the census was conducted in years ending with "1") suggests that the GNP per capita increased from roughly $124 in 1870, to $135 in 1880, to $167 in 1890, and to $196 in 1900. By way of explanation, it should be noted that the purchasing power of a dollar then was at least twenty times, and perhaps thirty times, what it is today.

This progress was not entirely smooth, for the economy, then as now, fluctuated between periods of growth and periods of recession. Research has demonstrated that the Canadian economy in the late nineteenth century followed essentially the same business cycle as that of the United States, even though the two economies were much less closely linked to one another by flows of trade and investment than they would be a century later. The Canadian economy entered a pronounced recession in the latter part of 1873, almost coincidentally with John A. Macdonald's resignation and the swearing in of a Liberal government headed by Alexander Mackenzie. Unluckily for the Liberals, this recession did not bottom out until 1879, by which time the electorate had already removed them from office. The Canadian economy rose from that low point to a peak in the summer of 1882, at which time a smaller recession began that lasted until the spring of 1885, when growth resumed. Another recession began early in 1887 and lasted only a year. Expansion resumed early in 1888 and lasted until the summer of 1890, when there was a brief recession followed by two years of expansion from March 1891 until February 1893. There was a further recession until March 1894, then expansion until August 1895, then recession until August 1896. (This time fortune finally smiled on the Liberals, who had been elected a month earlier, and the period of Laurier's first mandate proved to be one of continuous growth.) To summarize the period from Confederation until 1896: expansion was disrupted by a long and serious recession in the 1870s, coinciding closely with the Mackenzie interlude, and by relatively minor and short-term fluctuations from 1879 until 1896.[4]

During the same period Canada's external trade grew slowly and not continuously. Domestic exports increased from about $48.5 million in 1868 to about $76.7 million in 1874, but declined during the recession, with the result that the level of 1874 was not exceeded until 1881. The level of exports was fairly stable for the next decade and had reached only $85.2 million by 1890. In the next three years it increased rapidly and then levelled off, reaching $109.7 million in 1896.[5] Imports exceeded exports in every year, apart from 1880 when there was a slight surplus of exports. The trade deficits were particularly large in the early 1870s, and to some extent in the early 1880s, when they were probably augmented by the import of equipment and supplies for the Canadian Pacific Railway (CPR). By the 1890s the trade deficits were becoming insignificant. These deficits in trade were more than compensated for by heavy imports of foreign capital, almost all of which came from the United Kingdom in the form of portfolio, rather than direct, investment. Government and railway bonds accounted for most of the capital inflow. Net inflow of foreign capital from 1868 to 1899 was about $1 billion, or almost one-and-a-half times the accumulated trade deficit.[6]

When the export data are compared with the estimates of GNP referred to earlier, it appears true that, in the words of one economic historian, "staple exports no longer dominated Canadian economic fortunes by 1867."[7] Exports of all kinds amounted to only 13 per cent of GNP in 1870 and 1880, and a mere 11 per cent in 1890. These percentages are much lower than those of a century later. The relative decline of exports from 1880 to 1890 may suggest that the National Policy tariff made the country's economy more self-contained. However, it is important to emphasize that for the whole period under consideration most goods produced by Canadians were consumed in Canada. It is also true, although to a slightly lesser extent, that most of the goods consumed by Canadians were of Canadian origin.

Most of Canada's trade was with either the United Kingdom or the United States, and over the whole period these trading partners were of roughly equal importance. Up to 1871 the United States took more than half Canada's exports, as it had done when the Reciprocity Treaty was in force before Confederation. Exports to the United States declined in the 1870s, and a decade after Confederation more than half Canada's exports were going to the United Kingdom. The two export markets were of roughly equal importance in the 1880s, but in the 1890s the British market again accounted for more than half the total. Apart from the two main trading partners, the rest of the world took about one-tenth of Canada's exports throughout the period.[8]

The distribution of imports between British and American sources followed contrary trends to those regarding exports. Up to 1873 more than half Canada's imports came from the United Kingdom, but by the late 1870s more than half were coming from the United States. In the 1880s the two sources of imports were roughly equal in importance. Towards the end of the decade the British share began to fall rapidly and by 1895 it was below 30 per cent, while the American share from then onwards was consistently above 50 per cent. Interestingly, more duty was always collected on imports from the United Kingdom than on imports from the United States.[9]

Canada's farms supplied about half its exports throughout the period from Confederation to 1896. In the early years field crops accounted for most of the agricultural exports, but beginning in 1884 and continuing past the end of the century most farm exports were animal rather than vegetable products, with livestock and cheese as the main items. By 1896 more than 70 per cent of the farm exports and more than one-third of all exports were in this category. Exports of manufactured goods were about one-third of all exports

Table 2.1
Percentage of Labour Force in Agriculture

Province	1871	1881	1891
Ontario	49.3	48.3	40.5
Quebec	47.1	46.6	39.1
Nova Scotia	41.9	44.9	33.7
New Brunswick	46.7	51.8	41.9
Manitoba	—	58.3	55.4
British Columbia	—	14.5	13.0
Prince Edward Island	—	60.1	54.2
Territories	—	26.2	54.1
Canada	47.5	47.7	39.5

Source: Calculated from data in Canada, Census, 1871, vol. 2, 345; 1881, vol. 2, 327; 1891, vol. 2, 140–81

soon after Confederation, but did not grow significantly over the next twenty years, so that their relative importance declined. They recovered somewhat from 1887 onwards, but were still less than 30 per cent of the total in 1896. Exports of forest products generally stagnated, falling from about 12 per cent of the total in 1868 to about 6 per cent in 1896. Exports of the fisheries grew from about 7 per cent of the total to about 10 per cent. Mineral exports were the smallest category until 1891, when they finally surpassed forestry exports in importance. They were almost 8 per cent of the total by 1896.[10]

The importance of agriculture (including the raising of livestock) in Canada's export trade reflected its importance in the economy as a whole and in Canadian society and politics. In 1871 agriculture employed almost half Canada's labour force. A decade later its predominance in this regard was unchanged; in fact there had been a slight, although insignificant, increase in the percentage of Canadians who were employed in agriculture. By 1891, however, the share of agriculture in the Canadian labour force had fallen below 40 per cent, probably because of the economic diversification produced by the National Policy tariff. Nonetheless, agriculture still far exceeded any other sector of the economy as a source of employment.

Table 2.1 shows the percentage of the labour force employed in agriculture in each province, and in Canada as a whole, in each of the three census years. Some interesting facts emerge from these data. In the first place, the regional specialization of the Canadian economy, to which the acrimony of federal-provincial relations is sometimes attributed, scarcely existed at the outset, and had only emerged to a limited extent by 1891. Second, and contrary to persistent stereotypes, Ontario was always more agricultural than Quebec, and more agricultural than Canada as a whole. Quebec was always close to the national average in the percentage of its labour force employed in agriculture. Nova Scotia, with its fisheries and coal mines, was always somewhat below average. New Brunswick was slightly below average in 1871, but above average in 1881 and 1891. British Columbia in all three years is conspicuous for its overwhelmingly non-agricultural population. Manitoba and Prince Edward Island, in contrast, had more than half their labour force in agriculture in both 1881 and 1891. The sudden change in the territories between 1881 and 1891 reflects the influence of the CPR on the area that subsequently became the provinces of Saskatchewan and Alberta.

One fact not shown, although possibly suggested, by table 2.1 is that between 1881 and 1891 there was an absolute decline in agricultural employment in each of the eastern and central provinces. In the Maritimes and Quebec, this decline was significant. In the same decade agricultural employment more than doubled in Manitoba, nearly tripled in British Columbia, and increased by a factor of ten in the territories. The regional specialization of the twentieth century, with all its consequences for metropolis-hinterland relations, was beginning to appear.

Although it remained a predominantly rural and agricultural country in 1891, Canada was beginning to industrialize. The number of persons employed in industrial enterprises had increased from 187,942 in 1871 to 370,256, an increase of almost 100 per cent. Although there were still nearly twice as many persons employed in agriculture as in industry, industry was clearly the more rapidly growing sector of the economy. Its productivity was not growing rapidly, however. The value of industrial production increased from $222 million in 1871 to $476 million twenty years later, a rate of increase only slightly greater than the rate of increase in employment.[11]

At the beginning of the period, and to a slightly lesser extent at the end, Canadian industrial production consisted mainly of transforming indigenous raw materials into relatively simple products. In 1871 the ten leading categories of industrial enterprises, in order, were flour and grist mills, sawmills, boot and shoe factories, tailoring and clothing factories, tanneries, foundries, bakeries, blacksmiths, carriage factories, and sugar refineries. The first two categories accounted for more than a quarter of the value of industrial output, and the ten leading categories for more than half. Twenty years later these ten categories of industrial enterprises still accounted for

46 per cent of industrial production. The rank order was little different, except that sugar refineries (a major beneficiary of the National Policy tariff) had moved into fifth place and blacksmiths and carriage makers had both dropped out of the top ten to fourteenth and twelfth place, respectively. The categories that had moved ahead of them in importance were dressmakers; sash, door, and blind factories; cheese factories; and carpentry shops.[12]

Contrary to what is generally assumed, industrial activity did not become increasingly concentrated in Ontario. Ontario accounted for 46.4 per cent of industrial employment in 1871, which was almost identical with its share of the total population. Ten years later Ontario's share was stil 46.4 per cent, and by 1891 it had dropped slightly to 44.9 per cent of industrial employment. Quebec, and especially New Brunswick, suffered more serious declines in their share of industrial employment. Nova Scotia was the only one of the original provinces to increase its percentage over the twenty-year period. British Columbia by 1891 had more industrial workers than farmers. In Ontario at that date, employment in agriculture still exceeded employment in industry by a ratio of nearly two to one.

In 1871 Canada's leading industrial centres, measured by value of output, were, in order, Montreal, Toronto, Quebec City, and Hamilton. In 1881 their rankings were unchanged. By 1891 Hochelaga, the area immediately to the east of Montreal, had moved ahead of both Quebec City and Hamilton. If it is included with Montreal, which later annexed most of it, the rank order was unchanged from that of 1871. Saint John was the fifth ranking industrial centre in 1871. Twenty years later it had fallen behind Ottawa, London, Halifax, New Westminster, Winnipeg, and Victoria. Toronto had fallen further behind Montreal in the 1870s but appeared to be catching up again in the 1880s. However, Montreal and Hochelaga together still had nearly twice the industrial output of Toronto in 1891, a ratio little changed from twenty years earlier.[13]

As a natural consequence of industrialization, trade unions were gaining adherents and industrial disputes were becoming more numerous. John A. Macdonald followed Disraeli's example by legalizing unions in 1872, partly to spite his political and personal enemy, George Brown, whose employees at the *Globe* were on strike.[14] Fourteen years later, however, the prime minister was somewhat disturbed when the Knights of Labor organized a strike against the horse-powered Toronto Street Railway, which was owned by Tory senator (and minister without portfolio) Frank Smith.[15] Macdonald asked his minister of justice, John Thompson, to prepare a memorandum asserting that the relations between labour and capital fell

Table 2.2
Percentage of Population in Cities of 10,000 or More

Province	1871	1881	1891
Ontario	8.2	9.5	17.5
Quebec	14.0	14.9	21.1
Nova Scotia	7.6	8.2	8.6
New Brunswick	10.1	12.9	12.2
Manitoba	—	0	16.8
British Columbia	—	0	31.1
Prince Edward Island	—	10.5	10.4
Territories	0	0	0
Canada	10.3	11.0	17.2

Source: Calculated from data in Canada, Census, 1871, vol. 1, 428; 1881, vol. 1, 406; 1891, vol. 1, 370

under federal jurisdiction as part of "the regulation of trade and commerce."[16] Possibly he feared that the Liberal government of Ontario would adopt legislation encouraging strikes against other Conservative enterprises, but if so his fears were apparently unfounded.

Despite episodes such as these, or the far larger and more significant Grand Trunk Railway strike of 1877, the potential impact of unions and industrial conflict was limited by the extreme fragmentation of Canada's relatively primitive industrial structure. The average industrial establishment in 1891 had only five employees, although admittedly some were much larger. Public utilities and transportation enterprises were actually more congenial environments for unions than the industrial sector itself. The rapid growth of the Knights of Labor in the 1880s suggests that a working class with some collective consciousness was emerging, but Canada remained an agricultural country with scattered enclaves of industrialization, and this was just as much true in Ontario as elsewhere.

Closely related to, although not identical with, industrialization is urbanization. Table 2.2 shows its uneven progress across the provinces, and across the two decades from 1871 to 1891. Canada was not significantly more urbanized in 1881 than it had been in 1871. Ontario was still less urbanized than the country as a whole, and even less than Prince Edward Island. In the next decade there was a significant trend to urbanization, largely because of the rapid growth of Toronto and the even more rapid growth of cities in the West. Ontario was still less urbanized than Quebec, but had finally overtaken the national average.

The varying rates of growth of different cities reflected a gradual westward shift of population and economic activity. Quebec City and Saint John grew hardly at all in the three decades after Confederation, and the rate of growth in Halifax was fairly modest.. Montreal and Ottawa more than doubled between 1871 and 1891, and Toronto more than tripled in size. Hamilton, the sixth largest city at the time of Confederation, did not quite double but moved ahead of the two Maritime seaports and maintained a narrow lead over Ottawa. London doubled but remained in eighth place. Winnipeg, which counted only 241 inhabitants in 1871, had 25,642 twenty years later and was in ninth place. Victoria, the capital of the other western province, increased over the same period from 3270 inhabitants to 16,841. Vancouver, which did not exist until 1887, counted 13,685 inhabitants four years later. Other cities that had attained a population of ten thousand or more by 1891 were Kingston, Brantford, Guelph, St Thomas, and Windsor in Ontario, St-Henri, Hull, and Sherbrooke in Quebec, and Charlottetown in Prince Edward Island.

Most nineteenth-century Canadians probably regarded ethnic and religious differences as more important than distinctions based on class, occupation, or place of residence. Certainly politicians appeared to take them more seriously. The Canada of the nineteenth century was a collection of distinct ethnic and religious communities, the product of different streams of immigration, which were socially and to some extent geographically isolated from one another. The tendency in the latter part of the twentieth century to see provincial boundaries as the main component of Canada's diversity should not be uncritically applied to the nineteenth century when government, particularly at the provincial level, had a limited impact on people's lives. Ethnic and religious loyalties were probably more intense than provincial ones, particularly when so many Canadians were immigrants or the children of immigrants. Concerns common to a particular group, such as separate schools for Catholics, temperance for many Protestants, or the contrasting responses of French and other Canadians to the fate of Louis Riel, were not easily confined within provincial boundaries.

Fortunately for the social scientist or historian, the Canadian census provided exceptionally good data on ethnicity and religion; these figures were more reliable in the nineteenth century than in the twentieth, when political considerations influenced both the collection and the presentation of the data. Table 2.3 depicts the ethnic origins of Canadians as of 1881. Except in the case of Manitoba, whose ethnic composition changed significantly between 1870 and

Table 2.3
Ethnic Origin by Province, 1881 (per cent)

Province	French	Irish	English	Scottish	German	Aboriginal	Other
Ontario	5.3	32.6	27.9	19.7	9.8	0.8	3.9
Quebec	79.0	9.1	6.0	4.0	0.7	0.6	0.6
Nova Scotia	9.4	15.0	29.3	33.1	9.1	0.5	3.6
New Brunswick	17.6	31.5	29.1	15.5	2.0	0.4	3.9
Manitoba	15.1	15.4	17.4	25.0	13.1	10.3	3.7
British Columbia	1.9	6.4	14.8	7.9	1.7	51.9	15.4
Prince Edward Is.	9.9	23.3	19.7	44.9	1.0	0.3	0.9
Territories	5.1	0.5	2.4	2.2	0	87.6	2.2
Canada	30.0	22.1	20.4	16.2	5.9	2.5	2.9

Source: Calculated from data in Canada, Census, 1881, vol. 1, table 3, 300–1

1896, these data may be taken as representative of the whole period with which this book is concerned.

French Canadians were the largest single group, representing exactly 30 per cent of the population. They were of course dominant in Quebec, although less so then than now; several counties in the so-called Eastern Townships and in the Ottawa Valley had non-French majorities. French Canadians were already fighting a desperate rearguard action in officially bilingual Manitoba. They were the largest ethnic group in three Ontario counties (Essex, Prescott, and Russell) and in three New Brunswick counties (Gloucester, Kent, and Victoria), but still they lacked political visibility in either province. They ranked a distant third in size among New Brunswick's ethnic groups, and a distant fifth among Ontario's. The Acadians in New Brunswick and the other Maritime provinces had practically no contact with Quebec, and the people of Quebec were hardly aware of their existence. The French Canadians of the West, although more remote, had more historical links with Quebec, whose explorers, fur traders, and priests had helped to develop that region.[17]

The Irish were Canada's second largest ethnic group in 1881, and the largest group in both Ontario and New Brunswick. Although the twentieth-century tendency is to equate "Irish" with "Catholic," most Irish Canadians in the latter part of the nineteenth century were Protestants.[18] Their large numbers were the consequence of massive immigration that had taken place principally in the middle third of the nineteenth century. They were the largest ethnic group in the seaport cities of Halifax and Saint John, and in the nation's capital. They were dominant in southern New Brunswick and on both banks of the Ottawa River, but their main area of strength was a broad belt of counties extending through central Ontario from Dundas in the east to Perth in the west. More than half of all Canadian Irish lived in Ontario.

English Canadians (in the strict sense) were the third largest ethnic group. Interestingly, they were not the largest group in any province, although in British Columbia, which denied the franchise to its aboriginal majority, they were the largest group entitled to vote and to participate in politics. In contrast to the Irish or the French, their migration to North America had been a continuous process extending over more than two centuries. They were somewhat more likely than other Canadian ethnic groups to live in cities, and were the largest ethnic group in Toronto, Hamilton, London, and Victoria. They also dominated some of the best agricultural land in Canada, including the Annapolis and Saint John valleys, the Quebec counties of Brome and Stanstead, and most of the counties with frontage on Lake Ontario. Most of these were areas where United Empire Loyalists had settled after the American Revolution, and the Loyalist migration may be considered the nucleus of English settlement in Canada. Later migration directly from England had substantially reinforced their numbers, however, and would continue to do so for many decades to come.

Scottish Canadians seem to have had a particular penchant for politics in the nineteenth century. John A. Macdonald and Alexander Mackenzie, the first two prime ministers, were both born in Scotland, as was George Brown, who headed the Reform party in Canada West before Confederation. Ontario's first premier, Sandfield Macdonald, and its most successful one, Oliver Mowat, were the sons of Scottish immigrants. The prominence of these men, and the photographic image of Donald A. Smith driving the last spike on the CPR at Craigellachie, have created the misleading impression that Canada was a Scottish country. In fact the Scots were only the fourth largest ethnic group, being one-sixth of the population. They were the largest group, however, in three provinces. In Prince Edward Island they made up almost half the population and were the largest group in every county. They also dominated the eastern half of Nova Scotia and were strong in Manitoba, where the first permanent European settlement had been founded by the Earl of Selkirk in 1812. In Ontario they were the largest group in three eastern counties (Glengarry, Stormont, and Lanark) and were also numerous in the area between Lake Huron and Lake Erie.

Unlike the groups previously mentioned, German Canadians were not commemorated in the nation's coat of arms, but they ranked high in both numbers and seniority. Many United Empire Loyalists were of German ancestry, and other Germans arrived in the nineteenth century, although the number who came to Canada was only a fraction of those who went to the United States. In 1881 the Germans outnumbered the French in Ontario and were not far behind them in Nova Scotia and Manitoba. They were the largest group in three counties: Lunenburg, Waterloo, and Welland.

The aboriginal peoples, as table 2.3 shows, were an extremely small minority in the four original provinces. Canada's expansion to the West, however, brought many more of them under Canadian control and made the federal government's jurisdiction over them a significant responsibility. They were virtually excluded from participating in politics. As of 1881 they were an overwhelming majority in the territories (including present-day Saskatchewan and Alberta) and on the British Columbia mainland. On Vancouver Island and in Manitoba they had already been reduced to the status of a minority.

Although ethnicity was important to nineteenth-century Canadians, religion was probably more so. The churches provided much of the social and intellectual, as well as the spiritual content of Canadian life. At a time when secular entertainments were few and the state played little part in people's lives, personal identity was largely anchored to religion. Religion also played a large part in politics. In constructing a federal cabinet, for example, the representation of the major denominations was almost as important a consideration as the representation of the provinces.

Religion and ethnicity were not entirely unrelated. Although the census did not do cross-tabulations of religion and ethnicity, a sampling of more than ten thousand individual returns from the 1871 census has revealed what is probably an accurate religious breakdown of the main ethnic groups.[19] French Canadians, as might be anticipated, were almost entirely Roman Catholic. Almost two-fifths of the Irish were Catholic and almost one-quarter, a surprisingly large proportion, were Anglican. Canadians of English ancestry were about one-third Anglican, one-third Methodist, and one-third miscellaneous. About three out of every five Scottish Canadians were Presbyterians. Methodists and Lutherans together accounted for about half the German population. Few aboriginals were enumerated in the 1871 census, and even in 1881 few were asked about their religious affiliation. Most probably adhered to their traditional beliefs, although Catholic and Anglican missionaries had made some inroads.

Table 2.4 shows the relative strength of the major denominations in Canada and in each province as of 1881. Like table 2.3, it may be

Table 2.4
Religious Affiliation by Province, 1881 (per cent)

Province	Roman Catholic	Anglican	Methodist	Presbyterian	Baptist	Other/ Not Stated
Ontario	16.7	19.0	30.7	21.7	5.5	6.4
Quebec	86.1	5.1	2.9	3.7	0.6	1.6
Nova Scotia	26.7	13.7	11.5	25.5	19.0	3.6
New Brunswick	34.0	14.5	10.7	13.3	25.2	2.3
Manitoba	18.5	21.7	14.3	21.7	14.3	9.5
British Columbia	20.3	15.8	7.1	8.3	0.9	47.6
Prince Edward Is.	43.3	6.6	12.4	31.1	5.7	0.9
Canada	41.4	13.3	17.2	15.6	6.8	5.7

Source: Calculated from data in Canada, Census, 1881, vol. 1, table 2, 202–3

taken as representative of the entire period with which this book is concerned. The territories are excluded since religious data are available for only a small fraction of their inhabitants. Data are also missing for most of the aboriginal people in British Columbia.

The Roman Catholic church enjoyed a quasi-official status and a numerically dominant position in Quebec, where its primacy had been recognized by the imperial government in the Quebec Act of 1774. In that province it provided an essential social network for its numerous adherents, including not only schools and colleges but the "Hospitals, Asylums, Charities, and Eleemosynary Institutions" mentioned in the British North America Act. Elsewhere Catholics were a minority, although they were the largest religious group in each of the Maritime provinces. It is interesting to note that Ontario had the lowest Catholic percentage of any province, and the constitutional entrenchment of separate schools in that province was something of an anomaly.

The Anglican church was not the largest denomination in any province, and ranked only fourth in Canada as a whole. It had never achieved the privileged position in Canada it enjoyed in some other parts of the empire, but it did have a certain social status in relation to the other churches. Its members were less likely to be farmers, and more likely to be in business, professional, or white-collar occupations than most other Canadians. The pre-eminence of Anglicans in the federal public service was remarkable. As of 1872, nineteen of the thirty-one officials who earned at least $2600 per annum (the minimum rate for a deputy minister) were Anglicans, as compared with only seven Catholics, three Presbyterians, and two unspecified "Protestants."[20]

Unlike the Catholic and Anglican churches, the other major denominations were not hierarchically organized and cohesive bodies. Their individual congregations were largely autonomous and they had a tendency to divide into distinct groupings.[21] The 1881 census, for example, specified five different varieties of Methodists, four of Presbyterians, and three of Baptists. This type of organization (or lack of organization) was well suited to a rural country with poor communications, and outside Quebec these denominations dominated the countryside, although the Anglicans were relatively stronger in the cities. As table 2.4 suggests, the overwhelming majority of Canadian Methodists lived in Ontario, where they were the largest religious group. More than half the Baptists lived in either Nova Scotia or New Brunswick. Baptists were not the largest denomination in any province, but they were not far behind the Catholics in New Brunswick. Presbyterians were quite evenly spread across Canada (with the exception of Quebec), but were not really dominant anywhere.

No account of religion in nineteenth-century Canada would be complete without a reference to the Loyal Orange Order. This broadly based popular movement catered primarily to Irish Protestants, although it was open to Protestants of any ethnic background. The order existed in both Canada West and the Maritimes before 1867 but became a nationwide movement after Confederation, with lodges in every province. Its greatest strength was in the predominantly Irish parts of rural Ontario, where it provided a strong institutional and social network for the Protestant population comparable with that which the Catholic parishes provided for French Canadians in Quebec.[22] The Orange network was particularly significant as a means of integrating Protestant immigrants from the British Isles into Canadian society and was perhaps an early equivalent of the "multiculturalism" policies professed by Canadian governments more recently.[23] Although in principle antagonistic to one another, these two social networks – the French Catholic in Quebec and the Orange Protestant in Ontario – served jointly as the backbone of the Conservative party in Canada throughout the second half of the nineteenth century.

Federal-provincial relations in late nineteenth-century Canada cannot be fully understood without some knowledge of the party system. Intergovernmental relations were not conducted by impersonal bureaucracies as is often the case today. Public servants were few in number and largely partisan in orientation; bureaucracy, in the Weberian sense, could hardly be said to exist. Party labels were meaningful both to voters and to elected office-holders, particularly in central Canada, and the intense competitiveness of partisan struggle pervaded every aspect of governmental activity, and not least the relations with other governments. Both John A. Macdonald and Oliver Mowat frequently referred to the opposing party as "the enemy," and the conditions in which constituency contests took place, particularly before the introduction of the secret ballot, often made the military metaphor seem appropriate.

Patronage – the trading of benefits and favours for political support – was universally considered to be an essential aspect of representative government. Jobs in the public service were one form of patronage, although, in contrast to the United States, a new government in Canada did not dismiss the employees appointed by its predecessor. Other forms of patronage included licences for tavern keepers, printing contracts for friendly newspapers, or the right to cut timber on public lands. Politics was a continuous battle, not so much over principles as over the power to dispense favours and thus to win support from voters, or from those who could influence voters.

The historian Gordon Stewart has attributed these characteristics of Canadian political life to the difficult and occasionally violent conditions under which responsible government was won in the middle of the nineteenth century.[24] These conditions, including the armed rebellions that broke out in both Upper and Lower Canada in 1837, distinguished Canada from the Maritimes, the Australasian colonies, or the United Kingdom itself, in all of which the transition to responsible government was peaceful.

In winning responsible government, Canadians wrested control of patronage away from the governor and his irresponsible advisers, but they did not in doing so abolish patronage or even spread the control over it more widely. Patronage was merely transferred from a Château Clique or Family Compact to a centralized political machine controlled by a party leader. These people in turn held office for as long as they could persuade or manipulate the electorate to keep them in office. Provided they could do so, the system remained almost as centralized as before. In English constitutional history, as Stewart and others have noted, the centralized, executive-dominant model of government was challenged by an alternative "country" model according to which power and patronage would be widely distributed among local elites who sat in both houses of Parliament. Although the centralized "court" model did eventually triumph in England, it faced serious challenges, and the alternative model decisively influenced the development of the thirteen English colonies that became the United States. In Canada, according to Stewart, the "country" model had few adherents. Both sides in the struggles over responsible government agreed in rejecting it, if they agreed on nothing else.[25]

These struggles were recent memories in 1867 to men like Macdonald, Cartier, Mowat, and Brown. Confederation, and the annexations that followed, extended their peculiar vision of politics over a much wider territorial domain, now including the smaller colonies that had not experienced Canada's history of conflict. Within a few years, half a continent was incorporated into a political system based on the Canadian model. Confederation also added the complication of federalism. How could two levels of government, both based on the centralized, executive-dominant model of politics, share jurisdiction over the same territory and population? If the same political machine controlled both levels, as in Mexican, Soviet, or Indian federalism more recently, few problems would arise, but what if this did not happen?

John A. Macdonald was selected by Lord Monck as the first prime minister of Canada because he was the principal architect of the British North America Act and the most talented politician in the largest province. His popular support was less than overwhelming, however, as the election that followed later in the year revealed. In both Maritime provinces the opposition outpolled the government. In the second election five years later the government gained significantly in Nova Scotia but was outpolled by the opposition in Ontario. Without the two new western provinces, Macdonald would not have had a majority in the House of Commons. The revelation of the Pacific Scandal administered the *coup de grâce* to a government that appeared moribund, despite its considerable achievements. Alexander Mackenzie formed a Liberal government that received an overwhelming majority in the election of 1874.

The Liberal government proved a disappointment, however, and its arrival coincided with the beginning of a severe recession. Macdonald won re-election in 1878 by promising to protect and encourage Canadian industries with higher tariffs. From then until his death in 1891 he was indeed the Old Chieftain, whom the voters endorsed four times in a row at the expense of three Liberal leaders: Mackenzie, Edward Blake, and Wilfrid Laurier. Party discipline had become more rigid, partly because the tariff gave the parties something to disagree about and partly because of the electoral reforms introduced by the Liberals. Macdonald's control of Parliament, and of the country, was never in doubt.

Macdonald died in office soon after winning the 1891 election, and the party leadership fell by default to an undistinguished and elderly Quebec anglophone, Senator John J. Abbott. In December 1892 Abbott stepped aside in favour of the young minister of justice, John Thompson of Halifax, but Thompson died prematurely after two years as prime minister. Senator Mackenzie Bowell, an Ontario Orangeman and former newspaper editor, succeeded him. Bowell's ineffectual response to the controversy over separate schools in Manitoba inspired a cabinet revolt against his leadership in 1896, and Charles Tupper returned from his high commissioner's post in London to take control of the government. In the election that followed immediately afterwards the Conservatives won more votes than the Liberals but fewer seats. This was the first Canadian election in which minor parties, the anti-Catholic McCarthyites (led by D'Alton McCarthy) and the agrarian populist Patrons of Industry, won representation in the House of Commons.

Macdonald had hoped, like most founders of new states, that his own party would be a hegemonic, broadly based coalition, excluding only separatists, radical agrarian populists, and other marginal groups, and thus able to control the federal, Quebec, and Ontario governments more or less indefinitely. Although George Brown left the coalition even before Confederation was achieved, Macdonald's first post-Confederation government included other Reformers like James C. Aikins, William P. Howland, William McDougall, and even old Sir Francis Hincks. Joseph Howe, who had led Nova Scotia's opposition to Confederation, was soon lured into the fold. Erstwhile opponents of Confederation served, with Macdonald's approval, as premiers (and political allies) in Ontario and New Brunswick. Macdonald granted patronage to men like these because he wanted to stay in office, but also because he believed their support was essential if the fragile new dominion was to survive. He included them even at the cost of excluding former friends like Richard Cartwright, who never forgave Macdonald for not giving him a seat in the first dominion cabinet.[26]

Despite Macdonald's efforts, the two-party system of the old Province of Canada reasserted itself almost immediately, quickly spread to the new provinces of the dominion, and proved remarkably durable. In the first general election, held in the late summer of 1867, government candidates received only 50.1 per cent of the votes in the ridings that were contested. In the eight elections between 1867 and 1896 inclusive, the candidates of Macdonald's party never achieved more than 52.5 per cent of the popular vote and their average was only 49.5 per cent.[27]

One of Canada's leading political theorists, C.B. Macpherson, has argued that a quasi-colonial economy and an electorate consisting mainly of independent small farmers together provide conditions in which competitive party politics are unlikely to emerge.[28] Canada in the years just after Confederation certainly possessed both of the characteristics that Macpherson associated with a quasi-party system, and yet a competitive two-party system emerged instead. The reasons why this occurred would make an interesting subject for further research. Other models besides Macpherson's might be tested in the process. The defection of Cartwright from the Macdonald camp, for example, might give some credence to William Riker's theory of political coalitions, according to which limited resources of patronage are likely to be used to build a coalition just large enough to win a majority, but no larger.[29]

Escott Reid has alleged that the two-party system in Canada did not really emerge before 1878.[30] Voting behaviour in the House of Commons was certainly less predictable before that date than afterwards (see chapter 13), but Reid's assertion seems an overstatement. Using his criteria, one would have to conclude that neither the United Kingdom nor the United States had a two-party system in the 1870s. It is true that Manitoba and British Columbia had not yet accepted the two-party system, that New Brunswick had coalition governments, and that even Ontario elected a certain number of "loose fish" to the House of Commons. Nonetheless, no one doubted that John A. Macdonald was the leader of one major political party and that Alexander Mackenzie led the other. Although attitudinal surveys are obviously impossible a century after the fact, electoral data for the first four federal elections suggest that most voters were already quite firmly attached to one or the other party, and that a relatively small number of uncommitted voters decided the outcomes of elections. In the whole period up to 1896 the Conservative vote of 45.4 per cent in 1874, immediately after the Pacific Scandal, was the lowest percentage ever won by that party. The low point for the Liberals came in 1896 when they won only 45.1 per cent, but ironically won the election.

Voting behaviour, then as now, was probably influenced by the familiar variables of province, ethnicity, religion, occupation, and class, but none of these factors by itself can explain the outcome of any election. Ontario was more Liberal than Quebec, as had been true before Confederation. Nova Scotia inclined to the Liberals because that party expressed the continuing anti-Confederation sentiment in the province. British Columbia was Conservative, in federal elections, because the Conservatives promised to, and actually did, build the CPR On the whole, however, interprovincial differences in voting behaviour were not particularly pronounced by modern standards.

Macdonald's party, as noted earlier, derived strong support from the Catholic church in Quebec and from the Orange lodges in Ontario, and these two networks provided it with a solid core of reasonably safe seats in central Canada. In Quebec the most Conservative ridings tended to be north of the St Lawrence. The Richelieu Valley, a centre of *Patriote* activity in 1837, was still the *Rouge* heartland half a century later. Most of the anglophone ridings, like Argenteuil, Compton, Montreal West, Pontiac, Sherbrooke, and Stanstead, were Conservative strongholds, but Huntingdon and Brome inclined to the Liberals.

In Ontario the predominantly Irish ridings, where the Orange network was particularly effective, had a tendency to vote Conservative. Predominantly Scottish ridings, both in the extreme east of the province and in the southwest, had an even more pronounced tilt towards the Liberals. The most striking contrast in Ontario voting behaviour, however, was between the urban industrial ridings and the agricultural ridings. The very strong Conservative tendency of the former group was apparent in 1867 and 1872, and thus cannot be attributed to the National Policy tariff Macdonald promised in 1878. In the eight federal general elections from 1867 through 1896 the Conservatives won a total of sixty-three constituency contests in urban Ontario, while the Liberals won only nineteen. Apart from 1874 and 1896, the Liberals never won more than one urban Ontario seat in any election, and in 1887 they were shut out entirely. In agricultural Ontario, in contrast, the Conservatives won 309 constituency contests in the eight elections and the Liberals 310. Six rural ridings in 1896 were won by candidates running under other labels. The only Ontario riding that was neither industrial nor agricultural, Algoma, elected Conservatives five times and Liberals three times.

This is perhaps the best place to discuss nineteenth-century Canadian attitudes towards democracy and the evolution of the franchise. It is generally known that "democracy" was not a respectable word in nineteenth-century Canada, or in any other part of the British Empire at that time. Political thinkers from Aristotle to John Stuart Mill had argued that universal suffrage would mean mob rule and an end to liberty and property, and their views were still widely accepted in the late nineteenth century. Although the United States provided evidence to refute this pessimistic view, the Civil War did not increase the prestige of the American experiment. In Canada, or at least in central Canada, anti-American sentiment dating from 1812 also tended to reinforce anti-democratic prejudices. Almost all prominent politicians considered voting a privilege that should be reserved for those who met some property qualification or, as they often put it, to those having a stake in the country.

Until 1885 the precise qualifications required to vote in a federal election were left to be determined by the provinces, with the result that there were some interprovincial variations. All provinces excluded women, native Indians, and persons who were not British subjects either by birth or by naturalization. All except British Columbia and Prince Edward Island imposed a property requirement as well, although the details varied.[31]

There are serious difficulties in determining just how liberal the franchise was and how many people were excluded as a result of the various property qualifications imposed by the provinces. Age-specific population data are available only in census years. Data on the numbers eligible to vote are available only for years when elections took place, and are far from complete even for those years.[32] In ridings where the member won by acclamation (roughly a quarter of the seats in each of the three elections that preceded the introduction of the secret ballot), no voters' lists were compiled, and in many other ridings, particularly in the smaller provinces, no data are available. A sampling of the ridings for which data are available, however, suggests that in 1872 about three-quarters of men over twenty-one were eligible to vote in Ontario, about two-thirds in Quebec and New Brunswick, and about three-fifths in Nova Scotia. If native Indians and persons born outside the British Empire are excluded from consideration, the proportion enfranchised in Ontario was probably about four-fifths. This is not surprising since agriculture was the dominant industry, so that most adult males owned land. Nova Scotia, the least agricultural of the original provinces, predictably had the smallest proportion of its residents eligible to vote.

A similar exercise can be done with regard to the 1882 election, which also fell only a year after a census. As compared with ten years earlier, the percentage of adult males eligible to vote remained about the same in Ontario, but it had increased significantly in New Brunswick, which had about caught up with Ontario, and very significantly in Quebec, where about four-fifths of the adult male population were eligible. There was little change in Nova Scotia, which lagged far behind the other original provinces in the percentage of its residents who could vote. In British Columbia more than half the adult male population were excluded on racial grounds. Data are not available for Prince Edward Island, but there was no property qualification there and a racial qualification would have excluded few people. In Manitoba the high rate of population growth and questionable accuracy of the census makes it futile to attempt any calculation.

In 1885 the Macdonald government caused Parliament to adopt the Electoral Franchise Act, which took control over the franchise, as far as federal elections were concerned, away from the provinces.[33] The elections of 1887, 1891, and 1896 were conducted under the terms of this measure. A voter could qualify by owning either $300 worth of real estate in a city, $200 worth in a town, or $150 in a rural county. Tenants could qualify if they had lived at the same location for a calendar year and had paid rent of at least $2 per month, $6 per quarter, $12 per half year, or $20 per year. Farmers' adult sons living on the family farm could vote if the father was eligible. Commercial fishermen could count the value of their boats and equipment towards the property qualification in lieu of real estate. Residents of British Columbia and Prince Edward Island, which had no property qualifications at the provincial level, could vote in federal elections if they met the provincial requirements. Even Indians could vote in the eastern provinces, although not in the west, if they owned houses or "improvements" on a reservation worth at least $150. Clearly the measure was designed to exclude very few adult males from voting, which may be why it was so controversial. Macdonald might not profess allegiance to democracy, but he was close to accepting it in practice.

In the 1887 election, the first fought under the terms of the Electoral Franchise Act, the number of ballots cast was 40 per cent greater than in 1882, although the population at that time was growing very slowly. By 1891 the number who voted was 50 per cent greater than in 1882.[34] A comparison of those eligible to vote in a sampling of ridings in 1891 with age-specific census data for the same year suggests that virtually universal male suffrage had been achieved in New Brunswick, Ontario, and Manitoba. In Quebec, about five out of every six adult males apparently met the qualifications, and in Nova Scotia, about four out of every five. Data are not available for Prince Edward Island. In British Columbia the exclusion of native Indians and Chinese, and the large number of transients and non-British immigrants, still had the consequence that fewer than half the adult males possessed the franchise. This was an ironic situation for a province that had abolished property qualifications while it was still a crown colony, and that had been regarded as an outpost of radical democracy for more than twenty years.

What consequences did the party system, the elections, and the gradual movement towards de facto democracy have for federal-provincial relations? Differences in policy between the two parties were not very great except, after 1874, with regard to the tariff. The tariff as such was not really an issue in federal-provincial relations since it fell under exclusive federal jurisdiction and since most of the provinces had essentially similar economies, so that the benefits and costs of the tariff were equally shared.

Partisanship was, however, an independent variable that affected federal-provincial relations, particularly with regard to Nova Scotia, Ontario, and Quebec where party allegiance was deeply divisive. In those provinces, at least, relations with the federal government were significantly worse when the two levels of government had contrasting party labels. In practice this usually meant, during the period under consideration, that the federal government was Conservative and the provincial government was not. In Nova Scotia and Quebec, to make matters worse, the Liberal parties consisted largely of persons who had opposed Confederation in the first place. Yet even in Ontario, where the parties had not differed significantly in their views on Confederation or even on the details of the Quebec Resolutions, the Conservatives came to be regarded as the party of centralization and the Liberals as the party of provincial rights.[35]

With the relative lack of economic diversity among provinces and with the gradual broadening of the franchise at both levels, federal and provincial governments did not differ significantly in the constellation of class and economic interests they represented. Land reform in Prince Edward Island was one of the few class-related issues that provoked serious federal-provincial conflict (see chapter 5). British Columbia, the other province that did not impose economic restrictions on the franchise, had more than its share of conflicts with the federal authorities, but would probably have done so in any event. Ontario finally abolished property qualifications for the franchise in 1888, but by that time they had become nugatory at the federal level as well. Certainly Ontario's relations with the Macdonald government could not have become much worse than they were already.

One subject that did prove to be a perennial source of conflict between the federal government and all of the provincial governments was public finance. Many if not most of the intergovernmental disputes that arose in the thirty years after Confederation were disputes over money, and it is not unfair to suggest that the terms of the British North America Act made such disputes practically unavoidable.

In any political system the nature of public finance is largely a product of economic and social circumstances. Canada in 1867 was a predominantly rural society in which most adult males were self-employed and in which most families had little cash income. The family farm provided much of its own food, fuel, and other necessities and was a largely, although not entirely, self-sufficient economic unit. In such a society, as in many non-industrialized countries today, the most convenient and effective modes of taxation were to tax imports at the border or to tax certain goods and commodities that were not normally produced on the family farm at the point of production or sale. These two types of taxation, known respectively as customs and excise, were considered "indirect" taxes because they were collected from the importer, producer, or merchant rather than from the consumers who would ultimately bear their cost.

As is generally known, the British North America Act placed customs and excise taxes under the exclusive control of the federal government. To do otherwise would have permitted provinces to impose taxes indirectly on residents of other provinces if, for example, a Montreal merchant paid customs duty on goods destined for Ontario. It would also have created artificial barriers to the movement of goods among the provinces, barriers that would have reduced the traffic on interprovincial railways and drastically lessened the economic benefits that proponents of Confederation insisted it would provide. In any event, the central government was expected to have the most expensive responsibilities, such as military defence, the construction of canals and interprovincial railways, and protecting the fisheries from foreign encroachments. The provinces' responsibilities were mainly of a regulatory nature and were not expected to be very expensive.

For all these reasons it was natural to give the most significant sources of tax revenue to the central government. The provinces could theoretically impose direct taxes, but taxes on real property were anathema to farmers, although they were beginning to be imposed in urban municipalities. Taxes on income had been imposed by the United States government during the Civil War, and by the British government during the war against Napoleon Bonaparte, but they were not considered a normal feature of peacetime public finance and they could only be conveniently collected from persons with unusually high incomes, of whom Canada had very few. In practice this meant that the provinces would rely mainly on revenue from their public lands and resources, the sale of licences and permits, and grants from the federal government.

Table 2.5 shows the volume and distribution of government revenues and expenditures in the years 1870, 1880, and 1890. Federal revenues always relied mainly on the customs tariff, although excises on alcohol and tobacco made a significant contribution, and non-tax revenues, such as profits from the post office, interest on investments, and revenues from public lands, were increasingly important

Table 2.5
Government Revenues, Grants, and Spending

	1870	1880	1890
Federal revenue	15,512,226	23,307,407	39,879,925
Provincial revenue			
(excluding federal grants)	2,821,949	3,491,699	6,023,815
Total government revenue	18,334,175	26,799,106	45,903,740
Federal grants			
to provinces	2,588,605	3,430,846	3,904,922
Other federal spending	11,756,905	21,419,788	32,089,109
Provincial spending	4,465,163	7,366,106	11,132,175
Total government spending	16,222,068	28,785,894	43,221,284

Source: Calculated from tables in The Statistical Yearbook of Canada for 1890, 456–8, 462, 469–70

towards the end of the century. Total federal revenues grew rapidly and the proportion of them distributed to the provinces in the form of grants fell from about one-sixth to one-tenth. Provincial revenues grew slowly in the economically depressed 1870s but more rapidly in the 1880s, particularly as some provinces began to impose direct taxes on corporations. Federal grants accounted for almost half the provincial revenues in 1870 and for about 40 per cent in 1890. Federal spending, excluding grants to the provinces, always accounted for nearly three-fourths of the total spending by both levels of government. If these data are compared with the estimates of GNP referred to earlier, it appears that both levels of government together collected, and spent, roughly 4 per cent of GNP in 1870, 5 per cent in 1880, and 6 per cent in 1890. While the trend was clearly upward, the data illustrate the limited involvement of the nineteenth-century state in the economy, and its limited impact on people's lives.

Nineteenth-century governments did not always balance their budgets. Revenues were sensitive to fluctuations in the economy, and efforts to cut spending, then as now, were politically hazardous. The federal government spent more than it collected in every year from 1876 to 1880 inclusive, in 1885, 1886, and 1888, and in the years 1894 through 1896: a total of eleven out of twenty-nine years. The provinces fared even worse. Ontario and Quebec each had deficits in seventeen years, Nova Scotia in eighteen, and New Brunswick in thirteen. British Columbia balanced the budget in only three of its first twenty-five years as a Canadian province. Manitoba and Prince Edward Island each had deficits in eighteen years out of the years from 1874 to 1896 inclusive. (There are no data for Manitoba's first few years as a province.)[36]

One reason why governments at both levels could indulge in deficit financing was that interest rates were relatively low and declining. In 1868 the average rate of interest paid on the public debt of Canada was 4.64 per cent, but thereafter it declined steadily. It fell below 4 per cent by 1880 and was down to 3.23 per cent in 1896.[37] These were real, and not merely nominal, rates of interest, since inflation was practically non-existent. At the same time, the provinces had the great advantage of beginning with clean slates, since the dominion assumed their debts as they entered Confederation.

This abbbreviated account of public finance in the Canada of the late nineteenth century may make the subject appear deceptively simple. In practice it was not at all simple. Every province entered Confederation (or in the case of Manitoba was created) under specific financial terms that differed at least slightly from those of every other province. These initial differences were embellished by a bewildering variety of special deals and arrangements made between the federal government and the various provinces over the years.[38] Differences in the revenue bases and spending priorities of the provinces complicated the picture still further.

Economics, ethnicity, religion, partisanship, and the complexity of public finance all contributed to the lengthy agenda of relations between the federal government and each province. Chapters 3–6 will describe the main issues that arose between the federal government and the provinces up to 1896 and will indicate their outcomes. Later chapters will examine the contribution of particular institutions, practices, and procedures to dealing with issues that found their way onto the intergovernmental agenda.

THE ANGUS L. MacDONALD LIBRARY
ST. FRANCIS XAVIER UNIVERSITY
ANTIGONISH, N. S.

3 The Intergovernmental Agenda: Ontario

Ontario was perhaps the only province where Confederation was greeted with widespread enthusiasm, and only a handful of its representatives had voted against the Quebec Resolutions in 1865. Nonetheless, it emerged within a few years as the most redoubtable champion of provincial autonomy. There were underlying socioeconomic reasons for this apparent paradox, but the abrupt transition can only be understood with reference to the partisan politics involved.

One circumstance that distinguished Ontario for almost a quarter century after 1867 was that the two prime ministers, Macdonald and Mackenzie, were both deeply involved in, and knowledgeable about, Ontario politics. Macdonald had been a dominant figure in the Liberal-Conservative party of Canada West since its emergence in the early 1850s. Mackenzie, a Reformer, had also sat in the old pre-Confederation Parliament and, after Confederation, served briefly as provincial treasurer in Edward Blake's Ontario government. Both had their own friends and enemies, their own prejudices and preferences; their involvement in Ontario politics was inevitably more intimate and direct than their dealings with other provinces, about which they knew little. This fact reinforced the impact of Ontario's highly polarized, and highly developed, party system in giving a strong partisan flavour to federal-provincial relations.

Confederation had been carried in Ontario by a shaky coalition of Liberal-Conservatives and Reformers, a coalition that actually began to disintegrate before the British North America Act was passed by the Parliament at Westminster. Despite this inconvenient fact, and despite the weakness of his own party in Ontario, John A. Macdonald tried to ensure that the largest province would have, after Confederation, a provincial government that was friendly, not to say subservient, to his own government. An appropriate premier was found in the unlikely person of his namesake and erstwhile opponent, John Sandfield Macdonald, who was not only a Reformer but one of the few Reformers who had opposed Confederation.[1] Despite these odd circumstances, post-Confederation relations between the two Macdonalds, and between their respective governments, were cordial, but the experiment was not destined to last. The allegedly non-partisan provincial government was widely perceived as Conservative, a label that was not an asset in Ontario politics, and it suffered serious losses in the 1871 election. This fact, combined with his deteriorating health (he died of tuberculosis the following year), forced Sandfield Macdonald to resign a few months after the election. He was succeeded by Edward Blake at the head of a Reform government. When Blake decided to pursue his political career at the federal level a year later, Oliver Mowat resigned from the judicial bench to take over the provincial government. He continued to lead it until 1896 when, at the age of seventy-five, he entered Laurier's cabinet as minister of justice.

No account of Ontario's relations with the federal government can ignore the impact of Mowat's forceful, effective, and seemingly interminable leadership. His record of longevity in office has been exceeded by only one subsequent premier, George Murray of Nova Scotia, and his influence on Canadian politics has been equalled by no other provincial politician, and by very few at the federal level. He established a prototype for all subsequent provincial premiers, in Ontario and elsewhere, just as Macdonald established a prototype for federal prime ministers. Both were skilled politicians who used patronage and other devices to build strong centralized and highly effective political machines, Since the two machines had to coexist and compete on the same territory, a clash was inevitable. Since federalism made it possible for both machines to be simultaneously in power, they competed on more or less equal terms. Mowat's greater strength within the province was counterbalanced by Macdonald's ability to draw on resources from outside its borders.

Macdonald and Mowat had known each other at least since 1836, when the twenty-one-year-old Macdonald opened his law office in Kingston and the fifteen-year-old Mowat began the study of law in the same office. Their notorious antipathy to one another apparently began in 1861 when Macdonald, probably in his cups, came

close to physically assaulting his former pupil on the floor of the provincial Parliament.[2] Whatever its real cause, the antipathy cannot be
attributed to any fundamental differences in political philosophy.
Despite their different party labels, both were essentially moderate
pragmatists who accepted the existing social and economic relationships in their society rather than trying to change them, but who
were flexible enough to change with the times. Mowat was certainly
not a populist Clear Grit of the kind sometimes encountered in the
newer and more turbulent southwestern part of Ontario, and he was
not a doctrinaire opponent of the tariff, in contrast to Alexander
Mackenzie.[3] Even on the subject of federalism his private views were
more centralist than his reputation. Like Macdonald, he had been a
delegate at the Quebec Conference of 1865 and a supporter of the
resolutions that resulted from it. In a letter written towards the end
of his premiership, and quoted by his son-in-law and biographer,
Mowat criticized the United States Constitution for leaving the criminal law, the militia, and various aspects of economic policy in the
hands of the states, and praised the BNA Act for confiding such matters to the central government.[4]

Why, then, did Mowat, and Ontario, wage a battle for provincial
rights? Ontario in the nineteenth century can perhaps best be compared with the western provinces in the twentieth century. In fact,
the term "Western Canada," until the completion of the CPR, was
usually understood to mean the area southwest of the Niagara es-
carpment. Mowat's Ontario was less than a century removed from
the beginnings of European settlement. It had experienced populist
upheavals in the first half of the nineteenth century, as the prairie
provinces did in the first half of the twentieth. In the 1850s the radicalism abated, but the resentment directed against Montreal merchants remained. Demands for "rep by pop" and for freedom from
Montreal domination struck a responsive chord in Canada West and
undermined the legitimacy of the Province of Canada and its unitary constitution. When that constitution finally became unworkable,
Confederation appeared as the best way out of the impasse. After
1867 Ontario had a government of its own, but one that had to share
power with a dominion government supported by the Montreal
merchants and by Cartier's French-Canadian Conservatives. "Rep by
pop" had been won, at least in the House of Commons, but the addition of the Maritime provinces meant that Ontario was still outnumbered even in that house, not to mention the dominion cabinet
and the Senate. As a prosperous and rapidly growing region and the
producer, in its own perception at least, of most of Canada's wealth,
Ontario demanded political recognition. It resented the political

power exercised in Ottawa by the older provinces to the east. The struggle on behalf of Ontario's interests, which George Brown and the Grits had waged before Confederation, continued in a new institutional framework.[5]

Although it accounted for more than 45 per cent of Canada's population in 1871, Ontario had not yet attained a dominant position of control over the Canadian economy, let alone the Canadian state. Montreal was the unchallenged centre of Canadian capitalism and the headquarters of Canada's two major enterprises: the Grand Trunk Railway and the Bank of Montreal. Even Quebec City, the centre of shipping and the timber trade, had a slightly larger population than Toronto. Ontario was still an overwhelmingly rural province, with an economy based mainly on agriculture. A few years before Confederation, John A. Macdonald had argued that the two sections of Canada complemented one another because Canada East (Quebec) was better suited for industry and Canada West (Ontario) was better suited for agriculture.[6] That may have seemed a reasonable assumption at the time, and the fact that Macdonald believed it should undermine the oft-repeated myth that his National Policy tariff was designed to benefit Ontario at the expense of the other provinces. In his own lifetime Macdonald was more often perceived as the political spokesman for Montreal interests than for those of his own province.

If Ontario was not yet an industrial powerhouse, it was in many ways a fortunate province. It had an abundance of good soil and, by Canadian standards, a fairly mild climate. Ontario agriculture approximated the commercial pattern of the American middle west, rather than the subsistence farming found in Quebec and the Maritimes. As in the United States, industrial strength was built on the foundation of a prosperous agriculture that provided markets for its products.[7] Living standards and incomes in Ontario were almost certainly higher than elsewhere in Canada, although reliable data are difficult to come by. This prosperity had one very significant impact on federal-provincial relations. In contrast to all the other provinces, whose endemic financial problems appeared to resist any conceivable solution, Ontario had no need to beg the dominion for financial assistance. The statutory subsidies guaranteed by Section 118 of the British North America Act, its extensive public lands, and the significant revenue it could extract by way of taxation from a large prosperous and growing population were together sufficient to meet its needs. This fact removed a lot of potential issues from the agenda of federal-provincial relations and limited the amount of conflict. At the same time, Ontario's financial independence enabled it to promote its own interests more forcefully when those interests appeared to clash with the policies of the dominion government. It also enabled Mowat to build a formidable political machine and to win six consecutive provincial elections, even though his party (apart form the brief Mackenzie interlude) received no federal patronage.

In addition to general prosperity, some more specific reasons for Ontario's financial independence may be suggested. First, there may have been some economies of scale in governing a province with a large population. Second, Ontario had a well-developed system of municipal government, even in rural areas, which was financed through local property taxes and which assumed much of the burden that would otherwise have been carried by the province. Third, and very importantly, southern Ontario's railway network was almost entirely built by private enterprise and was already extensive by 1867. Ontario thus escaped the heavy financial burden of railway-building that afflicted other provinces after Confederation. Furthermore, although 1200 miles of the CPR main line, or almost 40 per cent of the total, lay within Ontario, the provincial government, as Sir John A. Macdonald complained on more than one occasion, made no financial contribution to it whatsoever.[8] The unhappy experience of Quebec in this regard makes an interesting contrast (see chapter 4).

A further characteristic of Ontario that had some bearing on its relations with the dominion was its relative freedom from internal conflicts, apart from those of a strictly partisan character. Even the partisan conflict, while often conspicuous, was relatively superficial, and had more to do with patronage than with serious ideological cleavages. Many Ontarians, especially Irish Catholics and businessmen, voted for both Mowat and Macdonald.[9] The ideological intensity of the struggle for (and against) responsible government had disappeared long before Confederation, and Confederation itself met with little serious opposition within Ontario. Conflict between business and labour, and between city-dwellers and farmers, had not yet become significant, since the province was overwhelmingly rural and agricultural. The sudden rise of the Patrons of Industry in 1894, just two years before the end of the Mowat era, was the first response by rural Ontario to the threat of urbanization, but the Patrons proved to be a short-lived phenomenon. Although the province was ethnically and religiously diverse, it seemed to avoid the polarization along ethnic or religious lines that existed in some other provinces. The relatively small Catholic minority was not threatened with the loss of its separate schools, perhaps because the issue was deemed to have been settled permanently by Section 93 of the BNA

Act. Oliver Mowat, a devout Presbyterian at the head of the traditionally anti-Catholic party, appears to have received most of the Catholic vote. Orangemen and other anti-Catholics directed most of their wrath against external targets like Louis Riel and Honoré Mercier, rather than against the relatively small Catholic minority within their own province. Ontario's largest denomination, the Methodists, had abandoned their radical and pro-American sectarian origins long before Confederation, and had become a pillar of the status quo.

In short, the largest province, then as now, was a remarkably stable and successful society, with a growing economy and an expanding, diverse, population. These sources of strength were significant assets to Ontario in its battle against Macdonald's vision of a highly centralized quasi-federal empire of the St Lawrence.

The history of Ontario's relations with the dominion up to 1896 divides naturally into four phases, based on the partisan affiliation of the governments concerned. From Confederation until December 1871 the allied governments of the two Macdonalds maintained a close and cordial relationship. For the next two years the Conservative government of the dominion faced Liberal governments, headed first by Blake and then by Mowat at Queen's Park. This was followed by a five-year period of Liberal governments at both levels. Finally, from 1878 until 1896, there were again Conservative governments in Ottawa to do battle against the Liberals at Queen's park, although the intensity of conflict abated after John A. Macdonald's death in 1891. Although these changes contributed significantly to the development of the relationship, there were elements of friction between friendly governments and instances of cooperation between those that were publicly opposed to one another. Furthermore, some of the issues that arose were independent of partisan considerations, and many of them remained on the agenda through more than one of the phases outlined above.

During the first phase, as might be expected, relations between the two governments were generally placid. John A. Macdonald wrote frequent letters to his namesake in Toronto, usually beginning with the salutation, "my dear Sandfield." (Premiers of more distant provinces were usually addressed as "my dear Attorney-General.") It appears that these letters were not always answered, since there are relatively few letters from Sandfield Macdonald in the John A. Macdonald Papers. Reflecting the close ties between the two governments, a large proportion of the letters dealt with patronage. John A. would frequently recommend one of his supporters for some provincial office or favour. On other occasions he would express unhappiness that an individual who was not a supporter of the dominion government was receiving patronage. Some of these letters hint at the unsavory political mores of the times. On one occasion the prime minister asked Sandfield to pay $100 to a certain Catholic priest and charge the disbursement to "election expenses." He added cryptically that the reasons for this request would be explained at their next meeting.[10] Two months later he urged Sandfield to "make an example of" a journalist whose comments about the dominion government were "unbearable."[11] There is no evidence to suggest that the premier made similar requests regarding patronage at the federal level, but he may have done so when the two heads of government met, as they did fairly frequently. Sandfield was a member of the House of Commons as well as of the Legislative Assembly, since this combination of roles was permitted until 1872. John A. also visited Toronto from time to time. In November 1870 he advised the premier of an impending visit to Kingston, and suggested that Sandfield could travel the short distance from Toronto to Kingston to meet him without attracting as much publicity as a meeting in either Ottawa or Toronto would do.[12] Apparently John A. realized that not all Ontarians looked kindly on the close relations between the two governments. The results of the provincial election, four months after this letter was written, suggested that his apprehensions were justified.

Even though Sandfield was two years older than Sir John A., and surpassed him in length of political experience, the style and content of this correspondence leave little doubt as to who was the boss. In his capacity as the dominion's minister of justice, John A. carefully examined and reviewed all of the province's legislation, at times recommending its amendment or repeal. Usually his advice was followed and the implicit threat of disallowance did not have to be carried out. He also bombarded the Ontario premier with advice on issues of public policy ranging from pensions for University of Toronto professors (which he favoured) to the decline of the Ottawa Valley timber trade (which he regretted), and from the need for a provincial corporations act to the desirability of encouraging construction of a railway from Kingston to Pembroke. (In the last case John A. made clear the fact that he was speaking on behalf of his Kingston constituency.)[13] Advice of this kind seems usually to have been followed, but John A.'s efforts to involve the Ontario government in the building of the transcontinental railway were apparently rebuffed even before the fall of the Sandfield Macdonald government.

Another instance in which the prime minister failed to influence the Ontario government concerned an act that the Legislative Assembly adopted in the fall of 1868, entitled an Act to Secure the Independence of the Legislative Assembly.[14] This statute provided that no one holding any public office, federal or provincial, could sit in the Legislative Assembly, apart from members of the provincial cabinet who had submitted themselves to re-election following their appointment. It further provided that no member of the dominion Privy Council, or of the Senate, could sit in the Legislative Assembly. Finally, it provided that no member of the Ontario cabinet could sit or vote in the dominion House of Commons, and that any member who did so would forfeit his cabinet office. Sandfield had little enthusiasm for this measure, and the last provision affected him personally, for he represented Cornwall in the House of Commons as well as in the Legislative Assembly. His majority in the assembly was shaky, however, and the opposition did not consider the measure strong enough, since it wished to prohibit any member of the Legislative Assembly from sitting in the House of Commons. Apparently the beleaguered premier had to make some concession to this sentiment. In November 1868, while the bill was still before the house, John A. Macdonald wrote to Sandfield Macdonald that it went "a little too far." In particular, he suggested that it was inconsistent to prohibit senators from sitting in the provincial house while allowing members of the House of Commons to do so, since senators were more independent of the dominion government.[15]

In December 1869, a year after the act had become law, John A. Macdonald wrote two letters to Sandfield Macdonald, three weeks apart, urging its repeal.[16] Like his original advice on the same subject, these suggestions apparently received no reply. Sandfield Macdonald was meanwhile disregarding his own measure by retaining his seat in the House of Commons, which he held until his death. It seems likely, however, that he attended the Commons only rarely, if at all, after the end of 1868 so as to remain within the letter, if not the spirit, of the law. The act was never repealed, and in 1872 Blake's Liberal government accomplished what it had failed to accomplish as an opposition party in 1868 by prohibiting any member of the House of Commons, after the dissolution of the current Parliament, from sitting in the Ontario Legislative Assembly.[17] Blake promptly resigned his provincial seat, and later in the year his premiership, so as to retain his seat in the House of Commons.

Sandfield Macdonald resigned as premier of Ontario on 9 December 1871, and Edward Blake was sworn in eleven days later. On the day that Blake took office John A. Macdonald received a telegram from Richard Scott, the Speaker of the Ontario Legislative Assembly, the political boss of the Ottawa Valley, and an ally of both Macdonalds. Scott reported that Blake had offered him a cabinet post and had promised in return that Blake's government would adopt a position of neutrality in relation to party politics at the federal level. Scott wanted to accept so that he could continue to represent, in the new government as in the old, the interests of eastern Ontario, the timber trade, and the Canada Central Railway.[18] He did not need to add that without his presence a Blake government would disproportionately represent the Grittish peninsula of southwestern Ontario, which John A. Macdonald had distrusted throughout his political career.

Macdonald replied that he would not discourage Scott from joining the government, but asked that the pledge of neutrality be secured in writing.[19] Apparently it was, and Scott joined the government as commissioner of crown lands. By the summer of 1872 a federal election campaign was in progress. In a letter to Scott, Macdonald complained of rumours that Scott was not working for the government candidates, and was perhaps even working against them. He professed not to believe the latter accusation, but urged Scott to campaign in favour of Macdonald's followers, since "the radical wing," as he put it, of the Blake government were working for the opposition. Scott replied by telegram that it was inconsistent for Macdonald to denounce the Ontario government on the hustings and then seek the support of one of its members. Macdonald's reply was prompt:

I have persistently drawn distinction between you and the liberal wing of local Govt. Such wing contrary to solemn agreement is using power of the Govt. against you and me. I have not published private correspondence altho' perfectly justified in doing so from your inaction and the activity of your colleagues. I have stood by you like a man although I disapproved of your colleagues' course. I expect a fitting return. I shall be in Toronto on Monday night and would like to see you. Meanwhile keep your hands out of any dirty mess.[20]

The meeting, if it took place, was to no avail, and Macdonald had to face the fact that the Ontario government was now entirely in the hands of his opponents. Scott became a minister in Alexander Mackenzie's Liberal government after the Pacific Scandal and also the Liberal leader in the Senate, retaining the latter position until 1908.

During the two years that followed Sandfield Macdonald's departure, John A. Macdonald continued to correspond with his provincial counterpart about Ontario legislation, addressing his comments now to "my dear Blake." Nonetheless, he resented the Blake government's support of the federal opposition. When Mowat took over at Queen's Park, Macdonald wrote to him expressing the hope that relations between the two governments would be more "pleasant" than they had been recently, despite the differences of party label, and added the astonishing assertion that he had never had any "difficulty" with the Liberal government of Nova Scotia. He even offered his old acquaintance a somewhat ambiguous compliment: "with all your political sins you will impart a respectability to the Local Government which it much wanted."[21] Mowat replied by expressing a hope that was not to be realized, especially after 1878: "I heartily concur in the hope which you express that the relations between the dominion and Ontario governments may be pleasant. I have ever felt greatly interested in the success of Confederation, and I agree with you that its success will be aided by proper relations being maintained between the dominion and Local Governments as such, even when these are not in the hands of the same political party."[22]

By the time these words were written the revelations concerning the Pacific Scandal were only a year away so there was little opportunity to put these good intentions to the test. Two major issues had already emerged between the governments that would last well into the 1880s – the appointment of queen's counsel and the definition of Ontario's western boundary. Since both evolved over a lengthy period, they will be examined below.

When Alexander Mackenzie became prime minister of Canada in November 1873, a period of unusually intimate relations between the dominion and Ontario governments began. Mackenzie had been provincial treasurer in Blake's government, and Blake was a minister in Mackenzie's federal cabinet for almost three years, including two years as minister of justice. Questions of patronage and partisan advantage again loomed large in the correspondence between Ottawa and Queen's Park although, in contrast to the era of the two Macdonalds, the advice now seemed to flow more from the provincial level to the federal than vice versa. For example, in 1875 Mowat warned Blake as minister of justice not to appoint a certain Liberal MP to the bench since he did not think the Liberals could win the by-election that would follow.[23] The appointment was not made. On at least two occasions Mowat urged Mackenzie to appear at political picnics in various parts of Ontario, a form of campaigning that John A. Macdonald was employing with considerable success but that was less congenial to the dour Mackenzie.[24] On another occasion Mowat passed on to Mackenzie, who was also minister of public works, a disturbing rumour that the railway construction labourers at Prince Arthur's Landing (Thunder Bay) were "warm sympathizers with the enemy."[25] They were obviously not alone in that regard, for a year later John A. Macdonald returned to office with sixty-two of Ontario's eighty-eight seats, the best showing he ever achieved in the province.

During the Mackenzie interlude, Ontario and the dominion succeeded in removing at least one item of business from the intergovernmental agenda. At Confederation the public property of the old Province of Canada had been divided among the three successor governments. Among the property acquired by the dominion was a building in Kingston known as the Rockwood Asylum, which was legally a part of the Kingston penitentiary. Since asylums, unlike penitentiaries, now fell under provincial jurisdiction, Sandfield Macdonald had asked John A. Macdonald in 1870 to sell the building to the province. The prime minister agreed in principle, and an Act of Parliament given royal assent in April 1871 authorized the minister of public works to reach an agreement with his Ontario counterpart on terms and conditions for the sale or lease of the property.[26] Meanwhile, mental patients who were the responsibility of the province were accommodated at Rockwood, with the dominion periodically billing Ontario for the cost of their upkeep. When he became premier, Mowat adopted the position that the province should be given the building without having to pay for it, since "lunatic asylums" were included among the provincial property enumerated in the Fourth Schedule to the BNA Act. In August 1874 he so advised the dominion government, but Blake and Mackenzie were not impressed by the argument and Mowat reluctantly agreed to pay $50,000. Mackenzie, a building contractor by profession, described this offer as "ridiculously low" and claimed it would cost four times as much to build a comparable facility.[27] Agreement was eventually reached on a price of $96,500, not including the furniture in the building, and Parliament approved the agreement in April 1877.[28]

A similar episode with a less happy outcome concerned some improvements to the Trent River system which dated back to the 1830s, and had apparently been forgotten in compiling the Fourth Schedule. As early as 1870 the dominion minister of public works, Hector Langevin, recommended that these works were of purely local significance and should be handled over to Ontario. An order in council to authorize discussions with the province was approved, but no transfer ever took place. Ontario seemed in no hurry to accept these facilities until four days before the resignation of the Mackenzie government, when Mowat wrote to the prime minister requesting that the transfer be completed.[29] An order in council was passed just hours before the government left office, but it was too late. The incoming Conservative government reversed the decision.[30]

The various *causes célèbres* that marked the Macdonald-Mowat relationship after 1878 are well-known to students of Canadian history.[31] Most of them had actually appeared on the intergovernmental agenda during the previous decade; an examination of how they progressed through various changes of government provides evidence of the impact of partisanship and personality on intergovernmental relations, but also shows evidence that to some extent the sources of conflict were independent of these variables.

The longest, most complex, and perhaps most important of these controversies concerned the definition of Ontario's western boundary. The origins of the confusion over this issue could be traced back to the exploration of northern North America by the British and French in the seventeenth and eighteenth centuries. Neither the peace treaty of 1763 nor the Quebec Act of 1774 clearly specified the boundary between the territory previously granted to the Hudson's Bay Company and the territory of "Quebec" or "Canada" that lay to the south and east. The latter territory of course was subsequently divided into Upper and Lower Canada, later known as Canada West and Canada East, and still later as Ontario and Quebec. Not until late in the nineteenth century did the precise location of the boundary appear to be a matter of great concern.

In 1869 the Hudson's Bay Company territories were surrendered to the crown and became part of the dominion of Canada, administered directly by the federal government. "Canada," meaning the dominion government, thus ironically stood to benefit from a narrow definition of what had been "Canada" before 1869, since Canada's original territory, whatever it was, belonged to the provinces in accordance with Section 109 of the BNA Act. Everyone agreed that the precise location of Ontario's western boundary had something to do with the Mississippi River. The dominion claimed that the western boundary of the territory to which the Quebec Act applied was a line running due north from Cairo, Illinois, the junction of the Mississippi and the Ohio. Projected north of Lake Superior, this line would place Prince Arthur's Landing (Thunder Bay) outside Ontario and within the North-West Territories of the dominion. The province claimed that the appropriate line should run due north from the source of the Mississippi: Lake Itasca in the state of Minnesota. This would place Ontario's boundary six degrees further west, and not far from the little province of Manitoba that the dominion had reluctantly created in 1870. At stake were many millions of acres of softwood forest, an important source of revenue and of political patronage, and some 340 miles of the projected Pacific railway, to which Ontario refused to contribute either land grants or any other form of assistance.

In July 1871 the Ontario government, still headed by Sandfield Macdonald, suggested to the dominion that steps should be taken to define the boundary. The dominion promptly appointed Eugene Taché as its representative on a two-member commission to perform this task. Ontario appointed William McDougall, who had served briefly in the dominion cabinet and who was still a member of the House of Commons as well as the Legislative Assembly. (He had left the dominion cabinet in 1869 to serve as lieutenant-governor of the North-West Territories, in which capacity he suffered the indignity of being denied entrance to his bailiwick by Louis Riel.) McDougall was an expansion-minded Ontario Grit by background, and his previous federal ties did not suffice to reconcile him to the federal position. By the spring of 1872 the Blake government, on McDougall's advice, decided that no agreement was possible. It also took exception to a federal proclamation, under the terms of a statute adopted three years earlier, restricting the possession of firearms and prohibiting the sale of liquor in large portions of the disputed territory. It instructed McDougall to refrain from further cooperation with his federal counterpart.[32]

John A. Macdonald, concerned as minister of justice about the potential vacuum of law and order in the disputed territory, now suggested another approach. The two governments should submit the boundary dispute to the Judicial Committee of the Privy Council. While awaiting its decision they should devise some joint arrangement for the government of the territory, including the administration of justice and the granting of licences to exploit the natural resources. Blake's government proposed instead that the boundary should be determined by a commission of inquiry and that in the interim the province should be responsible for the administration of justice. The dominion could not agree to either suggestion, but did agree to rescind its proclamation regarding weapons and liquor, which it claimed was no longer required, subject to the proviso that this concession did not imply any acceptance of Ontario's territorial claims.[33]

There matters rested when Alexander Mackenzie became prime minister in November 1873. The new government, with its strong ties to Liberal Ontario, suggested a compromise. Ontario's idea of defining the boundary by arbitration, rather than referring it to the Judicial Committee, would be accepted. In the meantime the disputed territory would be divided by an interim boundary approximately down the middle, with Ontario administering the eastern half and the dominion the western half. This offer was accepted and the two governments agreed on the interim boundary in June 1874, although neither agreed to abandon its claims on the other side of the line.[34] Later in the year the dominion appointed L.A. Wilmot, a former lieutenant-governor of New Brunswick, as its commissioner, and Ontario appointed Judge W.B. Richards. The two commissioners were supposed to select an impartial third party as chairman, but this proved difficult, for few if any Canadians were likely to be impartial. Towards the end of the year the British minister at Washington, Sir Edward Thornton, was persuaded to accept the thankless task, but Ontario's reluctance to agree to his appointment caused further delay. Richards was appointed to the new Supreme Court of Canada in 1875 and resigned from the Boundary Commission. In 1878, with the commission having still failed to achieve anything, Wilmot died. He was replaced by Sir Francis Hincks, a political veteran of ambiguous party allegiance who had served the dominion as minister of finance in Macdonald's government.

While all this was going on, both governments undertook a search for obscure documents and maps that would buttress their respective arguments. Ontario apparently had more success, largely through the efforts of David Mills, an able lawyer who ironically joined the dominion government as minister of the interior in October 1876. Blake, as dominion minister of justice after 1875, tried to interest the Hudson's Bay Company in lending support to the dominion's efforts, but the company, having lost its empire in any event, indicated that it was no longer interested in taking sides. Mackenzie tried to persuade Mowat to share the information that Ontario had collected to support its case, but Mowat politely indicated that political friendship had its limits.[35]

In the last few months of the Mackenzie government two important developments took place. Mills suggested that the provisional boundary, which had originally applied only to the administration of justice, should also be used to divide responsibility for issuing timber licences and land grants. Knowing how strong Ontario's case was, since he had largely prepared it himself, he perhaps thought this the best way to salvage anything from the dominion's claims. Mowat agreed to the arrangement, and it was embodied in orders in council by both governments.[36] Although it had no historical justification, the interim line, running through what is now Quetico Park, would have been a geopolitically appropriate boundary between Ontario and Manitoba. That it did not become one was largely the result of the second development that followed in 1878.

Mowat, who had few illusions about the durability of the Mackenzie government, had been pressing for a solution of the boundary dispute before he would again be faced with Sir John A. Macdonald as an opponent. With the appointment of Hincks to succeed Wilmot, the three-member commission was at last prodded into action. It held a brief meeting in August and issued a report completely endorsing Ontario's claims. With Parliament already dissolved, the Mackenzie government had no time to react, and two months later Macdonald was back in office.

Macdonald laid great stress on the fact that the commission was not a court and therefore its decision was not legally binding and need not be complied with. Technically this was true, but the decision had seriously weakened the dominion's position. Ontario adopted legislation in 1879 to provide for the administration of justice in the whole of the disputed territory, but the dominion disallowed it the following year.[37] The Legislative Assembly twice adopted nearly unanimous resolutions calling on the dominion to recognize the decision of 1878. Macdonald ignored the resolutions, despite a threat by McDougall, who had returned to the House of Commons after a six-year absence, that he and other ex-Reformers might rejoin their old party and "fight once more the old battle against French domination" if Ontario did not receive satisfaction.[38] Macdonald encouraged Manitoba to seek an enlargement of its own boundaries so as to border on Ontario, an initiative that would require both dominion and provincial legislation. In this way he hoped to transform the boundary dispute from one between the dominion and a province into one between a large province and a small one, in the hope that other provinces would sympathize with Manitoba. Because Manitoba was still considered a francophone, or at least a bilingual province, opinion in Quebec might be particularly sympathetic. The result from the dominion standpoint would be the same whether the disputed territory became part of Manitoba or of the North-West Territories. Since Section 109 did not apply to Manitoba, the dominion would issue the timber licences and control the public lands in either event. In May 1881 Macdonald wrote to his old friend, Alexander Campbell, whom he had just promoted from postmaster-general to minister of justice: "I wish you would tell Norquay [the Manitoba premier] to pass his bill re. the boundary. As soon as it has passed, get out the proclamation under our act of last session. It is important that the dominion should be rid of the boundary question and that Manitoba and Ontario should be left to fight it out."[39]

The legislation extending Manitoba's boundaries was adopted by the Manitoba legislature and by the dominion Parliament that year.[40] Manitoba had originally asked for an eastern boundary at the 89th meridian, east of Prince Arthur's Landing, but the final version stated more ambiguously that the eastern boundary of Manitoba was a line due north from the point at which the western boundary of Ontario intersected the border with the United States. This change, apparently made at Macdonald's request, was interpreted by Mowat as a deliberate effort to set the two provinces at loggerheads. Mowat's interpretation was correct, but the change also suggested that Macdonald no longer had serious hopes of keeping the lakehead out of Ontario's hands and was inclined to settle for the provisional line of 1874 as Ontario's western boundary. The land north of the Albany River, claimed after a fashion by both provinces but not a high priority for either, would be retained by the dominion.

Mowat tried unsuccessfully to arrange a meeting with Macdonald and in October 1881, he wrote to Campbell, a mutual friend, suggesting "some mutual arrangement" for "our still disputed territory" and offering to meet either Macdonald or Campbell if there was any hope of agreement. Macdonald informed Campbell that he would be willing to meet Mowat when he was in Toronto for a Conservative party convention in November, but Mowat either had second thoughts or deemed the occasion unsuitable, and no meeting took place.[41] Macdonald used the convention to impress Ontario Tories with the justice of the dominion's cause, with the result that the provincial opposition party withdrew its support for Ontario's claim. In 1882 the Legislative Assembly divided on party lines when Mowat moved his annual resolution on the boundary. Macdonald's majority in the House of Commons responded with a resolution calling for the boundary to be settled by either the Supreme Court of Canada or the Judicial Committee of the Privy Council, with administration of the disputed territory by a joint commission in the meantime. Mowat responded with an order in council incorporating a lengthy statement of Ontario's position.[42]

In the summer of 1883 attempts by both Manitoba and Ontario to administer justice in the western part of the disputed territory led to violence at Rat Portage, the present city of Kenora. This episode inclined both Ontario and the dominion towards a compromise. Although Mowat had argued that no judicial decision was necessary, he agreed with Manitoba to submit the question of the boundary between the two provinces to the Judicial Committee, a step that required the consent of the dominion. Macdonald agreed, despite his own preference for referring the question to the Supreme Court in the first instance. However, he now insisted on the dominion's rights to some of the land and timber regardless of where the boundary lay, since the lands in question had been the subject of treaties with the Indians.[43]

The Judicial Committee took only a few months to decide, in August 1884, that the decision of the arbitrators in 1878 had been substantially correct, and that Ontario's western boundary was at Lake of the Woods and its northern boundary on the Albany River. To Macdonald's distress, the Judicial Committee at least implicitly suggested that the territory north of that river was part of Manitoba. Finally, it recommended that the Ontario boundary be confirmed by an Act of the Imperial Parliament.

Macdonald had lost, but he was not quite ready to give up. His government continued to renew timber licences in the western half of the disputed territory, although their original justification – the heavy demand for timber caused by the construction of the CPR – was no longer relevant. He also continued to insist that the dominion owned lands ceded by the Indians, until the Judicial Committee ruled otherwise in the St. Catharines Milling and Lumber Company decision of 1888. Finally, he managed to delay the passage of imperial legislation for five years, despite the urging of Mowat, the colonial secretary, and the governor general.[44] The imperial government would not act without Canada's consent, and Macdonald, although he grudgingly accepted the western boundary, was reluctant to extend either Ontario or Manitoba to the shores of Hudson Bay lest Quebec demand a comparable enlargement of its territory. In the end the imperial statute of 1889 left the land between the Albany River and the bay as part of the dominion's North-West Territories, and so it remained until 1912, when the Borden government rewarded both Ontario and Manitoba for their help in defeating reciprocity.

Although the boundary tended to overshadow all other subjects of dispute between Ontario and the dominion, it was by no means the only question at issue during these years. Controversies concerning the status of the lieutenant-governor, while apparently trivial, had vast implications, as both Mowat and Macdonald realized, for the future of Canadian federalism.

Beginning at least as early as Blake's premiership, Ontario had claimed that the lieutenant-governor was as much the representative of the crown as was the governor general, and that prerogative powers should be shared between the two levels of government. This claim fundamentally challenged John A. Macdonald's view of the constitution, according to which the provinces were subordinate quasi-municipal governments and the lieutenant-governor a mere official of the central government, similar to a departmental prefect in France. The BNA Act gave credence to Macdonald's interpretation by referring to the queen as part of the dominion Parliament in Section 91 while making no reference to her in Section 92, which outlined the powers of provincial legislatures. Immediately after Confederation, however, both Ontario and Quebec began to enact their statutes in the queen's name, just as the Province of Canada had done before Confederation, and thus implicitly claimed that she was a part of their legislatures. (Nova Scotia and New Brunswick did not invoke the queen's name, but they had not done so before Confederation either, so their practice did not clearly indicate support for Macdonald's claim that the direct link between the crown and each province had been broken by Confederation.)

The issue first arose in relation to the appointment of queen's counsel, traditionally a prerogative power of the crown. Although these appointments were an important form of political patronage, the record suggests that both the dominion and the Ontario government were more concerned with the symbolic aspects of the question, and with the broader implication of deciding whether provinces did or did not share in the prerogatives of the crown. As he would do on many future occasions when constitutional issues arose, John A. Macdonald sought the advice of the attorney general and solicitor general of the United Kingdom, also known as the law officers of the crown. In the fall of 1872, after these two officials had endorsed Macdonald's view of the matter, the dominion cabinet adopted an order in council protesting against some recent appointments of queen's counsel by the Blake government in Ontario. It cited the recent opinion by the law officers of the crown that since a lieutenant-governor lacked prerogative powers, the appointments were probably invalid. However, if Ontario adopted legislation conferring the power to appoint queen's counsel on its lieutenant-governor there would be no objection, since the question of prerogative would not arise. Furthermore, since the dominion government judged that the individuals appointed were worthy of the honour, it advised the governor general to exercise his prerogative powers and appoint them all.[45]

By this order in council Macdonald shrewdly kept the issue on the high ground of constitutional principle rather than the low ground of political patronage. The fact that the appointees he was willing to endorse included Samuel Blake, the premier's brother, and E.B. Wood, who had defected from the Sandfield Macdonald government to support Blake, underlined the point. The appointees received letters from the dominion government offering them new commissions, and the Blake government was left with no cause for complaint other than the fact that it had not been informed of the law officers' opinion in time to prevent it from making the appointments. It also promised that Ontario would adopt legislation at the next session giving the lieutenant-governor the power to appoint queen's counsel, and thus implicitly conceding that he did not already have it. However, it suggested that the whole question be referred to the Judicial Committee of the Privy Council, since it "involves question of local and federal jurisdiction far wider than the single question under discussion."[46]

Macdonald's government responded with an order in council stating it had no objection to Ontario adopting legislation as suggested but rejecting the idea of a reference to the Judicial Committee. It also indicated its intention to continue appointing queen's counsel of its own, and suggested that the dominion and the provinces should enter into agreements to recognize one another's appointments. The Ontario government, now headed by Mowat, introduced the promised legislation to confer appointing power on the lieutenant-governor, and the statute was adopted by the Legislative Assembly in 1873.[47]

The Mackenzie government did not make any queen's counsel appointments, but it is not clear whether this was out of deference to the provinces or for some other reason. Apparently the gratitude of those who were appointed could be outweighed by the resentment of those who were not. Mowat cited this fact of human nature as a reason for delay after Blake, as dominion minister of justice, hoped that the Ontario government would make some appointments. Significantly, Blake indicated he was under pressure to make some federal appointments, and action by the province would give him an excuse not to do so.[48]

Meanwhile, the issue of whether prerogative powers were shared by the provinces had arisen in another context. In 1874 Ontario adopted legislation providing that the attorney general of the province could take possession of any property of a person who died intestate and without lawful heirs, or any property confiscated in accordance with criminal justice.[49] Both types of property, known respectively as escheats and forfeitures, belonged to the crown under the common law of England. By providing for their seizure by the province, Mowat was asserting a provincial claim to this part of the prerogative. On the advice of the deputy minister of justice (who was John A. Macdonald's brother-in-law), the dominion government advised Mowat that the stature was *ultra vires* and should be repealed at the next session. Mowat responded with a lengthy memorandum expressing the hope that the minister of justice, Télesphore Fournier, would not defer to the views of his deputy and arguing that prerogative powers since Confederation were shared between the two levels of government. Fournier was not impressed, and the Escheats and Forfeitures Act was disallowed in April 1875.[50]

A month later Fournier resigned, having been promised a seat on the new Supreme Court of Canada, and was succeeded by Blake. Mowat now had reason to hope for a more sympathetic hearing on the question of escheats and forfeitures. He promptly wrote to Blake indicating that he still believed escheats to be a provincial matter. Blake, who privately agreed, suggested that the issue should be decided by the courts, either in the course of ordinary litigation or on a reference from the governments. Mowat preferred a reference to the Supreme Court of Canada, and Blake agreed in May 1876. Shortly afterwards, however, the Quebec Court of Appeal unanimously upheld provincial jurisdiction over escheats. Since this confirmed Blake's own opinion, he argued that the reference was now unnecessary. Instead he proposed a compromise to which Mowat agreed: the dominion would recognize the provincial right to escheated property while the province would recognize the dominion's right to property forfeited in the course of criminal justice.[51] Since Mowat's primary concern was with the principle of the divided prerogative, rather than with financial benefits, this gave him everything he wanted.

A few years later the issue erupted again, with the appointment of queen's counsel being again the focus of attention. In 1879 the Supreme Court of Canada decided the case of Lenoir *vs* Ritchie, in which the issue was whether a queen's counsel appointed by the province of Nova Scotia could be given precedence over one appointed by the dominion. The Supreme Court ruled that he could not, and in doing so repudiated the whole notion that the lieutenant-governor could exercise royal prerogatives. Recognizing the implications of this decision, Mowat wrote to John Thompson, the Nova

Scotia attorney general, suggesting that the provinces jointly appeal the decision. Thompson, a Tory and a future prime minister of Canada, had no desire to do battle. In a letter to Mowat he suggested that Nova Scotia's previous Liberal government had made a number of unsuitable appointments, and that the rebuke administered by the Supreme Court was probably deserved.[52] Despite this setback to interprovincial cooperation, the episode began a friendly relationship between Mowat and Thompson that helped to smooth some troubled waters after Thompson became the federal minister of justice.

On the issue of queen's counsel, however, Thompson and Mowat continued to disagree. In January 1886, shortly after Thompson succeeded Campbell in the Justice portfolio, Mowat seized the occasion of what he viewed as a slight by the dominion government to provincially appointed queen's counsel to revive the whole issue. In one of the lengthy constitutional memoranda for which he was famous, he reminded the dominion government that the provincial legislation providing for the appointment of queen's counsel had been adopted in 1873 at the suggestion of John A. Macdonald. However, Mowat argued that the legislation was not really the source of the power but merely provided the means of exercising a prerogative power that had belonged to the lieutenant-governor since Confederation. Prerogative or executive powers were divided between the two levels of government in the same way as the legislative powers to which they corresponded. Suggesting that Lenoir *vs* Ritchie had not really decided the issue, he urged that it be submitted to the Judicial Committee of the Privy Council for a final solution.[53]

This memorandum was embodied in an order in council and formally communicated to the dominion government, which waited several months to respond. In the meantime Mowat wrote directly to the governor general, Lord Lansdowne. Lansdowne wrote to Thompson expressing some sympathy for the provincial arguments, and suggesting that the Judicial Committee was the proper authority to decide serious constitutional disputes between the dominion and the provinces. Thompson replied with a detailed explanation of the background and consequences of Lenoir *vs* Ritchie, including Mowat's unsuccessful effort to interest Thompson, as attorney general of Nova Scotia, in appealing the decision. The decision had been a good one, he wrote, and he had hoped that Mowat had accepted it. Furthermore, Thompson was not impressed by the Judicial Committee's handling of Canadian issues. Lansdowne replied that he found Thompson's arguments convincing, and there the matter rested for the time being.[54]

Mowat, however, did not give up. Three years later he raised the question again in another letter to Thompson, and this time he appeared to argue that the appointment of queen's counsel was an exclusively provincial power, and that appointments by the dominion were invalid. He also promised to refer the question to the courts, and had the temerity to suggest that Thompson defer any federal appointments until after it was decided.[55] The reference did not actually take place until 1892, apparently because Mowat gave priority to a reference on another issue related to prerogative powers: the lieutenant-governor's power to pardon persons convicted of violating provincial laws. The decision in that case upheld provincial power, and in 1892 the Judicial Committee's desision in the Maritime Bank case indicated that the highest tribunal in the British Empire now accepted Mowat's notion of the divided prerogative. Mowat knew he had won, and he now asked the Ontario Court of Appeal to decide on the validity of the 1873 statute regarding the appointment of queen's counsel. The case was not argued until September 1896, by which time, ironically, Mowat was the minister of justice in Laurier's cabinet. The decision in November of that year upheld the statute, and the dominion did not appeal.

Another issue that preoccupied the two governments throughout the Mowat years had less obvious implications for the theory of Canadian federalism but would become even more familiar to generations of law students. The issue was that of jurisdiction over the regulation of alcoholic beverages. Sir John Willison's judgment of this complicated story is harsh, but perhaps appropriate: "There has been no greater comedy in Canadian politics than the manoeuvres between the federal and provincial authorities to evade responsibility for prohibitory legislation. Generally the object was not to establish jurisdiction but to evade and confuse. There was mortal apprehension lest the Imperial Privy Council should discover that definite and complete authority was vested in either the Provinces or the dominion. There was a desperate apprehension that under evasive plebiscites the popular majority for prohibition would be decisive enough to require actual legislation."[56]

In practice this was largely an Ontario issue. There was little prohibitionist sentiment in Catholic Quebec or in the frontier settlements of the West. In the Maritimes prohibitionist sentiment was strong, but in spite of this fact, or perhaps because of it, provincial governments seemed content to let the dominion take responsibility for the whole issue. Only in Ontario did the two levels of government wage a protracted struggle over the beverage industry. As Willison suggests, neither really wanted prohibition, because alcohol was an important source of revenue and the licensing power an important source of political patronage. Both governments, however, were under pressure from the Baptist, Methodist, and Presbyterian churches, and from voters and politicians affiliated with those churches, to restrict or prohibit the consumption of alcohol. These cross-pressures were felt by both levels, because the constitution did not assign exclusive responsibility for the subject to either government. The pressures would have existed with or without federalism, but federalism provided both a source of conflict when governments wished to act and an excuse to evade responsibility when they did not.

Three years before Confederation the Province of Canada had adopted a statute known as the Dunkin Act, which provided for prohibition by local option. This was an ideal solution because it passed responsibility to the local councils and because it appeased prohibitionist sentiments without either destroying the beverage industry or imposing prohibition on French Canadians, apart from the few who lived in predominantly Protestant cities or counties. Like other existing legislation, the Dunkin Act continued in force under Section 129 of the BNA Act until repealed or amended by the level of government having the authority to do so after 1867. In the case of the Dunkin Act, it was far from clear which level of government that was.

In 1869 Ontario adopted a statute giving any municipality the power to limit the number of tavern licences within its boundaries and also allowing municipalities to impose total prohibition if the by-law was approved at a referendum.[57] The latter provision differed from the Dunkin Act, which had required a referendum only if at least thirty ratepayers petitioned for one to be held. Perhaps because his ally, Sandfield Macdonald, was still in office, John A. Macdonald did not object to this measure, but three years later, when the Blake government conferred the same powers on the newly established municipalities in northern Ontario, the prime minister objected that the province's licensing power (under Section 92(9) of the BNA Act) only authorized it to issue licences as a source of revenue and not for regulatory purposes.[58] However, he did not disallow the act.

Oliver Mowat, a strict teetotaller himself, had no scruples about using the licensing power to build his political machine, with or without the prime minister's approval. In 1873 his government adopted legislation enabling it to appoint provincial inspectors to enforce the provisions of the licensing act in each municipality.[59] Another enactment the following year gave it the additional power to appoint an issuer of licences in each municipality, who would hold office at the pleasure of the provincial cabinet.[60] In effect this transferred the licensing power from the municipalities to the province itself. The Department of Justice in Ottawa, still headed by Macdonald's brother-in-law although Macdonald himself was out of office, drew the province's attention to a possible conflict with the dominion's exclusive power to regulate trade and commerce, but the suggestion was politely ignored.[61]

At the same time as he was adopting these measures, Mowat incongruously allowed the Legislative Assembly to adopt three resolutions supporting total prohibition. The first of these, in 1873, suggested that the dominion impose prohibition. The second resolution, a year later, suggested a constitutional amendment that would allow a province to do so. The third resolution, eight months after the second, indicated that either of these courses of action would be acceptable.[62] Mowat did not believe, or perhaps did not want to believe, that the province had the authority to impose prohibition under the existing constitution. However, in 1876 he made another concession to prohibitionist sentiment by adopting a statute known as the Crooks Act, which imposed a province-wide limit on the number of licences in each municipality, depending on the size of the population. At the same time he gave himself further opportunities for patronage by establishing a three-member Board of Licence Commissioners in each city, county, or district.[63]

Mowat was still troubled by prohibitionist pressure and by constitutional uncertainties. In a letter to Blake, now the minister of justice of the dominion, he defended his decision to include the Dunkin Act in the consolidated statutes of Ontario on the grounds that it was essentially an act dealing with municipal institutions. He suggested that the question of liquor control, among others, should perhaps be referred to the Supreme Court. In another letter he warned Blake, early in 1877, that it might be impossible to prevent the Legislative Assembly from adopting a resolution requesting such a reference on the question of prohibition, and he asked whether this would seriously embarrass Mackenzie's government.[64] In the end Mowat averted the danger by assuring the legislature that the Supreme Court might decide the question anyway in the case of Severn *vs* the Queen.[65]

The Severn decision confirmed that prohibition at the provincial level would be *ultra vires*, and Mowat significantly did not appeal it to the Judicial Committee. The task of appeasing the prohibitionists now shifted to Mackenzie's government, which responded by enacting the Canada Temperance Act, actually a system of prohibition by referendum in a county or city where 25 per cent of the electors who were qualified to vote in a dominion election requested a vote.[66] Blake, who in several letters to Mowat had expressed the view that the dominion should not legislate in this field, was now out of the government. The measure was introduced by Secretary of State Richard Scott who, it will be recalled, had joined Blake's Ontario government in 1871 while proclaiming his continuing loyalty to John A. Macdonald. The Scott Act effectively superseded both the Dunkin Act and the local option provision of Ontario's 1869 statute. It was almost universally adopted in the Maritimes, where the alternative and less difficult procedure, the Dunkin Act, had never existed. In the 1880s most of rural Ontario, and some anglophone counties in Quebec, also voted for prohibition under the terms of the Scott Act.

Soon after the Scott Act became law, John A. Macdonald was back in office. The Tory prime minister was hardly a prohibitionist, but he knew an opportunity to broaden federal authority when he saw one, and he assisted the prohibitionists in defending the validity of the act before the Judicial Committee. When it was upheld in the celebrated decision of Russell *vs* the Queen, he told a public meeting that Ontario's licensing act was unconstitutional and promised to introduce licensing legislation in Parliament if his party won the 1882 election.[67] This promise was carried out in the form of the McCarthy Act of 1883, which required taverns and saloons to hold a licence from the dominion government.[68] Within a few months the Judicial Committee upheld Ontario's licensing act in Hodge *vs* the Queen. Liberals now argued that the McCarthy Act was unconstitutional, and Mowat's government enacted legislation imposing punitive taxation on holders of the dominion licences.[69] Macdonald disallowed this measure, but in 1885 the Judicial Committee declared the McCarthy Act *ultra vires* without even bothering to give reasons for its decision.

The Canada Temperance Act was still in force, but by 1890 its effective operation was confined to the Maritimes and two counties in the Eastern Townships of Quebec. All of the dry counties in Ontario had reversed their original decisions in subsequent referenda in 1888 or 1889, a circumstance that suggests a concerted campaign by the distillers and brewers.[70] In response, the Mowat government introduced a new local option statute similar to the old Dunkin Act.[71] Individual townships, rather than entire counties, could vote themselves dry, referenda would be administered by the local councils, and there was no need for a petition by 25 per cent of the electors to get the process underway. The statute explicitly stated that the province was not claiming any new powers but only reviving the Dunkin

Act. On a reference it was upheld by the Court of Appeal as valid legislation in relation to municipal institutions. Perhaps hoping for a reversal of Russell *vs* the Queen, Mowat in 1893 urged Thompson, who had retained the Justice portfolio as prime minister, to refer the whole question of liquor legislation to the Supreme Court, with the possibility of appeal to the Judicial Committee.[72] Thompson found excuses not to do so, but after his death his incompetent successors agreed to Mowat's request. Thompson's death thus led directly to the celebrated opinion of Lord Watson in the Local Prohibition case, which coincided with Laurier's election and symbolically ended the era of Macdonaldian federalism.

It remains to chronicle one further instance of conflict between Ontario and the dominion which had no real importance but has attained such notoriety that it can hardly be omitted. Some time before Confederation a Lanark County lumberman named Peter McLaren began to construct a series of dams and other improvements to facilitate floating logs down the numerous creeks and streams of that county to his sawmill at Carleton Place. Since the improvements were on his own land, McLaren considered that his competitors should pay tolls for the privilege of using them. In the spring of 1880 the rival lumbering firm of Boyd Caldwell and Sons, which also owned a sawmill at Carleton Place, attempted to use McLaren's improvements without his consent. This led to a lawsuit that McLaren won in the lower court, but the Caldwell firm took their case to the Ontario Court of Appeal, arguing that a pre-Confederation statute guaranteed freedom of passage on rivers and streams. McLaren's case was based on a court decision of 1863 which had interpreted that statute as applying only to rivers that were navigable in their natural state.[73]

The issue did not long remain out of the political arena. McLaren was a Conservative who had been recommended for a senatorship by John G. Haggart, the MP for Lanark South who subsequently became postmaster-general in Macdonald's government. The Caldwell firm had Liberal connections, and their appeal for help to the Mowat government was promptly answered. In March 1881, while the dispute was still before the Court of Appeal, the Legislative Assembly of Ontario adopted a statute affirming the right of all persons to float timber down the rivers and streams of Ontario regardless of any works or improvements that might have been constructed by other individuals.[74] While denying that anyone could have an exclusive right to a river or stream, the statute did recognize the right of persons who had constructed improvements at their own expense to charge reasonable tolls, but the amount of such tolls was to be fixed by the provincial cabinet. McLaren petitioned to John A. Macdonald for disallowance, which took place with unusual promptness, only two months after the Rivers and Streams Act had received royal assent. Two months after the disallowance the Ontario Court of Appeal ruled in favour of Caldwell.[75]

Over the next three years this dispute would preoccupy both governments and, for Macdonald in particular, it seemed to become almost an obsession. Both sides cited grounds of high principle – property rights for the Conservatives and freedom of navigation for the Liberals. Despite this, the incident seems to amount to nothing more than a case of the state's authority, at both levels, being misused for private and partisan advantage. Mowat enacted the statute again in 1882 and 1883, and on each occasion Macdonald disallowed it. Meanwhile McLaren had appealed to the Supreme Court of Canada, lost there, and carried his case to the Judicial Committee of the Privy Council, where D'Alton McCarthy, one of the rising stars of the Conservative party, argued on his behalf. Macdonald's insistence on repeatedly disallowing this measure, contrary to his usual caution in using the power of disallowance, is difficult to explain. Alexander Campbell, the minister of justice, W.R. Meredith, the Tory leader in Ontario, and even McCarthy all expressed doubts whether disallowance was an appropriate response.[76] Finally, in 1884, the Legislative Assembly adopted the Rivers and Streams Act a fourth time, with the slight change that the courts rather than the cabinet were now empowered to fix the level of tolls.[77] This time it was not disallowed. Almost simultaneously the Judicial Committee ruled in favour of Caldwell. McLaren did get his Senate seat in 1890 (his almost illiterate letter of thanks is in the Macdonald Papers) after his wife had written to Macdonald on his behalf.[78] He was a senator for nearly thirty years.

Mowat's many disputes with the Macdonald government led to his enthusiastic participation in the interprovincial conference of 1887, hosted by Premier Honoré Mercier of Quebec. Although the conference was Mercier's idea, most of the seventeen resolutions it adopted on constitutional matters were suggested by Mowat. Apart from the important resolution regarding statutory subsidies, which was Quebec's highest priority, and a provision to facilitate the abolition of legislative councils, they read like a list of the various disputes between Ontario and the dominion. About a year after the conference Mowat wrote to Macdonald on behalf of the five provincial governments that had attended, inviting the prime minister to attend a second conference which would discuss the resolutions. Macdonald naturally declined (unlike some twentieth-century prime ministers) to subject himself or the dominion to such an ordeal, but he agreed to meet Mowat privately, although it is not clear whether the meeting actually took place. Mowat expressed the hope, rather optimistically, that he and Macdonald could agree on most of the items. He admitted that agreement was unlikely on six resolutions, including those on statutory subsidies and legislative councils. The other difficult items were demands for abolition of the power of disallowance, provincial appointment of half the Senate, restriction of Parliament's power to declare works "for the general advantage of Canada," and concession to the provinces of the right to determine who could vote in federal elections.[79]

Despite his many battles with Macdonald, Mowat recognized the need for cooperation between the two levels of government. On several occasions he urged Macdonald's government to cooperate with Ontario by adopting an insolvency act (which Ontario needed but lacked the jurisdiction to enact), by attempting to harmonize federal and provincial legislation regarding insurance, or by taking steps to protect the scenic beauty of Niagara Falls, which the Canada Southern Railway threatened to destroy by placing a freight yard in the vicinity.[80] Such overtures never seemed to evoke a positive response from Macdonald. Campbell as minister of justice sometimes urged the prime minister to adopt a more conciliatory posture towards Mowat, but he met with little success. Nonetheless he continued his efforts after being shifted to the Post Office Department, and even as lieutenant-governor of Ontario. His successor in the Justice portfolio, Sir John Thompson, was tougher and less conciliatory than Campbell, but he was also prepared to cooperate with Mowat on occasion, provided the authority of the dominion was not threatened by doing so. He and Mowat corresponded from time to time on matters related to the administration of justice and occasionally other matters. On at least one occasion Thompson secured the passage of an act through Parliament at Mowat's request.[81] On another occasion he sent Mowat a copy of a bill before it was passed, although it is not clear whether Mowat had requested its passage.[82]

In general, however, the conventional impression of a predominantly conflictual relationship between the two governments is accurate, at least for the years when both Mowat and Macdonald were in office. Partisanship and personality explain much of this conflict. Both Mowat and Macdonald were determined, effective, and highly partisan leaders, and there was no love lost between them. Nevertheless, some friction between the two governments persisted even when one or the other was out of office. Macdonald's need to balance the interests of all regions, his dependence on Bleu support in

Quebec, and the importance of Montreal business interests to his nation-building plans would have guaranteed some conflict with Ontario regardless of who composed the provincial government. Furthermore, as Macdonald recognized (perhaps borrowing an idea from John Stuart Mill), federations do not run smoothly when one of the component provinces is very large in relation to the whole.[83] A province making up almost half of Canada's population could not be allowed to dominate, but neither could it be held in subordination.

4 The Intergovernmental Agenda: Quebec

In contrast to Ontario, Quebec entered Confederation in 1867 with mixed feelings. There was no enthusiasm widespread or deep enought to transcend, even temporarily, the difference between parties. Confederation in fact reinforced a polarization that was already based on more serious ideological conflicts than the distinction between Tories and Grits in Canada West. The Conservatives or Bleus, the party that was closer to the Roman Catholic church and to big business, supported Confederation, while the Liberals or Rouges opposed it. The vote on the Quebec Resolutions followed party lines, so that Quebec's party system remained essentially the same after Confederation as before. Only a few individuals, of whom Honoré Mercier was the most notable, found it necessary to change parties because they disagreed with their own party's position on the issue.

Even among the Bleus the new dominion seemed to inspire little popular enthusiasm. It was accepted mainly from a widespread conviction that the unitary constitution of the United Province had become unworkable. Its main attraction for those French Canadians who supported it was the restoration of a provincial legislature through which Quebec could manage its own affairs without interference from the rapidly growing and overwhelmingly Protestant western section of the United Province, the future Ontario.[1] Most Bleus found the attraction of this change irresistible, and realistically concluded that it was the best arrangement Quebec could hope for. The alternative, they feared, was "Rep by Pop" in a unitary Canada.

The Rouges did not oppose the idea of re-establishing a separate legislature for Quebec, but they doubted whether the powers given to it were sufficient to compensate for the fact that the new dominion would include a much larger anglophone population than the old United Province. Only a few French Canadians, mainly some of the businessmen of whom George-Étienne Cartier was the principal spokesman, saw much benefit to themselves in a political association with the Maritime provinces or in the acquisition of territory to the west.

Until the 1850s Canada East had been larger in population than Canada West, but by the time of Confederation Ontario had pulled ahead in the race, and the gap between the two provinces was growing. Nonetheless, Quebec was still a large province. Its population passed the million mark shortly before Confederation and, according to the first dominion census, in 1871, it had almost exactly one-third of Canada's population. The percentage fell slightly to 31.4 per cent in 1881 and 30.8 per cent in 1891, although growth in absolute numbers continued. Montreal was still by far the largest Canadian city in 1871 with almost twice the population of Toronto, and even Quebec City was slightly larger than Toronto in 1871. However, Quebec City grew very slowly over the next twenty years while Montreal doubled and Toronto more than tripled in size. Apart from the capital city and the metropolis, Quebec's other urban centres, then as now, were relatively insignificant.

Despite the myth of its agricultural vocation, Quebec was in fact much less well-suited to agriculture than Ontario. The winters were longer, the soil poorer, and the land suitable for serious farming was confined to the narrow St Lawrence Valley and some low-lying parts of the Eastern Townships. The rural areas were seriously overpopulated by 1867, and the exodus of their surplus population to the United States was beginning to cause concern. As John McCallum has pointed out, the weakness of Quebec's agriculture was the major reason why the province lagged behind Ontario in growth and prosperity, even before Confederation.[2]

Nonetheless, Quebec was beginning to industrialize. In 1871 its industrial output was more than two-thirds as large as Ontario's, a respectable figure considering the disparity in population between the two provinces. The number of persons and the amount of capital employed in Quebec industry were both about three-quarters of the Ontario figure, although the greater disparity in output suggests that productivity in Quebec was less. An even more revealing contrast is the fact that the average wage of an industrial worker in 1871 was $245.37 in Ontario and only $185.71 in Quebec.[3] For the much larger number of persons employed in agriculture, the disparity in living standards between the two provinces was probably just as great, if not greater. Although Quebec, and particularly Montreal, contained a disproportionate number of Canada's very rich people, most people in Quebec were much poorer than their Ontario counterparts. Partly for this reason, the provincial government was constantly in financial difficulties, a circumstance that was a major cause of its weakness, passivity, and dependence on the dominion. Financial problems also tended to dominate the agenda of dominion-provincial relations, in contrast to Ontario where they played a relatively insignificant role.

Another important contrast between the two provinces was that Quebec had few railways. Although the headquarters of the Grand Trunk were in Montreal, most of its trackage was in Ontario. Astonishingly, Quebec City was not served by any railway at the time of Confederation, although it was the second largest city in Canada. The first train arrived in the provincial capital in 1879, two years later than the beginnings of railroading in distant Manitoba. Since private enterprise showed little interest in serving Quebec with railways, much of the provincial government's scarce resources had to be devoted to this purpose by way of subsidies or, even more disastrously, public ownership. This expense accounted for no small part of Quebec's financial problems.[4]

Apart from economic and financial problems, Quebec governments had to deal with a complex social and cultural environment. Although the distinction between the two political parties, as in Ontario, had originally been related to the struggle for responsible government, and although the polarization in Quebec was reinforced by the issue of Confederation, the really dominant political issue was the relationship between church and state. It accounted for most of the intensity of conflict between Bleus and Rouges and for some, although not all, of the endemic factionalism within the Bleu party itself.

Pius IX, after whom one of Montreal's major boulevards is named, was pope from 1846 until 1878. During his long reign he proclaimed the doctrine of papal infallibility in matters of faith and morals (broadly defined). He also placed the church in determined opposition to liberalism, and indeed to most of the political, social, and cultural developments of the nineteenth century. This tendency was particularly strong in his last years, after he had been dispossessed of his temporal domains in Italy by the unification of that country, an event that coincided closely in time with Canada's Confederation.

These developments affected political and social life throughout the Catholic world, but their impact in Quebec was particularly strong. Not only was the province overwhelmingly Catholic but the influence of the church had expanded after 1840 to fill the vacuum created by the lack of strong secular elites and the defeat of the Patriot rebellion in 1837–38. As in Ireland and Poland, Catholicism was associated with nationalism, but it was also, in contrast to those two countries, associated with the established regime. Indeed, almost since the Conquest, the British authorities had encouraged clerical authority in Quebec as a bulwark against American-style revolution.

The ultramontane ideas of Pius IX were enthusiastically echoed by French-Canadian clerics like Bishop Ignace Bourget of Montreal and Bishop Louis-François Laflèche of Trois-Rivières around the time of Confederation. They also strongly influenced the Conservative party, particularly after the illness and death of Cartier. A political manifesto known as the *Programme catholique*, published two years before Cartier's death, became the rallying point for an extreme ultramontane and nationalist faction, known as the Castors, who functioned as a virtual party within a party.[5] The more moderate business-oriented type of conservatism represented by Cartier lacked a strong spokesman after his death, and the influence of the Castors increased. Much of the factionalism that characterized the party could be traced to this cause, although it was reinforced by personal rivalries and by the struggle for spoils between the Montreal region and the Quebec City region of the province.

Although the climate of religious opinion in Quebec created difficulties for the Bleus, it imposed a far worse handicap on their adversaries, the Rouges. Soon after the establishment of responsible government in the United Province, the moderate Rouge element had defected to the Bleus, leaving the Rouge party as a minority faction who were anathematized by the church and by much of the population for their alleged radicalism and anticlericalism. Their cooperation with the militantly Protestant Grits of Canada West contributed further to their notoriety. The effects of these events were still visible in the 1870s, when the young Wilfrid Laurier began his lifelong battle to demonstrate the compatibility of Catholicism and liberalism. Even as late as 1896 he was finding it an uphill struggle.

The ideological climate in Quebec soon after Confederation is perhaps most dramatically illustrated by the celebrated Guibord affair. Guibord, a printer and a member of the Institut Canadien, a liberal organization condemned by the church, died in Montreal in 1869, and was denied burial in consecrated ground by Bishop Bourget. The ensuing controversy divided the province for years and was litigated all the way to the Judicial Committee of the Privy Council. The bishop lost, but when Guibord's remains were finally conducted to the cemetery in 1875, six years after his death, the militia had to be called out to protect the belated funeral procession from violence. The bishop then had the last word after all by quietly deconsecrating the plot in which Guibord rested.[6]

While matters of this kind divided the francophone majority in the province, Quebec was further divided by the presence of an important minority of anglophones, making up more than one-fifth of the population. This minority was itself a congeries of various minorities, divided by ethnicity, religion, geography, and class. About half were of Irish ancestry in 1871, and 29 per cent of Quebec anglophones shared the Roman Catholic faith of their francophone neighbours.[7] Anglophones were disproportionately represented among the business elite of the province, but also among the wage-earning, non-agricultural, working class. Montreal was about half anglophone in 1867, and ten rural counties had anglophone majorities: three in the Ottawa Valley, one southwest of Montreal, and six in the Eastern Townships. Although some anglophones could be found in most parts of the province, the largest concentration was in the Townships, and the anglophone Quebec representative in the dominion cabinet customarily came from that region.

Many Quebec anglophones had feared and resisted Confederation, since it meant the restoration of a predominantly francophone legislature for the first time in almost thirty years. To allay their fears, the boundaries of the anglophone constituencies for provincial elections were entrenched in the BNA Act, as were the existence of an appointed Legislative Council, the Protestant school system, and the use of English as well as French in the legislature, in statutes, and in the courts. Quebec senators, unlike those of any other province, were required to own property in, and represent, specific districts, virtually ensuring that several of them would be anglophones. By convention, Quebec anglophones were given at least one representative in the dominion cabinet and several in the provincial cabinet. The provincial treasurer was usually an anglophone (a custom that continued until 1944), although in the nineteenth century this did not seem to make balancing the provincial budget any easier. These guarantees and practices succeeded in reconciling Quebec anglophones to Confederation, even before their imagination was captured by westward expansion and the CPR. Most of them voted for John A. Macdonald's party in both federal and provincial elections.

A numerically small but important group within the anglophone minority were the Montreal capitalists, who would play a large role in the National Policy of tariff protection and railway building. In a sense they were in Quebec but not of it, using Montreal as a base from which to dominate the whole Canadian economy and asking little from the provincial government except to be left alone. Their mixed feelings about their province were expressed by one of their political spokesmen, future Prime Minister John Abbott, in a private letter in 1880: "English-speaking people are rather tolerated than sustained here, and nothing less than a scrupulous attention to the ideas, and even caprices, of the French Canadian people will enable any Englishman to obtain any influence in public affairs. Public appointments are obtainable only of inferior quality."[8] Although they made strange bedfellows with the ultramontane and nationalist Castors, the Montreal business elite became a mainstay of the party that Macdonald built, a role they retained well into the twentieth century.

For Quebec, as for Ontario, Confederation meant the division of a single unitary government into three distinct but related parts: the governments of Quebec, Ontario, and the dominion. Relations between Quebec and the dominion were, for the first few years at any rate, relations among politicians who had known one another and worked together prior to Confederation. However, as noted in chapter 3, the fact that Prime Ministers Macdonald and Mackenzie were from Ontario made their knowledge of that province more intimate, and their dealings with it more direct, than their knowledge of and dealings with Quebec. Even before 1867 the two sections of the United Province retained a certain separation *de facto* and their party organizations were distinct, with each party having a recognized leader in each section. This separation continued after 1867, with the added complication that each of the four party organizations (Bleu and Rouge in Quebec, and Conservative and Liberal in Ontario) now had to operate at two levels in a federal state.

Partly because of this tradition, partly because of the different issues and problems that arose in the two successor provinces, and partly because of the language barrier (although Macdonald apparently could at least read French), prime ministers relied heavily on intermediaries in their dealings with the mysterious province across the Ottawa River. Until his death in May 1873, Cartier played an indispensable role in the dominion's relations with Quebec that had nothing to do with his ministerial portfolio of Militia and Defence, but everything to do with his recognized position, throughout the last seventeen years of his life, as the leader of the Bleu organization in Quebec. Unlike Macdonald, Cartier took advantage of the double mandate to occupy a seat in the Legislative Assembly of his own province as well as in the House of Commons. The first premier of post-Confederation Quebec, Pierre Chauveau, had been a close colleague and follower of Cartier since 1855.[9] Although Cartier spent little time in Quebec City after Confederation, he retained a strong influence over the Chauveau government.

Cartier's role as the prototypical "Quebec lieutenant" was never really filled after his death. Hector Langevin, the minister of public works, attempted to assume Cartier's mantle but was not strong enough to overcome the persistent factionalism in the Bleu party. Neither the extreme Castors nor their greatest opponent within the party, J.-A. Chapleau, accepted Langevin's leadership. Langevin returned to office with John A. Macdonald in 1878 and remained minister of public works until a scandal forced his resignation soon after Macdonald's death, but his influence gradually declined and was negligible after 1887.[10] During the Mackenzie interlude matters were even more unsettled. A.-A. Dorion, who had been the leading Rouge opponent of Confederation, took office with Mackenzie as minister of justice, but after only six months Dorion secured his own appointment as chief justice of the Court of Queen's Bench. None of the other French Canadians who served in Mackenzie's government could exercise effective leadership. In any event, no Rouge in Ottawa could have effectively managed relations with a Bleu government in Quebec, and by the time the Rouges took office in the provincial capital (under distinctly odd circumstances) the Mackenzie government's days were numbered.

Provincial politics in Quebec after Confederation were totally different from the politics of Ontario. The Bleus, or Conservatives, remained the dominant party, as they had been before 1867, in large part because the Rouges were suspected of anti-clericalism. An additional reason, after Confederation, may have been the consideration that Quebec's financial weakness made it desirable to stay on good terms with the dominion government. The Bleus thus controlled the provincial government from 1867 to 1878, from 1879 to 1887, and from 1891 to 1897. Since there was no distinction between federal and provincial party organizations, and since the dominion had far greater funds and more patronage at its disposal than the province, a Conservative government in Ottawa could exercise decisive influence over a Bleu government in Quebec City. More precisely, one could say that leading Conservative politicians in Ottawa could exercise such influence, for Macdonald did not interfere in the factional infighting of the Quebec party except on the advice of his lieutenants.

Partly because of the party's endemic factionalism, and partly because of external control from Ottawa, a Conservative premier of Quebec was not typically in any real sense the leader of his party.

This generalization may be illustrated by considering the eight Bleus who held the premier's office (two of them held it twice) between 1867 and 1897. Pierre-Joseph-Olivier Chauveau, the only one of the eight who lasted more than four years, was selected by Cartier in 1867 because he was moderate, acceptable to the anglophone minority, and had served as superintendant of education for Canada East since 1855.[11] Like Cartier himself, Chauveau was simultaneously a member of the Legislative Assembly and the House of Commons. A few months before Cartier's death Chauveau was appointed to the Senate and resigned his premiership. His successor, Gédéon Ouimet, was chosen by the federal leaders of Quebec conservatism, particularly Langevin. Langevin's rival, Joseph-Adolphe Chapleau, joined the Ouimet government as solicitor general.[12] In September 1874 the rising influence of the Castors led to the departure of both Ouimet and Chapleau from the provincial government. Ouimet was replaced by Charles-Eugène Boucher de Boucherville, who suffered the ignominy of being dismissed for flagrantly partisan reasons by a Rouge lieutenant-governor. Henri-Gustave Joly, a French-born Protestant, was installed as leader of a minority Rouge government.

When the Bleus returned to office, after a brief interval, in 1879, Chapleau became premier. Three years later he went to Ottawa as secretary of state in the Macdonald government, and the previous occupant of that office, Joseph-Alfred Mousseau, was sent to Quebec City as premier. In a letter to John A. Macdonald two weeks after the change, Mousseau assured the prime minister: "Though I am now Premier in Quebec I still consider myself of Ottawa, and continue to do your business here."[13] Perhaps understandably, Mousseau was not accepted as leader by the Castors, who succeeded in replacing him after two years with John Jones Ross, a francophone and a Catholic, despite his name, and a member of the appointed Legislative Council. In 1886 the Bleus suffered electoral defeat, largely because of the reaction to Louis Riel's execution the year before. They clung to office until the Legislative Assembly met in January 1887, but the replacement of Ross by Louis-Olivier Taillon as head of the Bleu government prolonged its life by only two days.

From then until December 1891 the provincial government was headed by Honoré Mercier, the most memorable of Quebec's nineteenth-century premiers. Mercier had been a Bleu but had left the party at the time of Confederation because he disagreed with its position on that issue.[14] A strong nationalist who disapproved of traditional Rouge anti-clericalism, he became leader of the Rouges in 1883 and, after Riel's death, was able to lure some disaffected Bleus into a coalition he called the Parti National. As premier he made common cause with Oliver Mowat's Ontario against the Macdonald government, although he was not on particularly warm terms with the federal Liberals.

In December 1891 Mercier was dismissed by the Bleu lieutenant-governor, the second such event Quebec had experienced in less than fourteen years. With a certain poetic justice, de Boucherville, the victim of the previous dismissal, was installed as premier to succeed Mercier. Throughout his second premiership de Boucherville was a member of the Senate, to which Macdonald had appointed him in 1879. Soon after celebrating his seventieth birthday in 1892 he handed over the premiership to Taillon, who had held it for two days in 1887. When Taillon left Quebec to become Sir Charles Tupper's postmaster-general in 1896 he was succeeded by Edmund Flynn, who led the Bleus to defeat a year later.

Thus the only two Bleu premiers not to receive federal patronage when they left office were Ouimet and Flynn, both of whom had the misfortune to leave the premiership at a time when the dominion had a Liberal government. Chauveau, de Boucherville, and Ross went to the Senate, Chapleau and Taillon to the dominion cabinet, and Mousseau to the Superior Court. The prospect of such rewards doubtless provided some consolation for the thankless task of governing an ideologically divided and chronically impecunious province. The patronage, one suspects, also contributed to making the province more docile in its dealings with the dominion, although its financial problems were even more significant in that regard.

In dominion elections Quebec generally lived up to its Conservative reputation. It provided Macdonald with a working majority in 1867 and saved him from what would otherwise have been a defeat in 1872. Although it voted for the incumbent Liberals in 1874, it did so by a far narrower margin than the rest of the country. Contrary to a widely believed myth, federal Liberal support did not increase significantly as a result of Riel's execution, and the Conservatives won a slight majority of Quebec's votes and seats in 1887. In 1891, after Laurier had become leader, the Liberals did win a majority of Quebec's seats, but the Conservatives still had a slight plurality of the popular vote. Only in 1896 did Quebec swing decisively towards the Liberals, enabling Laurier to form a majority government after winning only 69 of the 148 seats in English-speaking Canada.

In general, the relations of Quebec with the dominion in the years of John A. Macdonald's first government seem to have been cordial and free of controversy, with one exception. As minister of justice Macdonald examined Quebec's legislation, as he did that of all the provinces, and he freely offered suggestions to Premier Chauveau as to how legislation might be improved. Sometimes he corresponded directly with the premier while on other occasions he dealt with him through the intermediary of Cartier or Langevin. Chauveau made numerous requests for patronage to various ministers in the dominion cabinet on behalf of persons who had written to him. Apparently many Quebec voters were confused about which level of government was responsible for such matters as the census, lighthouses, and the post office. In January 1873, already contemplating resignation, Chauveau requested the office of lieutenant-governor for himself, but the office was given a month later to R.-E. Caron, a seventy-one-year-old judge on the Court of Appeal.[15] Chauveau had to be content with a seat in the Senate.

The first serious issue to emerge in Quebec's relations with the dominion concerned the province's finances, a subject that would continue to dominate the agenda for most of the next twenty years. Although the particular problem that arose immediately after Confederation concerned Ontario as well as Quebec, the much happier financial situation of that province, as well as the prominence of other issues, prevented it from having a major impact on Ontario's relations with the dominion. In Quebec, where financial issues were a much greater concern, their prominence was established at a very early date and arose directly out of the terms of the BNA Act.

The financial terms of Confederation established as a general principle that the dominion would "be liable for the Debts and Liabilities of each Province existing at the Union." In section 112, however, the BNA Act provided that Ontario and Quebec should jointly be liable to pay interest to the dominion on the amount by which the debt of the Province of Canada at the time of the union exceeded the sum of $62,500,000. The purpose of this section, essentially, was to ensure that the financial settlement would not appear too generous to the two large provinces, which had jointly incurred a much larger per capita debt before 1867 than either New Brunswick or Nova Scotia.

Because Ontario and Quebec had had no separate existence between 1841 and 1867, the period during which most of the public debt was incurred, some formula or procedure for apportioning their joint liability between them would have to be devised. The solution of this problem was postponed until after Confederation was achieved. Section 142 of the BNA Act provided that the decision on the apportionment of debts, and also of public property, between the two provinces would be referred to three arbitrators, of whom one would be chosen by Quebec, one by Ontario, and one by the dominion. To ensure that the federal appointee would be impartial, this section provided that he could not be a resident of either Quebec or Ontario.

The three arbitrators were duly chosen in 1868. Ontario selected Senator D.L. Macpherson, Quebec chose Charles Dewey Day, and the dominion nominated John Hamilton Gray of New Brunswick. They did not actually begin work until the following summer, after a preparatory meeting had been held between the three governments. This meeting, which lasted for three working days in July 1869, included the two premiers, the two provincial treasurers, the minister of finance of the dominion, Sir John Rose, and the minister of militia and defence, Sir George-Étienne Cartier. Prime Minister Macdonald appeared briefly on the last day. It was mainly concerned with defining what should be included in the debt, no easy matter in view of the multitude of special funds and accounts that had been established before Confederation, and therefore determining the size of the excess that would have to be apportioned. No agreement was reached on this question, which was turned over to the arbitrators, along with the far more difficult task of deciding how the excess debt, once determined, would be allocated between the two provinces.[16]

The arbitrators met twenty times between August 1869 and July 1870 but achieved no concensus. In the first few months little progress was made even in determining the amount of the debt to be apportioned. Ontario blamed Quebec for the delay, while Quebec blamed the dominion. The more difficult problem of apportioning the excess debt between the two provinces was apparently not even considered until early in the new year, and it soon became apparent that Quebec was fundamentally at odds with the other two governments concerning the methodology to be used. Ontario proposed, and the dominion's arbitrator agreed to, a procedure based on a distinction between debts incurred for provincial purposes (as defined by the BNA Act) and those incurred for what became federal purposes after 1867, such as railways, canals, and defence. Those debts in the former category, which were alleged to be about one-quarter of the total debt, were said to have been 52.8 per cent for the benefit of Ontario and 47.2 per cent for the benefit of Quebec, a finding based mainly on the physical location of the assets for whose construction the funds had been borrowed. Therefore the excess debt, which all three governments eventually agreed to be $10,400,000, should be divided between the two governments in those proportions.[17]

At the nineteenth meeting, in May 1870, Quebec submitted a totally different proposal. This was based on the assumption that the Union of 1841 should be considered as a business partnership.

Debts incurred while the partnership was in existence should be divided equally between the partners, but their respective balance sheets at the time the partnership was formed should also be taken into account. Lower Canada had entered the partnership with a credit balance, while Upper Canada had already had a substantial debt. When these facts were taken into account the procedure suggested by Quebec would have attributed almost 80 per cent of the excess debt to Ontario. This was totally unacceptable to Ontario, and the dominion arbitrator apparently found Ontario's case more persuasive, on the grounds that the analogy between a political union and a business partnership was inappropriate.[18]

Depending on which of these calculations was used, Quebec's share of the excess debt would range from $2,155,000 to $4,912,000 and its interest payments to the dominion at a rate of 5 per cent per annum would range from $107,750 to $245,600. The difference does not seem large by modern standards, but since Quebec's total revenues from all sources, including the dominion subsidy, were only in the neighbourhood of two million dollars per annum, the implications for its financial situation were considered to be serious.

After an interval of two months, the arbitrators met again in July 1870. Macpherson and Gray proposed that the formula on which they had agreed in May be adopted as the official and binding decision of the arbitrators. Day of course dissented and then, apparently on instructions from the Quebec government, resigned his position as arbitrator.[19] These developments superimposed a legal dispute on the original financial one. Quebec claimed that a binding decision could only be made unanimously by the three arbitrators, and that a decision by two out of the three had no legal effect. It also claimed that Gray, the dominion's nominee, had violated the requirements of his position by becoming a resident of Ontario, and that his impartiality was therefore questionable. (Gray argued that his permanent residence was still in New Brunswick, but that he had rented a house in Ottawa because the arbitration itself had required him to spend more than a year there.) Ontario and the dominion insisted that a decision by two arbitrators would be valid. The decision was officially handed down in September, but since Quebec still refused to comply with it, the dominion government referred the question of its validity to the Judicial Committee of the Privy Council. The Judicial Committee eventually ruled, in 1878, that the decision by two out of the three arbitrators was valid and legally binding.[20] By the time this ruling was handed down, however, an initiative by the dominion government had greatly reduced its significance.

In the second Parliament of Canada, elected in 1872, Macdonald was more dependent on his Quebec supporters than before, since he had lost heavily in Ontario. The Quebec government's poor financial situation, and its unhappiness about the decision of the arbitrators, were thus important subjects of concern. The solution arrived at by the government was to increase the debt allowance shared by Quebec and Ontario from the $62,500,000 specified in the BNA Act to $73,006,088, thereby eliminating any obligation by either province to make interest payments to the dominion. At the same time the debt allowances of all the other provinces were increased in the same proportion, with the result that their subsidies also increased. This change in financial arrangements was approved by the cabinet in April 1873, and by Parliament in May.[21] It appeared to please everyone except the Mowat government in Ontario, which now claimed that the excess debt of the Province of Canada had been overestimated by the arbitrators in 1870, and that the two central provinces could have been forgiven their interest payments without the generosity extended to the other provinces.[22]

The financial settlement of 1873 did not end the controversy over the allocation of the Province of Canada's debt, but it transformed it largely from a controversy between Quebec and the dominion into a controversy between Quebec and Ontario. The two provinces continued to disagree over the distribution between them of certain assets of the former United Province, such as the Municipal Loan Fund, the Common School Fund, and the Upper Canada Land Fund. Over the next few years inconclusive negotiations took place between Quebec and Ontario in an effort to resolve these issues.[23] The federal government was able, at least for a time, to let the two provinces fight them out between themselves. Quebec's financial situation was improved as a result of the increase in debt allowances, and there would have been little point in making financial demands on the tight-fisted and politically unfriendly Mackenzie government that took office in November of that year. Financial questions dropped to the bottom of the federal-provincial agenda, and did not become prominent again before the 1880s.

Meanwhile, a serious constitutional crisis erupted in 1878. Lieutenant-Governor Caron had died in December 1876, and in his place the Mackenzie government had appointed one of its own members, Luc Letellier de St. Just, the federal minister of agriculture. Letellier was a highly partisan Rouge while the premier, C.-B. de Boucherville, was an ultramontane Bleu. Furthermore, Letellier regarded the lieutenant-governor as far more than a ceremonial figurehead on the ship of state. He presided in person over the Executive Council and appeared to regard de Boucherville as his subordinate in fact as well as in form. He also demanded that his advisers share all their secrets with him. The provincial government, knowing him to be a political opponent and the representative of an unfriendly government in Ottawa, refused to do so.

On 7 March 1878 Letellier unexpectedly dismissed the de Boucherville government and appointed Henri Joly, the leader of the opposition, to head a new government. The immediate pretext for this action was a bill forcing municipalities to contribute to the cost of building the provincial railway system. More generally, Letellier charged in a letter to Prime Minister Mackenzie a few days later that his former advisers had conducted government business behind his back and without consulting him, and had "acted as though the lieutenant-governor was not part of the legislature."[24] In a subsequent letter he added that "constitutionally and necessarily I had to withdraw my confidence from men ignoring the position of the chief [sic] and keeping themselves in power through mischief and mendacity."[25] Mackenzie was apparently surprised but not shocked by his former colleague's action. He sent a message of congratulations to Premier Joly, whom he had wanted to succeed Letellier as federal minister of agriculture when Letellier went to Quebec. Mackenzie also urged Letellier to dissolve the Legislative Assembly as soon as possible, a desirable precaution since the Bleu opposition still held almost two-thirds of the seats.[26] The Bleus also, of course, dominated the appointed Legislative Council, which had adopted a resolution on the same day that de Boucherville was dismissed protesting against the lieutenant-governor's action.

The provincial election on 1 May 1878 returned a Legislative Assembly almost evenly divided between Bleus and Rouges. The Joly government survived its first session, which was brief, but its situation was clearly precarious and its assertion that the voters had endorsed Letellier's action somewhat questionable. A federal election followed in September and Mackenzie's Liberals were decisively defeated, particularly in Quebec where they won only eighteen seats. By October John A. Macdonald was back in office and the Conservative MPs from Quebec, who made up one-third of the new government's parliamentary supporters, were demanding Letellier's head.

Macdonald disapproved of Letellier's action and had said so in Parliament in April, but he also disapproved of the American practice whereby public officials were dismissed for partisan reasons by an incoming administration. He was on record as saying that a lieutenant-governor should enjoy security of tenure.[27] Letellier had acted in a flagrantly partisan manner, however, and had arguably violated the standards of impartiality and integrity which security of tenure was designed to protect. Furthermore, Macdonald had depended for all his political life on Conservative Quebec to counterbalance the weight of Liberal Ontario, and he had no wish to split his party or antagonize his Quebec followers.

On 7 November 1878 the Conservative members of Parliament from Quebec presented a formal petition to the governor general demanding that Letellier be dismissed on the grounds that his conduct was "of a nature to imperil the peace and prosperity of the dominion of Canada."[28] Since the recipient of this document, Lord Dufferin, was about to leave office, it was followed by similar petitions addressed to Macdonald, on 23 November, and to the new governor general, the Marquess of Lorne, on 19 December. J.-A. Mousseau told Macdonald that Quebec Conservatives were disappointed by his failure to dismiss Letellier and that a prompt dismissal would enable the party to win an impending by-election in St-Hyacinthe.[29] J.-A. Chapleau wrote to "mon cher Sir John" comparing the petition calling for Letellier's dismissal to Magna Carta.[30] Meanwhile, Letellier himself had sent a dispatch to the dominion government criticizing his former advisers for failing to consult him on important issues of policy and claiming that the power to dismiss a lieutenant-governor was held only by the governor general in his capacity as an imperial officer, and must not be exercised on the advice of the dominion cabinet.[31] This assertion was consistent with Oliver Mowat's view that a lieutenant-governor represented the crown, not the dominion government. It enabled Letellier, Joly, and their supporters to argue that the real issue was provincial autonomy, which would be endangered if Letellier was removed. Conservatives could reply, just as credibly, that Letellier himself had placed Quebec's autonomy in jeopardy by using his position as a federal officer to dismiss the elected government of the province.

The new governor general, who had arrived in Ottawa on 25 November, opposed the dismissal of Letellier. It is not clear that this was his original view, and he may have been influenced by a private memorandum from Alpheus Todd, Canada's foremost authority on constitutional law and practice, who wrote that a lieutenant-governor should have the same security of tenure as a judge and that the dismissal of Letellier would violate provincial rights.[32] Todd may have helped the governor general to write another memorandum which Lorne addressed to Macdonald on 30 December and which repeated Todd's arguments. This memorandum also argued that the people of Quebec had had the opportunity to turn Joly's government out of office and had not done so, an argument that was dubious given the closeness of the election result. Lorne sent a copy to the colonial secretary, explaining that Macdonald was under pressure from Quebec Conservatives and that Lorne thought it his duty to present the other side of the argument.[33]

Macdonald managed to delay a decision for another three months, but on 29 March he informed the governor general that the cabinet had decided to dismiss Letellier. When Lorne protested, Macdonald suggested that the question might be referred to the imperial government for a final decision. Lorne agreed, while emphasizing to the colonial secretary that this idea had been Macdonald's and not his own.[34] In response, the Joly government informed the governor general that it intended to make its own representations directly to the imperial authorities. This provoked an order in council from the dominion stating that it would be improper for a provincial government to offer advice to the queen on the appointment or dismissal of a lieutenant-governor. However, the dominion government stated that it had no objection to Letellier himself submitting a memorandum to the imperial authorities.[35]

Both sides hastened to London to present their views. Langevin presented the dominion government's case, accompanied by Senator John Abbott, a prominent Quebec anglophone and future prime minister. Premier Joly insisted on presenting Letellier's case in person, despite efforts by both the dominion and imperial governments to discourage him from making the journey. Letellier could not go since a lieutenant-governor required the dominion government's consent to leave his province. Joly arrived at the colonial secretary's office to discover that Langevin and Abbott, who already had an appointment, were expected in a few minutes. Joly had to be satisfied with an appointment the following day, and later blamed the failure of his mission on the fact that his opponents had been able to see the colonial secretary first.[36]

Joly remained in London for three weeks before giving up and returning home. Langevin and Abbott stayed about two months, and their perseverance was finally rewarded on 3 July 1879 when the colonial secretary sent a long dispatch to Lorne.[37] This document carefully avoided criticizing Letellier's conduct, but said that if Lorne's advisers were determined to dismiss the lieutenant-governor he must follow their advice. Lorne reluctantly agreed and Letellier was dismissed on 25 July, to be replaced by Théodore Robitaille, a Conservative member of parliament. Three months later the Legislative Assembly adopted a motion of non-confidence in Joly's government. Robitaille refused to grant Joly a dissolution, and Chapleau became premier of Quebec.

With Conservatives back in office at both levels, relations between the dominion government and Quebec returned to a pattern reminiscent of the first six years after Confederation. Although there were differences of opinion, relations were generally cordial and the agenda was dominated by relatively mundane issues of party politics and public finance. Chapleau's main objectives as premier were to defeat the Castor element in the party, which had become dominant after Cartier's death, and to improve the state of the province's finances.[38] He looked to the Macdonald government in Ottawa for help in achieving both objectives. Success with the second objective would, or so he hoped, contribute to the first. A successful term as premier and the resolution of Quebec's financial problems would facilitate moving to Ottawa as Macdonald's Quebec lieutenant, replacing Langevin as the dispenser of federal patronage in Quebec, and using that power to defeat the Castors. In fact, this plan was carried out only in part. Chapleau was a relatively successful premier and he did join Macdonald's cabinet, but he had to share control of the patronage with Langevin. Furthermore, his successor and lieutenant, Mousseau, proved unable to hold the fort against the Castors in Quebec City. Finally, although the Macdonald government was relatively generous it was, as usual, slow to act, with the result that Chapleau and his moderate wing of the party did not receive all the credit.

The main source of Quebec's financial problems was the ambitious railway-building program that had been launched in the early 1870s.[39] The Grand Trunk had used Quebec as a corridor between Ontario and the New England states but had ignored the part of the province north of the Ottawa and St Lawrence rivers. Thus the provincial government itself undertook, in 1875, to build a line from Ottawa to Quebec City by way of Laval and Trois-Rivières. By 1879 the project was complete, but the province had borrowed so heavily that it had difficulty paying the interest on its bonds. As usually happens with such projects, construction costs on the railway had exceeded expectations while operating revenues had not. During the interval between the federal election of 1878 and Mackenzie's resignation, the Joly government had sought financial help from the outgoing government, but all they had received was the partial payment of the statutory subsidy due to them on 1 January 1879 three months in advance. The advance amounted to $500,000.[40]

Within weeks of taking office in October 1879, Chapleau and his treasurer, J.G. Robertson, travelled to Ottawa to seek further help. They succeeded in gaining a further advance of $125,000, with the importance difference that this one would not be deducted from their next statutory subsidy payment. Instead it would be deducted from the total amount allegedly owing to Quebec upon settlement of the tangled financial affairs of the former United Province, whose trust funds were still held by the dominion on behalf of the two successor provinces. A few months later Quebec was back for more. Tilley, who was again minister of finance, was unwilling to make any further advance against the trust funds, but he did in April 1880 repeat his predecessor's action of paying $500,000 of the statutory subsidy three months in advance.[41]

Living from hand to mouth in this fashion was obviously no solution, and Chapleau needed a more permanent means of escape from Quebec's financial difficulties. In May 1880 he met with Macdonald and suggested for the first time that the dominion should buy Quebec's railway, thus enabling the province to retire some of its debt. Macdonald indicated that he could not yet commit the government to this expenditure, but he apparently held out some hope that he might do so in the future. Apart from his obvious interest in strengthening Chapleau's position vis-à-vis both the Rouges and the Castors, Macdonald was presumably thinking of the projected CPR, which would need access to one or both of the St Lawrence ports to be commercially viable. His government had not yet found anyone willing and able to build the transcontinental railway, but in September an agreement was reached with George Stephen and his associates, who promised to build it in return for $25 million cash and twenty-five million acres of western land. A month later Chapleau again raised the question of the Quebec railway system, writing to ask Macdonald whether either the dominion government or the CPR syndicate would take it off his hands. Chapleau claimed to have three other offers for the railway, but said he would prefer to give the dominion the first opportunity to purchase. However, his first duty was to improve the state of Quebec's finances. As an alternative to selling the line, he suggested that Quebec might keep it and grant running rights to the CPR in return for a subsidy.[42]

Macdonald had more than one reason for wanting to comply with these requests. He was deeply committed to the transcontinental railway project; he did not want Quebec's railway system to fall into the wrong, particularly American, hands; and he wanted Chapleau in Ottawa to strengthen his cabinet. Chapleau would not leave Quebec until he had brought about some significant improvement in the province's financial and railway problems.[43] In January 1881 Macdonald saw two members of the CPR syndicate on Chapleau's behalf and informed Chapleau that the CPR would probably purchase the Quebec railway "eventually" if the price was right. Chapleau told Macdonald in reply that he would accept $7 million, slightly more than half of what he claimed Quebec had invested in the railway.[44]

From this point onwards Chapleau concentrated his efforts on the CPR itself, although he still kept Macdonald informed of the progress of the negotiations and occasionally sought the prime minister's help. The CPR was definitely interested in the western division of Chapleau's railway, from Ottawa to Montreal, but access to Quebec City was a lower priority for them. In February 1882 Chapleau and the CPR reached agreement on the sale of the western divison, including the terminal facilities in Montreal, for $4 million. Chapleau credited Macdonald with persuading the company to raise its original offer of $3 million. A week later the eastern division, from St-Martin Junction (Laval) to Quebec City, was sold for another $4 million to a group of investors headed by L.-A. Senécal, a political ally and a friend of the premier. This transaction was controversial, partly because Senécal was not universally popular and partly because Quebec City wanted to be served by the CPR, not by a local company. J.G. Robertson, the provincial treasurer, and J.J. Ross, the minister of agriculture, both resigned from Chapleau's cabinet in consequence. Senécal kept his railway only a few months before selling it to the Grand Trunk at a profit.[45]

A secondary objective of Chapleau's government, which also required federal help, was to establish regular steamship service between Quebec and France. Presumably this was desired for both commercial and symbolic reasons. Chapleau first raised the question with Macdonald in November 1880, suggesting that the dominion should offer a subsidy to persuade a French shipping company to establish the service. Macdonald, as usual, did not commit himself one way or the other. The postmaster-general, Macdonald's old friend Alexander Campbell, was definitely opposed to including the subsidy in his department's estimates, describing it as a waste of money. Macdonald, however, told Chapleau that he hoped the service could be established as soon as possible. Campbell was shifted to the Justice portfolio in May 1881, and in August Chapleau was encouraged enough to inform French prime minister Jules Ferry, erroneously, that the dominion government had agreed to subsidize the service. In October Chapleau was still urging Macdonald to act, since he was about to request a dissolution of the Legislative Assembly in order to seek a fresh mandate. Macdonald finally committed himself in November, the day after the dissolution took place, and the subsidy was included in the estimates for 1882–83.[46]

Chapleau's interest in re-establishing relations between Quebec and France was not confined exclusively to the steamship service. His letter to Ferry expressed an interest in stimulating trade, drew attention to Canada's virtual independence in matters of tariff policy, and asked that France reduce its own tariffs on Canadian ships, petroleum, and farm machinery. Chapleau also asked Macdonald to consider establishing a Canadian government office in Paris. Macdonald was able to report that the imperial government had no objection to such an office, but two months later Chapleau was still imploring the prime minister to act on "the most pressing matter" of the Paris office, which he hoped would attract both capital investment and immigration. According to Chapleau, Quebec derived practically no benefit from the dominion goverment's expenditures on immigration. The Paris office was finally established in July 1882, just before Chapleau joined Macdonald's government. Senator Hector Fabre, whom Chapleau had recommended for the job, became Canada's agent-general in Paris.[47]

Meanwhile Chapleau had won a convincing victory in the provincial election. This fact, and the sale of the provincial railway (albeit after dividing it into two parts), enabled him to depart for Ottawa without being accused of abandoning the province in time of need. As noted above, Chapleau exchanged places with Mousseau, who had been secretary of state in Macdonald's cabinet since November 1880. Mousseau proved to be less successful than Chapleau in dealing with either the province's financial problems or the attacks of the Castors. He lost his seat in the obligatory by-election that followed his acceptance of the premiership and was forced to take refuge in a partially anglophone constituency. He also failed to persuade J.J. Ross to serve in his cabinet; instead, Ross became premier after Mousseau gave up the office in January 1884. Mousseau's letters to Macdonald are replete with descriptions of plots and conspiracies and with requests that Macdonald help to resolve his political problems, either by the use of federal patronage or by persuading the CPR to invest more heavily in Quebec.

Mousseau's government also renewed Quebec's financial demands on the dominion government. In March 1883 the Legislative Assembly adopted a long resolution pointing out that Quebec's expenditures, particularly on the asylums and the administration of justice, had increased rapidly since Confederation while its statutory subsidy from the dominion had remained fixed. It demanded that the statutory subsidy of eighty cents per capita be henceforth based on the most recent decennial census, rather than being permanently based on the last census prior to Confederation. The resolution also noted that the dominion's revenues from Customs and Excise had doubled since Confederation, while its payments to the provinces had grown more slowly. This resolution was formally transmitted to the governor general, and was followed soon afterwards by a long memorandum from Mousseau himself which explained Quebec's financial problems in more detail, and attributed them in large part to the construction of the north-shore railways. The provincial cabinet travelled to Ottawa to present its demands. In a personal letter to Macdonald, Mousseau again pleaded for financial aid for his province, but to no avail. By the end of 1883 Macdonald had apparently given up on Mousseau and was trying to persuade Senator Louis Masson to succeed the beleaguered premier.[48]

Quebec's financial demands increased significantly the following year. Within weeks of taking office, Premier Ross submitted a new memorandum "for the consideration of the Honourable the Privy Council of Canada." This document repeated the demand that statutory subsidies be based on the most recent census, but also suggested that the per capita rate be increased from eighty cents to one dollar. It also revived a traditional Quebec complaint: that the increase in Quebec's debt allowance granted in 1873 should have been made retroactive to 1867. Finally, it pointed out that Quebec had received less than half as much from the sale of its railways as it had invested in them, and demanded reimbursement from the dominion for at least some of the additional cost. The document was carried to Ottawa by the entire provincial cabinet, apart from Ross himself who remained in Quebec City because of illness. In a letter to Macdonald explaining why he could not make the trip, Ross expressed the hope that Quebec would be suitably reimbursed for its services to the dominion. This was a reference to the historically dubious allegation in his government's memorandum that the north-shore railway had been planned from the outset to serve as the eastern section of the CPR.[49]

This time Quebec's efforts were more successful, although less because of the provincial cabinet's journey to Ottawa than because the Conservative members of parliament from Quebec insisted that their province's financial problems must be resolved before they would agree to additional aid for the still uncompleted CPR. In April 1884, two months after the provincial ministers had met with Macdonald, royal assent was given to two statutes that represented at least a partial fulfilment of their demands in relation to both debt allowances and the railway.[50] The first of these made the increase in debt allowances authorized in 1873 retroactive to 1867 for each of the four original provinces. The interest payments that would have been made between 1867 and 1873 on the increased amount were deemed to be capital owing to the provinces, as would interest (not compounded) on that amount for the years 1873 to 1884 at the rate of 5 per cent. Each province would thus receive an additional annual subsidy (supposedly an interest payment) equal to 5 per cent of the accumulated amount. In Quebec's case this annual increase would amount to $127,381.

The second statute, which received royal assent on the same day as the first, provided that Quebec would be reimbursed for part of the cost of building both sections of the north-shore railway. To make this measure more palatable to other provinces and to their representatives, it took the form of an omnibus measure authorizing the cabinet to grant subsidies to an assortment of railways, both actual and projected. It included, however, the provision that Quebec would be granted $1,440,000 for building the railway from Montreal to Ottawa ($12,000 per mile for 120 miles) and $954,000 for building the section from St-Martin Junction to Quebec City ($6000 per mile for 159 miles). The total of the two amounts would be deemed to be capital owing to Quebec, on which the dominion would pay the province interest at the rate of 5 per cent. The annual value of this payment to Quebec would be $119,700. The same statute authorized the CPR to purchase the line from St-Martin Junction to Quebec City (which then belonged to the Grand Trunk) or to build its own parallel line.

This was not quite the end of the matter, however. In an astonishing manoeuvre, the Macdonald government decided that only the first part of the railway subsidy would actually be credited to Quebec's account. The second part, pertaining to the eastern division of the railway, would be used to help the CPR purchase the railway in question from the Grand Trunk. Furthermore, the increased subsidy or "interest payment" resulting from the retroactive adjustment of the debt allowance would not be fully paid to Quebec, because the problem of dividing the debts and assets of the former Province of Canada had still not been resolved. Tilley, the minister of finance, claimed that "there appears to be a balance due the dominion government of between $800,000 and $900,000. Until this matter is adjusted between the premiers we never will get a settlement."[51]

By the winter of 1885 Quebec was somewhat disgruntled by these developments, as well it might be. The Ross government now increased its own demands, claiming that the eastern division of the railway should be subsidized at the same rate as the western division, $12,000 per mile, since it was equally essential to the CPR Louis Masson, who had recently been appointed lieutenant-governor, urged Macdonald in writing on at least four occasions to comply with this demand, pointing out that Quebec had contributed more to the CPR than any other province. Ross travelled to Ottawa to discuss the matter with Macdonald and warned that failure to give Quebec satisfaction would severely damage the Conservative party in the province. Subsequently he proposed a solution, which he said would satisfy the Quebec City business community who wanted their city to be served by the CPR. If the CPR purchased only a 50 per cent share in the railway, it would require no help from the government, and the Grand Trunk could retain the other 50 per cent.[52] However, the CPR purchased full control of the line in September 1885. Two months later the last spike in the main line was driven at Craigellachie, ending any possibility that Quebec members of parliament could bargain on their province's behalf by threatening to withold support from the transcontinental railway. The almost simultaneous execution of Louis Riel provided French Canadians, or at least some of them, with another grievance, and paved the way for the rise of Honoré Mercier. Under his government, relations between the province and the dominion became more antagonistic than ever before.

Before discussing Mercier and his government, however, mention should be made of one other matter that caused discord between the dominion government and Quebec, as it did between the dominion government and Ontario. This was the McCarthy Act to regulate the sale of intoxicating liquors, which Parliament adopted in 1883. Macdonald's promise, after the Judicial Committee's decision in Russell *vs* the Queen, to introduce a dominion licensing act was viewed with concern by the Quebec government, which relied on its liquor licensing powers for a large share of its revenue. During the 1883 session of Parliament, Premier Mousseau wrote several letters to Macdonald expressing this concern, and the provincial treasurer, J.S. Wurtele, travelled to Ottawa to discuss the subject with the prime minister. Possibly on Macdonald's suggestion, Quebec adopted a new licensing act of its own that would be compatible with the dominion act and would take effect only if the latter were adopted, but Mousseau still expressed the hope that Macdonald would change his mind and leave the entire field to the provinces.[53] The McCarthy Act was nonetheless adopted by Parliament in May 1883, and scheduled to take effect at the beginning of the new year.

Within days of the Ross government taking office, J.G. Robertson, back for his third and last stint as provincial treasurer, wrote a letter to Robert Hall, who represented Robertson's Sherbrooke constituency in the House of Commons. Robertson estimated that the McCarthy Act, which had been in force for a month, would cost Quebec between $80,000 and $100,000 per annum. He asked whether Hall thought the act would be retained on the statute book, particularly since some authorities believed it to be *ultra vires*. What reply, if any, he received is not known, although the letter was apparently referred to Macdonald.[54] The Macdonald government did not relent, but the Judicial Committee resolved the issue by striking down the McCarthy Act in 1885.

Macdonald's relations with his Bleu allies in Quebec were sometimes difficult, then, but they were generally cordial. Mercier's arrival in the premier's office early in 1887 produced an unprecedented level of hostility between the two governments, which lasted until his dismissal almost five years later. Mercier was a Quebec nationalist in the twentieth-century sense of the term who never really accepted Confederation as more than a necessary evil. In its first throne speech, his government announced plans to invite other provincial governments and the dominion government to a conference which would examine financial and other aspects of federal-provincial relations and suggest possible changes in the constitution. It repeated Quebec's financial grievances and referred to "well-founded fears for the maintenance of our local institutions." Mercier requested a confidential meeting with Macdonald before the conference to discuss these matters, but Macdonald promptly refused. After meeting with his cabinet Macdonald relented so far as to offer Mercier a non-confidential interview, but this time it was Mercier's turn to decline.[55] Mercier nonetheless invited the dominion government to the conference, but Macdonald and his colleagues did not attend.[56]

The five provincial delegations that did attend the conference recommended seventeen constitutional amendments, most of which reflected the influence, and the priorities, of Oliver Mowat's Ontario. From Quebec's point of view the most important of these resolutions was the last, which concerned the financial relations between the two levels of government. It proposed that the grants to the provinces for the upkeep of their governments and legislatures be approximately tripled, while the per capita statutory subsidies would be based on the most recent census and adjusted periodically, with no limit. However, growth in population beyond the level of two-and-a-half million would produce increments of only sixty cents per capita, rather than eighty cents. Twenty years after the conference this proposal was embodied almost verbatim in the British North America Act of 1907, adopted at the request of Laurier's government.

At its 1888 session the Quebec legislature adopted three statutes that became, for different reasons, subjects of controversy involving the dominion government as well as the provincial government. Beyond the fact that they were controversial, and the coincidence that they were adopted in the same session, the three measures had nothing in common. Together they united in simultaneous controversy three perennial preoccupations of nineteenth-century Canadian politics: finance, the administration of justice, and religion.

The first statute was designed to lessen the burden of Quebec's provincial debt. It provided for the compulsory redemption of debentures that paid interest at a rate of 5 per cent and their replacement by new securities paying only 4 per cent.[57] Macdonald was furious about this measure, which he described as "simply confiscation." In a letter to Charles Tupper, Canada's high commissioner in London, the prime minister lamented the fact that none of the affected bondholders lived in Canada, so that no Canadians had an interest in fighting Mercier on the issue. Despite his own strong feelings, he was reluctant to disallow the measure because "there will be a howl in Quebec and a special appeal to the habitans [sic] against a Government which compelled them to pay 5% when they can get plenty of money at 4." Macdonald suggested a possible solution to Tupper: the imperial government might be persuaded to disallow the act or at least send a dispatch to the governor general directing him to do so. The prime minister predicted that the colonial secretary would probably say that disallowance was Canada's responsibility, and Tupper reported in his reply two weeks later that this was indeed the case. However, Tupper reported, the colonial secretary would send a dispatch to the governor general recommending disallowance if the bondholders petitioned the imperial government to do so. Tupper used his contacts in the City of London to orchestrate the petition, which materialized with remarkable promptness, and was duly sent to the governor general. However, by October Macdonald had second thoughts, fearing that his government would still lose Quebec votes by disallowing the act, even if it claimed to be doing so at the behest of the colonial secretary.[58] In the end Mercier avoided a confrontation by amending the act at his next session to make the conversion voluntary. The original measure had only passed through the appointed upper house on the basis of a promise by Mercier that the compulsory provision would not be enforced, so the whole episode was probably unnecessary.

Meanwhile another controversy had erupted over another statute: the District Magistrates Act.[59] This act provided for the establishment of a new court in Montreal, with two provincially appointed judges who would handle much of the minor litigation originating in that city and reduce the burden on the Superior Court of the province. (Unlike other provinces, Quebec had never had county or district courts, so the Superior Court exercised a broader jurisdiction than elsewhere.) John Thompson, the dominion minister of justice, recommended disallowance on the grounds that Section 96 of the

BNA Act gave only the dominion government the power to appoint district court judges. Macdonald readily agreed, although he blamed the understaffing of the Superior Court, which provided the rationale for Mercier's legislation, on his own Quebec ministers and their endless arguments over judicial patronage.[60] The act was disallowed with unusual promptness, and without the usual efforts to persuade the provincial government to amend it. A secondary controversy followed when Mercier refused to publish the official proclamation of disallowance in the provincial Gazette. The lieutenant-governor, with Macdonald's approval, insisted on this formality and finally persuaded Mercier to relent after two months delay.[61]

In the following year, however, the District Magistrates Bill was again introduced and passed by the legislature. The new version defined the jurisdiction of the proposed court in more detail, and its preamble explicitly blamed "the federal authorities" for failing to make enough appointments to the Superior Court, but in other respects it was virtually the same as its predecessor. Thompson recommended this time that the bill should be reserved by the lieutenant-governor and simply allowed to lapse, so as to avoid another controversy over disallowance. Macdonald agreed, but Lieutenant-Governor A.-R. Angers was reluctant to take the responsibility, so Macdonald allowed him to sign the bill, which was then disallowed by the federal government.[62]

The third statute was one to which Macdonald and his government took no exception, but which caused a far greater uproar than all the Mercier government's other initiatives combined: the Jesuit Estates Act. This involved some real estate that had been confiscated by the crown almost a century earlier, after the original Jesuit order had been dissolved by the Vatican, and subsequently transferred to the control of the Legislature of Lower Canada. The revival of the Jesuits under Pius IX led to demands that this property be returned to them, while other elements within the church claimed that it should properly revert to the dioceses in which it was situated. Mercier, who had been educated in a Jesuit seminary, decided to resolve the dispute and did so in a fair and reasonable manner with a compromise that had the blessing of the Vatican: $400,000, an amount far less than the value of the land, would be divided among the various Catholic claimants, and an additional $60,000 would be given to support the educational system of the Protestant minority in Quebec.[63]

This harmless measure provoked one of the most shocking episodes of bigotry and intolerance, particularly in Ontario, that Canada has ever witnessed. Militant Protestants objected to the Jesuits receiving any compensation whatever, and particularly to the implication that the pope had helped to settle a dispute over real estate which they claimed belonged to the crown. Macdonald did not share these sentiments, but as petitions and delegations poured into Ottawa to denounce the measure he was faced with a characteristically Canadian dilemma. Disallowance would offend the Catholics, while failure to disallow would offend the Protestants. In March 1889 a motion requesting disallowance was introduced by D'Alton McCarthy, but was easily defeated in the House of Commons with only twelve Ontario members and one Protestant from Quebec voting in favour.[64] The Protestants then turned to the imperial government, asking that it disallow the act, since the dominion government had already indicated its unwillingness to do so. Predictably the colonial secretary again asserted, this time publicly, that provincial statutes were the dominion's responsibility.[65]

Although Macdonald had himself tried to bring about an imperial disallowance in the case of the debt conversion act only a year earlier, he did not want one in this case. Nor did he want the question of whether the Jesuit Estates Act was constitutional referred to the Supreme Court, as urged by Edward Blake and also by the francophobic proprietor of the *Montreal Star*, Hugh Graham. Instead he wanted the law officers of the imperial government to issue a declaration that the act was valid, and that recourse to the courts would therefore be futile. Furthermore, he wanted this declaration to be published soon after the deadline for disallowance by the dominion had passed, but to be received slightly before the deadline so he could not be accused of deliberate procrastination. With all three avenues of attack – imperial disallowance, federal disallowance, and litigation – thus blocked, he hoped that the Protestant hysteria would subside well before the next election. After much correspondence, and with the cooperation of the Colonial Office and the governor general, this delicate feat was accomplished. The country moved on to more mundane matters, but the unity of Macdonald's party had been severely damaged.[66]

Another measure by Mercier's government that provoked some ire in Ottawa was an act depriving federal public servants of the right to vote in provincial elections. Macdonald described this as "outrageous" and wanted to take some action, but Thompson pointed out that Nova Scotia had had a similar measure on the statute books for many years. No action was taken.[67]

Following Mowat's example, Mercier also pursued the question of Quebec's northern boundary. In 1886, shortly before Mercier took office, a legislative committee proposed a boundary based on the

Eastmain and Hamilton rivers, which it claimed represented the territory claimed by France before the Conquest. Early in his premiership, Mercier sent a copy of a book on the subject to the governor
general, who acknowledged it politely but apparently did not raise it
with Macdonald.[68] Alexander Campbell, who was now lieutenant-
governor of Ontario, suggested that the boundaries of both provinces should be extended to Hudson Bay, but Macdonald believed,
erroneously, that the land north of Lake Abitibi was suitable for
farming and he feared that making the central provinces too large
would have a detrimental effect on Canadian federalism. Regarding
Quebec, he had more specific anxieties: "Quite entre nous, I look to
the future in this matter – farther ahead perhaps than I should. But
are we not founding a Nation? Now just consider for yourself what
a country of millions lying between English Canada and the Atlantic
will be. I have no objection to the French as French or as Catholics
but the block caused by the introduction of French law and the Civil
Code would be very great."[69]

In the summer of 1888, Mercier and Macdonald discussed the
boundary privately when the prime minister was taking his customary vacation near Rivière-du-Loup, but apparently made little
progress. A few months later Macdonald suggested that Quebec's
northern boundary be a straight line along the fifty-second parallel
and that it be confirmed by imperial legislation, but Mercier rejected
the offer. The federal government then offered a slight modification of the line in Quebec's favour, but Quebec was still not interested.[70] It continued to insist on its original demand even after
Mercier's fall, and its persistence was finally rewarded by the Laurier
government in 1898.[71]

Difficult as the boundary question was, it was simple compared
with the seemingly interminable and insoluble problem of the financial accounts among Quebec, Ontario, and the dominion. Representatives of all three governments met at Toronto late in 1890 and
agreed on a new effort to solve their disputes by arbitration. Quebec
now accepted the view that a decision could be made by two out of
three arbitrators, and all three governments adopted the necessary
enabling legislation.[72] Three judges were appointed as arbitrators:
George Burbidge of the Exchequer Court for the dominion, John
Boyd for Ontario, and Louis Casault for Quebec. Quebec and Ontario were now agreed on most questions, and the one matter on
which they were not – the Upper Canada Building Fund – was excluded at Quebec's insistence from the terms of reference of the arbitration. By the summer of 1896 the arbitrators had issued a total
of ten decisions on various issues, five of which concerned Ontario

and the dominion only. The first and most important of these gave the provinces the interpretation they wanted of the interest due to them under the terms of the 1873 and 1884 statutes regarding debt allowances. The dominion appealed, but the decision was upheld by the Supreme Court in 1895. The more complex question of the Common School Fund was not resolved and dragged on into the twentieth century, largely because of Ontario's unexpected claim in Deceomber 1895 that the fund belonged solely to Ontario and need not be shared with Quebec. The arbitrators found in favour of Quebec, and against the dominion, on the relatively minor issue of the Montreal Turnpike Trust, and in favour of both provinces against the dominion in relation to some Indian claims dating from before Confederation.[73]

Surveying the whole history of Quebec's relations with the dominion up to 1896, it appears that the province's demands were relatively modest and its gains even more so. The victories that it did gain were less the result of any power wielded directly by its provincial government than the result of discreet pressure by Quebec ministers in Ottawa and Macdonald's consciousness of his dependence on Quebec votes. Quebec, like other provinces, also benefited indirectly and in the longer term from Mowat's assertion of provincial status and authority (assuming that provincial autonomy is in fact a benefit). During Mercier's brief term in office, Quebec relied less on quiet diplomacy and more on Mowat-like assertions of its own authority and status, although with less success than Mowat himself. At the same time, the Mercier era suggested the potential of a popular premier and a fairly cohesive governing party free of federal entanglements. In doing so, it foreshadowed some twentieth-century developments.

5 The Intergovernmental Agenda: The Maritimes

Maritimers dislike generalizations about their region and many of them refuse to accept that it is a region, preferring to emphasize the uniqueness of each province. Although the three provinces of Nova Scotia, New Brunswick, and Prince Edward Island were each and still are unique, the fact that the Charlottetown Conference of 1864 was intended to discuss Maritime Union testifies to the existence of some regional sentiment even then among these neighbours. The idea of a Maritime region was also given official recognition in the arrangements that the British North America Act made for the allocation of senatorial seats among the provinces.

Apart from their geographical proximity to one another, the most obvious characteristic that distinguished the three Maritime provinces from Ontario or Quebec was the fact that none of them had had any previous political association with Canada. In contrast to central Canadians, for whom Confederation was really only an incremental change in political and administrative institutions that already existed, Maritimers who were asked to pay taxes and send representatives to Ottawa were facing a totally new experience.

Second, all three provinces were established and, with the possible exception of Prince Edward Island, reasonably successful political communities that commanded considerable loyalty from their inhabitants. All had acquired representative assemblies earlier than Ontario or Quebec. Nova Scotia's Legislative Assembly was the oldest in British North America, dating from 1758. The Legislative Assemblies of New Brunswick and Prince Edward Island had been established in 1784 and 1769, respectively, the dates at which those two colonies were separated from Nova Scotia. All had achieved responsible government more than a decade before Confederation, and had done so without the violence that Canada experienced in 1837–8. Although all had small minorities of French-speaking Acadians, none had experienced the acute problems of linguistic and cultural cleavage that pervaded and preoccupied Canadian politics.

Although proud of their own identities and institutions, the people of all three provinces were also attached to the crown and the British Empire. In this they were not unique, but there was perhaps a difference between Maritimers and central Canadians in the impact of imperial loyalty on the legitimacy of the new dominion. In central Canada, Confederation was in a sense a reaffirmation of loyalty to the crown and a rejection of the obvious alternative: annexation by the United States. In Ontario and Quebec it was plausible to accuse anti-Confederates of being pro-American and disloyal, an argument to which both Macdonald and Cartier resorted on more than one occasion. For Maritimers the American threat, if such it was, was more remote. Furthermore, Confederation seemed to imply a weakening rather than a strengthening of the imperial tie. Instead of being directly linked to London, the Maritime colonies after Confederation would be indirectly linked to London by way of Ottawa. Ottawa in a sense would be substituted for London as the external source of authority and power. Psychologically, Confederation invited Maritimers to turn their backs on the Atlantic Ocean and look inland to the backwoods of North America.

For all these reasons it is understandable that Confederation inspired even less enthusiasm in the Maritimes than it did in Quebec. In Nova Scotia a substantial majority of the population were hostile to Confederation and joined Canada against their will. How long this hostility lasted is difficult to say with certainty, but as late as 1886 a provincial government was re-elected on a separatist platform. Prince Edward Island waited until 1873 to join the dominion, and did so then only to escape from serious financial problems. New Brunswick was perhaps the least unenthusiastic, but it seems likely that only the Fenian raid of April 1866 shifted the balance of opinion in favour of Confederation. John A. Macdonald's comment in the Confederation debates of 1865 that the Maritimers were "as much Canadians as we are" was decidedly premature.

One generalization about the Maritime provinces that should not be made with reference to the period of time under consideration is one that has become sadly familiar in the twentieth century: poverty and underdevelopment. In the nineteenth century the Maritimes were not poor, and it is probable that actual living standards were not significantly lower than in Ontario, let alone Quebec. Data from the 1871 census show that New Brunswick and Nova Scotia, particularly the latter, were less industrialized than central Canada, but their diversified economies had other assets that central Canada did not have: coal mines, fisheries, and a still-impressive role in the trade, commerce, and shipping of the Atlantic world. Halifax and Saint John were important commercial, and to some extent industrial, centres. Each was more than half as large as Toronto in 1871; in fact, Saint John was two-thirds as large as Toronto if the neighbouring municipality of Portland, which it later annexed, is included. The provinces themselves were still growing at a respectable rate and they were much larger, relative to the size of the whole dominion, than they are today. Nova Scotia had 10.8 per cent of Canada's total population in 1871, 10.2 per cent in 1881, and 9.3 per cent in 1891. The comparable figures for New Brunswick were 7.9 per cent, 7.4 per cent, and 6.6. per cent. Prince Edward Island had 2.5 per cent of the total in 1881, the first census following its entry into the dominion, and 2.3 per cent in 1891. In fact, the Island had almost as many people in absolute terms in 1891 (109,078) as it would have a century later.

From the perspective of the dominion government, the Maritime provinces were geographically remote (until 1876 a visit to them normally involved travelling through the United States) and almost totally unfamiliar. Although there was perhaps less of a cultural barrier for anglophone politicians and civil servants than with Quebec, the sense of remoteness and unfamiliarity must have been even greater. Few Maritimers came to work in Ottawa in 1867; most of the public service of the dominion was inherited from the Province of Canada. No Maritimer was prime minister until Thompson in 1892, and his term was cut short after two years. Strong regional ministers bridged the gap to some extent but they were not always available, and Prince Edward Island had no representation in the cabinet at all for more than half of the period under consideration.

NOVA SCOTIA

Nova Scotia confronted the new dominion with its first major crisis soon after Confederation, when it not only defeated all but one of the Macdonald government's candidates for the House of Commons but elected a provincial government committed to seeking the restoration of the *status quo ante*. Although this crisis was eventually surmounted, with the support of the imperial authorities, Nova Scotia remained at least until 1896 the most discontented of the Maritime provinces and the most difficult for the dominion government to deal with. This was so despite the generally high quality, and quantity, of Nova Scotian representation in the dominion cabinet.

Geographically, Nova Scotia was remote. One large part of the province actually was an island (Cape Breton) and the rest was virtually so, being joined to the continent only by a narrow isthmus. Rail communication with the rest of North America was not established until 1876, and even then the journey from Halifax to Ottawa took about two days. Historically and culturally Nova Scotia, or at least its western half, had more affinities with the New England states than with Canada. It is probable that only British naval power prevented Nova Scotia from becoming part of the United States at the time of the revolution.[1]

Economically, Nova Scotia was the most distinctive province of the dominion, apart from British Columbia. Although agriculture was the largest source of employment, as it was elsewhere, Nova Scotia was unique in the importance of mining (mainly for coal) and fishing. At the time of the 1871 census, which included only the four original provinces, Nova Scotia accounted for 79 per cent of all Canadians employed in mining and for 59 per cent of all those employed in fishing. Fishing accounted directly for about one-tenth of all employment in the province, and indirectly for much more. Nova Scotia had about six times as many fishermen as New Brunswick.[2] Coal royalties were an important source of revenue for the provincial government, both before and after Confederation.

Party alignments in Nova Scotia after 1867 were based on the issue of Confederation, which had deeply divided the province. Although a two-party system using the familiar labels of Liberal and Conservative had existed before Confederation, it was almost totally shattered by the cleavage over Confederation, which made the old issues irrelevant and produced a realignment.[3] After 1867 persons who supported Confederation were called Conservatives and persons who opposed it were called Liberals, regardless of what they had been called, or called themselves, before. It follows that the Conservatives were not in any meaningful sense more conservative, nor were the Liberals more liberal, than their opponents. These labels were simply used because "Conservative" was the name of John A. Macdonald's party.

In provincial politics the Liberals dominated the province after sweeping to victory on an anti-Confederation platform in 1867. The Conservatives managed to win a victory in 1878, but they held office for only four years before being defeated, and they did not win another provincial election until 1925. In federal elections the Conservatives did better, having federal patronage to dispense. In every federal election from 1874 through 1891 Nova Scotia gave a majority of its seats and votes to the winning party, and in 1896 it divided its seats evenly between the two parties. The disparity between federal and provincial voting was most dramatically illustrated in 1882 when the two elections were held on the same day: the Liberals won 45.0 per cent of the federal vote and 51.8 per cent of the provincial, while the Conservative percentages were 51.4 and 46.9, respectively.[4]

Although no Nova Scotia premier before 1896 enjoyed the durability and success of Oliver Mowat, there was less instability and weakness of leadership than in Quebec. From Confederation until the summer of 1896 there were seven premiers. Hiram Blanchard, who took over the pro-Confederation government when Charles Tupper went to Ottawa, was soon replaced by a secessionist Liberal government led by a prominent newspaper editor, William Annand. On his retirement in 1875 Annand handed the reins to P.C. Hill, a former Conservative who had served in the Blanchard government. The Conservatives governed from 1878 until 1882 under Simon Holmes and, very briefly, John Thompson. The Liberals then returned under W.T. Pipes, who was replaced after two years by the most durable and successful of the seven premiers, William S. Fielding. Fielding remained premier until he joined Laurier's government as minister of finance in 1896. For twenty of the twenty-nine years up to 1896 Nova Scotia was governed by a different party from that which held office in the dominion, and it was thus more frequently in partisan opposition to the federal government than any other province. Because of its relatively small size, however, its opposition was not as threatening to the dominion government as that of Ontario. Furthermore, there was not the personal animosity of the Macdonald-Mowat relationship.

The federal and provincial elections in Nova Scotia were held simultaneously on 18 September 1867. As most observers probably anticipated, the pro-Confederation party was overwhelmingly defeated at both levels, electing only one member (Charles Tupper) to the House of Commons and only two to the provincial House of Assembly. The defeat was so total that Hiram Blanchard, to whom Tupper had entrusted the provincial government, resigned before the new legislature met, a course of action that was without precedent in the British Empire. John A. Macdonald's government took advantage of the seven-week interval between the election and Blanchard's resignation to appoint General Charles Hastings Doyle, the commander of the British garrison in Halifax, as the lieutenant-governor of the province. Doyle had some vice-regal experience, having administered the government of New Brunswick, for whose military defence he was also responsible, for about a year. At the urging of the governor general, Viscount Monck, the imperial government allowed Doyle to retain his military command while serving as the dominion government's proconsul in Halifax, conveying a clear message to secessionist Nova Scotians that both the imperial government and the dominion meant business.[5]

The secessionist government took office on 7 November 1867. On 13 February 1868 it introduced resolutions in the House of Assembly calling for the repeal of the British North America Act. Doyle immediately dispatched copies of the resolutions to both the Colonial Office in London and the governor general. A few days later the resolutions were adopted by the House of Assembly and, at the end of the month, a delegation headed by Joseph Howe, who had led the struggle for responsible government in Nova Scotia, set sail for the United Kingdom.

Long before Howe arrived in London, the British government was well informed about the situation. A dispatch signed by the governor general, but probably drafted by John A. Macdonald, had been promptly sent to the colonial secretary as soon as the content of the resolutions was known. It warned that if Confederation was dissolved, "the maintenance of British power and the existence of British institutions in America will soon become impossible," and suggested that Howe's delegation be told that the repeal of Confederation would be tantamount to the expulsion of Nova Scotia from the British Empire. The dispatch rejected the argument that Tupper's government should have consulted the electorate before committing their province to Confederation, asserting that this principle was foreign to the British Constitution and that the same objection had been made without success when the Scottish and Irish parliaments were abolished in 1707 and 1801, respectively. It also suggested that the outcome of the recent election had been affected by issues other than Confederation, and that fewer than half of the eligible voters had voted against the pro-Confederation government.[6]

However plausible these arguments might be, it is not clear that they were decisive. Tupper, who followed Howe to London to present the case against repeal in person, reported to Macdonald in April that several members of the imperial government had in fact been prepared to reconsider the British North America Act. In addition to lobbying at Westminster, Tupper began the delicate process of detaching Howe from the anti-Confederation forces. The two

Nova Scotians had at least two long conversations in London, during which Tupper offered Howe a seat in the dominion cabinet, patronage for other Nova Scotians, and the possibility of better financial terms for the province. Howe displayed some interest but expressed concern that he would be repudiated by his followers if he accepted Confederation before they were ready to do so – an argument he used for the next nine months to extract additional concessions from Macdonald. Tupper reassured him that "between us we could rally to his support three fourths of the wealth, education and influence of the country."[7]

Early in June the colonial secretary informed the governor general that the Disraeli government was committed to Confederation and would not consider repeal.[8] This news was promptly communicated via General Doyle to the Nova Scotia government. Howe and his delegation returned home. With the imperial government having performed its essential part in the drama, the stage was set for bilateral negotiations between Nova Scotia and the dominion. Adams Archibald, who had been appointed one of two Nova Scotians in the first dominion cabinet but who had resigned after failing to win a seat in the House of Commons, urged Macdonald to travel to Nova Scotia for this purpose, since Archibald believed that the more moderate supporters of repeal were open to persuasion. However, Archibald warned Macdonald that offers of patronage would not be enough: the Nova Scotians would have to be persuaded that the province itelf would receive significant benefits, particularly of a financial nature. This advice was repeated by the governor general, who suggested that "a few millions" to appease the Nova Scotians would be a better investment than spending the same amount on military defence against the Americans.[9]

Macdonald and Cartier visited Halifax in August. Macdonald spoke privately with Howe and held a more formal session with a committee representing the secessionist members of both the Nova Scotia legislature and the House of Commons. The prime minister tried to tempt them with patronage and was again told that this would not suffice. He commended them for using only peaceful and lawful means in their campaign for repeal – not that they had much choice with General Doyle's troops in their capital city – but suggested that Nova Scotians would benefit if their members of parliament played a more active part in its deliberations, as the Irish nationalists did at Westminister. In a report to Monck on his expedition, Macdonald was optimistic, predicting that Howe would eventually accept a position in the dominion cabinet "and then the danger will be over." He also noted that the provincial legislature had tacitly accepted the status quo by "getting on with its business."[10]

Matters were still far from a solution, however, as Howe warned Macdonald in a long letter in mid September. In the month since his visit, Howe went on, Macdonald had made no definite offer in writing of better financial terms for Nova Scotia, so it was difficult to put much credence in his oral assurances to the committee in Halifax. As far as the general public was concerned, Canada had offered nothing. Meanwhile Benjamin Butler, a United States general who favoured the annexation of Nova Scotia, had visited the province to fish in troubled waters. As a result, Howe alleged, "the cry for repeal or annexation is heard all over the province."[11]

Macdonald replied promptly, blaming the delay on the difficulty of assembling his ministers during the summer, and promising a formal letter that could be made public and that would re-state what he had said privately in Halifax. The formal letter was finally sent on 6 October but promised nothing beyond a willingness to "discuss" the differences between Nova Scotia and the dominion over taxation, commercial policy, and fisheries. Howe, who was obviously becoming impatient, wrote to John Rose, the minister of finance, urging that the financial terms of Nova Scotia's entry into Confederation be improved. To Macdonald he wrote that he feared "revolution or violence" if Nova Scotia's demands were not satisfied. Howe confessed that he no longer entertained any hopes of repeal since "the men who represent the Railway and Financial interests" and who favour Confederation appeared to dominate both houses of Parliament at Westminister. However, a general election was in progress in the United Kingdom, and other Nova Scotians believed that a Liberal government headed by Gladstone would be more sympathetic to their cause. Furthermore, it was widely believed that Britain would not intervene to prevent the annexation of Nova Scotia by the United States.[12]

It is doubtful whether Macdonald took the talk of annexation seriously, but the reference to Gladstone may have reinforced a far more serious cause for anxiety. In any event, the Canadians finally began to negotiate seriously with their reluctant province. Rose invited Howe to Ottawa for discussions on financial matters. Macdonald also promised to settle "the financial question" and urged Howe to accept the inevitability of Confederation and negotiate without waiting for "the extreme men, the political hacks, and those who have nothing to lose." He compared Howe with Mirabeau, whose moderation could have prevented the excesses of the French

Revolution but for his untimely death. Howe replied that "Mirabeau was an able man, but unprincipled and as ugly as the devil," and added that Nova Scotia's grievances were not only financial but constitutional: it wanted an elected Senate in which Ontario and Quebec would not have a majority of the seats. Furthermore, he called the senators appointed by Macdonald's government "the most unpopular men in the Province." Howe was still reluctant to move too far ahead of public opinion or the provincial government, while Macdonald's strategy was to concentrate his blandishments on Howe, whose popularity and influence he perhaps overestimated, and to ignore the provincial government. Macdonald knew there was no realistic prospect of reforming the Senate, whose composition was the result of laborious compromises among the provinces before 1867. Despite these obstacles, and despite the continuing uncertainty about Gladstone, who became prime minister in December, there was some progress in the long-distance financial negotiations between Howe and Rose. Macdonald also pointed out that there was already a Nova Scotian vacancy in the Senate and that two senators were prepared to resign to create vacancies for Howe's friends.[13]

Events finally moved to a conclusion in January 1869. Howe agreed to meet Rose on the neutral ground of Portland, Maine, to hammer out a financial settlement. Sir John Young, who had become governor general in November, urged the new colonial secretary, Lord Granville, to assert that the Gladstone government was committed to Confederation. Granville promptly did so, in a dispatch which Macdonald assured Doyle was "the deathblow to repeal."[14] The meeting between Rose and Howe was successful. On Rose's recommendation, the Macdonald government agreed to increase Nova Scotia's debt allowance to $9,188,756, thus increasing its annual subsidy by $59,438, and also to provide an additional special subsidy of $82,698 for each of the first ten years after Confederation. Howe joined the government as president of the Privy Council five days later and was re-elected to Parliament in a by-election on 23 April, running this time as a pro-Confederation candidate. Parliament approved the "better terms" for Nova Scotia in June.[15]

Despite the settlement with Howe, the fate of Confederation still hung in the balance. Although Granville had assured Young that the Gladstone government would not entertain any proposal for repeal, he also warned him in a later, secret, dispatch that the British garrison in Halifax "are not stationed there to aid the authorities of Canada in enforcing the laws of the dominion on the inhabitants of Nova Scotia and must not be used for that purpose."[16] Until the returns were actually in it was far from clear that Howe would win his by-election. Even after his victory a majority of Nova Scotia's other members of parliament voted against an amendment affirming the desirability of Confederation. Furthermore, the provincial government had been entirely excluded from the settlement between Howe and the dominion government, a settlement to which it never gave its consent. In May the House of Assembly adopted a resolution demanding changes in taxation, commercial policy and fisheries policy, election of senators by provincial legislatures, and the abandonment of "rep by pop" in the House of Commons. In October the Annand government formally requested a joint commission to arbitrate the continuing differences between Nova Scotia and the dominion. In April 1870, more than a year after Howe had joined Macdonald's government, the House of Assembly adopted an address to the queen expressing regret that her majesty's government had not liberated Nova Scotians "from a Confederation into which they have been cruelly forced by unconstitutional means." The address further inquired whether the queen herself would grant Nova Scotia its independence, if that were desired by the people of the province.[17] The generation of Nova Scotians that had known the status of a self-governing colony never really accepted Confederation, and their bitterness flared up again in 1886.

In these circumstances federal-provincial relations were bound to be difficult, even when the issues themselves were not always of great consequence. While the negotiations with Howe were proceeding, and for some time afterwards, the Annand government produced an assortment of initiatives that indicated its reluctance to accept the dominion's authority. A bill that would have prohibited members of the militia from leaving the province was reserved by General Doyle in 1868, since defence was now clearly under federal jurisdiction. Doyle also refused, in December 1869, to allow the provincial government to send a delegation to Washington to negotiate a new reciprocity agreement. A measure that was adopted in 1871 prohibited employees of the dominion from voting in provincial elections, ostensibly to protect the independence of the legislature from external influence. Macdonald objected to an act empowering the provincial secretary to issue marriage licences, claiming this should be done by the lieutenant-governor as a federal officer in view of Parliament's jurisdiction over "marriage and divorce." He refrained from disallowance only because he feared the consequences of invalidating marriages that had already taken place.[18] Two acts that were disallowed provided for the sentencing of juvenile offenders by provincially appointed judges and the provincial licensing of marine pilots. The provincial government also refused to surrender the new post-office building in Halifax to the dominion until the end of 1871, when the dispute was settled by arbitration.

After 1871 most disputes between the two governments concerned the closely related subjects of finance and railways. The increase in provincial debt allowances in 1873, discussed in chapter 4, benefited Nova Scotia among others, but gave rise to a dispute over its interpretation. Nova Scotia argued that the new increase, which was proportionate to the increases granted Quebec and Ontario, must be in addition to the increase Nova Scotia had already been granted in 1869. Macdonald's government argued that the $8 million debt allowance granted to Nova Scotia in 1867 should be the base figure, so that the increase of 1869 would be considered part of the increase granted in 1873. After Macdonald's resignation in 1873, Premier Annand and two of his ministers travelled to Ottawa to discuss the question, and the Mackenzie government agreed to the province's interpretation. The Mackenzie government also belatedly compensated Nova Scotia for various supplies and equipment turned over to the dominion in 1867, following the precedent of the Macdonald government, which had made similar compensation to New Brunswick in 1871. However, the Mackenzie government refused to extend the special temporary subsidy granted to Nova Scotia in 1869 beyond 1877, the date at which it had been intended to expire.[19] This decision probably explains the fact that Conservative candidates won more than 50 per cent of the Nova Scotian popular vote, both federally and provincially, in 1878.

The new Conservative premier, Simon Holmes, wasted little time before renewing the appeal for "better terms." In January 1879 he addressed a forty-one page "memorial" to John A. Macdonald setting out the province's financial woes in copious detail. Holmes claimed that Nova Scotia's financial problems were unique, and thus rejected the argument that any concessions to his province would have to be matched by concessions to all the others.[20] Although Nova Scotia had entered Confederation with debts lower than its original debt allowance, let alone the increased allowance granted it by the "better terms" of 1869 and the act of 1873, its financial situation had deteriorated during the years of the Mackenzie government. The main reason for this decline was an Act of Parliament adopted in 1874 which permitted the federal cabinet to advance funds to any province for the construction of public works, provided the province in question had a debt allowance larger than the actual debt the dominion had assumed when it entered Confederation.[21] Nova Scotia had made extensive use of this provision, mainly to encourage the building of railways, with the result that its annual subsidy from the dominion declined by 5 per cent of the total amount advanced. In effect, Nova Scotia had borrowed the cost of its railway system from the dominion at 5 per cent, although money would have been available at a lower rate on the market.

Holmes proposed, as did the Legislative Assembly and the Legislative Council in separate addresses to the dominion later that year, an ingenious solution. Under the Treaty of Washington of 1871 the United States had paid Canada and Newfoundland compensation for certain fishing rights to the total of $5.5 million. If the Canadian portion of this payment were distributed among the provinces in proportion to the economic impact they suffered from the loss of fishing rights, Nova Scotia would receive about $2 million, which could be credited to its debt and subsidy account with the dominion. This money would roughly pay for its expenditures on public works since Confederation and permit its total subsidy to rise to the level at which it would have been in the absence of those expenditures. Despite repeated pleas from Holmes, and despite Nova Scotia's Conservative party label, the Macdonald government refused to consider this, or any other, solution. A memorandum from the deputy minister of finance, John Courtney, admitted that Nova Scotia's annual expenditures exceeded its revenues but said that all governments were having difficulty making ends meet because of the worldwide recession. There was no reason to single out Nova Scotia for better terms, and the province should simply make greater efforts to live within its means.[22]

Nova Scotia's difficulties with railways in this period somewhat resembled those of Quebec, but were even more complicated. At the time of Confederation the province had owned three railways: a line from Halifax to Truro, a branch from Windsor Junction (near Halifax) to Windsor, and another branch from Truro to Pictou. Under the terms of Confederation the dominion took over all three and the first became part of the Intercolonial main line, which was completed by 1876. The province had also, in 1865, chartered a private company to build a line from Windsor to Annapolis, with a clause in the charter giving the province the option of taking over the line at a future date. This line began to operate in 1869. In 1871 it reached an agreement with the dominion government to exchange traffic and to operate its own trains over the Intercolonial line into Halifax.

Nova Scotia's long-term objective was to extend railway communication all the way from Yarmouth in the southwest to Cape Breton in the northeast. A company known as the Western Counties Railway received a provincial charter in 1870 to build from Annapolis to

Yarmouth. To build the line from New Glasgow to the Strait of Canso, known as the Eastern Extension, the provincial government in 1876 signed a contract with a group of capitalists headed by Harry Abbott, the brother of Senator John J. Abbott. Subsequently this group organized a company known as the Halifax and Cape Breton Railway and Coal Company, although it never reached either of the places referred to in its name.

In 1873 the Macdonald government had decided to encourage the Western Counties project by offering to give the Windsor branch to the Western Counties Railway as soon as the line to Yarmouth was completed. A resolution to this effect was carried in the House of Commons without a division, and the Liberals indicated their support for the idea by adopting the necessary legislation a year later, when they were in office. No one seems to have stopped to consider that the Windsor and Annapolis line separated the Windsor branch from the Western Counties, or that the Windsor and Annapolis had been granted exclusive running rights over the branch only three years previously and might not wish to share them with another company. In 1877 Alexander Mackenzie, as minister of public works, signed an agreement to transfer the branch to the Western Counties as authorized by the legislation, but reserved the right to repossess the line if the Western Counties did not complete its track from Annapolis to Yarmouth by October 1879. The Windsor and Annapolis then sued the dominion government and the Western Counties Railway for damages, claiming a violation of the agreement reached in 1871. The Western Counties completed a line from Yarmouth to Digby but stopped construction at that point, twenty miles short of Annapolis. As a result the Macdonald government repossessed the Windsor branch in 1879, and again granted exclusive running rights to the Windsor and Annapolis. Even convinced federalists, of whom there were not many in Nova Scotia, must have questioned the usefulness of the dominion government's transportation policy after these events.[23]

The situation was no better at the other end of the province, where events took a somewhat similar course. After Harry Abbott and his friends agreed to build the Eastern Extension, the dominion government again decided to offer one of its branch lines, in this case the branch from Truro to New Glasgow and Pictou, as a reward. The Pictou branch was a much more generous gift than its counterpart at Windsor, for it carried a heavy traffic in coal and was probably the only profitable part of the Intercolonial system. In 1877 an Act of Parliament nonetheless authorized the cabinet to transfer the branch to anyone who would build a railway from New

Glasgow to the Strait of Canso and agree to operate both railways as well as a ferry across the strait.[24] However, the Pictou branch's extensive collection of rolling stock would not be included. As an added incentive the statute provided that the contractors could actually take possession of the Pictou branch as soon as they had spent $400,000 on construction, rather then waiting until their task was completed.

By 1879 Abbott and his friends were ready to claim their prize, although the federal and provincial governments that had set them up in business had both been defeated. The Eastern Extension was obviously not completed, and the Holmes government claimed that the builders had not even done the necessary $400,000 worth of work. Their views carried some weight, because practically all the money actually spent had been provided by the provincial government out of its debt allowance, under the procedure discussed above. The Macdonald government therefore adopted a new Act of Parliament, which stated that the Pictou Branch would be transferred to the Halifax and Cape Breton only at such time as the latter had carried out its agreement with the Nova Scotia government to the satisfaction of the latter.[25] If at any time after the transfer the Halifax and Cape Breton failed to run the railways and the ferry service in a satisfactory manner, ownership of the branch would revert to the dominion. However, if the Nova Scotia government acquired the Eastern Extension, the dominion would transfer the Pictou branch to that government.

Premier Holmes had decided that government ownership was the best available solution to Nova Scotia's railway problems. The legislature adopted an act in 1880 envisaging provincial ownership of all Nova Scotia railways, apart from the Intercolonial.[26] The contract with Abbott and his friends allowed the province to take over the Eastern Extension if that line was not completed by April 1880. Abbott claimed it was completed, but a provincial engineer inspected it and claimed it was not. If the line was completed, Abbott and his friends were entitled not only to keep the Eastern Extension itself but to acquire the more profitable Pictou branch from the dominion. If it was not completed, both lines would go to the government of Nova Scotia.

Charles Tupper, Nova Scotia's Father of Confederation, was now Canada's minister of railways and canals. As an investor in Nova Scotia coal mines he had an interest in the welfare of the Pictou branch and he apparently doubted the ability of any provincial government, even a Conservative one, to run it efficiently. Thus the dominion offered no encouragement to Holmes in his efforts to acquire the

Eastern Extension.[27] Abbott still held possession of the line when the provincial Conservative government went down to defeat in 1882.

Meanwhile Holmes had abandoned his brief flirtation with the idea of public ownership in favour of another solution to Nova Scotia's railway problems. If a private company could be persuaded to take over all the railways in which Nova Scotia had an interest and run them as an amalgamated system, the cash received in return for the province's rights and interests could be used to reduce the province's debt to the dominion, on which it was in effect paying 5 per cent interest. In 1880 Holmes approached George Stephen of the CPR syndicate and also the Baring Brothers, who were the principal dealers in Canadian bonds in London. The CPR was not interested in Nova Scotia at this time, and the Barings replied that owning and operating railways was not their line of business. Finally Holmes received an offer from a Montreal entrepreneur, E.W. Plunkett, who was one of the shareholders in the Western Counties Railway. Plunkett offered to buy all the railways, including the Windsor and Annapolis, which was controlled by absentee British investors, and the Pictou and Windsor branches, which belonged to the dominion government. In 1881 an agreement was signed with Plunkett.[28] The Nova Scotia legislature adopted a statute authorizing the provincial government to expropriate the Windsor and Annapolis with only four weeks notice to the proprietors.[29] The British investors petitioned for disallowance, claiming that Nova Scotia's power to take over their railway had ended at Confederation, but the Macdonald government refused to intervene.[30] Nova Scotia adopted another statute in 1882 to authorize the amalgamation of the railways under Plunkett's control.[31]

The federal government did not object to amalgamation of the western Nova Scotia railways, and it even caused Parliament to adopt an act providing that the Windsor branch would be given to Nova Scotia as soon as the gap was closed between Digby and Annapolis.[32] Tilley, the finance minister, was at first cool to the idea of reducing Nova Scotia's debt, but after meeting with the provincial attorney general, John Thompson, in November 1881 he agreed to accept a deposit of $1.3 million to the province's account, which would have increased its annual subsidy from the federal government by $65,000. (The provincial government had proposed a deposit of $2.35 million.) However, as noted above, Tupper was unwilling to surrender the Pictou branch, which was intended to be the brightest jewel in the crown of Plunkett's Nova Scotia Railway. In any event, these plans became academic after Holmes resigned in

May 1882 and Thompson led the provincial Conservatives to defeat a month later. The new government pursued negotiations with Plunkett for a short time, but finally concluded that he was not to be taken seriously.

In 1883 Nova Scotia finally did purchase the Eastern Extension Railway, but that railway was of little use to anyone without the Pictou branch. Macdonald and his ministers were even less inclined to surrender the branch to a Liberal government of Nova Scotia than they had been to surrender it to their political allies two years before. After a year of negotiations the province gave up and sold the Eastern Extension to the federal government for $1.2 million, in addition to the cost of the rolling stock and interest on the purchase price from October 1883 to the date of settlement.[34] The Eastern Extension was then absorbed by the Intercolonial.

Nova Scotia also failed to get back the Windsor branch. Macdonald's government asserted that the province's claims to the branch were no longer valid, but expressed a willingness to sell it if the province acquired the other western railways and completed the line from Digby to Annapolis. The province did neither.[35] In 1887 Parliament adopted a statute that declared the Western Counties Railway to be a work for the general advantage of Canada, extended the deadline for completing the Digby-Annapolis railway to 1889, and authorized the Western Counties to acquire both the Windsor and Annapolis and, with the consent of the federal cabinet, the Windsor branch.[36] Premier Fielding denounced the measure as "a flagrant violation of provincial rights."[37] The Western Counties failed to take over its old adversary, but did complete the Digby-Annapolis line with the aid of a federal subsidy that Parliament had authorized in 1884. It was allowed to change its name to the Yarmouth and Annapolis Railway in 1893. A year later the Yarmouth and Annapolis was taken over by the Windsor and Annapolis, which was in turn declared a work for the general advantage of Canada and allowed to change its name to the Dominion Atlantic Railway. The Dominion Atlantic was taken over by the CPR in 1911.

Although Nova Scotia's railways played a less prominent role in federal-provincial relations after 1884, the province's financial demands on the federal government continued to escalate from year to year. Since Nova Scotia, unlike any other province, was earning substantial royalties from coal, and since it was frequently able to budget for a surplus, these demands cannot be attributed to genuine need. Rather, they were an expression of anti-federal feeling, lingering resentment over the events of 1867–69, and a widespread belief that federal expenditures were disproportionately devoted, in Premier

Fielding's words, to "supplying the Indians of the prairie and the Chinamen of British Columbia with railroads."[38]

The Nova Scotia speech from the throne in 1884, read shortly before Fielding replaced W.T. Pipes at the head of the Liberal government, set the tone for the next twelve years by asserting that: "the experience of each succeeding year strengthens the conviction that the allowances to Nova Scotia from the Federal Treasury for Local purposes are inadequate, and that they should be increased. Your attention will be directed to this very important subject, with a view to the adoption of such measures as may be calculated to most effectively present the claims of the Province."[39]

One minor irritant referred to in the throne speech was a demand by Baring Brothers for the return of £52,000 sterling which in 1881 they had deposited to Nova Scotia's account with the dominion government as security for the contract with E.W. Plunkett and his Nova Scotia Railway. Baring Brothers demanded repayment from Nova Scotia, with interest, and Nova Scotia agreed to pay, but the deputy minister of finance in Ottawa refused to release the funds. Fielding finally appealed directly to Macdonald, claiming that Nova Scotia's credit rating in London was suffering from the delay. The funds were released at the end of the year.[40]

In January 1885 a Nova Scotia delegation journeyed to Ottawa with a new "memorial" demanding "better terms," which both houses of the provincial legislature had approved the year before. The Macdonald government accepted one of the province's arguments by admitting to a small clerical error in the calculation of Nova Scotia's additional debt allowance in 1869, but rejected the rest. A federal order in council adopted in reply asserted: "to concede the principle that when, through exceptional expenditures, any of the provinces of the Union become financially embarrassed it is the part of the dominion Government to go to their relief would destroy the whole financial basis of Confederation."[41]

Fielding and his attorney general, J.W. Longley, also revived Holmes's idea of depositing some surplus funds with the federal government to reduce the province's debt and increase the interest payment on its debt allowance. As the deputy minister of finance pointed out in a memo approved by the Macdonald government, the dominion was in no hurry to borrow money from Nova Scotia at 5 per cent when it could borrow on the ordinary financial market at 3 or 4 per cent. If the request were accepted it would be a precedent for any province to borrow at 4 per cent and earn 5 per cent by lending money to the dominion.[42]

In 1886 the Nova Scotia legislature adopted another joint address, which was supported by the opposition as well as the government. It pointed out that the agreement between Macdonald and Howe in 1869 had never been accepted by the government of Nova Scotia, and that the province was not bound to regard it as a final settlement. Among other claims, it demanded compensation for the cost of subsidizing the Eastern Extension, ignoring the fact that the federal government had already bought and paid for the line in 1884.[43] Fielding then secured a dissolution and went to the voters on a platform of separation from Canada, with a union among the Maritime provinces and Newfoundland to be considered as a possible alternative. He was returned with an increased majority.

The second "repeal" crisis of 1886 gives some credence to the celebrated remark that Marx attributed to Hegel about historical events occurring once as tragedy and a second time as farce. Canadian federalism was well established and reasonably successful and there was not the slightest prospect that the British government, let alone the Canadian government, would take the agitation seriously. Macdonald reminded the lieutenant-governor that Nova Scotia's representatives in Parliament were its proper spokesmen on constitutional matters and that provincial legislatures had authority to deal only with matters under provincial jurisdiction. In response to the governor general's inquiry whether the "separatists" should be taken seriously, Macdonald wrote: "If the matter becomes serious we have means of coercion by stopping all subsidies to Railways and other improvements but the time for that has not yet arrived."[44]

As Macdonald anticipated, Fielding soon retreated from separatism to more mundane matters, such as a demand that the federal government compensate the province for all its expenditures on public harbours, piers, and breakwaters. This matter had been first raised by the delegation sent to Ottawa in January 1885, which claimed reimbursement to the amount of $153,677.45. In 1887 the Macdonald government agreed to pay $71,512.98 on condition that certain public works be transferred from provincial to federal ownership. This amount was actually paid in May 1888, but Fielding was not satisfied and continued to demand some additional payment from John Thompson, who was now the federal minister of justice and Macdonald's Nova Scotia lieutenant.[45]

Fielding also strengthened his relationship with Oliver Mowat, with whom he had corresponded occasionally since taking office in 1884, and participated enthusiastically in the interprovincial conference at Quebec City. Prior to the conference, Mowat sent his provincial secretary to Halifax to find out whether Fielding was genuinely committed to separatism or whether he might be interested in Mowat's ideas for a more decentralized federation. Fielding replied that he was still a separatist, but continued: "I do not suppose that the question of separation will arise at the conference, except so far as may be necessary to make it clear that our participation in the gathering shall not prejudice our right to take any action that we may deem best in the future on that subject."[46]

In fact the conference marked the end, rather than the beginning, of Nova Scotia's years as the *enfant terrible* of Confederation. The province was entering a period of relative prosperity, largely based on Cape Breton coal and steel, that lasted for some thirty years, and the generation that remembered the days before Confederation was passing from the scene. Fielding himself joined Laurier's cabinet in 1896 and did not retire from federal politics until 1925, which by co-incidence was the year in which the Liberals ended their unbroken reign of forty-three years at Halifax.

NEW BRUNSWICK

New Brunswick entered the dominion more willingly than Nova Scotia, and its relations with the dominion proceeded much more smoothly than those of its neighbour to the east. Admittedly the decisive victory of the pro-Confederation forces in the election of 1866 was in large part a reaction to the Fenian raid a few weeks previously, but if New Brunswickers had any second thoughts, they were not serious enough to have any visible consequences after 1867.

The contrast may perhaps be explained, at least in part, by the fact that New Brunswick had more in common with central Canada than did Nova Scotia. Like central Canada, it had a long undefended border with the United States and it also shared a border with central Canada itself, in contrast to the quasi-insularity of Nova Scotia. In their economic pursuits, New Brunswickers were also more continental and less "Maritime" than Nova Scotians. Fishing was relatively insignificant, and forestry and agriculture were the dominant industries. Like the central provinces, New Brunswick still had empty land in 1867 that was considered suitable for settlement and cultivation, so it was interested in attracting immigrants.

One aspect of New Brunswick society that seems to have had little direct impact on nineteenth-century politics was the presence of the Acadians. At the time of Confederation they made up only about 16 per cent of the population, and politically they seemed almost invisible. It may nonetheless be significant that Gloucester and Kent counties, both with Acadian majorities, voted against Confederation in 1866, and that Westmoreland, about one-third Acadian, was the only other county to do so. The only other county with a significant Acadian population was Victoria, which did vote for Confederation.[47] Perhaps Victoria's geographical situation, bordering on the United States, contributed to this outcome. It seems that, for whatever reason, most Acadians opposed Confederation while most anglophone New Brunswickers supported it. This is particularly surprising since the Intercolonial Railway, which was promised as one of the terms of Confederation, would inevitably run through the Acadian counties.

Party labels in New Brunswick had little meaning. In contrast to Canada or Nova Scotia, responsible government had been granted by the imperial authorities without any real struggle on the part of the people themselves. After this event, which occurred in 1854, most successful politicians called themselves Liberals, but the issue of Confederation a decade later confused and complicated, rather than reinforced, whatever tendency towards polarization existed. From Confederation until the end of the century, provincial governments were really coalitions held together by patronage rather than principle. Such governments adopted a position of neutrality in relation to federal politics, although their individual members were free to support one or other of the federal parties. This practice contributed to the placid and uneventful character of federal-provincial relations, which were not seriously affected by changes of government at either level.

New Brunswick had six premiers between 1867 and 1896, one of whom held the office twice. The first, Andrew Wetmore, had been an opponent of Confederation until the spring of 1866. He became a supporter, whether out of opportunism or conviction, in time to retain his seat in the legislature when the pro-Confederation forces swept the province in that year's election. Although he never formally declared any party affiliation he was a *de facto* political ally of Sir John A. Macdonald, who appointed him to the Supreme Court of New Brunswick in 1870. His successor, George King, was ostensibly a Liberal, but he too accepted a judicial appointment from the Macdonald government, and was eventually appointed to the Supreme Court of Canada by Sir John Thompson. King was premier for all but one year between 1870 and 1878. In 1871 he ceded the leadership of the coalition government to George Hathaway, but upon Hathaway's death the following year King, who had remained attorney general, assumed control once more. In 1878 John J. Fraser became premier and, four years later, he followed King's example by accepting an appointment to the Supreme Court of New Brunswick. Daniel Hannington, who like Fraser called himself a Conservative, lasted only a year as premier but remained in the legislature for another decade as leader of the opposition before receiving his reward on the bench. Finally, Andrew Blair, a Liberal, governed with the aid of Conservative votes until he joined Laurier's government as minister of railways and canals in 1896. Whether the province itself benefited from Confederation is difficult to say, but its premiers certainly had no cause to complain.

In dominion elections, New Brunswick voters were somewhat more inclined than other Canadians to support the Liberals, up to and including the election of 1887. The Liberals won a majority of votes and of seats in 1867, 1872, 1874, and 1878. In 1882 the Conservatives won a narrow victory in New Brunswick and in 1887 the Conservatives again won the contest in seats, although the Liberals actually received more votes. In 1891, however, the Conservatives won decisively in New Brunswick, taking all but three of the seats with 56 per cent of the popular vote. Macdonald's accusation that the Liberals favoured annexation to the United States may have contributed to this untypical outcome in a province where the Loyalist tradition was very strong. In 1896 the Conservatives again outpolled the Liberals in New Brunswick, but by a far less decisive margin.

New Brunswick's practice of non-partisan government and lack of strong anti-Confederation sentiment contributed to a generally mild and uneventful pattern of federal-provincial relations, a pattern quickly established after 1867 that has largely endured to the present day. Insofar as difficulties did arise between the two levels of government, they were mainly concerned with financial questions. In common with all the other provinces except Ontario, New Brunswick had trouble making ends meet under the financial terms of Confederation. New Brunswick's problems in this regard were similar to those of Nova Scotia, with the difference that New Brunswick did not enjoy substantial revenues from royalties on coal. As an original province without a strong anti-Confederation movement, New Brunswick did not have to be lured in with particularly generous terms of union or kept in with "better terms" like those that Nova Scotia received in 1869. It also did not enjoy the rapid population growth that led to dramatic increases in the statutory subsidies paid to Manitoba and British Columbia.

An early exception to the general rule that New Brunswick's disputes with the federal government were over financial questions was a relatively minor controversy over marriage licences that arose in 1869. As in Nova Scotia, the distinction between the federal jurisdiction over "marriage and divorce" and the provincial jurisdiction over "the solemnization of marriage" was the source of some understandable confusion in New Brunswick. In May 1869 the lieutenant-governor of New Brunswick reserved a bill regarding marriage licences because he doubted whether the provincial legislature had the authority to enact it. Macdonald referred the issue to the law officers of the crown in England, who decided in January 1870 that the matter lay within provincial jurisdiction. Meanwhile no new licences had been printed in New Brunswick, with the result that by October none were available. When the lieutenant-governor telegraphed to the federal government for help he was sent a fresh supply of a thousand licences. However, he was advised that in future he could issue the licences on his own authority, and not as the governor general's deputy, and could arrange to have them printed in Fredericton.[48]

Disputes over financial matters also began to appear in 1869, perhaps in part because the better terms granted to Nova Scotia suggested that complaints stood a good chance of being rewarded with concessions. New Brunswick's need to complain was not immediately obvious. Its debt allowance was larger, in relation to the size of its population, than that originally granted to Nova Scotia. It was also given two special concessions: a subsidy of $63,000 per annum for ten years after Confederation and the right to continue imposing an export duty on timber. Nonetheless, there were conflicts. The two governments did not agree in their estimates of the size of the net debt with which New Brunswick entered Confederation. By the federal calculation it exceeded the province's $7 million debt allowance by some $384,560, but the province denied that any excess existed. Part of the problem, as usual, concerned railways, while the rest of it concerned the valuation of "stocks, cash, banker's balances and securities" that the province transferred to the dominion at Confederation in accordance with Section 107 of the BNA Act. In regard to the latter item, the province submitted a claim for $92,340 in January 1869 and again in July 1870, but without success. To make matters worse, the federal government committed the egregious error of deducting from the annual statutory subsidy an amount of $12,000, which should have been deducted only once from a special payment on account of the railway from Saint John to Woodstock. This error was not discovered and corrected until the summer of 1870.[49]

In 1871 both houses of the New Brunswick legislature unanimously adopted resolutions protesting against the better terms granted to Nova Scotia and demanding that New Brunswick be given the same debt allowance as Nova Scotia and a ten-year special subsidy equal to that of Nova Scotia, despite its much smaller population. The resolutions also claimed that New Brunswick received an inadequate share of federal spending and that spending on the Intercolonial Railway should not be included when making such calculations, since the railway had been promised as one of the terms of Confederation. A number of miscellaneous grievances were also mentioned, including the cost of keeping prisoners serving sentences of less than two years under the criminal code in provincial jails, as opposed to federal penitentiaries. Late in the year Premier Hathaway and two of his ministers travelled to Ottawa to present New Brunswick's case to the federal authorities. The federal government accepted some minor claims regarding provincial property surrendered at Confederation and suggested referring two larger claims, involving the valuation of railway shares, to the law officers of the crown. New Brunswick's major demands concerning the debt allowance and the temporary subsidy were rejected.[50]

In 1873 another delegation was sent to Ottawa with somewhat better results. In return for abolishing its export duty on timber so as to comply with the terms of the Treaty of Washington between the United Kingdom and the United States, New Brunswick was given a generous subsidy of $150,000 per annum, considerably more than the revenue that the duty had provided.[51] Less valuable to the province, but still welcome, was its share in the increase of debt allowances granted to all provinces by the Macdonald government in that year. Although designed primarily to benefit Quebec and Ontario, this measure had the effect of increasing New Brunswick's debt allowance by more than $1 million, and its annual revenue by 5 per cent of that figure.

Meanwhile, New Brunswick found itself at the centre of a nationwide controversy that lasted for four years, as a result of its decision in 1871 to abolish tax-supported Roman Catholic separate schools. These schools had been allowed to exist *de facto* for some years before and after Confederation, but their existence was not explicitly recognized by statute as was that of their Ontario counterparts, so there was some doubt whether they were entrenched by Section 93 of the BNA Act. Their abolition was incidental to a general modernization of the school system but it may also be true, as one historian has suggested, that they fell victim to hostile sentiments that were directed against Irish Roman Catholics as a result of the Fenian scare of 1866.[52] (This interpretation does not explain why their abolition was delayed for five years.) It is undeniable, however, that in New Brunswick, unlike other provinces, most Roman Catholics were Irish and most Irish were Roman Catholic.

Petitions requesting that the legislation be disallowed were soon pouring into Ottawa. Macdonald, contrary to myth, was usually cautious about exercising the power of disallowance, and he had no desire to antagonize a friendly and generally cooperative provincial government for the sake of an issue about which he cared little. He may also have feared a backlash from Ontario Protestants if he did recommend disallowance. In any event, he decided in January 1872 that the federal government should not intervene.[53] In April the House of Commons requested that the correspondence between the two governments be made public, and a month later there was an extensive debate on the whole issue. John Hamilton Gray of Saint John, one of New Brunswick's Fathers of Confederation, introduced a resolution to the effect that the law should be left undisturbed since it did not adversely affect any national interest and since as a general principle the provinces should be free to manage their own affairs.

Gray's motion was challenged by three amendments striking out his original words and expressing very different sentiments. Premier Chauveau of Quebec, still sitting in the House of Commons since the double mandate had not yet been abolished, introduced an amendment calling for Catholic educational rights in both Maritime provinces to be entrenched in the British North America Act. Charles Colby, a Quebec anglophone who later entered Macdonald's cabinet, also wished to strike out Gray's words but contented himself with a mild expression of regret at New Brunswick's interference with minority rights and a wish that the province might reconsider. The third amendment, by A.-A. Dorion, rather incongruously expressed regret that the legislation had not been disallowed, an improbable sentiment for an anti-clerical Rouge who was also a Quebec nationalist. Both the Chauveau and the Dorion amendments were lost, although many Catholic supporters of the government broke ranks to vote for them. The Colby amendment was supported by the government and passed, but forty-two members, almost all of them Catholics, voted against it, presumably because they recognized it as an empty gesture. Opposition leader Alexander Mackenzie, seconded by Edward Blake, then moved that the New Brunswick legislation be referred to the law offices of the crown in England, and if possible to the Judicial Committee of the Privy Council, to determine whether Section 93 of the BNA Act was applicable. This motion was adopted without a roll call.[54]

Macdonald's government waited more than five months before acting on this suggestion but finally did so, provoking a formal protest from the government of New Brunswick.[55] In February 1873 the Supreme Court of New Brunswick ruled that the act was valid, a conclusion with which the law officers of the crown agreed soon afterwards. The New Brunswick government introduced new legislation regarding school taxes and assessments, which was promptly approved by the legislature.[56] These measures led to a new round of protests and petitions from the province's Roman Catholics, who would now be forced to pay taxes for the support of schools to which they could not in good conscience send their children.

The issue soon returned to the House of Commons, where Macdonald's majority had been reduced almost to vanishing point by the general election of the preceeding year. John Costigan of Victoria County, New Brunswick, a Roman Catholic who normally supported the Macdonald government, introduced a resolution suggesting that the legislation regarding school taxes and assessments should be disallowed. Although opposed by the government, this resolution was adopted by a decisive vote of 98–63, with the Conservative party dividing along religious lines.[57] Macdonald informed the governor general that he would not recommend disallowance, which would disrupt the whole system of local taxation in New Brunswick. He also said that he would oppose any move to amend the BNA Act without New Brunswick's consent, since "Education is a local matter, and rightly so." However, the government did appropriate $5000 to assist New Brunswick Catholics in appealing to the Judicial Committee of the Privy Council.[58]

Macdonald's government was already in deep trouble over the Pacific Scandal at the time of these events, and a few months later it was out of office. The new government did not really differ from the old in its approach to the New Brunswick school question, but after the winter election of 1874 it had much firmer control over the House of Commons. As Macdonald had predicted, Costigan introduced a resolution in May 1874 asking that the queen be petitioned to bring about the amendment of the BNA Act so as to give New Brunswick's Roman Catholics the same protection as their counterparts in Ontario.[59] The motion was withdrawn a few days later, but was reintroduced the following year. This time Prime Minister Mackenzie succeeded in amending it so as to condemn the idea of an imperial act encroaching on provincial powers and to state "that it would be inexpedient and fraught with danger to the autonomy of each of the Provinces for this House to invite such legislation." A subamendment moved by Edward Blake, who was temporarily out of the government, recalled the Colby amendment of 1872 and suggested an address to the queen asking Her Majesty to urge the government of New Brunswick to reconsider its actions. Both amendment and subamendment were adopted, although a number of Liberals, mainly from the Maritimes and including three ministers, joined the Conservatives in voting against them.[60]

The day after the vote, Blake wrote to Mackenzie suggesting that the government and the Liberal party had now gone as far as they could safely go in supporting the New Brunswick Catholics but that the agitation for further interference could be ended if the colonial secretary would endorse the sentiments of the address just voted by the House of Commons, including the view that provincial rights should not be interfered with. Mackenzie took up the suggestion in a memorandum to the governor general the same day, and Dufferin promptly made the same request to the colonial secretary, Lord Carnarvon.[61]

Carnarvon's reply came in October, and presumably carried added weight because he had been the minister responsible for the British North America Act in 1867. He expressed the hope that the majority in New Brunswick would be generous to the minority, but stated he could not advise the queen to intervene since this would be an undue interference with provincial rights. He also suggested that the Canadian Parliament should refrain from discussing "a controverted question which may possibly engender much heat and irritation, and over which it has no jurisdiction."[62]

Carnarvon's dispatch had the desired effect, and no more was heard of an issue that had convulsed Canadian politics for more than four years. Having endured its moment of notoriety, New Brunswick went quietly about its business, and for the next two decades its dealings with the federal government were mainly concerned with financial matters. Only a brief summary of these is needed, since they raised no issues of great complexity or importance.

The special subsidy given to New Brunswick by Section 119 of the BNA Act for a period of ten years after Confederation expired in 1877. Two members of the provincial cabinet travelled to Ottawa in January of that year to urge that it be continued, but their interview with the minister of finance, Richard Cartwright, was not successful and the grant was allowed to expire, as was the similar temporary allowance granted to Nova Scotia in 1869. This apparently caused a fiscal crisis for New Brunswick, which on four occasions in 1879 and 1880 had to request that its statutory subsidy be paid in advance of the usual date. All of the requests were granted by Leonard Tilley, who was back in the finance department after the Conservative election victory of 1878, but more substantial relief was needed.[63] In the winter of 1880 another delegation was sent to Ottawa in the perennial search for "better terms." Tilley accepted two minor claims concerning immigration expenditures and a hospital for victims of leprosy, and he informed the delegates that a long-standing New Brunswick complaint regarding the upkeep of prisoners serving sentences of less than two years had been referred to the Supreme Court.[64] He also agreed to consider and investigate New Brunswick's most substantial demand, concerning the Intercolonial Railway. The province continued to live from hand to mouth, frequently requesting and receiving advances on its statutory subsidies, until 1884. In that year the increases in debt allowances that had been granted in 1873 were made retroactive to 1867 and the provinces credited with the accumulated interest on the increase (see chapter 4). In addition, a further adjustment in debt allowances was made to compensate for increases in population, based on the census of 1881.

New Brunswick's main grievance, however, concerned its contribution to the building of the Intercolonial Railway, and specifically the section of the main line between Moncton and the Nova Scotia border. This line had been completed before Confederation and had been handed over to the federal government at that date. In the list of demands presented to Tilley in 1880, New Brunswick claimed to have spent about $400,000 on its construction but to have been credited with only $250,000. Tilley and the cabinet agreed that the minister of railways and canals, Charles Tupper, should be asked to prepare and submit all the relevant information on the subject as soon as possible. In 1883 Tupper told the House of Commons that he supported New Brunswick's claim to the additional $150,000, and the money was placed in the estimates the following year.[65] However, Tupper left the cabinet soon afterwards to serve as high commissioner in London, and New Brunswick did not receive payment. In 1887 Premier Blair travelled to Ottawa to request payment and, several months later, Tilley, who had become lieutenant-governor of New Brunswick, repeated the same demand on behalf of his province.[66] In 1890 Blair wrote to John Thompson, who was now the most influential Maritimer in the government, regarding the $150,000. Blair claimed that since the payment should have been made at the time of Confederation, New Brunswick was entitled to the accumulated interest on it as well. Thompson replied that Tupper's statement to the House of Commons in 1883 had been merely an expression of personal opinion, which Thompson did not share. Thompson nonetheless promised to raise the issue with George Foster, a New Brunswicker who was now minister of finance and who might be more sympathetic.[67] The provincial government adopted orders in council reiterating its claim in December 1890 and again in February 1893, but without success.[68] Satisfaction was deferred until after 1896, when Blair became minister of railways and canals in the Laurier government. In 1900 the federal and provincial governments agreed to submit the claim to arbitration, and in 1901 the province was awarded $145,218.75, plus interest from 1884 onwards.[69]

The only other significant dispute between New Brunswick and the federal government in the last years of the Macdonald era concerned an Indian reservation in Victoria County. In 1890 the Blair government claimed that the Indians were using only about 500 acres of more than 15,000 that made up the reservation. It proposed that the Indian title to the allegedly unused land be extinguished so it could be turned over to the province and opened up to white settlement. The government further proposed to pay the Indians the princely sum of fifty cents per acre for the land that would be taken from them, to place the proceeds in a trust fund, and to contribute the interest on the trust fund, or less than $400 per annum, towards the Indians' welfare. The federal government waited more than a year before rejecting this astonishing proposal, at least in part. In March 1892 it finally responded, pointing out that the forty-eight Indian families required 5000 acres, not 500, and that the land surplus to their requirements was worth $1.15 per acre. This somewhat more generous settlement was accepted by the Indians a year later.[70]

PRINCE EDWARD ISLAND

Prince Edward Island, a reluctant convert to Confederation, joined in 1873, becoming the seventh province. The chief and perhaps only attraction of Confederation for the islanders was the financial settlement, which was uncommonly generous. Prince Edward Island's public debt was large in relation to the size of the population, mainly because of excessive railway building, so the dominion's offer to take over both the debt and the railway was tempting. The province was given a debt allowance about twice as large, in relation to its population, as that of the original provinces. In addition, and perhaps even more significantly, the dominion agreed to lend Prince Edward Island $800,000 at 5 per cent interest to buy out the absentee English landlords who owned most of the province. Furthermore, the "loan" was in fact a gift, because the province was given a special annual subsidy, which more than covered the cost of the interest payments, to compensate for the fact that it had no crown land.[71] The absence of crown land resulted from the fact that the entire island had been granted, in 1767, to the ancestors of the landlords who still owned most of it in 1873. The problem of the absentee landlords dominated Prince Edward Island's politics and impeded its development for decades before, and for some years after, it joined the dominion. It also led to the major issue in dominion-provincial relations after 1873. Finally, it created an understandable dislike and fear of absentee land ownership that was still reflected in the statute book of Prince Edward Island more than a century later.

Although small size, then as now, was the most noticeable chaːacteristic of Prince Edward Island, its population when it joined the dominion was larger than that of either Manitoba or British Columbia. It did not actually become the smallest province in population until British Columbia surpassed it in about 1892. However, it was unquestionably the smallest province in area, being about one-tenth the size of Nova Scotia. As in other provinces, agriculture was the main industry, but inshore fishing was also important. Almost half the population was of Scottish origin, making Prince Edward Island the most ethnically homogeneous province apart from Quebec. Population growth virtually ended with Confederation, perhaps because it was now both physically and psychologically easier to move to the mainland.

In its first quarter-century as a Canadian province, Prince Edward Island had six premiers. J.C. Pope, who had governed the colony intermittently since 1865, remained in office for a few months after union was consummated before resigning to run for the dominion Parliament. He was succeeded by Lemuel Owen, whose "Conservative" government brought about one of the most radical changes in property relations in Canadian history by expropriating the estates of the absentee landlords. When this task had been largely accomplished, in 1876, a coalition government was formed under Louis Davies, a Liberal, who had previously led the opposition to Confederation and who campaigned in 1876 against separate schools. The Davies government consisted entirely of Protestants, although more than 40 per cent of the population were Roman Catholics.[72] Normal party competition resumed in 1879 and the Conservatives governed the province for twelve years under William Sullivan (a Catholic who had changed parties because of the separate school issue) and then Neil McLeod. Frederick Peters, a Liberal, took office in 1891 and governed for six years, until he resigned and moved to British Columbia. As in New Brunswick, the premiers benefited personally from federal patronage. Pope served in John A. Macdonald's cabinet for four years. Sullivan became chief justice of the province, and McLeod was appointed a county court judge, significant in Prince

Edward Island where there were only three counties. Davies was a member of Laurier's cabinet and subsequently the first (and to date the only) Prince Edward Islander on the Supreme Court of Canada. He was chief justice of Canada from 1918 to his death in 1924.

The Prince Edward Island penchant for choosing a provincial government with the same party label as the dominion government probably contributed to the island's generally harmonious relations with the dominion. In federal elections islanders showed no tendency to favour the incumbents. Although they voted heavily for the Liberals in 1874 they turned against them in 1878, but then voted against Macdonald's Conservatives the next three elections. In 1896 they elected three Conservatives and two Liberals, although the Liberals received slightly more votes.

The land question, which had dominated Prince Edward Island politics for decades before Confederation, was predictably the first source of federal-provincial friction to emerge after Confederation, even though there was no fundamental disagreement between the two governments. Prince Edward Island had made some progress in buying out its absentee owners since the achievement of responsible government two decades previously, but the proprietors still owned two-thirds of the island in 1873. One-sixth of the island was owned by nine individuals, none of whom resided there.[73]

Having been promised up to $800,000 by the dominion to complete the purchase, Prince Edward Island wasted no time, and the legislature adopted the Land Purchase Act in 1874. This provided in effect for compulsory expropriation of the estates and compensation at a price to be determined by the provincial government. Lieutenant-governor Sir Robert Hodgson, the grand old man of island politics, reserved the bill on the obscure grounds that it allegedly affected the governor general's prerogatives. However, he warned the federal government of "the very general impression prevailing among the people of this Province of the absolute necessity of the adoption of such a measure."[74]

The governor general, Lord Dufferin, was an Irish landlord who felt an instinctive sympathy with the proprietors. Immediately on being informed of Hodgson's action, he told Prime Minister Mackenzie that he would not allow the federal government to assent to the reserved bill, which he described as "monstrous." He also reported to the colonial secretary, Lord Carnavon, who sent Dufferin two secret dispatches on the subject. Dufferin assumed that Mackenzie agreed with his decision and would inform the provincial government promptly that the bill would not receive royal assent. Mackenzie, however, had not made up his mind and did not tell the provincial government anything. Presumably he was waiting, as was customary in such cases, for the deputy minister of justice to report on the bill.[75]

In November, more than six months after Hodgson had reserved the bill, Dufferin received a letter from Carnarvon, informing him that some of the proprietors had petitioned the imperial government complaining of the delay and uncertainty about the Land Purchase Act. After discussing the issue with David Laird, Prince Edward Island's representative in the federal cabinet, Dufferin suggested a way to make the bill less objectionable. Provision might be made for disputes over compensation to be settled by three arbitrators: one appointed by the provincial government, one by the proprietors, and one by the governor general.[76] A month later the report by the deputy minister of justice singled out the absence of a procedure for "impartial arbitration, in which the proprietors would have a representation" as the grounds on which he would not recommend approval of the bill. Mackenzie agreed and the order in council withholding assent was passed a few days later.[77]

In 1875 Prince Edward Island adopted a new version of the Land Purchase Act, including the procedure for arbitration that Dufferin had recommended.[78] Hodgson again exercised his power of reservation, but this time the bill was promptly approved by the federal government. Meanwhile Dufferin, who apparently assumed that the appointment of one of the three arbitrators was his personal prerogative, had persuaded Mackenzie to agree to the appointment of Hugh Childers, a prominent British MP and personal friend of the governor general. Childers served as an arbitrator for a few months but in September 1875 he resigned on the grounds that other business left him no time to remain in Prince Edward Island. He was replaced by L.A. Wilmot, the former lieutenant-governor of New Brunswick, who also represented the dominion in the Ontario boundary arbitration.[79]

Although Dufferin was satisfied with the amended legislation, the proprietors were not. Some of them petitioned the imperial government to disallow the legislation, a power that it had surrendered when Prince Edward Island became a Canadian province. Dufferin and Mackenzie, who both visited England in the summer of 1875, attempted to smooth ruffled feathers with some success. However, towards the end of the year some of the proprietors, dissatisfied with the amount of compensation awarded to them, appealed the arbitrators' awards to the courts. The provincial government deferred payment until the appeals were decided, the proprietors complained to the Colonial Office, and Carnarvon sent a telegram to Dufferin demanding an explanation. This episode revived Dufferin's instinctive antipathy to land reform and, in a letter to Mackenzie, he accused the provincial government of delaying payment so it could collect the interest on the funds advanced by the dominion government. Mackenzie explained that this was not possible and that only the proprietors who appealed to the courts were suffering delays. Dufferin insisted that proprietors whose compensation was delayed must receive 6 per cent interest on the balance owing.[80] The Prince Edward Island government agreed, but also amended the act to bar access to the courts by any proprietor who had not appealed already.[81] Hodgson reserved the amendment, which never went into effect, but it was not needed. By July 1876 the process of land reform was essentially complete, except for one large estate that was dealt with by special legislation in 1895.[82] The Owen government secured a dissolution and was defeated on the issue of Catholic schools in an election that split the province along religious lines.

In surprising contrast to New Brunswick's experience, Prince Edward Island's abolition of tax-supported Catholic schools in 1877 attracted virtually no attention in the rest of the country. Although the bishop of Charlottetown petitioned for disallowance, the Mackenzie government allowed the legislation to remain in effect and no parliamentary debate ensued, even though John Costigan was still a member of the House of Commons.[83] Presumably Catholics saw no point in waging a serious battle over Prince Edward Island after their defeat in New Brunswick, where the legal arguments for invoking Secion 93 of the BNA Act had been stronger.

During William Sullivan's long premiership both the federal and provincial governments were Conservative, but relations between them were not particularly cordial. Sullivan claimed a share of the financial compensation received from the United States for fishing rights surrendered under the Treaty of Washington, on the grounds that Prince Edward Island had been a separate colony at the time of the treaty, but the federal government did not accept this argument.[84] An even more serious grievance concerned the steamship service that the terms of union required the dominion to operate and maintain between Prince Edward Island and the mainland. (Contrary to a belief that still lingers, there was no obligation to maintain railway transportation *on* the Island.) The steamship service provided by two wooden vessels was notoriously unreliable, especially in winter when it frequently failed to operate at all. A series of protests and representations to the federal government had little effect. In 1881 Prince Edward Island's five Conservative MPs and one Conservative senator addressed a petition to Charles Tupper, the minister of railways and canals. In 1882 the lieutenant-governor protested, and in 1883 the provincial cabinet adopted an order in council giving formal expression to its discontent. Sullivan visited Ottawa twice in 1884 to complain to John A. Macdonald. Finally, in 1885 the long-suffering provincial legislature addressed a petition directly to the queen, having failed to receive satisfaction from the governor general the year before. This led to a conference in London between Premier Sullivan, the colonial secretary, and Tupper, who was now the Canadian high commissioner.[85] The idea of a "subway" or railway tunnel under the Northumberland Strait was apparently discussed. In 1886 Macdonald agreed to a preliminary survey and soundings in the strait to determine the feasibility of the project, but the government was in no hurry to begin. Five years later the minister of public works informed the House of Commons of the estimated cost of the project, but no funds were ever appropriated.[86]

Dissatisfaction with the steamship service, and persistent grievance over what was perceived as inadequate federal expenditure on the maintenance of wharves and harbours, probably contributed to the Liberal success in every Prince Edward Island seat in the federal election of 1887. Sullivan's response was to suggest that the provincial government be given control over all the federal patronage on the Island, a power formerly exercised by the defeated members of Parliament.[87] When the new Parliament assembled, Macdonald's government introduced legislation to give Prince Edward Island a special additional subsidy of $20,000 per annum, ostensibly to compensate for the fact that the island had not shared in the expenditures on either the Intercolonial Railway or the CPR.[88] Relations with the provincial government seemed to improve after this concession, and the Conservatives managed to win two of the six seats in 1891.

By and large, Prince Edward Island, like New Brunswick, caused few problems for federal governments in the nineteenth century. Unlike Nova Scotia, both provinces had joined Canada with the acquiescence of most of their people, and they lacked either Quebec's distinct cultural identity, the peculiar problems of the new frontier provinces in the West, or the wealth and power that enabled Mowat's Ontario to challenge the federal authority. Their most dramatic initiatives – the abolition of separate schools in both provinces and the expropriation of the landlords in Prince Edward Island – did not challenge any fundamental interest of the dominion government, however controversial they might be to those directly affected. Such grievances as the two provinces had could generally be resolved by modest disbursements from the federal treasury. Both provinces established a tradition of harmonious relations with the federal government that has lasted to the present day.

6 The Intergovernmental Agenda: The West

For at least some Canadians, the prospect of territorial expansion to the west was a significant motive for Confederation. The motto "a mari usque ad mare," inscribed on the new nation's coat of arms, expressed a dream that captured the imagination of Canadians even before it became a reality.[1] The acquisition of the Hudson's Bay Company's territories in 1869 and the negotiated entry of British Columbia into the dominion two years later transformed Canada from a small country in the northeastern corner of North America into one of continental proportions. These events also confronted Canadians with the task of governing and civilizing a vast and almost empty land that few of them had ever seen. Although not without its share of mistakes, tragedies, and disappointments, the task was on the whole done well, and with remarkable speed.

The full story of that achievement is beyond the scope of this volume but one significant aspect of it, to which historians have given relatively little attention, is the early relations between the dominion government and the first two provincial governments to be formed in the region: Manitoba and British Columbia. Although, or perhaps in part because, the two provinces at that time made up an extremely small part of Canada's population, they accounted for a disproportionate share of the issues on the federal-provincial agenda. Their extreme remoteness, unfamiliarity, small size, economic weakness, and political immaturity presented nineteenth-century politicians with unique problems that were not encountered in dealing with the older provinces. A federal constitution designed for the needs of well-established and reasonably well-populated provinces whose origins dated back to the reign of George III or Louis XIV had to be adapted to include remote frontier settlements, thinly populated with a mixture of rootless fortune-seekers and native Indians or Métis, that had barely begun to experiment with representative government.

Generalizing about Manitoba and British Columbia is in some respects an even more questionable exercise than generalizing about the Maritime provinces. The two western provinces had totally different physical environments and economies, had no association with one another previous to 1871, and were geographically as remote from one another as Denmark is from Spain, or Florida from Massachusetts. Nonetheless, the fact that they became provinces of Canada within a year of one another was not the only characteristic they shared. Both were extremely remote, to the point of being almost inaccessible, from Canada. Both had small populations. Both were at an early stage of political, social, and cultural development when they joined the dominion. Neither had any previous experience with responsible government. Both were financially and politically dependent on a dominion government over which they could hope to exercise little or no influence. It goes without saying that both were almost totally unfamiliar to the Canadian politicians who had to deal with them.

By most objective criteria it would be fair to say that neither province was ready for provincial status in 1870–71. Their American neighbours – North Dakota, Montana, Idaho, and Washington – had to wait another twenty years for statehood, and by that time those four states had populations ranging from 88,548 in the case of Idaho to 357,232 for Washington. Nebraska and Colorado, which became states at about the same time as Manitoba and British Columbia became provinces, each had populations of over 100,000 at the time statehood was achieved. Alberta and Saskatchewan each had about 250,000 when they became provinces in 1905. In contrast, Manitoba and British Columbia attained provincial status when they had no more than a few thousand settlers. They could not be refused this status because Manitoba's Provisional Government had negotiated in 1869 from a position of strength and because British Columbia was already a crown colony with a legislative assembly. Nonetheless, they were not ready for it. Certainly they were in every respect more primitive, and smaller, than the Yukon and Northwest Territories would be a century later.

These remote provinces contributed a disproportionate share of the issues on the agenda of Canadian federalism, and both experienced considerable friction and conflict with the dominion authorities. The phenomenon that would later be known as "Western alienation" was not slow to emerge, particularly in Manitoba where the familiar litany of prairie complaints was clearly articulated as early as the 1880s. On the other side, central Canadian politicians did not always regard the new acquisitions as an unmixed blessing, for they seemed to require far more than their fair share of public expenditure and of governmental attention. Sir John A. Macdonald's description of British Columbia as "the spoilt child of the dominion" would have been echoed by many of his compatriots, most of whom were far less interested in the Pacific province than he was.[2] Some of his private comments about Manitoba, although less quotable, were even less flattering. Even the fact that his son, Hugh John Macdonald, moved to Manitoba in 1882 (he eventually became its premier) did not seem to bridge the psychological gap between east and west.

Unlike the other provinces, Manitoba and British Columbia had no Fathers of Confederation who could represent their interests in the dominion cabinet after they became provinces. In fact, Manitoba had no representative in the cabinet until 1892, and British Columbia none until 1895. Although Macdonald represented Victoria in the House of Commons after losing his own seat in 1878, and although Cartier briefly represented a Manitoba riding for the same reason, this sort of "representation" by persons who had never even visited the provinces concerned was hardly an adequate substitute for the presence of a local political leader around the cabinet table. Furthermore, the two western provinces had too few seats in the House of Commons to exercise much bargaining power over any government, even though they were represented somewhat more generously than they should have been on a strict basis of population. It is not surprising that their governments were sometimes shrill in defending their interests vis-à-vis the dominion.

MANITOBA

Manitoba was a deeply divided society that entered the dominion under peculiar circumstances. Situated in the centre of North America, the area near the mouth of the Assiniboine River had been a cockpit of ethnic and economic rivalries since the days of Lord Selkirk some sixty years before. Canada acquired it from the Hudson's Bay Company in 1869 as part of a much larger package, with no regard for the views of the local population and with scarcely a realization that they existed. It was soon forced to negotiate with their

Provisional Government, led by Louis Riel, and to give them provincial status. Not until an expedition of British troops arrived the following year was Canadian authority really established.

A local census conducted in 1870 counted a population of just under twelve thousand, of whom 48 per cent were francophone Métis, 34 per cent anglophone "half-breeds," 5 per cent Indians, and the rest Caucasians.[3] The last group, unspecified as to language, would practically all have been born in Canada, the United Kingdom, or the United States. Slightly more than half the population were said to be Roman Catholic. This motley assortment of persons were mainly concentrated within a fifty-mile radius of Fort Garry, although Fort Garry itself had only a few hundred residents.

The new province was extremely remote and inaccessible – a major reason for the bargaining power that the Provisional Government had used to win provincial status. Manitoba's only effective communications with the outside world were with, or through, Minnesota, and even those communications were by river boat in the summer and by horse-drawn sleigh during the lengthy winter. The absorption of the Montreal-based North West Company by the Hudson's Bay Company a half-century before had disrupted the east-west links of commerce and transportation to which Harold Innis has attributed the emergence of a Canadian nation. However, the French-speaking and Roman Catholic Métis retained some tenuous links with Quebec. Their bishop, Alexandre Taché, was a French Canadian who had gone to the Northwest as a missionary in 1844. Even Louis Riel had lived and studied in Quebec for a while before achieving his notoriety. Riel's bitterest enemies, the small number of English-speaking and mainly Liberal settlers recently arrived from Ontario, were another, and far more disruptive, source of Canadian influence.

With the fur trade and the buffalo hunt already moribund by 1870, Manitoba's economy as a Canadian province was based on agriculture, which became even more dominant there than elsewhere. Over the next two decades railways connected Manitoba with the outside world, and it enjoyed spectacular growth. By 1891 it had a population of 152,000, of whom one-third had been born in the province, another third were central Canadians, and the rest were from various parts of the world. Winnipeg, as it was now known, had become the ninth largest city of the dominion, with a population of 25,642. In the process, francophones, Métis, and Roman Catholics (who to a large extent were the same people) had been reduced to the status of small and beleaguered minorities. Rarely has any political entity changed so much in so short a period of time.

The first provincial government was established in September 1870, within a month of the Provisional Government's collapse and before the election of a legislature. In the circumstances its real head was inevitably the lieutenant-governor, Adams Archibald, who had himself arrived in the province only a few days before and who had previously represented a Nova Scotia riding in the House of Commons. Archibald initially selected two advisers: Alfred Boyd, an Englishman who had lived in Manitoba for some time, and Marc-Amable Girard, a recent arrival from Quebec where he had been a follower of George-Étienne Cartier. Three months later Archibald appointed Henry Clarke, an Irish Catholic lawyer from Montreal, as attorney general of the province. Although the Parliamentary Guide to this day lists Boyd, Girard, and Clarke as the first three "premiers" of the province, there was in fact no premier until at least July 1874, when Girard formed a more or less responsible administration. By this time both Boyd and Clarke had left the government. After Manitoba's second provincial election, which took place in January 1875, the government was headed by Robert A. Davis, a Quebec anglophone who had served as provincial treasurer under Girard and who retained that office as premier. Premier Davis was succeeded in 1878 by John Norquay, a native-born Manitoban and a Métis in the modern sense of the term (although not in the nineteenth-century sense, since his mother tongue was English). Norquay lasted until 1887, when a railway scandal forced his resignation.

Political parties emerged only gradually at the provincial level. Norquay tried to discourage their appearance and to steer a middle course between francophone Bleus from Quebec and anglophone Grits from Ontario, for neither of which he had much sympathy. The latter group increased rapidly in numbers with the construction of the CPR, and a full-fledged Liberal party emerged by 1886 to oppose Norquay in what proved to be his last election. Norquay was then forced reluctantly to identify himself as a Conservative, although his relations with the Macdonald government in Ottawa were cool at best. Following Norquay's resignation, his minister of agriculture, D.H. Harrison, attempted to govern the province for a few weeks. The Liberals then took office under Thomas Greenway, a former Liberal MP from Ontario, and governed until the turn of the century.

In federal politics, a clear distinction between Liberals and Conservatives appeared almost immediately after Manitoba became a province. Manitobans divided their vote evenly between the two parties, and in every Parliament from 1872 onwards they were represented on both sides of the House of Commons. The Liberals won more seats than the Conservatives in 1874 (when they swept every province except British Columbia) and in 1882. In 1878 Conservatives were acclaimed in three of the four ridings, but a Liberal won the fourth.

Writing to Lieutenant-Governor Archibald on the first day of November 1870, a few weeks after Archibald took office, John A. Macdonald congratulated him, perhaps prematurely, for "bringing order out of chaos." He also indicated his belief, which he would express many times over the next twenty years, that the new province required a firm hand. Among other advice, he informed Archibald that it was important to encourage immigration into the province.[4] This would help to counter the accusations of Ontario Liberals who charged that Manitoba had been created by Cartier as a Catholic and francophone counterweight to Ontario's predominance. In fact this was far from being Macdonald's intention. In another letter to Archibald more than a year later he asserted that the loyal response of British (sic) Manitobans to a recent Fenian raid "gave you an opportunity of putting the French in their right place." He also predicted that the construction of a transcontinental railway "will be the best thing to make you a civilized country, and will send you a large and healthy population among you."[5] Macdonald may have reconsidered these sentiments later on, for the anglophone settlers whom the CPR brought to Manitoba caused him and his party considerable difficulty in the last years of his life. Certainly Macdonald's low opinion of Manitobans did not mellow with advancing years, despite the changing ethnic composition of the province.

Tension between old and new Manitobans and Macdonald's preference, at least initially, for the latter contributed to one of the earliest differences of opinion between Manitoba and the federal government. In July 1871 the prime minister urged Archibald to secure passage of a statute that would allow lawyers from any part of British North America to practise in Manitoba. As Macdonald explained, his reason for this request was to ensure that suitable persons were available for judicial appointments, since the BNA Act provided that judges must be members of the bar in the province where they exercised jurisdiction. Archibald, who agreed with this rationale, instructed Clarke to draw up a bill and to introduce it in the legislature. Either Clarke misunderstood the instructions or had contrary ideas of his own, for he drew up and introduced a bill that gave the attorney general (himself) complete discretion to decide who could be admitted to the Manitoba bar. Archibald "told him [his] mind fairly freely," as he put it to Macdonald, and the bill was withdrawn.[6] In the next session, however, the legislature passed an act to constitute and incorporate the Law Society of Manitoba, which would give existing members of the legal profession in Manitoba, like their counterparts in other provinces, the power to admit or exclude new members. Describing this as "premature" in view of the small number of lawyers in Manitoba, and fearing that it would restrict the number of potential appointees to the bench, Archibald exercised his power of reservation. Since the federal government refused to approve the bill, it did not take effect.[7] In the following year a similar bill was again introduced and again reserved by the new lieutenant-governor, Alexander Morris. A few months later Morris had second thoughts and suggested that the bill should be approved.[8] It was not approved, even though the Liberals, ostensibly more sympathetic to provincial autonomy, had by this time taken control of the federal government.

In 1877 Manitoba finally adopted an innocuous statute giving any Canadian lawyer in good standing almost automatic admission to its bar. In 1881, however, the law was amended again to require lawyers from other provinces to undergo re-examination of their qualifications before they could be admitted to practise in Manitoba. Macdonald, perhaps because his own son was already planning to begin a law practice in Manitoba, wrote to Premier Norquay to protest against the "illiberal" measure and to suggest its repeal. Commenting sarcastically that he supposed the legislation must be "in consequence of the higher standards of education with you than in Toronto or Quebec," the prime minister threatened retaliatory legislation that might make it difficult for Manitoba lawyers to practise before federal courts or to receive judicial appointments. Norquay replied that his govenment had already decided to amend the legislation, but could not resist a parting shot of his own: "I may add that although we don't profess to have a higher standard of education than in Toronto or Quebec none of those educated with us spell Christ with a K as was the case with some of those applying for admissions to our Bar."[9]

Apart from this early dispute over what would later be called mobility rights, most of Manitoba's differences with the dominion government during its first decade as a province concerned its financial circumstances. While it was certainly not the only province to complain about the inadequacy of of its revenues, it had far more reason to do so than any of the others. The financial terms on which it achieved provincial status lacked both generosity and realism, and it seems incredible that experienced politicians like Macdonald and Cartier could have thought it possible to operate a provincial government on the revenues they provided. Because of its small population, Manitoba was given a debt allowance of only $472,090. The annual grant for the upkeep of its government and legislature was only $30,000, although the comparable grants for the original provinces ranged from $50,000 to $80,000. In contrast to Prince Edward Island three years later, it was given no compensation for the fact that it had no public lands, all of the land purchased from the Hudson's Bay Company being retained by the dominion. Admittedly the population was overestimated by about five thousand for the sake of calculating the statutory subsidy, but even so Manitoba's annual revenue was only $63,253 plus whatever it could raise from licences, permits, and direct taxation.[10]

Although controversies regarding the Provisional Government and the Fenian raid consumed the energies of Manitoba politicians for about two years after provincial status was attained, they began in 1872 a lengthy and eventually successful campaign to extract more money from the federal government. In that year the legislature adopted a joint address requesting that public buildings for the provincial government's use be erected at the dominion's expense, something that had allegedly been promised in 1870. The joint address was sent to Ottawa and politely acknowledged, but no action followed.[11] In the following year a delegation of Manitoba ministers travelled to Ottawa to describe the province's financial difficulties and to propose that its boundaries be extended to the sixtieth parallel on the north, to Lake Superior on the east, and also some distance to the west. Since the dominion would presumably retain the public land, the enlargement was desired mainly as a pretext for re-estimating the population and increasing the statutory subsidy. The Manitoba delegates proposed, absurdly, that the statutory subsidy be based on an assumed population of 200,000, although there were probably not that many people between Sault Ste Marie and the Pacific. They also suggested that the amount granted annually for the support of the government and legislature be increased from $30,000 to $90,000. The Macdonald government accepted the principle of enlargement, although not the other demands.[12] At its suggestion, the provincial legislature adopted a statute authorizing the acceptance by Manitoba of whatever additional territory Parliament saw fit to add to the province.[13]

In 1874, with a new government in Ottawa, another delegation of Manitobans descended on the capital to repeat essentially the same demands. Alexander Mackenzie's characteristic response was to suggest that the province should curtail its expenditures, particularly the expense of operating the legislature. Specifically he thought that Manitoba should abolish its appointed Legislative Council, modelled on that of Quebec, and adopt the unicameral system of Ontario. If this were done and some other economies imposed, Manitoba might be given some financial concessions, although its actual demands were declared to be "at present inadmissable." The provincial government agreed, but the Legislative Council refused to vote for its own demise. David Laird, the minister of the interior, travelled to Manitoba and returned somewhat more sympathetic to its demands than his colleagues, but the only concession he could persuade them to offer was an advance of $20,000, to be subtracted from the debt allowance on which the province received 5 per cent interest from the dominion.[14]

In October 1875 yet another Manitoba delegation travelled to Ottawa and met with greater success than its predecessors. The federal government agreed that Manitoba required total revenues of $90,000 per annum from the dominion. In return for the abolition of the Legislative Council, Mackenzie's government promised to increase the total annual grant (including the statutory subsidy, the grant for the legislature, and interest on the debt allowance) to this level, which would require an increase of $26,746. The new arrangements would last until the end of 1881, at which time the census would be expected to show a greatly increased population in Manitoba, permitting a recalculation of the statutory subsidy. Parliament adopted legislation to this effect in 1876, and the Legislative Council finally agreed to its own abolition, although Lieutenant-Governor Morris privately expressed regret at its disappearance.[15] In the following year Parliament extended Manitoba's boundaries to the east and west, although the northern boundary was unchanged and a large *cordon sanitaire* was retained between Manitoba and Ontario.[16] The Mackenzie government's final concession was an annual advance of $10,000 for three years, which was in effect a loan on the security of certain public lands reserved for the support of public education in Manitoba.[17]

John A. Macdonald and John Norquay took office almost simultaneously in October 1878, and before the end of the month Norquay was writing to Macdonald that Manitoba's financial situation was "desperate." He requested a further extension of boundaries, which he anticipated would lead to an increased subsidy, and he renewed the plea for the construction of public buildings at the dominion's expense with the following memorable argument: "We also are in great need of Parliament Buildings as we are reduced to the extremity of holding our Sessions of the Legislature in the Court Room, the lower storey of which is our Provincial jail. Just imagine the deliberations of the Assembly sometimes interrupted with the howlings of the lunatics confined in the jail and you can form some idea of the unpleasantness of our cramped financial position."[18] Unfortunately, the reactions of the "lunatics" to the proceedings of the legislature upstairs have not been preserved for posterity.

Macdonald's government agreed to finance the construction of public buildings and also increased the total subsidy from $90,000 to $105,653, retaining the proviso that a further increase would follow the 1881 census. The temporary increase was based on the arbitrary assumption that the population had reached 70,000, even though Norquay admitted it was only 53,540. Soon afterwards Manitoba was also allowed to borrow $100,000 from the dominion to build some flood control works around Winnipeg.[19]

Macdonald also supported Manitoba's boundary claims, despite his low opinion of the province, so as to involve Manitoba in his feud with Oliver Mowat's Ontario (see chapter 3). For the second time in seven years, Manitoba was asked to adopt a statute authorizing the acceptance of new territory, while an Act of Parliament defined the territory to be added. With deliberate ambiguity, Manitoba's eastern boundary was declared to be the western boundary of Ontario.[20]

Meanwhile Norquay and his provincial secretary, the durable M.A. Girard, had visited Ottawa in February 1881 to request "better terms" as well as an explicit statement that their boundary was east of Thunder Bay. Neither request was granted, since the Macdonald government was unwilling to consider any lasting financial settlement until after the census.[21] The census was a disappointment to Manitobans, revealing a population of only 65,954, although this may have excluded a number of Indians. Nonetheless, an Act of Parliament the following year credited Manitoba with a population of 150,000 for the purpose of computing the statutory subsidy, which was thus fixed at $120,000 per annum for the next decade. The grant for the support of the legislature was increased to $50,000 per annum (the same level as New Brunswick's) and the province was credited with $900,000 as compensation for the dominion's retention of the public lands, entitling it to interest payments of $45,000 per annum.[22]

Although this was a fairly generous settlement, Manitoba was back for more a year later, leading Macdonald to describe Norquay's demands as "insatiable."[23] The province accused the federal government of selling portions of the so-called school lands, which were supposed to support the cost of education, and pocketing the proceeds. It also demanded further advances on the security of those lands, in addition to the third and last advance authorized by Parliament in 1878, which had never actually been paid. The federal cabinet agreed to these demands in December 1883 and the necessary legislation was introduced in Parliament that winter, but in March 1884 Norquay was again describing Manitoba's financial situation as "desperate," the same word he had used, with somewhat greater justification, nearly six years before. Meanwhile the lieutenant-governor, J.C. Aikins, had urged that all public lands in Manitoba be transferred to provincial ownership, a suggestion that would not be acted upon for another forty-six years.[24]

Although Norquay had an obvious interest in making Manitoba's circumstances appear as bad as possible, poor economic circumstances and the rise of a radical populist movement, the Manitoba Farmers' Union, lent some credence to his warnings. In April 1884 the federal cabinet considered the situation in Manitoba and decided against either a transfer of the public lands or a further enlargement of the province's boundaries. It did, however, promise to pay Manitoba the interest on any further proceeds from the sale of school lands and to recalculate the population and the statutory subsidy every two-and-a-half years until the population reached 400,000, the same ceiling provided for the Maritime provinces in 1867. Norquay rejected these terms a month later, ostensibly because the federal government insisted on a clause describing them as a final settlement of the province's claims.[25] Although the minister of the interior, David Macpherson, blamed the impasse on "that Indian Norquay" and called the Manitoba premier "a treacherous fellow," Macdonald responded more temperately, and the two sides returned to the bargaining table almost immediately. The province was given a loan or "advance" of $150,000 for various local works, including a "lunatic asylum," and was offered a larger debt allowance, an increase in its annual grant in lieu of public lands from $45,000 to $100,000, and the transfer of those public lands deemed to be "swamp lands" and thus unfit for settlement. The offer to recalculate the statutory subsidy every two-and-a-half years was also renewed. These terms were accepted, even though the federal government still insisted on the finality clause that had been the ostensible point of contention earlier in the year, and were embodied in an Act of Parliament "for the final settlement of the claims made by the Province of Manitoba on the dominion."[26]

With this settlement Manitoba was finally placed in a financial situation roughly the same as that of the other provinces, and the volume and frequency of its financial complaints diminished sharply, although they did not entirely disappear. In 1886, for example, Norquay complained that the federal Department of Finance insisted on treating the funds that the dominion had spent on the provincial government buildings as a loan rather than a gift. The minister of finance, Charles Tupper, overruled his deputy minister and recommended accepting the province's interpretation, but cabinet did not agree, the necessary legislation was not adopted, and Tupper soon resigned his portfolio to return to England as high commissioner. Manitoba was still unsuccessfully pursuing the matter in 1896, as the era of Macdonaldian Conservatism entered its last days.[27]

After 1884, however, finances ceased to be the dominant issue in Manitoba's relations with the dominion. They were replaced in that role by the equally contentious issue of railways, until railways in their turn were overshadowed by the controversy over Roman Catholic schools which lasted from 1890 until 1896.

Manitoba's concerns over railways differed from those of the other provinces and in fact foreshadowed the prairie grievances over freight rates and transportation which would last far into the twentieth century. The main point of contention was the so-called monopoly clause in the contract the Macdonald government and the CPR syndicate signed in October 1880. It read as follows:

For twenty years from the date hereof, no line of railway shall be authorized by the dominion Parliament to be constructed South of the Canadian Pacific Railway, from any point at or near the Canadian Pacific Railway, except such line as shall run South West or to the Westward of South West; nor to within fifteen miles of Latitude 49. And in the establishment of any new Province in the North-West Territories, provision shall be made for continuing such prohibition after such establishment until the expiration of the same period.[28]

The purpose of this clause was to protect the young transcontinental railway from American competition and to ensure that railway traffic to and from the Canadian west would travel north of Lake Superior, from and to central Canada, rather than south of Lake Superior, from and to the American middle west. Even before the contract was signed, Macdonald's government regarded such a provision as essential. Although the provinces, generally speaking, had the power to charter railways that operated exclusively within their boundaries, Macdonald's government proposed an exception to the rule as early as April 1879: "The Government think it very desirable that all Railway legislation shall originate here and that no charter for a line exclusively within the Province of Manitoba should be granted by its legislature without the dominion Government first assenting thereto."[29]

Manitoba had no intention of complying with such a condition and Norquay made clear his opposition to the syndicate and their "monopoly" by moving condemnatory resolutions in the legislature within weeks of the signing of the contract. The federal government, however, had a powerful weapon in the power of disallowance, which was used twelve times over the next seven years to protect the monopoly clause from Manitoba legislation. These episodes made up almost a third of the forty-one instances in which the power of disallowance was used against any province during the thirteen years of the second Macdonald government. Four of the twelve railway disallowances took place in 1882, two in 1886, and the rest in 1887.[30] Ten of the disallowed acts were charters for specific railways that violated the terms of the monopoly clause, while the other two, one adopted in 1882 and one in 1887, were more general measures to encourage railway construction in Manitoba. Ironically the first charter to be disallowed was that of the Winnipeg Southeastern Railway, whose promoters included the same Peter McLaren on whose behalf Ontario's three Rivers and Streams acts were disallowed at about the same time. After this and two other charters were disallowed in 1882, Macdonald reassured the governor general that the "little tempest in Manitoba" would "blow over soon although it may bring down Norquay." Neither part of this prediction was accurate, and Macdonald's assertion in the same letter that the arrival of new settlers in Manitoba would end the "agitation" was decidedly premature.[31]

By 1884 public opinion in Manitoba was in an even more unsettled state and was beginning to attract the attention of such distant observers as George Stephen and the colonial secretary. Although a poor harvest and the province's financial difficulties were contributing factors, the CPR was already assuming a prominent place in the demonology of prairie populism. Meanwhile the Norquay government had temporarily changed its tactics and had thought of a new way to challenge the CPR monopoly without violating the letter of the contract. Rather than chartering railways to build south of the transcontinental line, it decided that a railway could be built north of the CPR all the way to Hudson Bay, thus reopening Manitoba's historic line of communication with the British Isles. It was mainly for this purpose that Manitoba requested the extension of its boundaries to the bay in 1884. Neither the federal government nor the CPR took the Hudson Bay Railway (HBR) project seriously, but for that reason they encouraged it, up to a point, as a harmless diversion from the more serious threat of competing lines to the south. As early as 1880 two groups of promoters had received federal charters to build railways from Winnipeg to Hudson Bay, at their own expense. Predictably neither had made any progress and in 1883 an Act of Parliament authorized the amalgamation of the two fictitious railways.[32] Macdonald promised Norquay in 1884 that he would encourage this development by offering the successor company a land grant if it made provisions satisfactory to the Manitoba government for early construction of the line, reasonable freight rates, and a pledge not to amalgamate with the CPR.[33] Macdonald may have made this promise in the hopes of appeasing Manitoba's demand for an extension to its boundary or because he feared the growing popularity of the Farmers' Union, a phenomenon that revived his memories of 1837. The companies amalgamated, but still made no progress and no land grant was given. In 1886 Norquay offered to guarantee $4.5 million worth of HBR bonds on the security of lands that belonged to the dominion, an indiscretion that led to the fall of his government a year later.[34] No more was heard of the proposed railway until the federal government finally built it after the First World War.

Meanwhile Norquay had returned to his southern strategy, chartering two more railways in defiance of the monopoly clause in 1884 and one in 1885, all of which were disallowed. Lieutenant-Governor Aikins warned Macdonald in April 1887 that the repeated disallowance of railway charters was making the federal government unpopular in Manitoba, and in another letter two months later he apparently warned of growing unrest in the province. Macdonald replied to the second letter by reminding Aikins that Parliament had endorsed the policy of disallowing charters that violated the monopoly clause, and that he did not fear the consequences of doing so. He added that "your bankrupt population at Winnipeg must be taught a lesson, even if some of them are brought down to trial in Toronto for sedition."[35] Four more charters and a general act to facilitate railway building were adopted by the Manitoba legislature that year, and all were disallowed with unusual promptness. Prominent Conservatives in Manitoba warned Macdonald that his railway policy was destroying the party in their province. The governor general, Lord Lansdowne, privately urged Macdonald to make some concession to Manitoban sentiments, perhaps by announcing that the monopoly clause would not be enforced for the full twenty years.[36] In August 1887 tempers were further inflamed when a Toronto newspaper published a fictitious report that Macdonald had threatened to use imperial troops against Manitoba. The colonial secretary wired the governor general to request that Macdonald be asked to deny the rumour.[37]

By this time Norquay's government was approaching its final crisis, and by January 1888 the Manitoba Liberals took office, for the first time, under Thomas Greenway. Macdonald, who had never regarded Norquay as a political ally, was not particularly displeased by these developments. However, the new government was just as eager to break the CPR monopoly as its predecessor. One of its first acts was to address a "memorial" to the imperial government complaining that the disallowance of railway charters was contrary to the terms of the BNA Act. The colonial secretary proposed to refer this question to the Judicial Committee of the Privy Council, a course of action strongly resisted by the Canadian government. A series of dispatches from Lord Lansdowne, and an order in council adopted by Macdonald's government on 10 March, persuaded the colonial secretary to abandon the idea of a judicial reference.[38] However, whether by coincidence or otherwise, negotiations between the federal government and the CPR regarding the termination of the monopoly clause began almost immediately after the colonial secretary suggested the possibility of referring the question to the Judicial Committee. In March Greenway visited Ottawa and was informed by Macdonald that there was a good prospect of legislation to end the monopoly clause. After an expensive financial settlement with the CPR, the company agreed to revise the contract, and the legislation was adopted by Parliament in May.[39]

Manitoba's troubles with the CPR were not quite over, however. The Red River Valley Railway, one of those whose charter had been disallowed in 1887, was chartered again by the legislature in 1888. Although the CPR was willing to lease one of its two parallel lines between Winnipeg and the border to the Manitoba government, the province claimed it would be cheaper to build its own line than to pay the price demanded by the CPR While still under construction, the Red River Valley line was leased to a major American railroad, the Northern Pacific, with which it connected at the border. Two weeks after this transaction was completed, the CPR tried to obstruct the constuction of the Red River Valley line, and a pitched battle between employees of the two systems took place at a point where their lines crossed. Macdonald refused to be drawn into this quarrel and informed the Manitoba government that the CPR was acting on its own authority.[40] When the CPR alleged that the Red River Valley charter was *ultra vires*, the federal government referred the question to the Supreme Court and was neither surprised nor dismayed when the court upheld the charter's validity.

Less than a year after these events a far more serious controversy, on a completely different issue, loomed on the horizon. In August

1889 Lieutenant-Governor John Schultz warned Macdonald that the Greenway government intended to abolish Roman Catholic separate schools and also the official status of the French language, both of which were entrenched in the Manitoba Act. Schultz doubted there was much popular support for either measure and thought the government should secure a fresh mandate from the voters before introducing them, but Greenway ignored the suggestion. In January, not long before the opening of the legislature, Macdonald told Schultz that the province had "no power to interfere with separate schools" and instructed the lieutenant-governor to send him any bills relating to the subject as promptly as possible. Macdonald also advised that if such bills were introduced, Manitoba Catholics should petition the dominion government and Parliament for redress.[41]

The acts establishing a department of education and abolishing denominational schools were adopted by the legislature in March, as was the act making English the only official language of Manitoba.[42] Petitions against the educational statutes soon began to arrive in Ottawa. The abolition of bilingualism was somewhat overshadowed in the controversy over schools, although the petition signed by all the Roman Catholic bishops of Canada, and forwarded by Archbishop Taché from St-Boniface, protested against the educational legislation.[43]

In April 1891, following Macdonald's last election campaign and two months before his death, the federal cabinet decided to leave all the Manitoba acts in operation. Justice minister John Thompson predicted that the language legislation would be almost certainly challenged and probably overturned in the courts, and argued that a judicial decision would resolve the question in a more permanent and satisfactory way than a disallowance. In a separate report on the educational acts, Thompson noted they were already before the courts in a case brought by a Catholic ratepayer, Dr Barrett, against the city of Winnipeg. Even if they were upheld by the courts, Manitoba Catholics would still be able to appeal to the federal government for redress under Section 22 of the Manitoba Act, so there was no need to take action at the present time.[44] Macdonald alowed Chapleau, the most influential of the three francophone ministers, to convey private assurances to the Catholic clergy that remedial action would be taken by the federal government if Dr Barrett lost his case.[45]

By July 1892, when the Judicial Committee ruled against Dr Barrett, Macdonald was dead, Chapleau's star was in eclipse, and Senator J.J. Abbott presided over an increasingly incoherent government. The cabinet formed a committee headed by Thompson, who became prime minister just as the committee was completing its report in December. The report in effect urged further delay by suggesting a reference to the Supreme Court on the question whether the provisions of Section 93 of the BNA Act regarding appeals to the federal cabinet and remedial legislation by Parliament applied to Manitoba. Chapleau, dissatisfied by the report, refused either to sign it or to serve in Thompson's government, and departed for Quebec as lieutenant-governor.[46]

As the Supreme Court prepared to consider the questions submitted to it, Lieutenant-Governor Schultz assured Thompson that some compromise between the Manitoba government and the Catholics might still be possible. With Thompson's encouragement, Schultz pursued this faint possibility through the year 1893, in December of which he expressed the hope that the Supreme Court would delay its decision until after the next session of the legislature, during which a solution might be worked out. Thompson replied with thanks for Schultz's efforts and expressed the hope that his optimism would be justified.[47] The Greenway government introduced some ambiguous amendments which, according to Schultz, were intended to make it possible for Catholic schools to receive public funding if they "substantially" followed the provincial curriculum. Unfortunately, a backbench revolt, after an opposition member had called attention to the ambiguity, forced the government to amend its amendments so that their eventual effect was to make the School Act even less satisfactory to the Catholics than the version adopted in 1890. These amendments were adopted by the legislature with all the Protestants voting in favour and all the Catholics against. Archbishop Taché asked Schultz to reserve the bill but Schultz refused, and on the same day the Supreme Court ruled that no right to remedial legislation existed, a decision the federal government appealed to the Judicial Committee of the Privy Council. Schultz still insisted that Greenway was inclined to compromise and that a *modus vivendi* acceptable to most Catholics could be worked out.[48] Thompson died suddenly in December 1894, as the Judicial Committee was hearing the appeal. Mackenzie Bowell, an elderly Orangeman from eastern Ontario and the fourth prime minister in four years, was left to consider the implications of the Judicial Committee's decision, which unexpectedly overruled the Supreme Court and found that remedial action on behalf of the Manitoba Catholics would be valid.[49]

Bowell urged Schultz to warn Greenway that remedial legislation would entrench the rights of the Catholics for all time to come and that this would be inconvenient for Manitoba "when it becomes more Protestant than at present." A timely concession giving him an excuse not to impose remedial legislation would be in the long-term interest of Manitoba Protestants.[50] A few days after this message was sent a mass meeting in Toronto, chaired by the city's mayor and addressed by D'Alton McCarthy, adopted a resolution that denounced remedial legislation as "humiliating" and contrary to the principles of federalism.[51] On 18 March 1895, a week after the meeting, Bowell's cabinet adopted a remedial order directing Manitoba to restore the rights and privileges of the Catholic minority. Some ministers favoured a dissolution of Parliament to give the government a fresh mandate before the agitation grew worse, but Bowell refused to request a dissolution, although more than four years had passed since the last election. C.H. Tupper, the son of Sir Charles and the successor of Thompson as minister of justice, sent Bowell his resignation, claiming that the prime minister was not serious about remedial legislation. Nonetheless, he remained in the cabinet until January of the following year.[52]

Manitoba ignored the remedial order, realizing that the federal government's time was running out and that most of Ontario supported the province's cause. In June Schultz dispatched to Ottawa a defiant "memorial" from the Legislative Assembly which declared Catholic schools to be lacking in "the attributes of efficient modern public schools." Bowell's cabinet caved in and adopted an order in council urging "further discussion" and "friendly negotiation" with Manitoba. With the federal government now clearly on the run, Manitoba waited five months before even bothering to reply, and then issued an order in council that left no room at all for compromise.[53] Several of Bowell's ministers resigned, but all except C.H. Tupper agreed to return ten days later after the embattled prime minister promised to introduce remedial legislation. The elder Tupper, who had been Canada's high commissioner in England for the past eight years, joined the government in place of his son. The remedial bill was introduced and it passed second reading on 20 March 1896 with twenty Conservatives, all but one of them from Ontario, voting against the government.[54] The government betrayed its lack of sincerity by sending the new minister of justice, A.R. Dickey, on a negotiating mission to Manitoba while the parliamentary debate was in progress. Before third reading could take place Parliament's term expired, making a dissolution unavoidable. Bowell resigned and Sir Charles Tupper led the divided party into the election that ended the era of Macdonaldian Conservatism in Canadian politics.

BRITISH COLUMBIA

Despite its remoteness and political immaturity, Manitoba shared some tenuous links and common characteristics with Canada even before 1870, and these connections were decisively and rapidly reinforced in the years that followed. British Columbia, however, was another story. Not only was it almost unimaginably distant – more than twice as far away as Manitoba – but it had practically nothing in common with the country of which it became part in 1871. To the few Canadians who saw it before the completion of the CPR it must have conveyed the exotic appearance it has never completely lost, even in the age of air travel and telecommunications.

Apart from Alexander Mackenzie's epic journey across the continent in 1793, which had no lasting consequences, the pre-Confederation history of British Columbia had practically nothing to do with British North America. Although the Hudson's Bay Company operated extensively on the mainland of the future province, the company was run from England and it discouraged white settlement beyond the Rockies even more effectively than it did on the prairies. Vancouver Island, which was not annexed to the mainland until 1858, was where most of the Caucasian population, such as it was, still lived in 1871. The island, which dominated the province socially and politically, was less a part of North America than an outpost of British naval power in the Pacific similar to New Zealand or the Australian colonies. Few North Americans had reason to go there, and it is revealing that eight of British Columbia's ten premiers between 1871 and 1898 were born in the British Isles. (By way of contrast, only one of the thirty-three premiers in the five eastern provinces during the same period was not born in the province he governed.)

As in Manitoba, but to an even greater degree, the physical remoteness of British Columbia from Canada impeded any possibility of communication that might have existed. As late as 1883 when Alexander Campbell, as minister of justice, was sent on a mission to British Columbia, he had to travel from Ottawa to Oakland, California, on a series of trains and then for a thousand miles up the coast to Victoria on one of the slow and infrequent ships that linked the various Pacific outports.[55] The dominion government of 1871 was so ignorant of the geography of its new acquisition that for several years it seriously entertained the bizarre notion of running the CPR on a bridge across the Strait of Georgia.[56] The British Columbians, who wanted a railway on Vancouver Island as well as a transcontinental line, did not bother to point out that the idea was ridiculous.

British Columbia's economy was distinguished from that of Canada by the insignificance of agriculture, for which the mountainous terrain was not well suited and for whose products there would have been few accessible markets. In 1881, a decade after the province joined the dominion, there were only two thousand farmers, or about one-eighth of the employed population. Labourers, many of them engaged in constructing the CPR, were the largest occupational category at that time, while the main primary industries were mining and fishing.[57]

British Columbia looked impressive on a map, for its boundaries in 1871 were exactly the same as they are today. It was larger, at that time, than either Quebec or Ontario. However, for political purposes it was almost a city-state, since most of the politically active population lived in or around Victoria. The only mainland settlement of much consequence was New Westminister. (The city of Vancouver did not exist until 1887, and its present location was a forest in 1871.) The majority of the persons living in British Columbia in 1871 were native Indians, but they were totally excluded from the political process, and many of them lived in such isolated locations that their numbers were never precisely determined. Also excluded from politics were the Chinese who, as in Australia and New Zealand, were the target of much hostility. The small Caucasian population was distinguished from that of Canada by the total absence of francophones and the scarcity of Roman Catholics. British Columbians, then as now, were also more likely than other North Americans to declare they had no religion.

British Columbia was the only province in the 1870s that claimed to have universal male suffrage, but since the privilege was confined to the Caucasian minority it was a rather barren boast. In contrast to Manitoba, a legislative assembly had been established in 1858, coincidentally with the joining of the island and the mainland in one colony. Responsible government, however, did not come before 1871. Even after that date, parliamentary government in British Columbia did not function in precisely the way Walter Bagehot described it in his classic description of the Westminster model. In fact Pacific coast politics, then as now, were somewhat bizarre. In dominion elections, as noted above, British Columbia voted solidly Conservative. In provincial elections political parties did not formally exist until after the turn of the twentieth century, but the governments were generally pro-Conservative. Significantly, British Columbia, unlike Manitoba, refused to participate in the Interprovincial Conference of 1887.

British Columbia had ten premiers in its first twenty-seven years as a province, the same number as Quebec in the same period, but more than any other province. One of the British Columbia premiers held the office twice. Only three of the eleven governments lasted as long as three years. The instability, however, was more superficial than real, for there were no real ideological or partisan cleavages and essentially the same small political elite were always in office. Nine of the eleven governments included at least one minister from the previous government. The number of ministers in each government, including the premier, ranged from three to five, and there were a total of forty-nine positions in the eleven governments. Thirteen individuals, seven of whom were premier for part of the time, occupied thirty-eight of these positions. Eleven other individuals, three of whom were premiers, occupied the remainder.

Three of the changes of government were caused by the death of the premier, a remarkable mortality rate since only one other provincial premier died in all of Canada during the same period. Of the remaining premiers one was dismissed by the lieutenant-governor, two were appointed to the bench, one resigned because he lost his seat, one chose to devote his time to the House of Commons, and the rest were defeated on votes of confidence. Five of the ten premiers represented Victoria in the Legislative Assembly, although the city and its environs had only six seats.

The first premier, John McCreight, had opposed both responsible government and Confederation. He lost the confidence of the assembly at its first session and resigned. He was succeeded by the colourful journalist and crusader for Confederation Amor de Cosmos, an ex-Nova Scotian who had changed his name from the more prosaic William Smith while prospecting for gold in California. De Cosmos was already a member of parliament and, like Edward Blake, he opted for federal politics when the double mandate was abolished. He handed over the provincial government to his right-hand man, George Walkem, who was defeated on a vote of confidence two years later and resigned. Walkem returned to the premiership when his successor, Andrew Elliott, lost his seat and most of his followers in the 1878 election. Walkem was given a judicial appointment by Sir John A. Macdonald in 1882, just before a provincial election, and succeeded by his minister of finance, Robert Beaven, who failed to win the confidence of the new House. The next three premiers, William Smithe, A.E.B. Davie, and John Robson, all died in office. Theodore Davie, the brother of A.E.B., succeeded Robson in 1892 and was appointed chief justice of British Columbia three years later. His successor, John Turner, was dismissed by the lieutenant-governor in 1898, the first of three such episodes over the next five years.[58]

In federal politics British Columbians were Conservatives because they correctly perceived that only the Conservative party was seriously committed to building the CPR. Even the populist de Cosmos, although he styled himself a Liberal, generally supported the Macdonald government in the House of Commons. All of British Columbia's members of parliament until the 1896 election were *de facto* Conservatives. Richard Cartwright in his memoirs accused Macdonald of admitting British Columbia to Confederation for the sole purpose of providing six additional Conservative votes in the Commons, a suggestion that perhaps reveals more about Cartwright than it does about Macdonald.[59] Although Macdonald did call British Columbia the spoilt child of Confederation, the metaphor does not suggest a total lack of affection, and Macdonald himself was the indulgent parent who did most of the spoiling. Liberals, although they coveted prairie land, seemed to regard the province beyond the Rocky Mountains as more of a nuisance than an asset. British Columbia voters and politicians understandably reciprocated their sentiments.

Perhaps reflecting the Conservative sympathy for the province, as well as the fact that Canada acquired it by negotiation rather than purchase, British Columbia's terms of union were far more generous than those given to Manitoba. Its population was estimated at sixty thousand, which was at least three times the actual number, excluding Indians who had no political rights and received no services from the provincial government. British Columbia's debt allowance and statutory subsidy were both about three-and-a-half times as large as those Manitoba received. It also received $35,000 for the support of its government and legislature, compared with Manitoba's $30,000. It retained all its public lands and resources, apart from some lands that were surrendered to help finance the CPR, and in return for those it received a generous allowance of $100,000 per annum. (Prince Edward Island, with a larger population, received less than half as much as compensation for having no public lands at all.) The dominion agreed to provide steamship service between British Columbia and the United States, to provide pensions for British Columbia public servants, to pay the interest on a loan of up to £100,000 sterling to build a graving dock for the repair of warships at Esquimalt, and, above all, to ensure that the CPR was built within ten years.[60] One is tempted to paraphrase Winston Churchill by observing that never in the field of human government was so much promised by so many to so few.

In spite of, or perhaps because of, their generosity, these terms of union were the source of acrimonious, and seemingly endless, conflict between British Columbia and the federal government. Charges of bad faith on the one side, and of ingratitude on the other, were freely exchanged, countless meetings were held, and mountains of documents accumulated. The governor general, and even the Colonial Office, were brought into the fray to an extent unmatched by the dominion's relations with any other province. Although animosity between the two governments was particularly intense during Alexander Mackenzie's ill-fated government, British Columbia's suspicion of the federal authorities and their motives transcended any considerations of partisanship or personality. Even Macdonald, although his patience towards the Pacific province was remarkable, often found the maintenance of friendly relations to be an uphill struggle.

The most important of the terms of union, and the most onerous for the federal government, was the commitment in Article 11 to bring about the construction of the CPR. Macdonald was sincerely committed to this project, even though he knew that a great many Canadians were unconvinced that the acquisition of a small and remote province was worth the cost of the undertaking. However, as he told the lieutenant-governor of British Columbia early in 1873, sectional jealousies between Ontario and Quebec made it difficult to organize a syndicate to build the railway. For this and other reasons little was accomplished in 1872, and the bad publicity of the "Pacific scandal," even before it brought down Macdonald's government, had placed the future of the CPR project in considerable doubt.

The Liberals had always doubted the feasibility, and the wisdom, of Canada's commitment to build the railway, and they had little interest in British Columbia. Their commitment to low taxes and economical government, which in Mackenzie's case bordered on fanaticism, was reinforced by the recession that struck the Canadian economy at about the time they took office. They also knew that the transcontinental railway project had brought about the fall of their predecessors from office. For all of these reasons they were inclined to escape from Canada's commitment if at all possible, and their arrival in office was bad news for British Columbia and for all supporters of the transcontinental project. One of their first actions after the 1874 election was to send J.D. Edgar, a prominent young Liberal who had just lost his seat in the House of Commons, as a special emissary to British Columbia. Edgar's hopeless mission was to persuade the British Columbians to accept a relaxation of the terms of Article 11. Instead, he suggested, the Mackenzie government would build a short railway from Esquimalt to Nanaimo on Vancouver Island, which might some day become the western link in the transcontinental. It would also build a wagon road through the mountains and a telegraph line from British Columbia to Ontario, would survey possible routes for the transcontinental, and would spend $1.5 million per annum on railway-related construction in British Columbia, once the survey was completed.[61]

This offer was predictably rejected and the mission was a failure. Lord Carnarvon, who had acted as Canada's godfather in 1867, was back in office as colonial secretary, and expressed regret over the difficulties. With good intentions, but perhaps unwisely, he offered to serve as a mediator between British Columbia and the federal government. Mackenzie rejected the offer, but when the governor general, Lord Dufferin, informed him that Carnarvon considered his reply discourteous, the prime minister reluctantly changed his mind.[62] The British Columbians welcomed Carnarvon's suggestion and Premier Walkem made the long journey to England to acquaint the colonial secretary with their grievances. They also sent, by way of Dufferin, a petition to the queen from residents of Victoria complaining of Canada's failure to comply with Article 11. Carvarnon, who found Walkem to be "temperate and reasonable," proposed a compromise that came to be known as the Carvarnon terms. Canada should begin the Vancouver Island railway at once, increase its expenditures on the survey, set a deadline for the survey's completion, and compensate the province financially if the deadline was not met. It should also spend $2 million per annum on the transcontinental line, which it should pledge to complete no later than 1890. The idea of the wagon road, which the province did not want, should be abandoned, and the telegraph line should be postponed until the route of the railway was definitely settled.[63]

The Mackenzie government insisted that the wagon road and the telegraph would be necessary to build the railway, accepted the proposed level of expenditure with obvious reluctance, and refused to consider building a railway through northern Ontario by 1890. After consulting Walkem, who was still in England, Carnarvon modified his proposal to include the wagon road and the telegraph and to set the deadline of 1890 for construction from British Columbia to Lake Superior only. Although Mackenzie expressed unhappiness with the colonial secretary presuming to decide on a question of federal-provincial relations, his government more or less accepted the terms.[64] Walkem, passing through Ottawa on his way home, had a friendly meeting with Mackenzie, and a bill was introduced in Parliament to authorize construction of the Esquimalt and Nanaimo line. In April 1875, however, this bill was rejected by the Conservative-dominated Senate, making implementation of the Carnarvon terms impossible. Mackenzie then suggested the alternative of paying British Columbia in cash what the Esquimalt and Nanaimo line would have cost, an amount estimated at $750,000. Although Carnarvon thought this reasonable, British Columbia definitely did not. Most politically active British Columbians lived on Vancouver Island, and they professed to interpret Article 11 as implying a railway link to their provincial capital. The island railway would bring them more immediate benefit than the larger project on the mainland. Furthermore, the transcontinental project itself seemed threatened by the Mackenzie government's increasing tendency to curtail expenditures in response to the recession. Matters were not improved when the Mackenzie government's formal offer of compensation for the island railway was misplaced by a clerk and not sent to Victoria until two months after it was made.

In 1876 relations between British Columbia and the federal government reached perhaps their lowest point in history. The year opened with the provincial cabinet's rejection of Mackenzie's offer and a simultaneous petition to the queen from the Legislative Assembly. The provincial cabinet minute contained language Dufferin described to Carnarvon as improper, reprehensible, and unseemly.[65] In reply the federal cabinet claimed that Article 11 did not commit Canada to build the Esquimalt and Nanaimo, that the government could not be held responsible for the action of the Senate, that its offer of compensation had been refused, and that it was building the transcontinental line as fast as Canada's financial situation permitted. As if to reinforce the latter observation, the House of Commons almost unanimously endorsed a resolution by a backbench Liberal that the Pacific railway project should be pursued only insofar as this could be done without increasing rates of taxation.[66]

In March Dufferin offered to visit British Columbia in an effort to improve relations, and in August and September he actually did so. In a lengthy speech at Victoria he suggested that Article 11 had been unrealistic, defended Mackenzie's policies (while claiming that he did not intend to do so), and urged British Columbians to be patient. He also deprecated the talk of secession that was increasingly heard in Victoria: "a governor general is a Federalist by profession, and you might as well expect the Sultan of Turkey to throw up his cap for the Commune as the Viceroy of Canada to entertain a suggestion for the disintegration of the dominion."[67]

A.N. Richards, the Ontario lawyer whom Mackenzie had appointed as lieutenant-governor of British Columbia, thought the viceregal visit had had the desired effect. Dufferin himself reported to Mackenzie that anti-Canadian sentiment in Victoria was much stronger than he had expected, but that no one outside of Victoria cared about the Esquimalt and Nanaimo Railway. Like most visitors to British Columbia, the governor general was more impressed by the scenery than by the people or the politicians, whom he described in very unflattering terms in his private correspondence with Carnarvon. He warned Mackenzie that the threat of secession was real and that the federal government should make some additional concessions, particularly as opinion in the United Kingdom was likely to be biased in favour of the province. Specifically, Dufferin suggested that building a railway from Yale to Kamloops would satisfy British Columbians for the time being and permit the indefinite postponement of the CPR. He also thought that representatives of the federal and provincial governments should meet with Carnarvon to negotiate a compromise.[68] Mackenzie and Blake were offended by this suggestion and refused to make any further concessions to British Columbia. Eventually Mackenzie agreed in December 1876 that the proposed conference might take place in early 1878 if construction of the transcontinental railway in British Columbia had not begun by that time. Although Dufferin still claimed to be on good terms with Mackenzie, he had become convinced that relations with British Columbia would not improve until Macdonald was back in office.

Although construction did not really begin in 1877, the survey was more or less completed. In March 1878 Dufferin informed Sir Michael Hicks-Beach, who had succeeded Carnarvon as colonial secretary, that discontent in British Columbia had significantly declined, a circumstance he attributed to an improvement of economic conditions.[69] Later in the spring, Mackenzie's government appropriated funds to begin construction from Yale to Kamloops and announced that the transcontinental line would terminate at Burrard Inlet. Nonetheless, Vancouver Island was still discontented because the Esquimalt and Nanaimo was not included in the government's plans. Islanders may also have realized that the choice of Burrard Inlet would eventually end the island's domination of the province. In September 1878, almost simultaneously with the federal election, the Legislative Assembly in Victoria sent a petition to the queen asking her to allow British Columbia to secede if Canada failed to carry out the Carnarvon terms.[70] The petition was never acknowledged.

A month later, Macdonald was back in office, with construction of the CPR as his first and highest priority. "Until this great work is completed," he had written earlier in the year, "our dominion is little more than a geographical expression."[71] His election as MP for Victoria, a place he had never seen, seemed to underline his commitment. British Columbia was not quite convinced and the legislature refused to adjourn in March 1879, when it would normally have done so, until Macdonald made a definite pledge to build the railway as quickly as possible. In May he obligingly did so and was thanked by Premier Walkem.[72] In the following year the celebrated contract was signed with George Stephen and his associates, and the CPR, as it was henceforth known, at last became a reality.

British Columbia was still not satisfied, for, as Macdonald informed Walkem in October 1880, the CPR syndicate did not want to build a line on Vancouver Island. Walkem promptly replied that in that case the federal government would have to build the Esquimalt and Nanaimo line itself.[73] When Macdonald's government refused to do so the Legislative Assembly addressed yet another petition to the queen, and the provincial cabinet appointed de Cosmos, who was still a member of parliament, to convey its grievances to both the dominion and the imperial governments. Macdonald noted that the Carvarnon terms had never been accepted by Parliament and that the island railway was a "local work," and thus not the federal government's responsibility. He told Walkem that the CPR might still be persuaded to build the line.[74] When this proved not to be the case, and when the provincial government refused to finance the island railway itself, the federal government pursued the possibility of having it built by James and Robert Dunsmuir, of Nanaimo, who owned coal mines on Vancouver Island. The Dunsmuirs were willing to build the railway in collaboration with the group of American capitalists who controlled the Central Pacific Railroad, and who hoped to ship Dunsmuir's coal to California where it could be used as locomotive fuel. Premier Walkem, who distrusted the Dunsmuirs, was cool to this proposal, and recommended that Macdonald support another group of entrepreneurs who were allegedly willing to build the line. Macdonald disposed of Walkem by appointing him to the bench, but the impasse over the Esquimalt and Nanaimo continued. The Dunsmuirs now insisted on a contract with the federal government, while Macdonald insisted that the line was a provincial responsibility.[75] Anti-Canadian sentiment continued to flourish on Vancouver Island, so alarming the governor general, Lord Lorne, that he followed his predecessor's example by undertaking a personal mission to British Columbia in the fall of 1882.

Perhaps as a result of Lorne's visit, it was agreed that the province would grant a charter and a land grant to whomever the federal cabinet designated to build the railway. In the following year the agreement almost collapsed because Macdonald objected to the wording of the statute adopted by the Legislative Assembly, which seemed to suggest that the railway was a federal responsibility. Alexander

Campbell, the minister of justice, was sent on a diplomatic mission to British Columbia, in the course of which he met the Dunsmuirs' American partners in San Francisco and signed a contract with them on the federal government's behalf.[76] Parliament and the Legislative Assembly endorsed this contract in 1884, and the Esquimalt and Nanaimo Railway was completed two years later. Ironically it was sold to the CPR, along with its valuable lands and resources, in 1905.

Despite its zeal to expedite the construction of the CPR, British Columbia followed Manitoba's example by attempting to charter other railways in defiance of the monopoly clause. In 1883 the Legislative Assembly adopted acts chartering three different railways, the Columbia and Kootenay, the Fraser River Railway, and the New Westminster Southern. On Campbell's instructions, the lieutenant-governor sent the three acts promptly to Ottawa. Lord Lorne, a firm supporter of the CPR, expressed concern about the New Westminster Southern in particular, and was assured by Macdonald that its charter would be disallowed if necessary. On his visit to British Columbia, Campbell arranged a compromise regarding the Columbia and Kootenay whereby the charter would be amended to prohibit it from approaching the U.S. border. George Stephen of the CPR urged disallowance of the other two charters, and on Campbell's recommendation they were disallowed in October 1883.[77]

Simultaneously with their lengthy dispute over Article 11 of the terms of union, British Columbia and the federal government locked horns over Article 12, which committed the dominion to assist in building a "graving dock" at Esquimalt. The two issues frequently became entangled with one another and, between them, largely accounted for the poisonous relations between the two governments, at least up to 1883. British Columbia wanted the dock for all the usual reasons for which provinces wanted public works, but also in the belief that it would increase the likelihood of the British Admiralty maintaining a squadron at Esquimalt. By another of the terms of union, Article 9, Canada promised to use its influence to encourage the continued maintenance of the naval station.

Article 12 stated that Canada would pay the interest at 5 per cent for ten years on a loan of up to £100,000 sterling which British Columbia would raise, presumably on the London money market, to finance the project. Within two years, however, the province suggested an entirely different arrangement whereby the dominion would make an interest-free "advance" to the province of £50,000, in the hope that the imperial government might be induced to contribute the rest of the necessary funds. The legislature adopted an address making this proposal to the federal government, as well as legislation to authorize its implementation.[78] Amor de Cosmos, who was both premier of the province and a member of the House of Commons in Ottawa, was appointed a special agent of the province to conduct the necessary negotiations in both Ottawa and London.

De Cosmos apparently received a favourable response from Leonard Tilley, but the Macdonald government left office before anything could be done. A few days after taking office, however, Prime Minister Mackenzie promised de Cosmos that the new government would submit to Parliament legislation to implement the British Columbia proposal "or some scheme equivalent thereto."[79] The British Columbians erroneously assumed from this letter that the thrifty prime minister had accepted their idea of an interest-free grant, but they were soon to be disappointed.

Having apparently succeeded in Ottawa, de Cosmos proceeded to London, armed with a letter of introduction from the governor general, where he proposed that the imperial government provide the other half of the necessary funds. The Admiralty was initially willing to commit only £30,000, rather than £50,000, and also suggested that payment should be made after the work was completed, rather than in advance.[80]

In the following year Mackenzie's government introduced, and Parliament accepted, legislation authorizing the federal government to advance up to $250,000 to British Columbia for the graving dock, in lieu of the original promise in the terms of union.[81] A second section of the same statute authorized additional advances to any province of funds for local improvements, such advances then to be debited against the debt allowance of the province concerned. Later in the year Walkem, who had succeeded de Cosmos as premier, proceeded to London where he managed to persuade the new Disraeli government to increase its contribution to the £50,000 originally requested. The original offer of £30,000 had been recommended by the Admiralty before the change of government, and approved by the new government shortly afterwards. The increase may be attributed in part to Disraeli's anti-Russian foreign policy, which made a base in the North Pacific a higher priority, and in part to Walkem's threat that without it British Columbia would build a smaller graving dock that would be suitable for merchant ships only. In any event, Walkem said, British Columbia no longer needed payment in advance, since it could spend the federal funds before drawing on those provided by the imperial government.[82]

In April 1875 British Columbia submitted to the federal government a request for $439,150 as payment for various public works in accordance with the federal legislation of the previous year.

The federal government interpreted this request as including the $250,000 advance for the graving dock, which it said could not be paid without evidence of actual progress in the construction. It agreed to pay the balance of the sum requested, but warned that in future no such payments could be made to any province unless the public works had been specifically authorized in advance by the federal government. British Columbia responded that its request had not been meant to include the advance for the graving dock, and also added that it had not been aware of any requirement that public works be approved in advance. It again requested payment of the full amount but was refused.[83]

A year after its first request, British Columbia submitted another. It now claimed to have spent over $50,000 on the graving dock, and requested payment. The Mackenzie government replied by asking the province to specify whether the advance should be charged against the debt allowance or whether the interest on it should be deducted from the statutory subsidy. The province replied indignantly that it understood the cost of the graving dock to be not a loan but a gift, since it was intended as a replacement for Article 12 of the original terms of union. The response was that the province could have either the interest guarantee under Article 12 or the advance envisaged by the 1874 legislation, but that in the latter case the province would be expected to pay interest. This was an entirely new, and highly questionable interpretation of the 1874 legislation. The province expressed its willingness to submit the dispute to any competent tribunal, a request the Mackenzie government ignored.[84]

Work on the graving dock, such as it was, ended in acrimony just before the Turkish crisis of 1876 exposed the British Empire to a real danger of hostilities in the North Pacific. The provincial cabinet accused the dominion of irresponsibly threatening the security of the empire, and of British Columbia in particular. The province then asked the imperial government to complete the dock, since the dominion was apparently unwilling to do so, forwarding its request by way of Ottawa. To make matters worse, the request was somehow lost by the federal government and never forwarded to London. In a letter to Lord Dufferin, Mackenzie regretted this loss, but denied the accusation of bad faith that had predictably come from the province. He insisted that his government had always considered the promised $250,000 advance as a loan rather than a gift. Dufferin agreed that Mackenzie was the best judge of what his own government's intentions had been, particularly since the deputy minister of finance, who had held that office since Confederation, agreed with Mackenzie's interpretation. He noted, however, a telegram from

Tilley, now serving as lieutenant-governor of New Brunswick, in which the former minister of finance assured the British Columbians that the Macdonald government really had intended to advance the funds as a gift rather than a loan.[85]

This impasse apparently convinced Dufferin that only through the action of the imperial government would the graving dock ever be built. Apart from its military significance, this would be desirable as it would remove one of several sources of conflict between British Columbia and the federal government, and perhaps facilitate resolution of other disputes. On the basis of what he termed a "hint" from the colonial secretary, he suggested that the imperial government should take over and complete the dock and then operate it. Mackenzie seemed to agree with this approach. The colonial secretary, Sir Michael Hicks-Beach, brought the idea before the British cabinet but met with great difficulties, perhaps because the threat of war with Russia had receded by 1878. Hicks-Beach, however, did not give up, and suggested that the idea might be made more acceptable if the $750,000 Mackenzie had offered as compensation for not building the Esquimalt and Nanaimo Railway could be used to complete the graving dock. The imperial government would thus acquire the dock without the need for any financial commitment beyond what it had already promised.[86]

Dufferin outlined this proposal to Macdonald as soon as Macdonald returned to office in October 1878, but Macdonald did not commit himself. In England the following summer Macdonald saw Hicks-Beach, who hoped that the imperial contribution might be raised from £50,000 to £75,000, although the Admiralty was cool to this suggestion.[87] In November 1879 Macdonald's government authorized an immediate advance to British Columbia of $100,000 for the graving dock. This would be regarded as a gift if British Columbia completed the dock within three years, but if not it would be debited against the province's debt allowance. Although the wording of the offer suggested there would be further advances on the same terms as the work progressed, the British Columbia government was indignant at this proposal. It demanded an immediate advance of the full $250,000 promised by the legislation of 1874, as a gift and without any conditions.[88] Premier Walkem travelled to Ottawa to discuss the matter with Tilley, who was again minister of finance, and managed to convince the Macdonald government to give the province $250,000 with no conditions: essentially what Tilley had suggested in 1873. However, the federal government reserved the right to take over the dock if work did not progress at a satisfactory rate, and in that case it, rather than the province, would receive the imperial subsidy of £50,000. This agreement was embodied in an Act of Parliament.[89]

By 1882 little work had been done on the dock and Macdonald blamed the British Columbia government for the delay. The federal government took over the project, with little apparent resistance from the province, and agreed to compensate British Columbia for its expenditures. These arrangements were embodied in an Act of Parliament in 1884. Soon afterwards the imperial government agreed to pay the promised subsidy to Canada, rather than to British Columbia, and to pay it by the first day of 1887. Although there were doubts that the dock would be large enough to service the latest warships, neither government wished to risk further controversy by increasing the cost of the project.[90]

A third major dispute over the terms of union, which continued long after the other were resolved, concerned the so-called railway belt. Besides requiring the dominion to build the CPR, Article 11 required the province to transfer to the dominion a belt of land for up to twenty miles on either side of the railway, to be used to facilitate its construction. In 1880 British Columbia enacted legislation to convey this land to the dominion, based on the assumption that the transcontinental railway would use the Yellowhead Pass through the Rocky Mountains.[91] When the CPR at the last moment selected a southern route through the Kicking Horse Pass, this legislation became inapplicable. The federal government argued that the rugged terrain along the southern route, and the many curves on the railway, would make it difficult to define the precise boundaries of the new railway belt, and that much of the land was in any event unfit for settlement and thus worthless. The provincial government blamed the federal government for the uncertainty that had withheld much of the province's best land from the market on the pretext that it might be needed to build the railway. It claimed this delay had imposed an artificial constraint on the growth of the population.

These difficulties were discussed when Alexander Campbell visited British Columbia in 1883. Campbell reached an agreement with the province to substitute a new railway belt for the one defined in 1880 and to give the dominion an additional block of land in the Peace River Country to compensate for the fact that much of the new railway belt would be unfit for settlement. In return, Campbell promised that those railway belt lands that were fit for settlement would be brought on the market without delay, although this could not be done until the precise limits of the new railway belt were defined.[92] Early in the new year the provincial cabinet formally urged the federal government to define the limits of the new railway belt, and Campbell repeatedly urged Macdonald to do so. Both the Legislative Assembly and Parliament adopted legislation incorporating the agreement of 1883, including the pledge that the land would be opened for settlement, but nothing was actually done about the survey. The task was nominally entrusted to Joseph Trutch, the former lieutenant-governor who was still on the federal payroll as Macdonald's agent in British Columbia, but Trutch lacked the means, and claimed that he lacked the authority, to perform the task.[93] Premier Smithe bombarded the federal government with indignant telegrams, including the claim that the province had received offers for railway belt lands which it had declined on the grounds that only the dominion had the authority to sell them. However, David McPherson, the minister of the interior, charged in 1885 that the province actually was selling railway belt lands that it had ostensibly conveyed to the dominion. Campbell noted that this practice was contrary to the agreement he had negotiated with the British Columbians two years previously, and on his recommendation the Macdonald government adopted an order in council declaring the sales null and void and warning the province against any further sales of lands within the railway belt. In the following year a provincial statue providing for the sale of a specific piece of land within the railway belt was disallowed, even though the province had granted the land in question to a private individual in 1878, before the railway belt was established.[94]

In 1887 the federal government finally proposed a detailed definition of the boundaries of the railway belt, almost two years after the last spike had been driven at Craigellachie, but the provincial government was not satisfied with the boundaries proposed. In fact the provincial government now suggested that the entire railway belt should be transferred back to provincial control, perhaps in exchange for an additional block of land in the Peace River Country. The arguments for this course of action were that the railway belt was obviously not needed for its original purpose, since the railway had already been built, and that having distinct federal and provincial administrative regimes in adjacent and not clearly separated lands was an inconvenience for settlers, miners, and lumbermen. Thomas White, who had succeeded McPherson as minister of the interior, wished to pursue this possibility, although Macdonald did not.[95] When White died unexpectedly in 1888, Macdonald took over the Interior portfolio himself, and no action was taken. Macdonald did agree to give the province 45,000 acres of the so-called Sumas Diking Lands, which it claimed and which had been the subject of the statute disallowed in 1886. With respect to an additional 16,000 acres, also claimed by the province, Macdonald maintained federal ownership but agreed to recognize the timber licences already granted by the province.[96] One of the beneficiaries of this agreement, incidentally, was the ubiquitous Peter McLaren of Lanark County, who was thus involved in the Macdonald government's disputes with three out of the seven provinces.

A major obstacle to the disposition of the remaining railway belt lands was the uncertainty regarding the ownership of mineral rights and royalties. This question was referred to the Supreme Court and eventually decided, on appeal, by the Judicial Committee of the Privy Council in 1889.[97] The Supreme Court had ruled that all the rights had been transferred to the dominion by the grant of a railway belt, but the Judicial Committee ruled that precious metals and royalties were prerogative rights of the crown and not incidental to land ownership, and were thus retained by the province, although ordinary minerals, such as coal, had been transferred. Following this decision the provincial government suggested that all minerals in the railway belt should be provincially administered, but that the province should remit to the dominion payments in relation to those minerals deemed to be federal property. The federal government proposed instead that coal should be administered by the dominion and all other minerals by the province, and on this basis agreement was reached in 1890.[98]

Meanwhile the precise boundaries of the railway belt were still in dispute. In 1891 and again in 1892 the British Columbia government proposed referring the question to the courts, but the dominion did not agree to do so. On the advice of the minister of the interior, Edgar Dewdney, the federal cabinet suggested that a literal interpretation of the twenty-mile limit was in fact feasible (a view that it had rejected in 1887), so that no judicial reference was necessary. Premier Davie discussed the matter with Justice Minister John Thompson in 1892, just before Thompson became prime minister, but the meeting was unsuccessful and was followed by an acrimonious exchange of letters. Finally, in 1895, after Thompson's death, the two sides reached agreement on the basis of the proposal that the federal government had made in 1887.[99]

Apart from the terms of union, the most serious disputes between British Columbia and the federal government concerned the two principal non-Caucasian ethnic groups in the province, the aboriginal Indians and the Chinese. Both controversies gave some credence to Lord Dufferin's observation, in a private letter to Lord Carnarvon, that British Columbians displayed the vulgar xenophobia of the English middle class from which many of them came.[100]

Although Indians were a federal responsibility according to the BNA Act, the federal government did not own the land in British Columbia and thus could not sign treaties with them as it did on the prairies. The province itself had done nothing to accommodate its aboriginal peoples before 1871, and showed little disposition to do so afterwards. In 1874 the Mackenzie government formally complained about the unsatisfactory status of the Indians in British Columbia, and in the following year it disallowed a provincial statute regarding crown lands on the grounds that it disregarded Indian claims. Subsequently the province reluctantly agreed to a federal proposal whereby a three-member commission (one federal and one provincial appointee, and a jointly selected chairman) would select lands to be allocated to the Indians. British Columbia rejected the federal appointee, a missionary known to be sympathetic to the native people, and insisted on his replacement by another individual, whom the federal government obligingly appointed.[101] Lord Dufferin, on his visit to British Columbia a few weeks later, devoted much of his public address to Indian affairs, reprimanded the province for disregarding Indian interests, and reminded his audience that since Indians had no representatives in Parliament, the governor general had a special obligation to intervene on their behalf.[102] Not in the least abashed, the provincial government soon afterwards demanded the repeal of those sections of the Indian Act, recently adopted by Parliament, that protected the Indians from being deprived of lands already reserved for them without their consent. Early in 1877 it proposed that the commission, which had been in operation for only a few months, should be wound up at the end of the year and replaced by a new procedure for settling Indian claims which would give a veto power to the province's chief commissioner of lands and works. The federal government at first agreed but a year later David Mills, the minister of the interior, had second thoughts, since the Indians seemed increasingly discontented. He proposed instead that Gilbert Sproat, the federally appointed member of the now-dissolved commission, should allocate land for reserves. The province reluctantly agreed but reserved the right to review Sproat's decisions in "exceptional" cases.[103]

A few years later, in 1884, the British Columbia government proposed what it termed the "rearrangement" of Indian reserves by removing the Indians to wilderness areas so that the more valuable land occupied by them could be made available to the growing white population. John A. Macdonald, who was at that time the minister responsible for Indian affairs in addition to his other duties, replied firmly that the reserves were "now the property of the Indians" and could not be taken from them without their consent.[104]

In 1890 the British Columbia government opened a lengthy campaign whose objective was to remove the Songhees, a small band of Indians whose reserve was considered too close to the provincial capital. The provincial cabinet claimed that "their close proximity to the city of Victoria is undesirable, and tends to retard the growth and prosperity of the said city." The federal government replied that the Songhees had been asked to move on several occasions but were attached to their land, which they had occupied from time immemorial, and were not interested in moving. It refused to move them without their consent. The provincial government renewed its request the following year, this time claiming that the Songhees were "demoralized" by their proximity to the city. A third request was made in 1893. This time Edgar Dewdney, who had been the minister responsible for Indian affairs at the time of the earlier requests but was now lieutenant-governor, offered to try to persuade the Songhees to move. The federal government, headed by Thompson, welcomed the offer, conceding that the removal of the band was desirable if it could be arranged with their consent, but Dewdney's efforts were apparently unsuccessful. In 1895 the provincial government offered an alternative site, further west on Vancouver Island, but action was delayed by a pending court decision about mineral rights, and nothing had been done when the Laurier government took office.[105]

Federal-provincial conflict over the Chinese minority in British Columbia began in 1878, when the Legislative Assembly imposed a heavy poll tax on persons of Chinese extraction. The head of the Chinese diplomatic mission in London protested to the imperial government, which communicated his protest to the governor general.[106] After the Supreme Court of British Columbia declared the tax unconstitutional, the Legislative Assembly unanimously petitioned the dominion government to adopt a statute empowering the province to impose such a tax, a course of action that would itself have been unconstitutional. Instead the poll tax was disallowed in August 1879, Macdonald informed Premier Walkem that he considered the agitation against the Chinese regrettable, particularly since more Chinese labour would be needed to build the transcontinental railway. This prediction was confirmed more than two years later, when the contractor building the CPR main line west of the mountains informed Macdonald that he needed six thousand additional Chinese labourers, but that hostility to the Chinese was growing among the white working class of British Columbia.[107]

In 1883 the provincial cabinet formally protested against Chinese immigration, to which the federal government returned the standard reply that Chinese were needed to build the CPR. In the following year Premier Smithe complained to Macdonald about the "hordes of Chinese" whom he alleged were bringing "disease and pestilence and degradation" to British Columbia.[108] The province adopted a statute to restrict their entry, claiming it could do so under the concurrent power to legislate regarding immigration in Section 95 of the BNA Act. A second statute, entitled "An Act to Control the Chinese Population," imposed various discriminatory restrictions and contained such overtly racist language that the head of the Chinese diplomatic mission in London, on hearing about it two years later, complained to the imperial government. Macdonald's government disallowed the immigration act almost as soon as it arrived in Ottawa, but the prime minister assured Premier Smithe that the dominion would study the question and restrict Chinese immigration itself unless this was found to violate a treaty obligation.[109] In 1885 the province again enacted a Chinese immigration law, almost identical to the first. In a message to the governor general, the legislature alleged that legislation was necessary "to prevent the province from being completely overrun." This act was also promptly disallowed, on the grounds that it interfered with trade and commerce, since the colonial secretary had earlier declared that no imperial interest was involved. However, as the governor general correctly predicted in a secret dispatch, anti-Chinese sentiment in British Columbia was now so strong that federal legislation to restrict Chinese immigration was inevitable.[110]

Parliament adopted a statute later in the year which imposed strict quarantine requirements on Chinese seeking to enter Canada, limited the number that could be carried on any ship, and imposed a heavy tax on each one that entered, apart from diplomats, tourists, scientists, students, and merchants who had been issued a visa by a British consul. Revenue from the tax would be shared with the province of entry, which was expected to be British Columbia in almost every case.[111] A few months after this measure came into effect the CPR main line was completed, and the railway dismissed most of its Chinese employees. The provincial cabinet demanded that the dominion take responsibility for what it termed "these Mongolian hordes" now that their services were no longer required, but the federal government refused to do anything.[112]

The restrictive legislation and the completion of the CPR drastically reduced the rate of Chinese immigration, but the provincial government was still not satisfied. In 1891 it formally requested that the entry tax be raised from $50 to a $100, that the permitted ratio of Chinese immigrants to ship tonnage be reduced, or that, better still, the entry of Chinese be completely prohibited. It also wished to abolish the provision of the act allowing Chinese who had been admitted to re-enter the country after a temporary absence.[113] The federal government acknowledged these representations but its only action, in 1892, was an amendment to make the provisions allowing re-entry slightly more restrictive.[114] Further complaints from the provincial cabinet in 1892 and 1893, alleging that the Chinese were bringing leprosy and smallpox into British Columbia, were ignored.[115]

A final dispute of a somewhat less unpleasant character marked the dominion's relations with British Columbia in the last years of Conservative rule. After the census of 1891 had been conducted, the preliminary count showed British Columbia's population as 92,767. The provincial government alleged that the actual population was between 111,000 and 135,000, in support of which claim they presented elaborate arguments. What was at stake, of course, was the level of the statutory subsidy for the next ten years. The final census return increased British Columbia's total slightly to 98,173, including 23,263 Indians, but the provincial cabinet cited an estimate by the federal superintendant-general of Indian affairs that there were 35,302 Indians in the province. It insisted that the statutory subsidy should be based on this estimate rather than on the number of Indians enumerated by the census. Despite repeated pleas from Premier Davie to Prime Minister Thompson, the federal cabinet rejected this claim in January 1894 on the basis that the BNA Act required statutory subsidies to be based on the census. It also presented elaborate arguments to demonstrate that the superintendant-general's estimate was faulty and that some migratory bands had been counted more than once. More than a year later the provincial cabinet issued another statement indicating that, although it still believed in its original estimate of the number of Indians, it would be prepared to settle for a statutory subsidy based on a total population of 100,894. The federal government appears to have ignored the suggestion.[116]

Surveying the history of the dominion's relations with the two western provinces up to 1896, one can find much evidence of a dialogue of the deaf that has largely continued up to the present day. The provinces believed, with more justification then than now, that they were too small and too remote to have much influence on the federal government, and that their legitimate interests were therefore ignored. The federal government, and probably most of the Canadian population, tended to become impatient with provinces that seemed to demand time, money, and attention out of all proportion to their size or real importance, and that rarely expressed any gratitude for the efforts expended on their behalf. While it is possible to apportion some blame on both sides, it is difficult to see how matters could have been made substantially different. The unpleasantness was perhaps the price that Canada paid, and continues to pay, for its territorial expansion.

7 Intergovernmental Relations: Issues, Processes, and Institutions

In addition to the major issues that dominated the agenda of relations between the dominion government and each of the seven provinces, there were a great many minor matters that briefly occupied the attention of officials and ministers in Ottawa and in the provincial capitals. Overall, the agenda of dominion-provincial relations was as crowded as it was controversial. In highly abstract theory, a federal constitution might be designed so as to minimize intergovernmental controversy, and indeed to minimize intergovernmental relations of any kind, by neatly dividing the substance of public policy into matters of federal and provincial jurisdiction. In such an ideal scheme there would be no overlap between matters of federal and provincial jurisdiction, and thus no friction between competing policy initiatives in the same field. Provincial jurisdiction would be confined to matters that had little or no impact outside the boundaries of the province concerned, and that would not be a source of conflict with any other government. Federal jurisdiction, in contrast, would be confined to matters of interest or concern to the whole polity, and in regard to which the provinces would share a common interest. Insofar as there were divergent views among the provinces about these subjects, the representation of each province in the institutions of the central government would provide means for such differences to be accommodated without the need for intervention by the provincial governments themselves.

None of these ideal, and in practice unattainable, conditions was achieved in the nineteenth century. Matters of federal and provincial jurisdiction overlapped considerably, either by design, as in the case of agriculture and immigration, or by unavoidable necessity. Provincial policies sometimes offended the beliefs or affected the interests of persons outside the province. Federal policies often had an adverse impact on a province or, perhaps even more frequently, failed to provide a province with benefits to which the province considered itself entitled. The institutions of the dominion government sometimes managed to accommodate divergent interests, but at other times conspicuously failed to do so (see chapter 13). Political parties, an essential component of representative government, complicated and exacerbated intergovernmental relations as often as they did the reverse.

A complete list of the matters that caused at least occasional friction between Canadian governments in the first three decades after Confederation would include virtually every subject enumerated in Sections 91 through 95 of the British North America Act, and a few subjects that were not. Despite this great variety, the most difficult and controversial issues between the dominion government and the various provinces could with few exceptions be placed under one of four headings: land, money, railways, and religion.

The prominence of issues related to land was virtually inevitable in a society where agriculture was the main industry and where forestry, another land-based endeavour, was its closest rival. Land was the source of wealth, power, and prestige, for individuals and for governments. As S.J.R. Noel has suggested in his study of Ontario politics, land was the basis of political relationships, from the lowest to the highest levels, just as it was directly or indirectly the basis of most economic activity.[1] Although as a general rule the British North America Act placed land under provincial jurisdiction and control, the dominion had important powers and responsibilities related to land as well: lands used for dominion purposes such as military defence, land reserved for the Indians, land ceded to the dominion by provinces, such as the railway belt in British Columbia, and, above all, the public land of the territories acquired from the Hudson's Bay Company, including Manitoba as well as the vast domains that were not organized into provinces.

Thus many of the major issues and controversies between the dominion and provincial governments concerned land. The conflict over the definition of Ontario's northwestern boundary, which lasted almost two decades, was in essence a conflict over land and over the economic wealth and political influence that could be derived from land. The same could be said of Manitoba's efforts to enlarge its territory, Quebec's and Ontario's desire to extend their boundaries to James Bay, and British Columbia's suggestion at one point that its already vast territory should be augmented by extending its boundary to the eastern foothills of the Rocky Mountains. The Caldwell-McLaren dispute, in both its trivial aspects and its broader implications, also concerned lands, as did the controversy over escheats and forfeitures. Land reform in Prince Edward Island involved that normally tranquil province in its only really serious confrontation with the federal authorities. Conflicts over Indians also involved land, as land-hungry settlers and provincial governments sought to encroach on aboriginal lands while the dominion government, generally if not invariably, sought to carry out its responsibility to protect aboriginal interests. The British Columbia railway belt was an important source of federal-provincial conflict. Manitoba sought the same control over public land as the older provinces enjoyed, a demand that would grow more strident, and more successful, when two more western provinces joined the chorus after 1905.

Disputes over money or what would today be called fiscal federalism were almost continuous and involved every province. The financial terms of the British North America Act were carefully drafted, complex, and fairly sophisticated, but they soon proved to be controversial and in some respects inadequate. Some intractable problems, notably the division of debts and assets between the two central provinces, were deliberately postponed. Others, including the fundamental fact that the statutory subsidies were inadequate to support the provincial governments, were not anticipated. The financial settlement Joseph Howe secured for Nova Scotia was money well spent from the dominion's point of view, since the alternative was to allow secession. However, as J.A. Maxwell pointed out many years ago, it created a precedent that led to constant demands for "better terms" and federal responses that were often dictated by considerations of political and partisan advantage.[2] The parsimonious terms on which Manitoba was grudgingly given provincial status produced animosity and conflict that should have been anticipated, and inevitably the terms had to be revised. The much more generous terms on which British Columbia and Prince Edward Island were added to the dominion produced more controversy than gratitude.

Fundamentally the problem for all the eight governments was financial stringency, although some suffered from it more than others. It was not easy to extract revenue from a society consisting largely of self-employed farmers, particularly during the long depression that afflicted Canada and the rest of the world after 1873. Although the dominion's financial resources seemed large by comparison with the provinces, they were less impressive from the standpoint of a minister of finance trying to make ends meet while resisting a chorus of provincial demands for financial concessions. The provinces varied in their financial circumstances from reasonably satisfied in the case of Ontario to desperate in the case of Manitoba, but all faced limited resources and constantly increasing needs. Conflict over money was thus unavoidable, and the complex financial terms of Confederation, including those terms pertaining to particular provinces, usually provided plausible arguments for both sides.

Railways, in the late nineteenth century, were considered the key to economic growth and development. They were also the most expensive function of government, regardless of whether they were publicly or privately owned, and a source of much corruption and scandal. They affected dominion-provincial relations in a number of ways. First, the Maritime provinces all entered the dominion with publicly owned railways that were a major cause of their financial problems. Although the dominion acquired both the railways and the debts, haggling over the details of these arrangements continued. Second, Nova Scotia and Quebec, whose geographical configurations ensured that much of their population would be bypassed by the major interprovincial railways, pursued ambitious and expensive programs of railway-building after 1867, and were soon forced to seek help from the dominion. Third, the dominion's obligations to bring about the construction of the Intercolonial and Canadian Pacific railways produced conflict with the provinces concerned, particularly in the latter case where British Columbia accused the dominion of not taking its obligation seriously. Fourth, the dominion government's determination to protect the Canadian Pacific from competition clashed with Manitoba's and British Columbia's efforts to charter additional railway lines within their own boundaries. Fifth, the dominion's use of its declaratory power to assume jurisdiction over railways by declaring them to be works "for the general advantage of Canada" was resented by Ontario, which wished to keep some lines under its own jurisdiction.

Much of this railway-related conflict could have been avoided if the British North America Act had placed all railways under exclusive federal jurisdiction in the first place, rather than dividing the field between the two levels of government. The Macdonald government appears to have realized, belatedly, that allowing the provinces to play a role in railway development had been a mistake. As can be seen from table 7.1, the use of the declaratory power increased sharply after the signing of the CPR contract in October 1880.[3] By 1896 practically the entire railway network of Canada had been

Table 7.1
Acts of Parliament Employing the Declaratory Power

Parliament	Railways	Other	Total
1st Parliament (1867–72)	15	5	20
2nd Parliament (1873–74)	4	1	5
3rd Parliament (1874–78)	9	2	11
4th Parliament (1879–82)	20	7	27
5th Parliament (1883–87)	37	1	38
6th Parliament (1887–91)	53	3	56
7th Parliament (1891–96)	54	8	62

Source: Andrée Lajoie, Le pouvoir déclaratoire du Parlement (Montreal: Les presses de l'Université de Montréal 1969), 123–37

brought under federal jurisdiction. This was also the period in which the power of disallowance was used to discourage provincial chartering of railways, particularly in the case of Manitoba. Thus one of the major mistakes in the British North America Act was repaired, but too late to prevent a great deal of unnecessary conflict, difficulty, and expense.

Religion, finally, produced relatively few episodes of intergovernmental relations, but several of those that it did produce were of great importance. As discussed in chapter 2, religion played a large part in Canadian life and Canadians took their religious affiliations seriously. No constitution could have been designed that would have prevented the animosity between Protestants and Catholics from affecting intergovernmental relations. The imposition of Catholic separate schools on Canada West by a majority drawn largely from Canada East had undermined the legitimacy of the old Canadian union and had thus been one of the immediate causes of Confederation. Although separate schools could not be abolished in Ontario, their abolition first in New Brunswick, then in Prince Edward Island, and finally and most conspicuously in Manitoba provided opportunities to keep the issue alive. The Manitoba episode produced one of the most serious crises in the whole history of Canadian federalism, and demonstrated the impracticality of the dominion's theoretical power to intervene.

Separate schools were by no means the only issue of public policy that divided Canadians along religious lines. Repeated efforts to incorporate the Orange Order, in Ontario, in Prince Edward Island, and at the federal level, illustrated the political importance of religion, as did the controversy over the Jesuit Estates Act. Mercier's settlement of the Jesuit Estates question, although reasonable and constructive, offended Protestants as much as the abolition of separate schools offended Catholics. Both stirred passions far beyond the boundaries of the province immediately concerned, and thus became issues to which the dominion government had to respond. The controversies over temperance legislation and the licensing power between Ontario and the dominion could also be attributed, in part at least, to religious sentiments. Although the two governments had other reasons to be interested in the licensing power, the issue was exacerbated by the prohibitionist views of the Protestant churches and the pressure the churches brought to bear on politicians at both levels. That pressure led to the Scott Act, which led to the decision in Russell *vs* the Queen, which led in turn to the McCarthy Act.

Although intergovernmental issues and conflicts involved all the provinces, they were not evenly distributed among them. "It seems that the smaller the Province the more troublesome it will be," lamented Alexander Mackenzie on one occasion. "Columbia, Manitoba and Prince Ed. Island each give me much more trouble than all Ontario and Quebec."[4] Prince Edward Island actually became one of the least troublesome provinces once the land question was settled, but Mackenzie's comments on "Columbia" and Manitoba were well deserved. The two western provinces accounted for an astonishingly large proportion of intergovernmental business, considering the relatively insigiificant size of their populations. John A. Macdonald's description of British Columbia as "the spoilt child of the dominion" has already been quoted. Even Lord Lansdowne, who often urged Macdonald to be more sympathetic to Manitoba, eventually expressed some disillusionment with that province: "The moral of it all is that we should be in no hurry to confer self-government upon young communities unfitted to be trusted with the future destinies of the country they inhabit."[5]

The relationship Mackenzie noted between smallness and troublesomeness was perhaps not entirely coincidental. Being small, the two western provinces had little influence in the dominion cabinet or in Parliament, and were thus forced to be more strident and demanding to prevent their interests from being ignored. Political and social immaturity, as noted by Lord Lansdowne, was also a factor, as was the geographical isolation of both provinces. Manitoba also suffered from severe cultural cleavages and a chronic scarcity of revenue. In British Columbia's case the vital necessity of the CPR, and the Mackenzie government's obvious lack of interest in the project, left a lasting legacy of bitterness.

Despite Mackenzie's observation, the two central provinces also produced a large share of intergovernmental issues and conflicts, particularly after 1878. This was especially true of Ontario, in part because of the partisan and personal hostility between Mowat and Macdonald but also because the province was large enough, strong enough, and rich enough to wage a battle against the dominion on more or less equal terms. Quebec's chronic financial and railway problems, as well as the ideological and ethnic cleavages within the province, generated a number of issues as well, but for the most part they were handled discreetly within the Quebec Conservative party, whose endless factional infighting prevented a strong Quebec leader from emerging at either the federal or provincial level and enabled Macdonald by default to dominate the province. The brief episode of the Letellier affair, and Mercier's turbulent premiership a decade later, nonetheless revealed Quebec's potential ability to rock the federal boat, which it would do to far greater effect in the twentieth century.

The Maritime provinces were relatively tranquil, once the crisis occasioned by Nova Scotia's efforts to bring about the repeal of the British North America Act had been overcome. Compared with this episode, the controversies over separate schools in New Brunswick, land reform in Prince Edward Island, and railways in Nova Scotia did not seriously threaten the stability of the dominion or the peace of mind of its government. Generally speaking, relations between the dominion and the three Maritime provinces were of a routine nature, apart from the financial problems that all provinces shared to varying degrees.

Perhaps more than any other factor, partisanship determined the character of a province's dealings with the federal government. To use Donald Smiley's terminology, nineteenth-century Canadian parties were integrated rather than confederal, which is to say that there was no real distinction between federal and provincial organizations or personnel.[6] From a prime minister's standpoint, most of the provincial governments with which he had to deal could be classified as either friendly or hostile, depending on their partisan label. Friendly governments were those with which one shared patronage, information, and advice. Dealings with them were largely informal, and conflicts with them could usually be resolved discreetly and quietly, if they arose at all. Hostile governments were dealt with at arm's length and in a more formal and official manner. There was little incentive to accommodate one's interests with theirs; public and noisy disputes with them might actually be useful in rallying one's own supporters, in Parliament and in the constituencies.

The first Macdonald government enjoyed the support of friendly administrations in the two central provinces, at least until Blake became premier of Ontario in 1872, and faced a hostile government only in Nova Scotia. Mackenzie, by contrast, was on good terms with the Ontario and Nova Scotia governments but faced hostile governments in British Columbia, Prince Edward Island, and, until Letellier dismissed his advisers, Quebec. For a brief period after Joly's defeat, the restored Macdonald Conservatives were on good to excellent terms with every province except Ontario. However, Nova Scotia joined the hostile camp in 1882, and Quebec became hostile under Mercier in 1887, Manitoba under Greenway in 1888, and Prince Edward Island under Peters in 1891. The long Conservative regime of Macdonald and his successors from 1878 to 1896 thus provided the first instance of the cycle later identified by R. MacGregor Dawson: a dominion government takes office with the support of most provincial governments but, as its policies become more controversial, its provincial allies are defeated one by one. Finally, it too loses office and the cycle begins all over again.[7]

Some support for Dawson's interpretation is provided by the fact that grumbling over the National Policy tariff began soon after it was adopted and was reported to Macdonald by premiers in the outlying provinces, including Walkem of British Columbia, Pope of Prince Edward Island, and Norquay of Manitoba.[8] Anti-tariff sentiment contributed to the rise of Fielding in Nova Scotia and of Greenway in Manitoba, premiers who were implacably hostile to Macdonald and the National Policy. Macdonald, however, gained little obvious gratitude from the province that the National Policy eventually benefited the most: Ontario.

Macdonald's policies towards the provinces frequently placed the provincial wings of the Conservative party in an awkward position. The Conservative opposition leader in Nova Scotia, Adam Bell, complained to Macdonald in 1883 that it was difficult for the provincial party to take a position on the controversial question of the Pictou branch railway when it did not know the dominion government's intentions.[9] Bell's Ontario counterpart, W.R. Meredith, disagreed privately with Macdonald's practice of bringing provincial railways under federal jurisdiction, but he also urged Macdonald to stand firm against the Mowat government's demand for financial compensation. Meredith regretted the dominion statute of 1884, which had made the increase in Ontario's debt allowance retroactive to 1867, because the improvement in the province's financial situation had allegedly made Premier Mowat more popular.[10] While in office, Manitoba Conservatives urged Macdonald to abandon his rigid defence of the CPR monopoly, but once they were in opposition they became apprehensive that he would do so and thus enable the province's new Liberal government to share the credit. Despite their pleas, the monopoly clause was soon abandoned, and the provincial Conservative leader, D.H. Harrison, privately expressed his disappointment.[11]

By 1890 at least one prominent politician had concluded that federal and provincial party organizations should be entirely separated from one another. Sir Charles Tupper made this suggestion in a letter to his son, who had joined the Macdonald government when the elder Tupper went to London as high commissioner. Sir Charles considered it inevitable that in a diverse federation the provincial wings of any party would differ among themselves on many questions, and he believed that the ties between federal and provincial parties were a source of inconvenience and embarrassment to both.[12] Later in the same year he repeated the same observation in a letter to Macdonald, urging the prime minister to "sever all connection between the dominion Government and Provincial parties.[13] Perhaps Tupper's advice was premature in an age when parties depended on patronage, but it would be increasingly followed in the twentieth century, although more by Liberals than by Conservatives.

Although most intergovernmental relations, and certainly most intergovernmental conflicts, were between the dominion and one of the provinces, there were some multilateral conferences in the early years (see chapter 13). In addition, there were interprovincial relations that did not involve the dominion. The conference held at Quebec City in 1887 is the most celebrated example of the latter phenomenon, but not the only one. A few instances may be cited to show that provinces did interact with one another, either to deal with joint or common problems, to exchange information or advice, or to seek one another's support in their conflicts with the dominion.

In the early years after Confederation, interprovincial relations were hampered by the fact that provincial politicians did not know their counterparts in other provincial capitals and had often not visited any province but their own. Ontario-Quebec relations were less inhibited by these circumstances than were those between other provinces, because the two central provinces had been combined under one government since 1841. After Confederation, contacts between the other provinces gradually developed, particularly as they were integrated into the two-party system of central Canada. Manitoba's interaction with other provinces, although handicapped by distance and limited financial resources, was reinforced to some extent by the many Manitoba politicians who had migrated from either Quebec or Ontario. This asset was not possessed by British Columbia, which remained by far the most isolated of the provinces, in every sense, even after the CPR was completed.

The difficulty of developing interprovincial relations in the early years is perhaps illustrated by the fact that when Sandfield Macdonald's Ontario government in 1868 made a financial donation for the relief of distressed Nova Scotian fishermen, the Nova Scotia government acknowledged the gift by sending a dispatch to the secretary of state for the provinces in Ottawa.[14] Since the Annand government could hardly have been motivated by a concern for protocol or by deference to the superior status of the dominion, one must assume that it simply did not know the address of its Ontario counterpart.

Over the next decade interprovincial relations developed slowly and for essentially pragmatic reasons. Ontario and Quebec were thrust into some unavoidable intimacy by the necessity of sorting out their financial assets and liabilities in accordance with sections 112 and 113 of the British North America Act. The two governments mainly dealt with one another directly on this issue, rather than indirectly via the intermediary of the dominion. Ontario and Quebec also cooperated with one another, and with the dominion, in jointly funding a bridge across the Ottawa River at Portage-du-Fort. In 1870 New Brunswick sought to interest Quebec in jointly funding a railway between the two provinces, perhaps because it was dissatisfied with the dominion's slow progress on the Intercolonial project, but Quebec was not receptive to the suggestion.[16]

After the Conservative victory in the federal election of 1878 set the stage for the lengthy confrontation between John A. Macdonald and Oliver Mowat, Mowat seems to have pursued a deliberate strategy of developing friendly relations with other provincial governments, particularly those of a Liberal persuasion. Mowat and Premier Joly of Quebec exchanged friendly letters on party politics and other matters during Joly's brief term in office, although when Joly sought Mowat's help in resisting the dismissal of Letellier he received nothing more than an expression of sympathy.[17] Mowat sought to gain the support of Premier John Thompson of Nova Scotia, a Conservative, in his battle with Macdonald over the appointment of queen's counsel.[18] Although Thompson did not share Mowat's views on this issue, the two remained cordial even after Thompson moved to Ottawa as Macdonald's minister of justice. Mowat was more successful with W.S. Fielding, who headed a Liberal government in Nova Scotia from 1884 to 1896. Both premiers were distressed by Macdonald's decision to wrest control of the federal franchise away from provincial governments, and their correspondence on this issue launched what proved to be a durable relationship.[19] Prior to the Interprovincial Conference of 1887

Mowat sent his provincial secretary, A.S. Hardy, on a mission to Nova Scotia (described as "a holiday visit" since it took place in July and August) to find out whether Fielding was serious about wishing to separate from the dominion and, if not, whether the two Liberal governments could work together to bring about a reformed and more decentralized federalism. The mission was apparently reassuring on both counts.[20]

The Interprovincial Conference itself was a major step in the direction of closer horizontal relations among the provinces. Of the five provinces that attended, only Ontario and Nova Scotia were truly Liberal. Mercier, who played host, headed what was really a coalition of Nationalists and Rouges. Blair of New Brunswick was a Liberal who headed a coalition including some Conservatives, and Norquay of Manitoba was a reluctant Conservative who had been forced to adopt that label when his political opponents, most of whom were recent arrivals from Ontario, began to call themselves Liberals. Conservative Prince Edward Island did not send a delegation, nor did ostensibly non-partisan British Columbia, to which Macdonald had recently paid a triumphal visit on the newly completed CPR. Premier A.E.B. Davie expressed to Macdonald his disapproval of Mercier's motives in summoning the conference, and told the prime minister that British Columbia would send a delegation only if Macdonald wished it to do so.[21]

Following the conference, Fielding, Mowat, Mercier, and Blair continued to correspond among themselves in an effort to maintain a common front and to bring about the reform of Canadian federalism along the lines suggested in the conference resolutions. Efforts were also made to bring Prince Edward Island into the alliance, although without success. On Blair's suggestion, Mowat even wrote to the premier of Newfoundland, since Macdonald still hoped to lure that colony into Confederation, suggesting that Newfoundland should declare it would never join the dominion unless the reforms suggested at the Interprovincial Conference were implemented. Although Fielding believed that Newfoundland's entry would be to Nova Scotia's benefit, he agreed that the resolutions of the Interprovincial Conference should be publicized in Newfoundland.[22]

The common front suffered a severe loss when Mercier was dismissed from office in December 1891. For the next decade relations between the two central provinces were dominated by a renewed effort to resolve the question of their joint debt by arbitration, and constitutional questions were pushed into the background. Nonetheless, the Interprovincial Conference may have paved the way for the rise of Laurier to power and for the success of his government,

which included Blair, Fielding, and Mowat in the three most important portfolios as well as two other ex-premiers: Joly of Quebec and
Davies of Prince Edward Island.

The structures and processes, as opposed to the content, of intergovernmental relations developed gradually and through trial and
error. They were apparently given little or no attention at the conferences leading up to Confederation, perhaps because no one realized how complex and extensive relations between the two levels of
government would have to be. Insofar as intergovernmental relations were thought about in advance, the Fathers of Confederation,
and Macdonald in particular, tended to make the misleading analogy with relations between the imperial government and the colonies. The imperial-colonial relationship, especially as it had evolved
since the achievement of responsible government, was familiar to
British North American politicians, so the analogy was perhaps congenial. Sections 58 through 68 of the British North America Act, describing the unique office of lieutenant-governor, suggest that the
analogy with imperial-colonial relations influenced prevailing con-
cepts of federalism and intergovernmental relations, and the curious wording of Section 90, the basis for what K.C. Wheare called the
"quasi-federal" powers of reservation and disallowance, makes the
analogy explicit.[23]

Apart from the issues on the agenda and the prevailing ideas
about colonialism and federalism, the third major influence that
shaped the early pattern of intergovernmental relations was the
technology of transportation and communication as it existed at the
time. Modern telecommunications and air transport, which would
play an essential part in intergovernmental relations a century after
Confederation, of course did not exist. Even the railway and the telegraph had not yet attained a high level of development. The impact
of distance and isolation on the western provinces was emphasized
in chapter 6, but these factors affected all the provinces to varying
degrees.

By far the most important medium of communication between
the dominion government and the various provincial governments
was correspondence, the volume of which was enormous. Nineteenth-century politicians, not only in Canada but elsewhere, spent
much of their time writing letters, a fact that would be a boon to later
historians although it may not have been a pleasure to the politicians
themselves. Until the 1880s, when the typewriter made its appearance, this correspondence was always written out by hand, either by
the politicians themselves (whose penmanship was frequently atro-

cious) or by secretaries (whose penmanship was usually much better). Postal service to the more remote provinces was very slow, particularly before the Intercolonial and Canadian Pacific railways were completed. Service between Ottawa and Toronto or Ottawa and Quebec City, however, does not seem to have been much slower in John A. Macdonald's time than it is today.

If ordinary correspondence was too slow, the telegraph was always available. Its chief disadvantages were the cost, which led to a certain terseness of expression and a reluctance to use it for any but the most urgent messages, and the lack of security, since anyone familiar with the Morse code could intercept confidential communications. Elaborate codes were devised to overcome the latter problem, based on the principle of replacing each word with a word located a certain distance from it on a list of words that was available to both parties. To preserve secrecy, the number representing the interval between the real word and the substitute word would be changed from time to time. The telegraph was important in communicating with the more remote provinces but was not extensively used to communicate with Quebec and Ontario, since it offered a relatively slight saving in time.

While correspondence was heavily relied upon, meetings between heads of government or between federal and provincial ministers also took place. These meetings were normally of a bilateral character, apart from the six conferences on immigration that took place betwee 1868 and 1874 and the Interprovincial Conference of 1887, which would have been a federal-provincial conference had the Macdonald government not refused to attend.

In the early years after Confederation, contacts between the dominion and certain provincial governments were facilitated by the practice of the "double mandate," whereby it was possible to be a member of parliament and of a provincial legislature simultaneously. The exceptions were Nova Scotia and New Brunswick, which never allowed the practice. Four early premiers were members of the House of Commons at the same time as they headed provincial governments: Pierre Chauveau of Quebec, Amor de Cosmos of British Columbia, and John Sandfield Macdonald and Edward Blake, both of Ontario. Conversely, Sir George-Étienne Cartier was a member of the Quebec Legislative Assembly, as well as the House of Commons, while serving as the second-in-command in John A. Macdonald's government in Ottawa. The practice of the double mandate facilitated political alliances between federal and provincial governments and gave an intimacy to federal-provincial relations that was lost after its abolition in 1873. Since the meetings that took place as a result were informal and generally unrecorded, their numbers cannot be ascertained, but were doubtless considerable.

Apart from the special circumstances created by the double mandate, there were numerous visits to Ottawa by provincial delegations, often including the premier. Almost invariably such visitors stayed at the Russell House Hotel, located not far from the present site of the Château Laurier, whose clientele appears to have consisted almost entirely of persons seeking to influence, or do business with, the federal government. In the case of provincial delegations, the desired outcome was usually some amelioration of their financial relations with the dominion government, on which they all depended for the major part of their revenues. An interview with the minister of finance, and possibly with the prime minister, would usually be granted, and stood a fair chance of leading to the desired result. Other meetings might be held with friendly members of parliament from the province concerned as a means of placing additional pressure on the federal authorities.

It will probably never be possible to make a complete list of such visits, but a number that certainly took place may be noted. In 1872 the premier of New Brunswick, George Hathaway, visited Ottawa to discuss "better terms" for his province. In 1873 similar missions were undertaken by a new premier of New Brunswick, George King, and by a delegation of several ministers from Manitoba. In 1875 the visitors to the Russell House included another Manitoba delegation and the premier of British Columbia, George Walkem. (Walkem's concerns were not financial, but related to the Mackenzie government's failure to build the transcontinental railway that his province had been promised.) In 1879 and again in 1880 Premier J.-A. Chapleau of Quebec visited the capital to discuss finances and his efforts to dispose of the province's publicly owned railway system. Premier Walkem appeared again in 1880, this time to discuss the uncompleted graving dock at Esquimalt, and another New Brunswick delegation arrived the same year. In 1880 there were visits from the premier of Manitoba, John Norquay, and the attorney general of Nova Scotia, John Thompson. J.G. Wurtele, the provincial treasurer of Quebec, travelled to Ottawa to discuss Quebec's finances in 1883, as did Premier J.J. Ross in the following year. Premier Norquay of Manitoba made another visit in 1884. Premier Sullivan of Prince Edward Island made two visits in 1884 and two more in 1886. Premier Fielding of Nova Scotia travelled to Ottawa for discussions in 1885, as did Premier Blair of New Brunswick in 1887, Premier Greenway of Manitoba in 1888, and Premier Theodore Davie of British Columbia in 1892. Even Oliver Mowat appeared in Ottawa to discuss the question of Ontario's boundary with John A. Macdonald in 1889.[24]

Federal-provincial meetings outside Ottawa were less common, apart from the fence-mending visits of federal ministers to the provinces they represented in cabinet and in Parliament. John A. Macdonald generally preferred to let provincial delegations come to him, rather than vice-versa, and his example was followed by subsequent prime ministers. Although he travelled frequently to Toronto and Montreal, and spent every summer near Rivière-du-Loup on the lower St Lawrence, Macdonald rarely used these occasions to conduct federal-provincial diplomacy. He did meet at least twice with Mowat in Toronto, and in the summer of 1888 he met at his summer retreat with Premier Honoré Mercier to discuss the definition of Quebec's northern boundary.

A truly serious crisis in federal-provincial relations might bring a more formal visit of federal politicians to a provincial capital. In 1868, for example, both Macdonald and Cartier travelled to Halifax to dissuade Nova Scotia from its efforts to withdraw from the dominion. Since the Annand government refused to alter its views, the mission was a failure. Negotiations thereafter were conducted with Joseph Howe, who was really a private citizen with no mandate to represent his province. Since negotiations in Halifax might have reflected favourably on the provincial government, and since negotiations in Ottawa might have been embarrassing to Howe, it was decided to hold them on neutral territory in Portland, Maine, which was the eastern terminus of the Grand Trunk Railway. Sir John Rose, the minister of finance, represented the dominion and worked out with Howe the financial settlement that ended the crisis in Nova Scotia.

Federal emissaries were also sent to the western provinces, despite the extreme difficulty of transportation. In 1874 the Mackenzie government sent David Laird, the minister of the interior, to Manitoba to discuss that province's financial problems, and in the same year J.D. Edgar, a recently defeated member of parliament, was sent on a mission to British Columbia to see if that province would consent to some lessening of federal obligations under its terms of union. The Edgar mission was a failure, and frustrations over the CPR and other matters strained relations between British Columbia and the federal government for another decade. In an effort to improve matters, two governors-general, Lord Dufferin in 1876 and the Marquess of Lorne in 1882, travelled to British Columbia on missions that were more diplomatic than ceremonial. They were followed by the minister of justice, Alexander Campbell, in 1883. Campbell had injured his spine just before his mission, which was almost cancelled as a result, and was probably in pain for much of the summer. His enthusiasm for transcontinental railway projects was not enhanced by his journey across the United States on the Union Pacific and the Central Pacific, which he described as "an abomination – heat and dust intolerable – a desert for a thousand miles to pass through."[25] On arrival in California he had to wait for one of the boats that ran on irregular schedules up the coast. (Lord Dufferin, on his mission seven years earlier, had requested the use of a British warship for this phase of the journey, since he did not think it became the dignity of his office to sail up the coast with "a crowd of gold-diggers and Chinese washermen.")[26] Federal-provincial diplomacy could be almost as arduous as a military campaign.

Transportation had at least improved by the time the crisis over Manitoba schools erupted in the 1890s. At the same time as Parliament was considering remedial legislation in support of the Manitoba Catholics, the minister of justice, A.R. Dickey, was sent to Winnipeg in a last-ditch effort to negotiate a compromise with the provincial government. To add to the confusion, the governor general, Lord Aberdeen, was a highly partisan Liberal who had little confidence in his advisers. Without consulting the cabinet, Aberdeen sent Donald A. Smith (who had driven the last spike at Craigellachie in recognition of his role in financing the CPR) to Winnipeg on another negotiating mission quite independent of the government's efforts. Neither Dickey nor Smith was able to accomplish anything.

In contrast to these exercises in crisis management, John A. Macdonald's western tour in 1886, which has been memorably described in the memoirs of his private secretary, was more of a ceremonial occasion.[27] Its purpose was to celebrate the completion of the CPR, which had left British Columbia in unaccustomed good humour, and to impress western voters, who gave Macdonald's party fourteen out of a possible fifteen seats in the general election a year later. This was the only occasion in his long life when Macdonald ventured west of Lake Huron, although he had represented Victoria in the House of Commons from 1878 to 1882. It was also the only western visit by an incumbent Canadian prime minister prior to 1910.

The extreme difficulty of communicating with British Columbia, as well as the many disputes between the dominion and that province, led Macdonald to adopt an unusual expedient following his return to office in 1878. Joseph Trutch, who had been appointed the first lieutenant-governor of British Columbia in 1871, had continued to correspond with Macdonald after the latter lost office in the wake of the Pacific Scandal. Trutch's term ended in 1876 and his successor, a Liberal lawyer from Brockville, Ontario, named Albert Richards, was unpopular with the British Columbia politicians. When Macdonald returned to office he retained Richards as lieutenant-governor but ignored him as much as possible. To handle the real business between the two governments he appointed Trutch as "dominion Resident Agent in British Columbia" at a salary almost equal to that of a deputy minister. This arrangement continued even after a Conservative lieutenant-governor was appointed in 1881. It was terminated shortly after the completion of the CPR main line, which both facilitated communication and removed the principal issue between the two governments.

While visits to and from the provinces were important, they could not deal with more than a fraction of the business that arose, and governments inevitably relied heavily on correspondence. Each year literally thousands of letters, memoranda, and other documents flowed back and forth between Ottawa and the provincial capitals. Major controversies over provincial boundaries, fiscal federalism, railways, separate schools, and other weighty matters could drag on for years, through the lifetime of several provincial governments. Other subjects of concern, such as Indians and liquor licensing, never attained quite the same level of intense controversy but were likely to recur from time to time. The nature of the federal constitution, despite Lord Atkin's celebrated and inaccurate metaphor of the ship with watertight compartments, contributed to a considerable amount of routine business involving both levels of government. The federal power of disallowance, and the knowledge by individuals and interest groups that it existed, brought a great deal of provincial legislation and policy under the scrutiny of the federal authorities, while federal policies regarding railways, fisheries, tariffs, banking, and other matters affected the economies and political interests of the provinces. Agriculture and immigration were explicitly stated to be shared fields of jurisdiction and the administration of justice was certainly so *de facto*, with responsibility for the subject being divided in a complex but generally effective way between the federal government and the provinces. Provincial governments frequently requested and received military aid to deal with riots, strikes, and other disturbances.[28] All of these various matters contributed to the high volume, as well as the heterogeneous character, of intergovernmental relations.

For either a federal or a provincial government, two choices had to be made in dealing with any item on the lengthy agenda. These choices might be described as vertical and horizontal classification.

Vertical classification means the level at which the matter would be dealt with; for example, by the full government in its formal capacity, by the prime minister alone, by another minister, or by subordinate officials. Horizontal classification means the way in which responsibility for dealing with the matter would be divided between departments.

In practise, vertical classification was a fairly simple matter in most cases. Government was smaller and simpler then than now, and appointed officials were not expected to exercise much independent authority. Almost any matter of consequence would require an Act of Parliament (or of the provincial legislature), the inclusion of an item in the estimates, an order in council (eg, disallowance), or at least a minute of council formally setting out the government's position on the issue. Horizontal classification involved choices that were less obvious: what channels would be used to communicate with the other level of government, how would incoming messages be processed and dealt with, and on whose recommendation would action be taken?

One approach would be to distribute responsibility for intergovernmental relations among the various departments of government, depending on whether the specific topic fell under the rubric of justice, finance, agriculture, or whatever. The other approach would be to centralize primary responsibility for intergovernmental relations in one agency in the same way that the British Colonial Office had primary responsibility for dealing with the subordinate governments of the empire or as the foreign office of any sovereign state dealt with the foreign offices of other sovereign states.

The second approach was perhaps suggested by the analogy that was frequently drawn between the imperial-colonial relationship and the dominion-provincial relationship. That analogy, of course, was given substance by the federal power to disallow provincial legislation, the financial dependence of the provincial governments on federal subsidies, and the ambiguous position of the lieutenant-governor as both a federal officer and the formal head of a provincial government. No one doubted in the early years that the British North America Act made the provincial governments subordinate to the federal government. For John A. Macdonald and others of like mind this fact was the principal virtue of the constitution, distinguishing it from American federalism. For opponents of Confederation the same fact was the principal reason for their opposition. Thus a "colonial office" in Ottawa might seem the natural and appropriate mechanism for dealings with the provinces.

Prior to Confederation the United Province of Canada, the regime under which federal politicians from central Canada had gained their early political experience, had had a provincial secretary responsible for conducting, receiving, and recording the government's official corresondence as well as for certain other functions such as being the custodian of official seals. Official correspondence included communications with the imperial government, via the governor general, as well as correspondence with assorted individuals, business enterprises, churches, interest groups, municipalities, and so forth that sought to influence government policy or to conduct some transaction with the state. Confederation added a new category of correspondence whose volume would be difficult to predict in advance: correspondence between the dominion and provincial governments. Would this be handled in the same way as other official correspondence or by a special agency? If the latter, would the special agency be merely a channel of communication or would it become a sort of "colonial office," a central agency for dominion-provincial relations? That was how the question posed itself to the federal authorities, but each province whether old (the Maritimes), new (Manitoba), or re-established after an interval of forced unification (Quebec and Ontario) had to make an analogous decision for itself.

When Sir John A. Macdonald formed the first dominion government in 1867 it included, in succession to the old provincial secretary of the United Province of Canada, two secretaries of state: Hector Langevin as secretary of state of Canada and Adams George Archibald as secretary of state for the provinces. Archibald was a Nova Scotian, one of four Maritimers in a government of thirteen members. It is possible that his office was designed to reassure the two smaller provinces that their interests would be taken into account by a central government that was inevitably dominated by, and located in, central Canada.[29] This reassurance was required particularly in Archibald's own province, where anti-Confederation sentiment was known to be widespread. In fact, Archibald, like all but one of the pro-Confederation candidates in Nova Scotia, failed to win a seat in the House of Commons when the first general election took place in September 1867.

Less than three weeks after Confederation, the four provincial governments were officially advised that all correspondence with the dominion should be directed to Archibald's department.[30] The position of undersecretary of state for the provinces, or deputy minister, was filled by E.A. Meredith, a veteran civil servant with twenty years of service in the United Province of Canada. The other personnel consisted of a chief clerk, two first-class clerks, a clerk, and a messenger. According to a report prepared by Meredith about a year later, the duties of these personnel were as follows. The undersecretary conducted the correspondence and generally supervised the office. The chief clerk helped with the correspondence and took the place of the undersecretary when the latter was absent. One of the first-class clerks was in charge of the register and letterbook records, while the other had the task of copying letters, dispatches, and other documents. All of these personnel had served for more than twenty years before Confederation. The other clerk, the only francophone in the department, had joined the public service only a few months before Confederation. Officially his duties were to assist in copying letters and documents, but may have included some translation.[31] The extent of bilingual capability among the more senior personnel is not known. While the size of the establishment seems absurdly small by modern standards, it might be noted that the Colonial Office in London, responsible for administering the largest empire in history and communicating with several dozen colonial governments, had only sixty-seven personnel in 1870.[32]

Although the lieutenant-governors of the provinces generally followed instructions and directed official correspondence to the secretary of state for the provinces, Archibald's failure to win a seat in Parliament undermined the effectiveness of his department and placed its future in considerable doubt. Archibald offered to resign from the cabinet as soon as his electoral defeat occurred in September, but was apparently persuaded to remain in office for another seven months, until April 1868.[33] However, he played practically no part in the negotiations with Nova Scotia that took place after that province elected a government committed to seeking the province's withdrawal from Confederation. Those negotiations were largely conducted on the federal side by Macdonald and by John Rose, the minister of finance, while on the provincial side, since the Annand government refused to negotiate, they were conducted by Joseph Howe, a member of the House of Commons who held no provincial office. Since Howe was not part of the provincial government, correspondence with him was unofficial and was not even routed through Archibald's department. Even if it had been, no substantive decision could have been made by a minister who had been discredited by his failure to win a seat.

The abolition of the department was apparently considered as early as March 1868. Not surprisingly, the most vigorous opposition to this course of action came from its deputy minister, E.A. Meredith. In a letter to Macdonald towards the end of the month, Meredith claimed that his department had dealt with 250 different questions or subjects since December.[34] He predicted that the volume of correspondence routed through the department would increase as new provinces were added and as a normal relationship between Nova Scotia and the central government was restored. For these reasons he argued that the department was needed and should be retained as a separate entity. However he suggested, somewhat inconsistently, that it should be given two new and unrelated responsibilities: to process requests for the pardoning of persons convicted of criminal offences in the provincial courts, and to be responsible for the Civil Service Board that the government hoped to establish and that would have general supervisory powers over the recruitment of personnel for the public service.

This letter was occasioned by the fact that Macdonald's government was in the process of giving a statutory basis to the departments that had been hastily established by order in council immediately after Confederation. A series of statutes establishing various departments were adopted and received royal assent in May 1868, but, despite Meredith's pleas, no specific legislative provision was made for the Department of the Secretary of State for the Provinces. Furthermore, no minister was appointed in succession to Archibald, and the office remained vacant for more than eighteen months after Archibald's resignation. The department, however, was not abolished. Provision was made in the Salaries Act for its personnel, and it continued under Meredith's direction to process official correspondence, even though the secretary of state for the provinces, to whom such correspondence was addressed, did not exist after Archibald's resignation was accepted. In June, two months after Archibald's resignation, Meredith actually predicted that "the work of the Department must of necessity increase," and he recommended that the number of personnel be increased from six to eight.[35]

The department received a new lease on life in November 1869 when Joseph Howe finally agreed to enter Macdonald's government and to fight the obligatory by-election on a pro-Confederation platform. Ironically, but perhaps appropriately, the man who had been Confederation's most prominent opponent only two years previously was sworn in as secretary of state for the provinces. A few weeks later, after Howe had won his by-election, he also became superintendant-general of Indian affairs, an office that was not considered a cabinet post in its own right but that had previously been occupied by Langevin as secretary of state. Langevin was shifted to the more important portfolio of Public Works, and Senator J.C. Aikins of Ontario, a former Grit, became secretary of state.[36]

Soon after assuming his portfolio, Howe instructed all lieutenant-governors to direct their official correspondence to his office.[37] At

Macdonald's suggestion, the departments of the federal government were officially advised not to correspond directly with their provincial counterparts, but to correspond by way of the secretary of state for the provinces.[38] This instruction was followed in most cases, but not universally. The Department of Agriculture, responsible also for immigration, found the rule inconvenient, because both of its responsibilities were shared with the provinces according to Section 95 of the BNA Act, and this overlapping jurisdiction required frequent communication between the two levels of government. In January 1872 an order in council specifically exempted the Department of Agriculture from the general rule, leaving it free to correspond directly with its provincial counterparts on the subject of immigration.[39]

In March 1870 a bill "to provide for the organization of the Department of the secretary of state for the Provinces" was introduced in the Senate and quickly adopted by that House, in which the government had an overwhelming majority. When Howe introduced the measure in the House of Commons, however, a debate ensued. Opposition leader Alexander Mackenzie introduced a motion to the effect that the exigencies of the public service did not require giving statutory basis to another department. Macdonald then moved to adjourn the debate and the measure was allowed to die.[40] For the rest of its brief life, the department continued to be based solely on an order in council. Howe's influence in the government, never very great, declined as the threat of separatism in Nova Scotia receded. In May 1873 he resigned from the cabinet to accept the position of lieutenant-governor of Nova Scotia, although his death on the first day of June prevented him from ever actually assuming the duties of that office.

A few days before Howe resigned, royal assent was given to an act that, when it came into effect in July, ended the department's existence.[41] In its place the act established the Department of the Interior, which was modelled after the department of the same name in the United States. It was responsible for the administration of the territories (including what are now Alberta and Saskatchewan) and of all crown land belonging to the dominion. The minister of the interior was also declared to be ex officio the superintendant-general of Indian affairs, although the two offices were separated temporarily from 1883 to 1887. Meredith became deputy minister of the interior, and most of the staff of the Department of the Secretary of State for the Provinces followed him into the new department. However, the act declared that the secretary of state of Canada, rather than the minister of the interior, would have charge of official correspondence with the provinces, and the lieutenant-governors were officially informed of this change a day after the act came into effect. Alexander Campbell, the first minister ot the interior, wrote to Macdonald a few weeks later suggesting that correspondence with the western provinces, although not with the others, should be directed through his department, and claiming that he had understood this to be Macdonald's original intention.[42] Macdonald's reply, if any, has apparently not been preserved, but Campbell continued to receive dispatches from the lieutenant-governor of Manitoba until the Macdonald government resigned over the Pacific Scandal in November. In this and other ways Manitoba, which had been granted provincial status with extreme reluctance, was treated more like a territory than a province during its first few years.

As a general rule, official correspondence with provincial governments was directed through the Department of the Secretary of State after 1873. However, that department did not become a central agency responsible for federal-provincial relations, any more than the Department of the Secretary of State for the Provinces had been one before 1873. A great deal of unofficial correspondence between federal and provincial politicians took place through other channels, just as it had done before 1873. Even the correspondence that did go through the secretary of state usually originated with, or was referred to, another department or the cabinet as a whole. The secretary of state's department was not really a policy-making, or even a policy-implementing, institution. At least two secretaries of state, Richard Scott (1874–78) and J.-A. Chapleau (1882–92), were politicians of considerable stature, but the portfolio gave them no political influence additional to what they would have possessed in any event as the acknowledged leaders of political machines in eastern Ontario and western Quebec, respectively.

Although neither the Department of the Secretary of State for the Provinces nor, after its demise, the Department of the Secretary of State, ever really attained the status of a central agency for dominion-provincial relations, a department that came much closer to doing so was the Department of Justice. Apart from any other circumstances, the pre-eminence of the Department of Justice in the first dominion government was assured by the fact that Sir John A. Macdonald occupied the position of minister of justice himself, in addition to being prime minister. He did so in part because the position of prime minister was not officially recognized and entitled its occupant to no salary, so that a prime minister was virtually required to hold a ministerial portfolio. (The same was also true of provincial premiers.) Justice was the logical choice for Macdonald because he was a prominent lawyer who had been attorney general for Canada West in the United Province of Canada, and because the administration of justice, more than any other aspect of public policy, was his lifelong interest. The minister of justice also controlled the most sought-after patronage: appointments to the superior, county, and district courts of the various provinces. His department provided legal advice to the dominion government and represented that government in litigation before the courts. No department could have better suited Macdonald's objective of moulding the new federal state and its constitution "until the gristle hardens into bone." In addition, it provided him with the administrative resources that modern prime ministers derive from the Privy Council Office, an institution that did not yet exist.

An important asset to Macdonald in the Justice portfolio was his deputy minister, Hewitt Bernard, with whom he enjoyed an unusually close relationship, both personal and professional. Like most senior public servants in the early years after Confederation, Bernard was a veteran of the public service of the United Province in which he had been deputy minister of justice for Canada West since 1864. The Macdonald-Bernard partnership went back even further than that, however, since Bernard had been Macdonald's private secretary between 1858 and 1864.[43] Bernard probably introduced Macdonald to his sister, Susan Agnes Bernard, whom the prime minister married a few months before Confederation.

Macdonald and his government resigned on account of the Pacific Scandal in November 1873, but Bernard remained as deputy minister of justice for almost three years under the Liberal government of Alexander Mackenzie. For most of that time Bernard effectively ran the department. Mackenzie was a building contractor by occupation rather than a lawyer, and logically took the portfolio of Public Works. There were four ministers of justice during the five years of his government, and all except Edward Blake, who held the portfolio from May 1875 to June 1877, were weak and ineffective. Blake, who was Macdonald's equal as a lawyer although not as a politician, took his duties seriously and performed them well. Two of the other three merely initialled the reports written by Bernard and by Bernard's successor, Zebulon A. Lash. Ironically for a government that ostensibly opposed the centralism of Macdonald, eighteen acts were disallowed in five years. Two-thirds of these were while Bernard was deputy minister. Thus while his famous brother-in-law languished in opposition, Bernard tried to perpetuate the Macdonaldian concept of federalism through much of the Liberal interlude. Lash, recruited by Blake, was an equally effective deputy minister and retained his position for almost four years after the Conservatives returned to office. Subsequent deputy ministers George Burbidge, Robert Sedgewick, and Edmund L. Newcombe maintained the position of the Department of Justice as the most important department of government and as the lead agency for federal-provincial relations.

As minister of justice, Blake maintained a close relationship with Oliver Mowat, who had succeeded Blake himself as premier of Ontario, although Blake firmly defended federal interests when the policies or interests of the two governments diverged. Thus the Mackenzie government was not dominated by Ontario, as it easily might have been, but at the same time it avoided open conflict between the dominion and the largest province such as occurred after the federal Conservatives returned to office in 1878. Blake played a less important role in relations with the other provinces, although his scepticism about the CPR contributed to the hostility between the Mackenzie government and British Columbia.

The Department of Justice retained an important role in federal-provincial relations after the Conservative restoration, although James McDonald, the minister from 1878 until 1881, was not particularly effective or successful. McDonald's successor, Senator Alexander Campbell, had been Sir John A. Macdonald's law partner but was also friendly with Oliver Mowat, with whom the prime minister was barely on speaking terms. Less of a centralist and more inclined to sympathize with provincial viewpoints than Macdonald, Campbell helped to maintain the necessary degree of cooperation between the dominion and the largest province, despite the mutual hostility of the two leaders. (After leaving the Justice portfolio he continued to play the role of go-between, although with less success, as postmaster-general and finally as lieutenant-governor of Ontario from 1887 until his death in 1892.) Campbell's diplomatic skills were also put to good use during his mission to British Columbia in 1883, which helped to resolve most of the outstanding difficulties between the two governments and paved the way for Macdonald's triumphant visit three years later.

Campbell's successor as minister of justice was John S.D. Thompson, who held the portfolio for more than nine years until his death. For the last two of these years Thompson was also prime minister, so that the combination of the two offices in one person was revived, for a brief period, after a lapse of nearly twenty years. Although his biographer claims that Thompson was less of a centralist than Macdonald, he was certainly more of a centralist than Campbell.[44] Nonetheless, he was on reasonably good terms with Mowat, with whom he had corresponded since about 1880 when Thompson was attorney general of Nova Scotia. Thompson was the most influential minister, next to John A. Macdonald, in the last six years of Macdonald's government, and he effectively ran the government during the nominal prime ministership of Senator J.J. Abbott after Macdonald's death. Thompson's reports on various legal issues, and his annual reports on provincial legislation, were as good as those written earlier by Macdonald and Blake.

Apart from Justice, the federal department that played the largest role in federal-provincial relations was the Department of Finance. Its involvement was unavoidable because the provinces, apart from Ontario, constantly bombarded the federal government with financial demands: higher subsidies, larger debt allowances, payment for railways and other public works built at provincial expense, and compensation for assorted injuries attributed to federal policies. Provinces also frequently requested that a portion of their subsidy be paid in advance of the usual date, a request that was almost always complied with although interest would be charged. The satisfaction of such demands, as well as the financial obligations to the provinces that were written into the BNA Act, made up a large portion of the total expenditure by the federal government. Perhaps the most important task of the minister of finance, apart from determining the rates of customs and excise in the annual budget, was to decide which of these provincial demands were reasonable and which the federal government could afford to respond to. His decisions were of critical importance to the provinces, for subsidies from the dominion accounted for well over half their revenues in the early years, and for 43 per cent of the revenues as late as 1896.

The task of guarding the public purse against provincial demands was ably performed by two capable deputy ministers, John Langton from Confederation until just before the election of 1878 and John M. Courtney from that date until 1906. Both served until they reached the age of retirement. Langton was not actually deputy minister of finance until 1870, when the position was established for the first time, but prior to that date he performed most of the same duties with the title of auditor.[45]

Although Langton and Courtney generally supplied the arguments against agreeing to provincial requests, their ministers were more inclined, for political reasons, to be generous. A notable exception to the rule, however, was Richard Cartwright, the minister of finance in the Mackenzie government, whose hostility to any kind of public expenditure bordered on fanaticism and who had little sympathy for any province except his own Ontario, which had no need for federal largesse. (In an often quoted comment on the 1891 election, Cartwright referred to the Maritime and western provinces as "the shreds and patches of the dominion.")[46]

Cartwright's rigidity contributed to his party's electoral defeat in 1878, although there were other reasons for its unpopularity. Other ministers of finance were far more flexible and responsive to provincial arguments, particularly in periods prior to a federal election. Conservatives were perhaps more fearful than Liberals of the possibility that frustrated provinces might impose direct taxation, which would fall mainly on corporations and the rich. In addition, the high protective tariffs imposed by the Conservatives after 1878, and the improvement in economic conditions, gave them more revenue with which to be generous than Mackenzie's government had enjoyed. However, Conservative generosity to the provinces had been apparent even before 1873 in the "better terms" granted to Nova Scotia, the financial inducements that lured British Columbia and Prince Edward Island into Confederation, and the increase in provincial debt allowances in 1873.

It may also be significant that apart from Cartwright and Francis Hincks, no minister of finance was from Ontario, the one province that required no financial concessions. Even Hincks had tenuous ties with Ontario, although he represented an Ontario riding in Parliament for most of the time he held the Finance portfolio. Leonard Tilley, who had led New Brunswick into Confederation, succeeded Hincks early in 1873 and began a tradition of Maritime ministers of finance that was not broken, except by the five years of Cartwright, until 1911. Tilley returned as minister of finance after 1878 and was then followed by Archibald McLelan and Charles Tupper, both Nova Scotians, and George Foster, a New Brunswicker. The Laurier Liberals continued that tradition with W.S. Fielding, previously premier of Nova Scotia, who held the Finance portfolio for fifteen years. Possibly their background inclined all these ministers to sympathize with provincial governments that found themselves in straitened circumstances.

Other ministers, regardless of the portfolio they held, played informal but important parts in maintaining relations with the governments of the provinces from whence they came, particularly if those governments were politically friendly, but sometimes even if they were not. This phenomenon was particularly important for Quebec, where political issues tended to be different from elsewhere and where prime ministers had difficulty in crossing the linguistic barrier, but some evidence of it can be found in other provinces as well. Sir George-Étienne Cartier was the prototypical Quebec lieutenant,

to whom Macdonald effectively delegated authority to deal with
Quebec and who largely controlled the provincial government. Cartier's power was reinforced by the double mandate, which was more
extensively used in Quebec than elsewhere. His shoes were never
really filled after his death, but prime ministers after 1873 still relied
on important Quebec ministers such as Letellier, Langevin, and
Chapleau to penetrate the political thickets of *la belle province*. In the
1880s the rivalry between Langevin and Chapleau, as well as between the factions they more or less represented, complicated relations with Quebec. To some extent the antagonism between Tupper
and Thompson, although less ideological in character, complicated
relations with Nova Scotia.

At the provincial level, arrangements for conducting intergovernmental relations were even less elaborate than at the federal level.
Provincial governments had limited functions and all, apart from
Ontario, suffered from serious financial problems. Their public services and cabinets were thus very small, and excessive specialization
in the functions of ministers and departments was a luxury that
could not be afforded. Presumably for this reason, no province is
known to have contemplated establishing a specialized agency or department for intergovernmental relations.

In any event, the key actor in a province's relations with the central government, then as now, was the premier. This office had no
formal existence in any province, but apart from Manitoba prior to
1874, where the lieutenant-governor was the effective head of the
administration, the existence of such an office was generally recognized.

Like federal prime ministers, provincial premiers were obliged to
hold a ministerial portfolio to receive a salary. A lawyer who was
asked to form a provincial government normally became attorney
general. This was the most prestigious portfolio in any government
and was also considered good preparation for a judicial appointment, which many provincial politicians considered more attractive
than the premiership itself. Premiers who were not lawyers usually
chose to be provincial secretary, an office whose miscellaneous duties resembled those of the secretary of state at the federal level,
and included responsibility for sending and receiving official correspondence.

The extent and character of a premier's correspondence with the
federal government and prime minister depended less on the office
he held than on political circumstances. The antipathy between John
A. Macdonald and Oliver Mowat reduced correspondence between
them to a minimum, but this was compensated for by Mowat's

friendly relations with two federal ministers of justice, Campbell and Thompson. Honoré Mercier, however, had no friends in the federal government and rarely corresponded with any one in Ottawa. For any provincial government, a certain amount of official correspondence with the central government was unavoidable, but unofficial political correspondence of the kind that was common between political allies varied enormously in volume from province to province and from time to time depending on the circumstances.

Apart from the premier, one provincial official who was inevitably involved in federal-provincial relations was the treasurer. The financial aspects of intergovernmental relations involved all provincial treasurers in voluminous correspondence, occasional visits to Ottawa, and negotiations that were sometimes difficult, acrimonious, and frustrating. Since the scope for provincial taxation was limited both by the BNA Act and by socioeconomic realities, extracting concessions from the federal government was in fact a more important aspect of the treasurer's job than formulating fiscal policy. Skill, patience, good timing, and good political connections, although not necessarily in that order, were the essential ingredients of success in this essential task. It might have been expected that provincial premiers would hold the Treasury portfolio themselves in view of its obvious importance, but William Annand of Nova Scotia and Robert Davis of Manitoba were the only premiers between 1867 and the turn of the century who combined the two offices for any considerable length of time.

Financial largesse was certainly an important way of influencing provincial governments, although J.A. Maxwell's assertion that no fiscal concession was ever made to a government headed by political opponents is exaggerated and excessively cynical.[47] Another instrument at the dominion government's control was patronage. In addition to the countless minor offices that were used to sway the loyalties of community leaders and ordinary voters, there were at any one time about 160 federally appointed judges, about half as many senators, a dozen or more positions in the dominion cabinet, and assorted other prestigious offices such as lieutenant-governorships, the high commissioner in London, and the agent-general in Paris. Some of these offices were important enough to interest prominent provincial politicians, and some provincial politicians were not shy about saying so. Even Martin Wilkins, the attorney general in the separatist government of Nova Scotia, brazenly informed John A. Macdonald in April 1870 that he would like to be considered for the bench.[48] Wilkins was not appointed, but others, perhaps more deserving, were more fortunate.

In response to Lieutenant-Governor Hastings Doyle, who had earlier informed Macdonald that Wilkins might be interested in a judicial appointment, the prime minister virtuously asserted: "I have always taken the position that fitness for the bench – not politics – must be the first consideration in judicial appointments." Macdonald qualified this principle slightly by admitting that "generally I think the attorney general of any province has a strong claim."[49] A more off-the-record comment by Prime Minister Mackenzie Bowell in 1895 was to the effect that "we will have to do the best we can in the interests of justice and – what is equally important – the party."[50] The context of the latter remark was an abortive scheme to get rid of the troublesome Premier Blair of New Brunswick by making him chief justice of the province.

Macdonald did appoint a number of provincial premiers to the bench, including Mousseau of Quebec, Wetmore and King of New Brunswick, Sullivan of Prince Edward Island, and Walkem of British Columbia. Others were appointed to the cabinet or the Senate. A decade before his own appointment Walkem wrote to Macdonald urging the appointment to the bench of John McCreight, premier and attorney general, whom Walkem hoped to succeed as head of the British Columbia government. Macdonald replied by reminding Walkem that provincial attorneys general were not automatically entitled to judicial appointments.[51] At about the same time the attorney general of Manitoba, Henry Clarke, wished to be appointed to the bench. Macdonald informed Lieutenant-Governor Archibald that he had a low opinion of Clarke and would not appoint him. Writing to Clarke himself, Macdonald made the more tactful excuse that "you are too young and active a politician to be laid on the shelf as a Judge just now," and added he had refused to appoint McCreight for the same reason.[52]

Both patronage and the power of the purse were political resources for the dominion, as were the more draconian powers of reservation and disallowance (see chapters 8 and 9), and the support of the imperial government (see chapter 10). Yet despite all of these assets, and despite Macdonald's remarkable gifts as a politician, the widely held belief that the provinces were mere subordinate appendages of the dominion during Macdonald's lifetime is totally inaccurate. With the exception of Manitoba and perhaps British Columbia, the provinces very rapidly escaped from the subordination to which Macdonald might have wished to consign them. By 1885 A.V. Dicey could observe quite accurately that Canadian government was closer in spirit to American federalism than to the unitary British constitution mentioned in the preamble of the BNA Act.[53]

In other ways as well the early history of Canadian federalism suggests the obvious fact that institutional arrangements, however ingenious, cannot easily overcome the social, economic, and political realities that determine the distribution of effective power. The Department of the Secretary of State for the Provinces was a notable failure. Whether it was ever intended to be a real central agency for federal-provincial relations, it was in practice no more than a sort of post office that received correspondence and directed it to the appropriate recipient, and even in that regard it was frequently bypassed. The same could be said about the Department of the Secretary of State after 1873. Intergovernmental relations were in practise conducted mainly by the prime minister, and only if the Department of the Secretary of State for the Provinces had been headed by the prime minister could it have acquired real importance.

The Department of Justice, in contrast, benefited from the fact that it was headed by the prime minister during the formative years up to 1873, as well as by the close relationship between Macdonald and his deputy minister, Bernard. Its importance was less thereafter, in spite of the fact that the power of disallowance continued to be exercised on its advice or on that of its minister. The Department of Finance assumed an equal or even greater importance in federal-provincial relations because so many provincial demands were financial. The prime minister, however, continued to dominate the process of intergovernmental relations, as is still the case today. This was particularly so when Macdonald held the office, in view of his great prestige and his extensive network of contacts and acquaintances across the country.

8 The Role of the Lieutenant-Governor

No aspect of Canada's constitution illustrates the awkwardness of attempting to combine federalism with monarchical government more clearly than the office of lieutenant-governor. In his classic book on this peculiar institution, John Saywell has rightly described it as unique.[1] Certainly it demonstrates the characteristically Canadian penchant for relying on experience and the incremental adaptation of existing institutions to new circumstances, rather than on logic and abstract principles or theories. It also perhaps illustrates the perils and disadvantages of that aspect of our national character. For the office of lieutenant-governor early fell victim to two insoluble contradictions that reveal the confusion in the political thought of the Fathers of Confederation.

These contradictions may be posed in the form of questions. In the first place, since federalism by definition consists of two distinct and separate levels of government sharing sovereignty over the same territory and population, how can one and the same person be both an agent of one level of government and the formal head of the other? In the second place, since responsible government by definition requires both competing partisan politicians and an impartial head of state, how can one and the same person be both a party politician and the queen's impartial representative? Because this is a book about federalism and not a book about the office of lieutenant-governor, the second question will be considered only insofar as it affected the conduct of, or became an issue in, dominion-provincial relations. The two questions in practice were sometimes posed simultaneously, most notably in the context of the Letellier affair, which posed them in a particularly acute fashion.

Neither the office nor the title of lieutenant-governor was entirely new in 1867. As early as 1791 the official who represented the crown at Quebec (the capital of the most important colony) was styled the governor general of British North America, while the crown's representatives in the lesser colonies, such as Upper Canada and Nova Scotia, were referred to as lieutenant-governors. Although all were appointed directly by the imperial government, and answerable to it, the lieutenant-governors were considered lower in status, as the title suggests. In practice, however, the pre-Confederation governor general, like a Habsburg Holy Roman Emperor, possessed little real power over his "lieutenants" and could best be considered as the first among equals.

Confederation made the title more appropriate and significantly modified the nature of the office. The power to appoint lieutenant-governors was transferred from the imperial government to the new dominion government, suggesting logically that the lieutenant-governor represented dominion rather than imperial interests. This new arrangement does not seem to have led to much controversy at the Quebec Conference, where Macdonald reassured the Maritime delegates that the lieutenant-governor would enjoy the same security of a tenure as a judge: "He should be independent of the Federal Government, except as to removal for cause, and it is necessary that he should not be removable by any new political party. It would destroy his independence. He should only be removable upon an address from the Legislature."[2]

Fourteen years later, when he was under irresistible pressure from his followers to remove Letellier from office, Macdonald may have regretted those words. At the time, the Maritimers seem to have raised few objections, but when the Quebec Resolutions were debated in the Canadian Parliament in 1865 the peculiar nature of the lieutenant-governor's office attracted some criticism. Members who pointed out the potential threat to responsible government at the provincial level included A.-A. Dorion, Christopher Dunkin, and, in one of the greatest ironies of Canadian history, Henri Joly.[3]

The British North America Act provided that the lieutenant-governor in each province would be appointed by the governor general (which everyone understood to mean on the advice of the dominion government) and would not be removable within five years of his appointment except for cause. (Despite Macdonald's remarks at Quebec, there was no mention of an address by the legislature, or by Parliament.) His salary would be paid by the dominion government, not by the province. Section 90 provided, in terse but awkward fashion, that a lieutenant-governor could either assent to or veto legislation, or else reserve it for the final decision of the governor general.

Since Confederation involved the re-establishment of distinct provinces of Quebec and Ontario, corresponding to the old Lower and Upper Canada, lieutenant-governors had to be found for those two provinces. Sir Narcisse Belleau, an experienced lawyer-politician who had been the nominal head of the last pre-Confederation government, was appointed for Quebec, and Major General H.M. Stisted, who commanded the British garrison in Ontario, was appointed the lieutenant-governor of that province. Military appointments were also made in the Maritimes, but these merely confirmed existing arrangements. Lieutenant-General William Fenwick Williams, who was already lieutenant-governor of Nova Scotia, was reappointed to that post by the dominion. Major-General Charles Hastings Doyle, who had administered the government of New Brunswick since the departure of Lieutenant-Governor Gordon in October 1866, became lieutenant-governor of New Brunswick. When Williams was recalled to England a few months after Confederation, Doyle replaced him in Nova Scotia (see chapter 5), and Colonel Francis Harding, who commanded the garrison in New Brunswick, succeeded Doyle as lieutenant-governor of New Brunswick. Stisted, Williams, Doyle, and Harding were all career British officers, although Williams had at least been born in Nova Scotia, and all returned to the United Kingdom after completing their terms.

This penchant for military appointments was a temporary expedient, and not intended to last. Of the forty appointments made between 1 January 1868 and the resignation of Tupper's government in 1896, all were Canadians, and practically all were politicians. Lieutenant-governors of the eastern and central provinces were all residents of the province to which they were appointed, although there was no legal requirement to this effect. Manitoba, reflecting its quasi-colonial status, had five of its first six lieutenant-governors appointed from outside the province. John A. Macdonald's three appointments to British Columbia were all British Columbians, although non-British Columbians were appointed by Prime Ministers Mackenzie and Abbott. Abbott's appointment of Edgar Dewdney, however, had been suggested by Premier Theodore Davie.[4]

If the forty appointments from 1868 through 1896 are classified in terms of the position that the lieutenant-governor held immediately prior to his appointment, the predominance of politicians, and indeed of federal politicians, becomes apparent. Thirteen were appointed directly from the dominion cabinet, and five others had served in a dominion cabinet at some time prior to their appointment. Excluding incumbent ministers, nine appointments were made from the Senate, seven from the House of Commons, and seven from the bench. Of the four who fall into none of these categories, Joseph Trutch (British Columbia) had been commissioner of lands and works in his province, Edward Chandler (New Brunswick) was a provincial politician, A.A. Macdonald (Prince Edward Island) was a postmaster and former provincial politician, and Albert Richards (British Columbia) was an Ontario lawyer who had served one term in the House of Commons.

Although Macdonald at least claimed that party politics was not the primary consideration in appointing a judge, the reasons for appointing a lieutenant-governor were almost always unabashedly political. Joseph Howe was appointed lieutenant-governor of Nova Scotia in 1873 because the Department of the Secretary of State for the Provinces, which he headed, had been abolished and Macdonald had no further use for him in the cabinet. Mackenzie planned to appoint Joseph Cauchon as lieutenant-governor of Quebec, but when Joly, the Rouge leader in Quebec, informed the prime minister that Cauchon was unacceptable, Cauchon was sent to Manitoba instead.[5] Macdonald reluctantly appointed L.-A. Masson, a Quebec judge and former cabinet colleague, as lieutenant-governor after repeatedly urging Masson to accept the more demanding position of premier.[6] Tilley was given a second term in New Brunswick, several years after his first, because the state of his health prevented him from continuing as minister of finance.[7] When Archibald McLelan accepted the vice-regal office in Nova Scotia "in order to facilitate the reconstruction of the Cabinet," Macdonald thanked him for his self-sacrifice and offered him a Senate seat at the end of his five-year term, but neither man lived long enough for the promise to be fulfilled.[8]

Nineteenth-century lieutenant-governors tended to be younger than more recent holders of the office. Most were appointed in their fifties, and a few in their forties. Although nine died in office and the four soldiers returned to the British Isles, some of the others pursued Canadian political careers after, as well as before, serving as lieutenant-governor. Tilley returned to his former position as minister of finance after serving five years as lieutenant-governor of New Brunswick, and then became lieutenant-governor again seven years later. Sir Adams Archibald was lieutenant-governor both of Manitoba and Nova Scotia, with a brief stint on the bench in between. Five former lieutenant-governors were appointed to the Senate before 1896 and three, including Archibald, to the bench. Archibald was elected to the House of Commons after serving as lieutenant-governor of Nova Scotia. Alexander Morris was elected to the Ontario legislature after serving a term in Manitoba. Joseph Trutch served as the dominion resident agent in British Columbia, a post he alone held, after his friend John A. Macdonald returned to power. A.-R. Angers was offered a cabinet portfolio by Macdonald, and again by Abbott after Macdonald's death, while serving as lieutenant-governor of Quebec.[9] He finally joined the Thompson government as minister of agriculture. Given these circumstances, it is hardly surprising that lieutenant-governors tended to carry out their duties in a partisan manner, and to offer highly political advice to the prime ministers who had appointed them.

It was natural for a lieutenant-governor to exchange political advice and information with his prime minister, particularly when the two were former cabinet colleagues who had worked together for years in Ottawa. Such political correspondence was entirely distinct from the official correspondence between the two levels of government, although that too was normally routed through the lieutenant-governor's office. The exchange of political information and advice with a friendly lieutenant-governor was particularly valuable to the dominion government when the provincial government was considered unreliable or hostile. Macdonald often relied on his lieutenant-governors for advice and information on developments in Quebec, the Maritimes, and the West, although he had other sources of information as well. Mackenzie was less fortunate in his viceregal appointments, although Letellier, who had been his minister of agriculture, was of some help in Quebec. Neither Macdonald nor Mackenzie needed much help from lieutenant-governors in Ontario, since both had extensive political roots in the province, and the office of lieutenant-governor was thus never as important in Ontario as elsewhere, at least until 1887, when Alexander Campbell was appointed. Campbell was one of Macdonald's oldest and most faithful followers, and had fifteen years of cabinet experience, but he was also more conciliatory towards Mowat than was Macdonald himself, so Macdonald did not always trust his judgment.

The relationship between prime minister and lieutenant-governor naturally became more distant when the lieutenant-governor was an appointee of the other party, a situation that first arose in several provinces when Alexander Mackenzie formed his government in 1873, and again when Macdonald returned to power five years later. Both prime ministers agreed that a lieutenant-governor in such circumstances should serve out his term of office, although Macdonald was forced to dismiss Letellier because of pressure from Quebec Conservatives who were understandably offended by Letellier's dismissal of the de Boucherville government. Macdonald did not correspond with the lieutenant-governors he inherited from Mackenzie. Mackenzie corresponded with only one of Macdonald's appointees: Alexander Morris in Manitoba.

Official correspondence between federal and provincial governments was supposed to be routed through the lieutenant-governor, in the same way that official correspondence between the imperial government and the dominion was routed through the governor general. Even this rule was violated in Ontario between 1874 and 1880. A few months after Mackenzie formed his government, Premier Mowat decided that official correspondence between the two Liberal governments should bypass the Conservative lieutenant-governor, J.W. Crawford, who had been appointed by Macdonald in 1872.[10] A provincial minute of council to this effect was communicated to the dominion. A year later, following Crawford's death in office, a dominion order in council stated that the privilege of bypassing the lieutenant-governor would be granted to Ontario, at that province's request, although not to any other province.[11] This anomalous situation lasted until February 1880, when the Macdonald government cancelled the special dispensation and directed Ontario to follow the same procedure for official correspondence as the other provinces.[12]

Although most lieutenant-governors enjoyed fairly tranquil terms in office, some did not. Possibly the most dramatic and unusual circumstances ever faced by a lieutenant-governor were those which Sir Charles Hastings Doyle faced as lieutenant-governor of Nova Scotia from October 1867 to May 1873.

Doyle came from a talented Anglo-Irish family (one of his cousins became famous as the creator of Sherlock Holmes) and was a professional soldier who had joined the British army at the age of fifteen. He had served in the Crimean War and had commanded the ground forces in the Maritime provinces since 1861. It is not clear whether his appointment was originally suggested by Macdonald or by Lord Monck, the governor general. Doyle did sometimes correspond directly with Monck and with Monck's successor, Sir John Young, an unconventional procedure for a post-Confederation lieutenant-governor. On one occasion he even asked Young to remove the first page of a letter before showing it to Macdonald.[13] Macdonald, however, seems to have had complete confidence in Doyle and wrote frequent and cordial letters to him. At times he would even make jokes: referring to his daughter Mary, born in 1868, the proud father invited the general to Ottawa to inspect his "infantry."[14]

Doyle brought with him from New Brunswick a private secretary named Harry Moody. More than half a century later Moody published an article claiming that Doyle had been lazy, politically naïve, and at best an amiable figurehead, and suggesting that Moody himself deserved the credit for keeping Nova Scotia in Confederation.[15] Little evidence has survived as a basis for evaluating these allegations and the historians seem to ignore Moody's role, whatever it was. Possibly the last word should therefore be left to John A. Macdonald, who wrote to Doyle in June 1872: "You have been of the greatest service to the cause of Confederation ever since the project was first mooted."[16]

Doyle arrived in Halifax a month after the September election that had given the anti-Confederates an overwhelming majority in both houses of the legislature. The old government, in accordance with normal procedure at that time, was still clinging to office. Doyle wrote to Howe, whom he considered the real leader of the anti-Confederation forces, even before leaving New Brunswick. He urged Howe to "give the dominion a fair trial" and to treat his defeated opponents with magnanimity, and at the same time he asked Howe's advice on who should be asked to form a government.[17] Howe, who had already met Doyle, made a friendly response, but his advice on the premiership was valueless since the anti-Confederation caucus rejected the person he proposed and chose William Annand as their leader instead. Doyle had nonetheless begun the task of detaching Howe from the militant anti-Confederates.

As lieutenant-governor, Doyle had to deal with a government whose behaviour was frequently provocative and bizarre, to prevent it from damaging the interests of the dominion but at the same time to avoid any crisis that would lead to its premature collapse and resignation. No alternative government could be formed from the existing legislature, where the anti-Confederate majority was overwhelming. A premature dissolution and election would almost certainly return another overwhelming anti-Confederate majority and would gravely weaken the cause of Confederation by demonstrating that the electorate were serious in their desire for repeal. Such an outcome might even cause the imperial government to reconsider its support for Confederation.

Doyle could do little but keep the dominion informed during the early months of his lieutenant-governorship, which were marked by the legislature's adoption of resolutions calling for repeal and by the dispatch of Howe's unsuccessful mission to the United Kingdom. In September 1868, about a month after Macdonald and his colleagues visited Halifax, an unusual situation arose. The attorney general, Martin Wilkins, made some remarks in the legislature suggesting that the Nova Scotia government might seek the help of the United States in extricating the province from Confederation. In the circumstances of British-American relations at the time, this was not considered amusing and could even be interpreted as treason. Doyle asked Wilkins to explain himself and Wilkins replied that he must have been misquoted, since he was incapable of disloyalty to the queen. Indeed, Wilkins wrote, it was precisely because of his loyalty to the queen that he opposed Confederation, which he believed would ultimately lead to the annexation of British North America by the United States. The legislature thereupon censured the lieutenant-governor for interfering with the free speech of one of its members.[18] This should logically have caused the government to resign or seek a dissolution, but the government, perhaps unwisely from its own point of view, did neither.

About a week after these events the legislature adopted a private member's bill that would prohibit the militia from leaving the province. This was obviously an anti-Canadian gesture rather than a measure having any practical significance, but it was just as obviously *ultra vires*. Doyle wired Macdonald for advice as to whether he should reserve it and Macdonald replied by telegraph the following day that he could send no official instructions, since there was no time to adopt an order in council. The prime minister advised Doyle to tell his ministers that the measure was *ultra vires*, but to assent if they persisted and if Wilkins officially advised that it was valid. Wilkins produced a memorandum, eccentric even for him, which in effect implied that defence was a concurrent jurisdiction. The following day he had second thoughts and produced an even stranger memorandum to the effect that the militia bill was not intended to alter the law, but merely to state what the law had been before Confederation. He now admitted that defence was an exclusive power of the dominion.[19] On the basis of this second opinion, Doyle decided to reserve the bill after all. Macdonald later told him that he had done the right thing.[20]

Early in 1869 Howe joined the dominion government and won his by-election, after the Macdonald government approved "better terms." Macdonald had no illusions that the Annand government would lose an early election. However, he was optimistic enough in June to write to Doyle that "you now, at last, have your ministry at your mercy." He congratulated Doyle for his handling of the situation. Doyle replied that he was glad to hear that Macdonald supported his efforts to avoid a confrontation with Annand, since both Howe and Charles Tupper had urged him to dismiss the government. Doyle considered he had no constitutional grounds to do so.[21]

In September Macdonald reported to Doyle a conversation he had had with Tupper. Tupper believed that Annand's control over his followers in the legislature was precarious and that Annand might therefore request, or try to provoke, a dissolution in order to win a fresh mandate. Macdonald advised Doyle that he still did not think a dissolution would be desirable and Doyle agreed, adding that he did not really expect Annand to ask for one.[22]

Meanwhile Annand was arguing that the "better terms" offered to Nova Scotia were inadequate and that further concessions should be made. Doyle appeared to have some sympathy for this viewpoint and decided to travel to Ottawa himself to present the province's case. He was dissuaded from this idea by Tupper, who thought it would embarrass the Macdonald government. Macdonald expressed relief that Doyle was not making the journey, since the lieutenant-governor's prestige might suffer if he returned from Ottawa without any concessions. Macdonald agreed, however, to meet a provincial delegation, as Doyle had suggested.[23]

In December 1869 Doyle risked a confrontation with Annand by refusing to authorize the premier's latest idea: a provincial mission to Washington to discuss commercial reciprocity.[24] This would have embarrassed both the dominion and the imperial government. The mission did not take place, but Annand still refused to resign. Perhaps the moment for doing so had passed, since anti-Canadian feeling was beginning to subside. The legislature was dissolved, at Annand's request, in April 1871 and the subsequent election returned the government with a greatly reduced majority and less than 52 per cent of the popular vote. In the same month the Treaty of Washington eliminated the faint possibility that the United States would intervene in support of the Nova Scotia separatists. The crisis was over. Doyle offered his resignation to Macdonald in 1872, but agreed to serve for another year when Macdonald declined the offer.[25] He returned to England in 1873 and was succeeded by Howe, who died within a month of his appointment, and then by Adams Archibald, who had already served as lieutenant-governor of Manitoba.

A task at least as difficult as Doyle's, although for somewhat different reasons, faced the first two lieutenant-governors of Manitoba. The prairie province attained provincial status long before it was ready for any form of self-government, and in the aftermath of what had virtually been a civil war. In 1870, when it became the fifth province of the dominion, Manitoba had never had either an election or a legislature, let alone responsible government on the Westminster model.

Adams Archibald, one of Nova Scotia's Fathers of Confederation, had been the secretary of state for the provinces for the first ten months of the dominion's existence and had finally entered the House of Commons in a by-election in September 1869. In a speech on the Red River uprising he expressed some sympathy for the Métis. Apparently for this reason he was appointed lieutenant-governor by Cartier, who was acting prime minister for three-and-a-half months in 1870 because Macdonald was seriously ill.[26]

Archibald arrived in Manitoba in September 1870 to find the new province in a state of chaos and without a functioning government of any kind. The only effective power was wielded by a detachment of British troops who had recently arrived in the province after a difficult and lengthy journey. To add to Archibald's woes, he was also lieutenant-governor of the North-West Territories, which were in an equally chaotic state and which continued to share a lieutenant-governor with Manitoba until October 1876.

Macdonald, who was back in his office and restored to health by late September, directed Archibald to play a more active role than the lieutenant-governors of the older provinces: "Although you are a Constitutional Sovereign, it is evidently necessary that, in the present state of affairs, you should be in fact a paternal despot. Much depends on the successful start of your legislative machine, and you would be quite justified in taking a personal interest in the result of the elections so as to secure the return of a body of respectable men representing the various races and interests."[27]

Archibald appointed Alfred Boyd, M.-A. Girard, and Henry Clarke (an Englishman, a French Canadian, and an Irish Catholic) to his executive council and followed Macdonald's advice by intervening decisively in the election, which took place in December. As Macdonald had hoped, the new legislature was reasonably representative of the province's diversity and the so-called Canadian party, mainly expatriate Grits from Ontario, occupied only a few of the seats. Archibald continued to be the effective head of the government, as he explained in a letter to Macdonald regarding the post-election shuffle of cabinet offices: "Before appointing them, I discussed with them individually the Policy which I had pursued, and intended to pursue, so as to see that they were prepared to give it a hearty support. This they have promised to do." Macdonald responded by congratulating Archibald on the outcome of the election and on the success of his administration to date.[28]

Less happy days were soon to follow. In October the Fenians attempted a raid against Manitoba, although the signing of the Treaty of Washington earlier in the year meant they could no longer expect any sympathy from the United States authorities. Louis Riel, who had returned to Manitoba after a brief exile, advised his armed followers to give the Fenians no support. Archibald, a Nova Scotian who did not understand the ethnic animosities of central Canada, publicly thanked the Métis leader and committed the politically fatal error of shaking his hand. The "Canadian party" now had the opportunity to repay Archibald for his role in the election campaign. The news of the handshake soon reached Ontario, where Riel's name was anathema. Joseph Howe, as secretary of state for the provinces, sent his fellow Nova Scotian a stiff rebuke: "You should not have shaken hands with Riel after the Fenian raid on Manitoba. This will cost us votes. Riel is a murderer. He didn't help to repel the Fenian raid anyway – merely armed his followers and waited to see the outcome before taking sides."[29]

Soon after receiving this letter, Archibald sent his resignation directly to the governor general. Receiving no reply, he sent another resignation letter to Macdonald in December.[30] The resignation was finally accepted in April, a few days before the House of Commons adopted a motion demanding the release of all the correspondence related to the notorious handshake.[31] There was no obvious successor, however, and when Archibald returned to Ottawa in October, Macdonald apparently asked him to consider another term. Archibald said he would return to Manitoba if the prime minister insisted, but would prefer not to do so.[32] Macdonald therefore appointed Alexander Morris, who as chief justice of Manitoba had been administering the government in Archibald's absence.

Morris was a lawyer-politician from Lanark County, Ontario, who had been in Manitoba only since his appointment as chief justice in July. He had a deep interest in the northwest and had even written a book on the subject before Confederation, so he was an appropriate choice. Macdonald's advice to the new incumbent was reminiscent of that he had given Archibald two years before: "Although you have got responsible government nominally, nevertheless you must be, for want of men, a paternal despot for some time to come."[33] Morris, however, devoted most of his time to the North-West Territories and to the problems of the native people, another subject on which he had written a book. Manitoba appeared to be settling down and to be ready for responsible government, and Macdonald was out of office after November 1873. After Girard accepted Morris's invitation to form a government in July 1874, the role of the Manitoba lieutenant-governor differed little from that of his counterparts in other provinces.

Although British Columbia had not known responsible government before joining the dominion in 1871, its transition to that form of regime was quicker and less complicated than Manitoba's. Unlike Manitoba, it had at least had an elected legislative assembly for several years. Its first lieutenant-governor was Joseph Trutch, who had apparently impressed Macdonald as a member of the delegation that travelled from Victoria to Ottawa to negotiate the terms of union.[34] Trutch had been born in England and had lived in the United States before moving to British Columbia in 1859. He was a civil engineer with extensive experience in different parts of North America. The commissioner of lands and works, the position he held when British Columbia became a province, was considered an administrative rather than a political office. Trutch wasted little time in finding a lawyer, John McCreight, to take over the task of leading the government as premier and attorney general in November 1871. Macdonald approved the choice and congratulated Trutch in January 1872 on how well the government of British Columbia was progressing. Three months later, as the legislative session closed, the prime minister predicted that Trutch's duties as lieutenant-governor would now be less onerous than they had been.[35] By November Trutch was complaining he was too young to hold an essentially ceremonial office and would rather be placed in charge of the British Columbia section of the transcontinental railway. Macdonald promised him this position in due course, but the Pacific Scandal prevented the promise from being carried out.[36]

By the mid-1870s the structure of Canadian federalism was taking shape and the office of lieutenant-governor was losing its original importance. The Mackenzie Liberals, with their deep ideological commitment to responsible government and their lack of rapport with the lieutenant-governors they inherited from Macdonald, hastened a process that would have taken place in any event. Letellier's arbitrary action in dismissing the de Boucherville government was widely regarded as an anachronism, and even members of his own party, apart from those he installed in office, had difficulty defending his behaviour with any enthusiasm. His own dismissal, although technically perhaps a violation of the British North America Act, does not seem to have been widely resented (Macdonald's majority in Quebec increased in 1882) and may have dissuaded other lieutenant-governors from similar adventures.

The reserve powers of the crown's representative remained, however, even if the lieutenant-governor was only indirectly the representative of the crown and primarily that of the dominion government. Although Macdonald did not believe that the provincial level of government shared in the prerogatives of the crown, he saw no inconsistency in urging lieutenant-governors to exercise the powers Bagehot attributed to the British monarch.[37] From time to time, when he was disturbed by some political development or impending crisis in a province, Macdonald would direct the lieutenant-governor concerned to play a more active role. For example, in 1883 he complained to John B. Robinson, whom he had appointed lieutenant-governor of Ontario three years before, about the Mowat government's attempt to assert its authority at Rat Portage. He told Robinson that the lieutenant-governor "must ask them for explanations."[38] Early in 1884 he informed the lieutenant-governors of the four original provinces, although apparently not the others, that some terrorist act might be expected around St Patrick's Day and that the premiers should be confidentially warned to place their public buildings under surveillance.[39]

In 1884 the ineffectual premier of Nova Scotia, William Pipes, resigned to return to his law practice. There was no consensus in Nova Scotia on who had the right to designate a successor in such circumstances, or even whether the resignation of the premier (an office that had no statutory basis) terminated the existence of the ministry. Macdonald advised Lieutenant-Governor Mathew Richey that he was free to send for whomever he chose, citing Bagehot's view that the choice of a prime minister was still the personal prerogative of the sovereign. However, if Richey wished to request or accept the advice of Pipes he was free to do so. Richey did so, and on the outgoing premier's advice chose William S. Fielding. Macdonald congratulated Richey on his handling of "the constitutional crisis."[40]

Two years later Richey faced another crisis when Fielding requested a dissolution to determine whether the voters wished Nova Scotia to secede from the dominion. Macdonald reminded Richey that a lieutenant-governor was entitled to refuse a dissolution and that the issue of secession could not be determined by a provincial election since Nova Scotia's representatives in the dominion Parliament were "the constitutional exponents of the wishes of the people with regard to such relations." The prime minister also informed Richey that if he decided to refuse Fielding a dissolution, "you will be supported by the whole weight of the dominion Gov't."[41]

Richey granted the dissolution anyway, claiming he had had little choice since it had been four years since the previous election, and that the issue on which Fielding chose to base his campaign was irrelevant. Macdonald was displeased with this decision and wrote that Richey should have tried to prevent a campaign based on the issue of secession by postponing the election until the last possible moment. However, he added philosophically that "there is no use looking back."[42] The Liberals won the election with the largest majority since 1867. Richey wrote that the situation was "very serious" and asked Macdonald for advice on what he should do if the Fielding government made a serious effort to secede from the dominion.[43] John Thompson urged Macdonald not to become involved, and to take the view that secession would require a decision at Westminster, not in Ottawa. Thompson argued that if Macdonald advised Richey to resist secession, the dominion would appear to be thwarting the people's will. Conversely, if he advised Richey to follow Fielding's advice, Richey might conclude that the province really had the authority to make a unilateral declaration of independence.[44] Macdonald apparently followed Thompson's advice and Fielding seemed gradually to lose interest in secession, although he remained premier for ten more years.

In the same year that these events took place a provincial election in Quebec left the Bleu government headed by J.J. Ross without a majority. Macdonald advised Lieutenant-Governor Louis Masson that the Ross government should not resign before the new legislature met to decide its fate, and expressed the hope that a Bleu government might be kept in office, even if Ross himself did not wish to continue. He explained his reasons for this view, in case there was any doubt: "I need not tell you that in my opinion the best interests of the dominion would be prejudiced by that discreditable person M. Mercier forming a government. I feel sure that you as an individual agree with me and that as a Governor you would do what you properly and constitutionally could to prevent such a calamity falling on Quebec."[45]

Ross remained in office for a few weeks, but Mercier had enough support in the new legislature to form a government that remained a source of anxiety to Macdonald for the rest of the prime minister's life. Masson resigned a few months after Mercier took office, claiming his health was not equal to the task of serving as lieutenant-governor.[46] He nonetheless was reappointed to the Senate (in which he had sat before becoming lieutenant-governor) and lived another sixteen years. His replacement was Auguste-Réal Angers, a judge with long experience in provincial politics, who proved to be made of sterner stuff. Angers made Mercier's life as difficult as possible for five years and finally dismissed him from office, an event Macdonald did not live to see. While he had better grounds for the dismissal than Letellier had had in 1878, an element of partisan revenge (or, if one prefers, poetic justice) is suggested by the fact that C.-B. de Boucherville, the premier dismissed by Letellier, was appointed to succeed Mercier almost fourteen years later. (The Letellier affair had an even more bizarre sequel which lies outside the chronological boundaries of the present study. In 1900 the Laurier government dismissed the lieutenant-governor of British Columbia and appointed former Quebec premier Henri Joly, who had changed his name in 1888 to Henri Joly de Lotbinière, as his successor.)

The collapse of John Norquay's Manitoba government in 1887 provided another opportunity for the exercise of viceregal powers. The lieutenant-governor was James Cox Aikins, an old Grit from Peel County, Ontario, who had changed parties at Confederation and served in Macdonald's cabinets both before and after the Mackenzie interlude. Macdonald chided Aikins for not being firm enough with Norquay, who was embroiled in a railway scandal, and reminded the lieutenant-governor that he was "a dominion officer." In a subsequent letter Macdonald said it was the lieutenant-governor's duty to refuse Norquay a dissolution. Still later he expressed the hope that Norquay would resign or, if Aikins could find evidence of "gross impropriety," be dismissed from office. Should either of these things happen, he suggested that Aikins should choose the person best able to form a strong and honest government.[47] Norquay resigned a month later and Aikins chose the minister of agriculture, David Harrison. Harrison soon found he had no support in the legislature and had to give way to Liberal leader Thomas Greenway, who governed Manitoba for the next twelve years.

With the possible exception of Mercier's dismissal, these episodes clearly show the limitations of the lieutenant-governor's office as a means of bringing federal pressure to bear on the provinces, or of installing or perpetuating congenial provincial governments. In the last analysis the will of the people, or at least of the legislature, would prevail. Although the reserve powers might be deployed occasionally on behalf of the dominion, most lieutenant-governors acted primarily as ceremonial figureheads, sources of information or channels of communication rather than as federal proconsuls.

At times lieutenant-governors would even make personal representations on behalf of their provinces, urging the prime minister to be more flexible or sympathetic. For example, Aikins told Macdonald in May 1884 that Norquay might have persuaded the legislature to accept the financial terms offered by the dominion had it not been for the clause stating that the terms were a final settlement, and he urged the prime minister not to insist on this condition.[48] At about the same time Lieutenant-Governor Clement Cornwall of British Columbia pleaded with Macdonald to open the railway-belt lands to settlement and to complete the Esquimalt graving dock before it collapsed.[49] A year later Lieutenant-Governor Masson urged Macdonald to agree to Quebec's request for a payment of $6000 per mile for its provincial railway.[50] In a subsequent letter to Macdonald, Masson expressed his personal regret at the execution of Louis Riel, arguing that the death penalty for treason was rarely carried out.[51] Sir Leonard Tilley, serving his second term as lieutenant-governor of New Brunswick, expressed the opinion that New Brunswick had "a strong case" in its claim to be entitled to an additional $150,000, plus interest, as compensation for the Eastern Extension Railway.[52] Lieutenant-Governor Angers urged Macdonald to make the Eastmain River Quebec's northern boundary in 1889, a recommendation actually carried out by Laurier nine years later.[53] Lieutenant-Governor Carvell of Prince Edward Island intervened to oppose a bill introduced by Macdonald's government that he claimed would effectively shut down the lobster fishery.[54] (The bill was withdrawn after second reading.) John Schultz, the first Manitoba lieutenant-governor to have spent most of his adult life in the province, tried unsuccessfully to find common ground between the provincial and federal governments with regard to separate schools.[55] James Patterson, Schultz's successor, urged Prime Minister Bowell to give sympathetic attention to Manitoba's financial needs.[56]

Section 90 of the British North America Act provided the lieutenant-governor with authority over provincial legislation. When a bill was adopted by the legislature the lieutenant-governor could either give or refuse assent or, as a third alternative, reserve the bill for the final decision of the dominion government. This third alternative, insofar as it was resorted to, clearly involved the lieutenant-governor in federal-provincial relations.

The lieutenant-governor's power of reservation and the dominion government's power of disallowance were both awkwardly provided for in Section 90 of the British North America Act and are frequently referred to in the same sentence, perhaps creating an impression that these two "quasi-federal" powers are closely related. In fact they are entirely distinct. The power of disallowance does not apply to reserved bills, but only to acts that have received the lieutenant-governor's assent. Disallowance was clearly intended to be, and in practice has been, an instrument of federal control over the provinces. Both the intention and the consequences of the power of reservation were more ambiguous, and in practise the power proved more of an inconvenience to the dominion government than an asset.

The ambiguity of reservation was part of the ambiguity that characterized the lieutenant-governor's office itself. Just as it was never entirely clear whether he was a federal or a provincial officer, or an embodiement of royal authority that somehow transcended the divisions of federalism, so it was not specified in the British North America Act or elsewhere either on whose behalf or at whose behest the power of reservation should be exercised. In practice the power was usually exercised at the lieutenant-governor's personal discretion, in one instance on the dominion government's instructions, and sometimes even at the request of his provincial advisers. The latter situation, more offensive to the philosophy of responsible government than to that of federalism, might arise because provincial governments, lacking disciplined political parties, were not always in full control of the legislatures on which their survival depended.

The power of reservation, like that of disallowance, was based on colonial precedent. In the far-flung British Empire, whose components were linked to the mother country by slow and unreliable sailing ships, colonial governors confronted with unexpected situations could not easily seek or receive instructions. Reservation allowed them to transfer the power of decision to a higher authority, without committing themselves or appearing to take sides. The power had been used from time to time in all the North American colonies that became part of the dominion in 1867 or afterwards. Therefore it was retained at the provincial level, but with the ultimate power of decision being transferred from the imperial government to the dominion. Yet the need for such a power was not obvious, when the provincial capitals were linked to Ottawa by telegraphs and in most cases by railways, particularly since the federal power of disallowance could be used to strike down any provincial statute up to a year after the dominion was notified of its passage.

Macdonald took the power of disallowance very seriously and devoted much attention to it, particularly in the first six years after Confederation (see chapter 9). It appears that he did not regard the power of reservation, even then, as an equally useful instrument of federal authority. No instructions or guidelines were sent to the lieutenant-governors during those years regarding the use of the power. Macdonald worked on a draft of such instructions, apparently in 1867, but it was never completed. Most of the grounds for reservation specified in this uncompleted draft were those that had

Table 8.1
Provincial Bills Reserved, 1867–96

Year	Ont.	Que.	NS	NB	Man.	BC	PEI	Total
1868		1	1	1				3
1869				3				3
1870								0
1871				1	4			5
1872					4	3		7
1873	2				6	1		9
1874			1	1			2	4
1875					1		1	2
1876							2	2
1877					2	1		3
1878							2	2
1879			1					1
1890		2			2			4
1891					1			1
1892		2		1			1	4
1893								0
1894				1				1
1895								0
1896								0
Total	2	5	3	8	20	5	8	51

Note: No bills were reserved in the years 1880 to 1889.

applied before 1867, when bills had been reserved for the imperial government, and there were no specific references to the interests of the dominion or the terms of the BNA Act.[57] Three of the four lieutenant-governors in office at this time were in fact British army officers, so perhaps the imperial flavour of the uncompleted instructions is not surprising. There were other and more reliable ways for the dominion to protect its interests.

As can be seen from table 8.1, a total of six bills were reserved during the first three years after Confederation, when Canada constituted only the four original provinces. The addition of three new provinces in the next few years contributed to a considerable increase in the frequency with which the power was exercised. In the years from 1871 to 1879 inclusive, there were thirty-five reservations, of which only six involved the four original provinces. Seventeen bills were reserved in Manitoba, five in British Columbia, and seven in Prince Edward Island. Thereafter the use of the power suffered a precipitous decline, so that, strictly speaking, there was not a single instance of a bill being reserved in the whole decade of the 1880s. Beginning in 1890, for reasons that are not entirely clear, the

Table 8.2
Disposition of Reserved Bills, by Ministers of Justice

Minister	Assent Given	No Action	Assent Withheld
John A. Macdonald (1867–73)	4	5	14
Dorion (1873–74)	5	0	1
Fournier (1874–75)	1	0	1
Blake (1875–77)	2	1	2
Laflamme (1877–78)	1	0	1
James McDonald (1878–81)	1	1	1
Campbell (1881–85)	0	0	0
Thompson (1885–94)	0	9	0
Tupper (1894–96)	0	1	0
Dickey (1896)	0	0	0

practice of reservation enjoyed something of a resurgence, so that ten bills from four different provinces were reserved over the next five years. There were no instances in 1895 or 1896 and, as it turned out, very few thereafter.

When a reserved bill was sent to Ottawa by the lieutenant-governor, the dominion government could choose among three options. Assent could either be given to the bill, or it could be refused. Alternatively, no specific action could be taken. In this case the bill would not become law, since it would not have received assent from either the lieutenant-governor or the governor general in council. However, the legislature would be free to re-enact the measure at a subsequent session.

Table 8.2 shows the disposition of reserved bills during the term of office of each minister of justice, the person on whose advice action was normally taken. During the first Macdonald government, when Sir John A. Macdonald was both minister of justice and prime minister, the majority of reserved bills were refused assent, although four received assent and five were allowed to lapse. A.-A. Dorion, the first of four ministers of justice in the Mackenzie government, gave assent to all but one of the six bills reserved during his term of office, a perhaps predictable response from the Rouge leader who had opposed Confederation only a few years before. The four Liberal ministers of justice as a group recommended assent to nine of the fifteen reserved bills during their terms of office, although apart from Dorion they were just as likely to withhold assent as to recommend it. One of the four bills refused assent, the Prince Edward Island Land Purchase Act of 1874, was turned down at the insistence of the governor general (see chapter 5).

After the Conservatives returned to office in 1878 the usual practise of the dominion government was to take no action on a reserved
bill. This tendency is particularly noticeable on the part of Sir John
Thompson, whose term of office coincided with the revival of the
practise of reservation in the early 1890s. Although this practice
caused the bill to lapse, it did not necessarily imply disapproval, but
rather a belief that the provincial level of government should take
responsibility for its own measures.

In most cases bills were reserved because the lieutenant-governor
had doubts, which were often well-founded, that the subject of the
bill fell within provincial jurisdiction. The relatively large number of
such cases in the early years might be explained by uncertainty regarding the meaning of the BNA Act and the fact that provincial politicians were still not accustomed to operating under a federal
constitution. The case of the Nova Scotia militia bill has already been
referred to. A New Brunswick measure of 1869 regarding marriage
licences raised more complex issues of constitutional law, since "marriage" was mentioned in both sections 91 and 92 of the British North
America Act. Macdonald expressed the opinion in a memorandum
that the bill was probably *ultra vires*, but he was uncertain enough to
recommend that a ruling be sought from the legal advisers of the
imperial government, known as the law officers of the crown. When
the law officers concluded that marriage licences in fact fell under
provincial jurisdiction, Macdonald's government assented to the
bill.[58]

The very large number of reservations in Manitoba in 1871, 1872,
and 1873 reflects the fact that responsible government had not
really been established in that province. The lieutenant-governor
was the effective head of the administration but had no direct control over the legislature, a situation that was more like a congressio-
nal than a parliamentary government. Macdonald withheld assent
from all the Manitoba bills reserved in 1871 and 1872. Four of the
six reserved by Morris in 1873 received assent from the Mackenzie
government.

In 1873, shortly after Oliver Mowat became premier, the Ontario
legislature adopted two bills to incorporate the Loyal Orange Asso-
ciations of Western Ontario and Eastern Ontario, respectively. Both
were reserved by Lieutenant-Governor Howland. Macdonald suspected that Mowat, who had voted for both bills, had advised
Howland to reserve them so as to embarrass the dominion government, which would offend Catholics if it gave assent and offend
Orangemen if it did not. Since Macdonald's government was largely
based on the support of Catholics in Quebec and Orangemen in On-

tario, the dilemma was a real one. Macdonald resolved it by refusing either to give or withhold assent, and justified his recommendation in a memorandum addressed to the governor general:

Under our system of government it is the duty of the ministers to recommend any measure passed by the legislature for the executive assent. The lieutenant-governor should only reserve a bill in his capacity as an officer of the dominion and under instructions from the governor general, just as the governor general should only do so as an Imperial officer and under the Royal Instructions. Otherwise they should assent to whatever their advisors recommend. A government, if the legislature adopts a measure of which it disapproves, should either accept it (and recommend executive assent) or resign. In this case the attorney general voted for and supported these bills as a member of the legislature. Your Excellency should take no action on these bills.[59]

Five years later another Orange Incorporation bill was reserved by the lieutenant-governor of Prince Edward Island. The post-1878 Macdonald government refused to take any action, citing the reasons in the prime minister's memorandum of 1873.[60]

Macdonald's lack of enthusiasm for the power of reservation is shown by the fact that no bill was ever reserved by a lieutenant-governor on explicit instructions from his government. One such instance did occur during the Mackenzie interlude, although even in that case the lieutenant-governor, Sir Leonard Tilley of New Brunswick, had independently decided to reserve the measure before the instructions were received. The bill in question extended the charter of a logging company that was empowered to restrict navigation on the Meduxnakik River. Some loggers in Maine had alleged that the restrictions violated the Webster-Ashburton Treaty of 1842, and the United States government complained to the British minister in Washington. By the time Tilley actually reserved the bill it had been extensively modified in response to these concerns, and the Mackenzie government, on Dorion's advice, assented to it.[61]

In the latter part of 1882 Macdonald again considered sending general instructions to lieutenant-governors, partly with the intention of discouraging the use of the power of reservation. A minute of council prepared by Macdonald complained of bills being reserved on the advice of provincial governments (although in fact there had been no reservations since 1879) and pointed out that communication between Ottawa and the provincial capitals had progressed to the point where the power need hardly ever be exercised without instructions from the dominion.[62] The draft instructions

provided that the lieutenant-governors should assent to all bills unless they were identical to measures that had previously been disallowed or denied assent by the dominion government. A specific
instruction to the lieutenant-governor of Quebec provided that assent should not be given to any bill in violation of Section 80 of the
BNA Act, which entrenched the representation of some predominantly anglophone constituencies. These instructions were printed,
but apparently were not sent to the lieutenant-governors until
1887.[63]

An interesting episode in 1884 was not a reservation, although it
was erroneously described as one in a book published by the Department of Justice about a decade later. The Ontario legislature
adopted a government measure entitled the Ontario Factories Act to
protect working people from industrial hazards and to impose penalties on employers who violated its provisions. A clause in the act
provided it would take effect on a date to be proclaimed by the
lieutenant-governor in council. Lieutenant-Governor John B. Robinson, who had assented to the bill in March, suggested to the dominion government in October that it should be referred to the
Supreme Court before proclamation. Justice minister Alexander
Campbell responded that he saw no reason to do so, since it could be
tested through ordinary litigation, and recommended that it be proclaimed, which it was soon afterwards.[64]

No single cause can be assigned to the apparent epidemic of reservations in the early 1890s. Only three of the ten bills, all in
Manitoba, met Macdonald's criterion that they should have been
previously disallowed. Three in Quebec were private bills to legalize
marriages contrary to canon law. One from Prince Edward Island
was an innocuous measure to abolish the upper house of the legislature, and Thompson reminded the over-zealous lieutenant-
governor that unnecessary reservations were an embarrassment to
the dominion government and that his instructions specifically directed him to use the power only in special circumstances.[65] The
three other measures were all probably *ultra vires*. In no case did the
dominion government either grant or withhold assent.

By 1896 the power of reservation was effectively obsolete and re-
dundant, and the office of lieutenant-governor had lost most of its
original importance. Except perhaps in British Columbia, which endured considerable political instability during the Laurier years, the
office had become essentially ceremonial, as it has remained. The
most distinctive feature of Canadian federalism virtually withered
away, and few regretted its passing. Canada had become a federation *comme les autres*.

9 The Disallowance of Provincial Legislation

The federal power of disallowance, like the lieutenant-governor's power of reservation, is usually regarded today as an anomalous and somewhat disreputable provision of the British North America Act: at best a curious anachronism, and at worst an unpleasant reminder of the colonial, undemocratic, and overcentralized character of Confederation. Even so careful a scholar as J.R. Mallory has contributed to the ill-repute of disallowance by portraying it as a means by which the hinterlands of Canada were subordinated to the business interests of Toronto and Montreal.[1] While disallowance certainly played the role attributed to it by Mallory on some occasions, it was neither always used nor solely intended for that purpose. An analysis of the occasions when it was used and, what is perhaps equally significant, the occasions when it was not, casts light on the multifaceted character of early Canadian federalism.

As Mallory points out, disallowance and reservation were both practices widely used in the British Empire as instruments by which the imperial centre could control the scattered peripheries, and the perpetuation of the same practices in the new federal state occurred naturally to political elites who had spent their public lives in the North American colonies of the empire. The idea of the two levels of government being equal in status – an idea that is itself open to criticism in terms of both intellectual coherence and pragmatic rationality – was not widely shared in 1867, if indeed it had emerged at all. Both supporters and opponents of Confederation tended to assume, for better or for worse, that one level of government must inevitably be superior in status and authority to the other. That the whole should be greater than its parts, and that a government representing the whole should exercise some supervisory power over legislatures representing the parts, was an idea quite consistent with federalism as the Fathers of Confederation understood it.

Even in the more decentralized United States, something analogous to disallowance had been considered. Not only Alexander Hamilton, but James Madison as well, had favoured placing a provision in the constitution that would enable Congress to overrule the legislatures of the states. The opposition of delegates mainly from the smaller states ensured that this idea did not survive the Philadelphia Convention. Its disappearance was one of several compromises made at the convention, compromises that collectively ensured that Madison would be commemorated in history as the inventor of a regime far less centralized than what he himself would have preferred.[2] In the end, however, the result that Hamilton and Madison had intended was ensured by the no more democratic device of having state legislation reviewed, and occasionally struck down, by the Supreme Court rather than by Congress. During the formative years of American federalism a Hamiltonian chief justice, John Marshall, played this role in a way that significantly reinforced the political and economic unification of the young republic.

Unlike the United States Constitution, the BNA Act established no Supreme Court, a fact that strengthened the case for providing a power of disallowance. Executive disallowance, rather than the legislative override Madison and Hamilton considered, was naturally suggested not only by the colonial precedent but by the very nature of executive-centred responsible government, "similar in Principle to that of the United Kingdom." No other alternative seems to have been considered.

Executive disallowance, however, could have more than one meaning. In the massive biography of Oliver Mowat written by his son-in-law and published shortly after Mowat's death, it is alleged that Mowat at the Quebec Conference of 1864 wished to give the imperial government, rather than the dominion government, the power to disallow provincial legislation. Mowat himself is cited as the source of this information, presumably in conversation since no letter or document is cited.[3] In the absence of any supporting evidence this allegation, published forty years after the alleged fact and based on an undocumented conversation with a man already deceased, must be treated as highly suspect, even if the conversation took place. Certainly imperial supervision of the legislation of the individual provinces would have reduced the dominion to a state of incoherence and the authority of the dominion government to the vanishing point. There is no reason to believe that anyone at the Quebec Conference, including Mowat, desired such a result. Joseph Pope's records of the conference, far from complete but the best available, show simply that Mowat moved the adoption of the provision for disallowance in what was essentially its final form.[4]

Another variation on the theme of disallowance, and one that was discussed quite soon after Confederation, was the idea that the power might be exercised by the governor general on his own authority and at his own discretion, rather than on the advice of the ministry. This in fact was an issue that should not have arisen. Section 56 of the British North America Act referred to the possible disallowance of dominion statutes by the queen in council, and since Section 90, providing for the disallowance of provincial legislation, was explicitly based on the analogy of Section 56, only substituting "governor general" for "queen," it must logically be read as giving the power to the governor general in council. In fact it was always exercised on advice, and no governor general seriously suggested doing otherwise.

The matter nonetheless gave rise to a lengthy controversy.[5] In 1869 a dispatch from the colonial secretary to the governor general conceded that the governor general must disallow any act he was advised to disallow by the ministry, but suggested that if he was advised not to disallow an act he considered illegal, he should refer it to the Colonial Office.[6] Not until 1877, following representations by Alexander Mackenzie's Liberal government, did the Colonial Office concede that the disallowance of provincial legislation was solely a power of the dominion government. More than a decade later, Sir John A. Macdonald attempted to revive the archaic notion of imperial disallowance of provincial legislation so as to avoid taking the political responsibility for disallowing Mercier's debt conversion act (see chapter 4).

Macdonald's more fruitful contribution to the theory and practice of disallowance, however, was made at a much earlier stage in his career. Macdonald assumed the portfolio of Justice in the first post-Confederation government and held it until his resignation terminated that government in November 1873. He selected as his deputy minister his brother-in-law and former private secretary, Hewitt Bernard. For both men these offices involved an element of continuity, since they had been, respectively, attorney general and deputy attorney general for Canada West immediately prior to Confederation. Bernard had also served as the executive secretary of the Quebec Conference in 1864.

Soon after Confederation all lieutenant-governors were reminded of their constitutional obligation (under Section 90, read in conjunction with Section 56) to dispatch to Ottawa at the end of each legislative session copies of all acts to which they had given assent, as well as bills reserved. On arrival in Ottawa, the acts were sent to the Department of Justice, where Macdonald as minister assumed the task of examining each one and writing a report to indicate which acts, if any, were constitutionally dubious or otherwise deserving of special attention. Since a province typically produced about a hundred acts (including private acts) during a session of its legislature, and since three new provinces were soon added to the original four, this was a considerable task. When it is recalled that Macdonald had numerous other responsibilities as minister of justice, prime minister, and party leader, the fact that the BNA Act allowed the government one year in which to decide the fate of any statute, counting from the time when it was received, does not seem excessive.

In June 1868, a few days prior to completing his reports on the first batch of provincial statutes, Macdonald produced a memorandum on the subject of disallowance which was approved the following day as a minute of council.[7] This document began by noting the imperial practice of disallowance as well as the fact that in recent years it had been used very sparingly with respect to colonies having representative institutions and responsible government. However, it forecast that "under the present constitution of Canada, the General Government will be called upon to consider the propriety of allowance, or disallowance, of Provincial Acts, much more frequently than Her Majesty's Government has been with respect to Colonial enactments." Macdonald did not explain the reasons for this forecast, presumably because he thought they were obvious. First, the dominion was intended to be an economic union, which the mid-Victorian empire was not. Second, the federal distribution of legislative powers confined the provinces to a much narrower range of legislative jurisdictions than they had enjoyed as self-governing colonies, and jurisdictional contests between the two levels of government in a federal Canada were inevitable.

Macdonald went on to specify the criteria by which provincial statutes should be evaluated: "In deciding whether any Act of a Provincial Legislature should be disallowed or sanctioned, the Government must not only consider whether it affects the interest of the whole dominion or not, but also whether it be unconstitutional, whether it exceeds the jurisdiction conferred on Local Legislatures, and in cases where the jurisdiction is concurrent, whether it clashes with the legislation of the General Parliament." The memorandum proceeded to specify the procedure to be used in considering and reporting on legislation, with the avowed aim of ensuring that the power of disallowance would be used sparingly, "with great caution, and only in cases where the Law and the general interests of the dominion imperatively demand it." It recommended that the minister of justice make separate reports on any acts that, in his opinion, fell into any one of four categories:

• as being altogether illegal or unconstitutional;
• as being illegal or unconstitutional in part;
• as clashing with the legislation of the general parliament, in cases of concurrent jurisdiction;
• as affecting the interests of the dominion generally.

Macdonald suggested that acts falling into the second, third, or fourth categories should not be disallowed until the provincial government and/or legislature had been informed of the dominion's concerns and given the opportunity to respond to them.

By and large these procedures were followed by Macdonald and his successors in the Justice portfolio, at least during the period of time considered in this book. Provincial governments were usually given the opportunity to modify or repeal questionable statutes. Given the shortness of legislative sessions and the long intervals between them, this practice often brought the dominion government dangerously close to the expiry of the one-year deadline for disallowance, and ran the risk that no disallowance would be possible if repeal or satisfactory amendment did not take place. During his first government Macdonald bypassed the formal channels of communication and corresponded directly with most of the provincial premiers regarding questionable legislation. In the cases of Nova Scotia, where the government was hostile, and Manitoba, where there was no recognized premier, he corresponded with the lieutenant-governor. This was also the practice in dealing with British Columbia for the short period before responsible government was established.

Following Macdonald's resignation, Bernard remained as deputy minister for almost three years, until September 1876. During this period there were three ministers of justice: Dorion, Fournier, and Blake. Dorion wrote his own reports, although only four of the seven provinces were the subject of reports during his brief term in office. Fournier allowed Bernard to draft the reports and merely signed them with the phrase "I concur." Blake wrote his own reports and eventually replaced Bernard with Zebulon A. Lash. After

Blake's resignation Lash wrote the reports and Toussaint Laflamme, Blake's successor, adopted Fournier's practice of concurring in his deputy's recommendations. This practice usually continued when the Nova Scotian James McDonald held the Justice portfolio in the Conservative government from 1878 until 1881. The next two ministers, Alexander Campbell and John Thompson, drafted their own reports, but both had to consider the views of John A. Macdonald, who was sometimes more inclined to use the power of disallowance than they were, and who grew more rigid and uncompromising towards the provincial governments as he grew older. However, Thompson could be tough himself and was not quite as disinclined to use the power of disallowance as his biographer, P.B. Waite, suggests.[8] As minister of justice under Macdonald he recommended several disallowances, and the fact there was none during the two years of Thompson's own government (when he was also minister of justice) appears to have been no more than a coincidence. After Thompson's death the minister of justice for somewhat more than a year was Charles Hibbert Tupper, the son of old Sir Charles who had led Nova Scotia into Confederation. Like Mackenzie and Abbott, Prime Minister Mackenzie Bowell left the responsibility for deciding the fate of provincial legislation to his minister of justice. None of the deputy ministers who followed Lash (George Burbidge in 1882, Robert Sedgewick in 1888, and Edmund Newcombe in 1893) enjoyed the influence Bernard and Lash had exercised in the 1870s, at least up to 1896. Newcombe remained deputy minister until 1924, but most of his term of office falls outside the scope of the present book.

A justice minister's report recommending disallowance would go to the cabinet to be embodied in an order in council and signed by the governor general. This decision would then be communicated to the province. The final stage in the process was supposed to be a proclamation by the province concerned to the effect that its act had been disallowed. On at least one occasion, the disallowance of the Mercier government's District Magistrates Act in 1888, the provincial government at first refused to comply with this requirement, but Lieutenant-Governor Angers, encouraged by Macdonald, finally persuaded Mercier to do so.[9]

Table 9.1 shows both the chronological and geographical distribution of disallowances between 1867 and 1896. The facts that stand out are the heavy concentration of disallowances both chronologically (in the period of Macdonald's second government) and geographically (in the provinces of Manitoba and British Columbia). For the other five provinces disallowance was clearly a rare event,

Table 9.1
Provincial Acts Disallowed, 1867–96

Year	Ont.	Que.	NS	NB	Man.	BC	Total
1869	1	1	1				3
1870	1						1
1871			1				1
1872							0
1873							0
1874		2			2	1	5
1875	1	1				2	4
1876		1			4	1	6
1877							0
1878						3	3
1879						3	3
1880	1						1
1881	1					2	3
1882	1				4		5
1883	1		1			3	5
1884	1					1	2
1885					1		1
1886					2	3	5
1887		1	1		8		10
1888		1				1	2
1889		1					1
1890					1		1
1891					2		2
1896					1		1
Total	8	5	6	1	25	20	65

Note: No Prince Edward Island acts were disallowed.

both after 1878 and before. Mallory's interpretation of disallowance as a means of controlling the western hinterland thus appears to be confirmed, at least in part.

It should be noted that table 9.1 refers only to disallowances in the strict sense: that is to say acts that were struck down by the dominion government after they had received assent from the lieutenant-governor. Reserved bills, of which there were many before 1878 although few thereafter, were sometimes explicitly vetoed rather than merely being allowed to lapse, a practice that was particularly common during Macdonald's first government (see chapter 8). Some of these instances are at times referred to, even in official publications, as disallowances, although strictly speaking they were not. Thus one reason for the scarcity of disallowances during Macdonald's first government, and their frequency during his second, was the early use, and subsequent decline, of the lieutenant-governor's power of reservation. During the early years a large number of the most questionable bills were reserved and thus did not need to be disallowed. Another reason was the fact that early provincial governments, particularly Sandfield Macdonald's in Ontario and Chauveau's in Quebec, were friendly towards and to some extent politically dependent on the dominion government. Many differences of opinion as to the validity or appropriateness of provincial legislation were thus resolved through quiet diplomacy, as recommended in Macdonald's memorandum of June 1868, so that the last resort of disallowance was not required.

Even after these conditions no longer applied, however, the scarcity of disallowances in the central and Maritime provinces continued. The thirteen years of the Mowat-Macdonald rivalry produced only five disallowances, and three of these were successive versions of the Rivers and Streams Act, the outcome of the Caldwell-McLaren imbroglio, which was repeatedly adopted and just as repeatedly disallowed until the Judicial Committee of the Privy Council finally settled the matter. Another premier who had his share of disagreement with Macdonald, W.S. Fielding of Nova Scotia, had only one statute disallowed. Prince Edward Island had none, but the penchant of its lieutenant-governors for exercising their powers of reservation, even after that practice had become rare in the other provinces, may be noted as a partial explanation. The most important issue involving the province, land reform, produced two reservations but no disallowance.

More informative and interesting than either the chronological or the geographical breakdown of disallowances is an examination of the reasons why disallowance did or did not take place as well as the kinds of statutes that were or were not disallowed. The former question may be answered, at least in part, by reference to the criteria for disallowance in Macdonald's memorandum of June 1868. These were that the legislation be either adverse to the interests of the entire dominion, unconstitutional, *ultra vires*, or clashing with dominion legislation in a concurrent field.

The third grounds for disallowance listed by Macdonald – that the act be *ultra vires* under the terms of the BNA Act – was the most important. At least forty-five of the sixty-five provincial statutes that were disallowed up to 1896, or just over two-thirds, were *ultra vires* or were believed by the dominion government to be *ultra vires* at the time they were disallowed. One had already been declared *ultra vires* by a superior court. Even if the few cases in which a subsequent judicial decision rejected the dominion's interpretation of the distribution of powers are excluded, it is apparent that disallowance was largely a substitute for judicial review as a means of keeping the provinces within the jurisdictional boundaries established by the BNA Act.

These forty-five disallowed statutes were considered to trespass upon the dominion's jurisdictional authority in a wide variety of ways. (Some did so in more than one way, but in such cases the most significant grounds for the disallowance is usually not difficult to identify.) The largest category, consisting of eight statutes, were those that trespassed on the dominion's control over the judiciary. Six related to the regulation of trade and commerce, five to dominion lands, four to criminal law or criminal procedure, and four to navigation and shipping. Transportation works or undertakings extending beyond the boundaries of the province accounted for three cases, the incorporation of companies for what were not deemed to be provincial objects for three more, and three dealt with the privileges of legislatures. Two disallowed statutes concerned the office of lieutenant-governor, two attempted to restrict the operations of companies incorporated by the dominion, two related to interest, one to Indians and lands reserved for the Indians, and one to naturalization and aliens. One was based on the assumption that the prerogative powers of the crown were shared between the two levels of government, an assumption that at that time was contested by the dominion government.

Macdonald's first grounds for disallowance – that the statute be contrary to the interests of the dominion as a whole – accounted for fourteen cases. Obviously this category was subjective since politicians, then as now, could define the interests of the dominion in different ways. It is significant that all fourteen of these cases occurred after 1878, in the epoch of Macdonald's National Policy, and all fourteen of the disallowed statutes were from either Manitoba or British Columbia. The ten from Manitoba were all railway charters, while the four from British Columbia included two railway charters and two statutes attempting to restrict Chinese immigration. In effect all fourteen were disallowed because they interfered with the construction or operation of the CPR. Clearly these instances of the use of disallowance lend strong support to the Mallory interpretation. However, it should be emphasized that they accounted for less than a quarter of all cases in which the power was used during the period under consideration.

Macdonald's second grounds for disallowance – that the statute be "unconstitutional" – may require explanation for modern readers. Most authorities, including Mallory and Eugene Forsey, assert correctly that Macdonald did not intend "unconstitutional" in this context to be a synonym for *ultra vires*.[10] It would have made no sense for him to do so, since he would merely have been repeating himself rather than establishing two distinct grounds for disallowance. Canadian federalism and the BNA Act were less than a year old when Macdonald wrote his memorandum on disallowance, and the American sense of the word "unconstitutional" as meaning contrary to the terms of a written constitution had not yet become established in the Canadian vocabulary. Instead Macdonald, as of 1868, used the word in the British sense as meaning contrary to convention, propriety, and the traditional rights of British subjects.

Like the interests of the dominion, this kind of constitutionality is a subjective concept, and its use as a grounds for disallowance in Canada illustrates the point. There appear to have been only four cases up to 1896 in which the disallowance of provincial statutes took place for this reason. Three of these were the repeated disallowances of Mowat's Rivers and Streams acts, disallowances that took place ostensibly on grounds of high principle but in fact on behalf of the Tory lumberman and later senator, Peter McLaren. It is not impossible, however, that Macdonald sincerely believed that the traditional property rights of British subjects were at stake in this affair, however strange this may seem from our vantage point a century later. In fairness to Macdonald it may also be noted that the interpretation of "due process" then prevailing among American judges would probably have caused the Rivers and Streams acts to be struck down had they been adopted by any American legislature.[11]

The fourth example is interesting in that the report on the basis of which disallowance took place was also written by Macdonald, and was in fact the last report on provincial legislation he ever wrote. This was a Manitoba statute adopted in 1887, and rather vaguely entitled "An Act for further improving the Law," which purported to make all persons employed on public works immune from liability for their acts.[12] The report was written by the prime minister because Justice Minister John Thompson was attending his mother's funeral in Halifax. According to Macdonald, the statute was "of such an unusual and extraordinary character and constitutes such a manifest interference with private rights that the undersigned is of opinion that the Act should be disallowed without delay."[13]

Only one statute was disallowed because it clashed with dominion legislation in an allegedly concurrent field, and in this case it was the dominion statute that eventually proved to be *ultra vires*. The Ontario act respecting licence duties, adopted and disallowed in 1884, was a response to the dominion's Liquor Licence Act, known as the

McCarthy Act, which Parliament had adopted in the previous year. The Ontario act imposed discriminatory penalties on innkeepers who held the dominion licences, and thus made it prohibitively expensive to comply with the McCarthy Act.[14] A year after the disallowance, however, the McCarthy Act was declared *ultra vires* by the Judicial Committee of the Privy Council.

One case of disallowance is difficult to place in any category, and the reasons for it are unclear. A Manitoba statute adopted in 1875 provided that Métis who had sold their land to white settlers and then had second thoughts could regain their land within a certain time period by repaying the price of purchase. Blake recommended disallowance on the grounds that it was "not to the advantage of the half-breeds" (which seems questionable) and also on the legalistic grounds that three months' notice of the passage of the act had not been given in the Manitoba *Gazette*, as required by an earlier statute that the new one amended.[15] The real facts behind this episode might make an interesting subject for further research.

While a classification of disallowances in terms of their ostensible grounds is of particular interest to students of the Canadian Constitution, students of Canadian politics and economic history might find a less legalistic classification in terms of broad subjects of concern to be more useful. By no means can all the disallowances be fitted into categories that appear both broad and meaningful, and several of those that cannot have already been discussed in this chapter. However, five broad categories of policy account for fifty-five of the sixty-five disallowances, and an examination of each should cast some light on the politics of Canadian federalism. These categories or fields of policy are justice, political institutions, transportation, corporations other than those involved in transportation, and public lands. Transportation (railways) and land were two of the four main subject areas of dominion-provincial relations, along with public finance and religion (see chapter 7).

Most of the disallowances falling into the broad category of justice related to the provisions regarding the judiciary in Sections 96 through 101 of the British North America Act. The most important effects and purposes of these provisions were, first, to protect judicial independence vis-à-vis the legislative and executive institutions of government and, second, to provide that the most important judges, those of the superior, district, and county courts in each province, would be appointed and remunerated by the dominion rather than by the provincial governments. While the latter provisions may be cynically regarded as a device to centralize judicial patronage in federal hands (which was certainly one of their consequences), their primary purpose was to integrate Canada's judicial and legal system, insofar as Quebec's peculiarities allowed, as a basis for integrating the country itself. This purpose was reinforced by the fact that jurisdiction over criminal law was confided to the dominion.

John A. Macdonald, a lawyer first and foremost, set great store by these provisions, and their defence against various provincial initiatives consumed a considerable part of his time and energy, as well as those of other federal politicians and officials. Particularly in the early years, up to 1878, statutes pertaining to the judiciary accounted for a large proportion of disallowances, and a number that were not disallowed were commented upon unfavourably in Macdonald's reports as minister of justice and in his private correspondence with provincial politicians. The very first act to be disallowed after Confederation was a Nova Scotia statute that empowered the police court in Halifax to sentence juvenile offenders to detention; Macdonald's report noted correctly that it pertained to criminal law and was *ultra vires*.[16] Macdonald persuaded Attorney General Martin Wilkins to repeal a provision of another act concerning the magistrate at Pictou, also on grounds that it interfered with criminal law.[17] In the following year Wilkins took the precaution of sending Macdonald a copy of his bill to reform the province's judicial system before it was enacted. He subsequently made a number of changes Macdonald suggested.[18]

Both Pierre Chauveau of Quebec and Sandfield Macdonald of Ontario followed John A. Macdonald's advice by deleting provisions of judiciary acts that trespassed on criminal law. In 1869, however, Sandfield's government introduced as part of an appropriations act a measure to pay a provincial stipend to district and county court judges in return for their performance of some additional duties. John A. Macdonald protested that this measure was contrary to Section 100 of the BNA Act, which provided that these judges would be paid by the dominion, but Sandfield refused to repeal it and it was eventually disallowed.[19]

The same issue soon arose in the new province of British Columbia, whose few judges before it joined the dominion had performed a variety of miscellaneous tasks in addition to their strictly judicial duties. In 1871 these judges began to receive their salaries from the dominion, but the province wished them to continue carrying out their non-judicial functions. Macdonald informed the lieutenant-governor that he did not object but that the dominion would not compel its judges to perform extra tasks on behalf of the province. Perhaps the province could pay them an additional stipend. In effect Macdonald was recommending that British Columbia adopt the same practice he had disallowed in the case of Ontario three years previously.[20] However, the British Columbia government decided for the time being to entrust the additional duties to other officials instead.

Meanwhile the Ontario legislature had re-enacted the measure to supplement judges' salaries. Edward Blake was now premier, and Macdonald wrote urging him to repeal it. Blake replied that he disliked the measure on principle and felt it should have been disallowed, but he suggested that before it was repealed the dominion government should increase the judges' salaries by the amount of the provincial stipend they would lose.[21] Nothing was done and both Blake and Macdonald were soon out of office. The measure remained in force.

In 1874 Ontario, Manitoba, and Prince Edward Island all adopted statutes relating to the organization and jurisdiction of the courts and all were criticized by Hewitt Bernard in his reports as deputy minister of justice for trespassing on the field of criminal law. The provinces stuck to their guns and none of the statutes was disallowed.[22] Efforts by British Columbia to reorganize its judiciary, however, continued to cause friction, both within and outside the province. No fewer than four such measures were disallowed by the Mackenzie government, contributing to the general unpleasantness of its relations with the Pacific province.

British Columbia's Superior Court, the only real court in the province, consisted of five judges who resided in Victoria. All five had been appointed before the province joined the dominion, and in most cases immediately after it became a crown colony in 1858. Unlike judges in other provinces, they were not qualified barristers. Having publicly supported Confederation because it would free them from dependence on the provincial government, the judges lobbied vigorously against any judicial reform, deriving whatever arguments they could from Sections 96 through 101 of the BNA Act.

Neither the Macdonald nor the Mackenzie government was particularly sympathetic to the province's efforts to reform the judiciary. Macdonald in 1873 saw no reason why the judges should be retired and replaced with more qualified successors, perhaps because under the terms of union this change would require the dominion to pay the pensions of the old judges as well as the salaries of the new ones.[23] The refusal of the judges to live outside Victoria limited their usefulness, but an act to enlarge the jurisdiction of local justices of the peace was disallowed at the last possible moment by the Mackenzie government in March 1874 on the grounds that it dealt with criminal procedure. British Columbia then decided to create five judicial districts, corresponding to its five constituencies for federal elections, and to require one judge to reside in each. In effect each would be a district court, whose decisions could be appealed to the whole bench of five. Horrified at the prospects of life on the mainland, the judges petitioned the dominion government to disallow the statute, which it did in 1875 on the questionable grounds that assigning the judges to specific districts trespassed on the federal power of appointment.[24] British Columbia tried again, but another disallowance on the same grounds followed in 1876. A third version, carefully worded so as to emphasize the federal power of appointment, was disallowed in 1878, this time on the grounds that it purported to dictate the level of judicial pensions to be paid by the dominion.[25] Finally in 1878 and 1879 the province adopted three statutes, which among other things established judicial districts and empowered the provincial cabinet to establish court rules of procedure. The judges again petitioned for disallowance but the Macdonald government, now back in office, was not impressed and all three were allowed to remain in force.[26] However, an act to confer some judicial functions on provincially appointed gold commissioners, adopted in 1882, was disallowed a year later, on the grounds that it encroached on the federal power of appointment.[27] Another act, to establish a court of appeal from the summary decisions of magistrates, was disallowed in 1888 because it interfered with criminal procedure.[28] An act to make the county court judge of New Westminster a judge of tax assessment appeals and to pay him an allowance of twenty dollars per day was described by Justice Minister John Thompson in 1889 as contrary to the BNA Act, but Thompson advised against disallowance on the grounds that the dominion had the remedy of declining to appoint a judge until the act had been amended.[29]

Although no other province had as much difficulty with judicial matters as British Columbia, a Manitoba act of 1875 dealing with criminal procedure was disallowed on Blake's recommendation.[30] An act to provide for the administration of justice in northwestern Ontario was disallowed in 1880, partly on the grounds that it dealt with judicial appointments, although the fact that the dominion disputed Ontario's claim to the territory obviously entered into the decision as well.[31] In 1882 a senior Ontario judge complained privately to John A. Macdonald about Ontario's practice of paying stipends to federal appointed judges, almost fifteen years after the prime minister had first objected to this practice. The judge described the practice as unconstitutional, but admitted it would be politically very difficult to take the stipends away from judges who had become accustomed to them.[32] Apparently Macdonald agreed, for nothing was done. A Manitoba act of 1889, narrowing the jurisdiction of the Court of Queen's Bench, gave "great offence" to the judges of that court, according to the lieutenant-governor, but no action was taken.[33]

The final disallowances related to judicial matters during the period under consideration were Mercier's two almost identical District Magistrates acts, disallowed in 1888 and 1889. These attempted to establish a provincially appointed court in Montreal to deal with minor cases involving civil law and thus to reduce the heavy case load of the Superior Court.[34] The Superior Court's difficulties in handling its docket were reinforced by the fact that some vacancies had not been filled, the result of conflicts over judicial patronage among the faction-ridden Quebec Conservatives.[35] Nonetheless, the acts were disallowed on the familiar grounds that they encroached on the dominion's power over judicial appointments.

In contrast to the courts, other provincial institutions occasioned only a few disallowances. The BNA Act empowered the provinces to amend their internal constitutions, except as regards the office of lieutenant-governor, and the dominion government generally respected their right to do so. Macdonald, for example, gave Premier Chapleau of Quebec friendly advice on how to abolish the Legislative Council at a time when that change was under consideration.[36] Almost a decade later his government officially informed Premier Blair of New Brunswick, who was also considering abolition, that "the federal government and parliament have no right to intervene in a matter of this kind. The province alone has jurisdiction."[37] Thompson was annoyed when the lieutenant-governor of Prince Edward Island reserved a bill on this subject (see chapter 8).

There were exceptions, however. In 1869 Quebec and Ontario almost simultaneously adopted similar statutes defining the privileges of their legislative assemblies as being identical to those of the House of Commons and protecting persons involved in the publication of sessional papers from any liability arising out of the contents.[38] John A. Macdonald, after consulting the law officers in England, considered these acts *ultra vires*, and since neither provincial government was apparently willing to take responsibility for securing their repeal they were disallowed on the same day in November 1869. Quebec adopted a more innocuous version the following year, which was allowed to stand. In 1875 Oliver Mowat, now premier of Ontario, sounded out Edward Blake, now the federal minister of justice, as to the dominion's reaction if Ontario were to adopt a new statute on legislative privilege. Blake responded by indicating that he agreed with John A. Macdonald's arguments against the original version, and might have to follow Macdonald's example by recommending disallowance, but that a statute similar to the Quebec version of 1870 would be acceptable.[39] Meanwhile Manitoba in 1873 had adopted a statute based on the Ontario statute of 1869, apparently unaware of the latter's fate. The confusion surrounding the Pacific Scandal and the fall of Macdonald's government prevented this measure from being disallowed within the one-year deadline, but the governor general solemnly asserted that it had not been "received" until November 1873, more than eight months after its passage, and could therefore be disallowed on Hewitt Bernard's recommendation in September 1874.[40]

Another Manitoba statute, in 1885, directly affected the office of lieutenant-governor and was disallowed more promptly. In the following year Quebec adopted "an act respecting the executive power" which empowered the lieutenant-governor in council and various agencies of the provincial government to conduct public inquiries, summon witnesses, and require evidence to be given under oath. Thompson's report stated that this measure exceeded provincial powers under Section 92 of the BNA Act and it was disallowed.[41]

Transportation, in all its aspects, accounted for twenty-six disallowances, or 40 per cent of the total number. Nineteen of the twenty-six were private acts to charter railway, bridge, or shipping companies, while the other seven were public acts of broader significance. Manitoba suffered by far the largest number of disallowances in this category, but most of the other provinces were affected at one time or another. It might also be noted that the twenty reserved bills from which the dominion government explicitly withheld assent included three railway charters, a charter to build a bridge and another for a telegraph company, a bill regarding harbours in New Brunswick, and a water-power charter that would have interfered with navigation on the St Lawrence River.

Of the twenty-six disallowed acts, strictly speaking, the earliest was a Nova Scotia statute to regulate pilotage in the Bras d'Or Lakes, disallowed in 1871 because it trespassed on federal jurisdiction over navigation and shipping.[42] Three Nova Scotia charters for international shipping companies were disallowed in 1874 and 1875.[43] Two charters to build bridges, one in Quebec and one in Manitoba, were disallowed in 1876 because of the possibility that the bridges might interfere with navigation.[44] Another bridge charter, in New Brunswick, was disallowed for the same reason in 1883.[45] A British Columbia act chartering a firm to engage in both food processing and shipping was disallowed in 1878, a few months before the Mackenzie government lost office.[46] The report by deputy minister of justice Zebulon Lash singled out the shipping aspect as the grounds for recommending disallowance.[47] Three British Columbia statutes imposing tolls on the Cariboo wagon road were disallowed, one in 1879 and two in 1881. (Premier Walkem offered to amend the latter two, but his offer came too late, as disallowance had already taken place.)[48] The reason given in all three cases was that they trespassed on federal jurisdiction over the regulation of trade and commerce, but the fact that the road was used to haul supplies for the construction of the transcontinental railway was probably the major consideration. Also disallowed, in 1887, was a Nova Scotia statute to regulate freight, warehouse, and wharfage changes. Both navigation and shipping and the regulation of trade and commerce were cited as grounds for this disallowance.[49]

The long struggle to protect the CPR monopoly against Manitoba, and to some extent British Columbia, involved the disallowance of no fewer than twelve private acts chartering railway companies, ten in Manitoba and two in British Columbia, between 1881 and 1887 (see chapter 6). Also disallowed were three public acts of Manitoba relating to railways.[50] The first was a general act to encourage railway-building in 1882, which was disallowed solely on the grounds that it affected the interests and policies of the dominion. The second was a measure adopted five years later permitting railways to be built by the Manitoba government itself, and was disallowed for the same reason. The last was the "Act for further improving the Law," described earlier in this chapter, which permitted railway contractors and their employees to escape liability.

Four other disallowances related to corporations and their charters, although not in the field of transportation. The BNA Act allowed provinces to charter corporations "with Provincial Objects," and the Mackenzie government disallowed two private acts for failing to comply with that restriction. The first was an act to incorporate the Winnipeg Board of Trade, disallowed in 1874 after the same long delay suffered by the act on legislative privilege.[51] The grounds were that a board of trade fell under "the regulation of trade and commerce" and therefore did not have a "Provincial Object." Lieutenant-Governor Morris, on behalf of his council, protested that Ontario had incorporated two boards of trade in 1868. A memorandum by Hewitt Bernard responded that John A. Macdonald had had doubts about those incorporations also and that, in any event, the Mackenzie government had since introduced a bill that would give Parliament a general power to incorporate boards of trade.[52]

The second disallowance of a private act relating to a non-transportation enterprise took place in 1878. The British Columbia legislature adopted an act incorporating a company to issue various types of insurance.[53] Since the Judicial Committee of the Privy Council had not yet decided the case of Citizens' Insurance vs Parsons, there were grounds for reasonable doubt whether a province could legally charter such an enterprise. A secondary grounds for the disallowance was the fact that the charter also dealt with interest, a subject placed under federal jurisdiction by Section 91.19 of the BNA Act.

In the 1890s Manitoba attempted to regulate the affairs of corporations chartered outside the province, including those with federal charters, insofar as they operated within Manitoba. In doing so the province entered a somewhat uncertain area of constitutional law. A public act of 1890 provided that any such company (apart from railways, banks, and insurance companies) would require a provincial licence to operate in Manitoba and that the licence could be revoked at any time by the provincial government. A company without a licence could not take or hold mortgages on any real estate in Manitoba. The statute was promptly disallowed. Five years later it was re-enacted in a slightly more restrictive form and with a different title, and again disallowed. The province tried again in 1897, perhaps expecting a Liberal government in Ottawa to be more tolerant of constitutional excesses, but a third disallowance followed in 1898.[54]

Public lands in the western provinces, an essential ingredient of the nation-building project of the dominion government, were of primary concern in six disallowances. The first of these was a British Columbia statute to amend and consolidate the laws relating to crown lands.[55] It was disallowed in 1875 mainly on the grounds that it disregarded the interests and claims of the native people, as well as the dominion's responsibility for "Indians and lands reserved for the Indians." A year later a Manitoba act to regulate legal proceedings against and by the crown was disallowed on the grounds that since the dominion owned the public lands in Manitoba, it might be deemed to apply to proceedings in which the dominion was a party.[56]

In 1878 British Columbia adopted a statute providing that the balances owing to the province on the purchase of surveyed crown land would be subject to interest at the rate of 24 per cent per annum. Since the normal interest rate at that time was 5 per cent, this was a somewhat unusual measure, even by British Columbian standards. The Macdonald government disallowed it on the grounds that interest was a federal responsibility.[57]

Land was also the issue when a Manitoba act relating to escheats
and forfeitures was disallowed in 1885. Although the dominion by
this time had had to concede that the older provinces, and particularly Ontario, had inherited the prerogative powers of the crown in
relation to these matters, it insisted that Manitoba was in a different
situation because its public lands belonged to the dominion. Therefore escheated or forfeited real estate must also revert to the dominion.[58]

The so-called Sumas Diking Lands, a part of the British Columbia
railway belt, accounted for one disallowance and caused consideration to be given to another. In 1878 the province had granted certain of these lands to an entrepreneur named E.L. Derby, who was
also empowered to construct certain works for the draining and reclamation of other lands in the vicinity. In return for doing this work,
Derby would receive an additional grant of land and also the right to
impose certain charges on settlers whose lands increased in value as
a result of the draining and reclamation. When Derby failed to complete the work in time, the legislature extended his privileges by an
amendment to the original act in 1883.[59] The settlers, whose lawyer
was Theodore Davie, later premier of the province, petitioned for
disallowance, but to no avail.[60] Two years later a new amendment
provided that the provincial cabinet could cancel the agreement with
Derby and then sell the unoccupied portion of the land, with the
proceeds going into a special fund to be used for the reclamation
work Derby had promised but not carried out.[61] This time the dominion did exercise its power of disallowance, on the grounds that
the Sumas Diking Lands were part of the railway belt and thus federal property. On the same day another British Columbia act relating to land, which retroactively validated certain sales and allowed
the provincial cabinet to place land reserved for public purposes on
the market, was disallowed on the grounds that it dealt with questions that were already before the courts.[62]

Controversial legislation at the provincial level was often followed
by petitions for its disallowance from private individuals or associa-
tions addressed to the dominion government. More often than not,
these acts were allowed to remain in force. In few if any cases, even
when the act was disallowed, do the petitions appear to have been a
decisive influence on the federal government's decision. As the contrasting fate of the two amendments to the Sumas Diking Act
suggests, the dominion was far more likely to use its power of disallowance on behalf of its own interests, powers, and property than on
behalf of those of private individuals or corporations. The Caldwell-
McLaren affair, and Macdonald's apparent obsession with it, appears to be the exception that proves the rule.

Of the petitions for disallowance that survive in the dominion government's files, and that were not acted upon, the majority appear to have been based on the economic self-interest of the petitioners. Two of these were sent from New Brunswick as early as 1869. One was from lumbermen on the Musquatch River who objected to the chartering of a firm to build dams on that river. The other was from shareholders in a railway company who refused to pay for their stock on the grounds that the company had not complied with its charter and who objected to an amendment requiring them to do so.[63] Another disappointed petitioner, a few years later, was the owner of the Toronto waterworks, whose enterprise was threatened by an act allowing the municipality to build its own waterworks.[64] In another instance, sixty-three members of the Montreal bourgeoisie, mainly anglophones, petitioned against a Quebec act authorizing the city to purchase stock in the Montreal Northern Colonization Railway, an enterprise promoted by the celebrated Laurentian priest, Curé Labelle.[65] A British Columbia bill imposing a tax on "wild land" was protested against by the Hudson's Bay Company.[66] Although it was reserved by Lieutenant-Governor Trutch and then refused assent by Macdonald, these actions appear to have been taken before Trutch or Macdonald were aware of the company's views, and to have been motivated by concern for the bill's effect on the transcontinental railway project.

In addition to the British Columbia judges and the Sumas Diking Land settlers, disappointed petitioners in the period after 1878 included a quarrying company near Toronto whose narrow-gauge railway along Kingston Road apparently disturbed the tranquility of the neighbourhood. The Ontario legislature enacted that the company must desist from the use of steam locomotives, which had been permitted by the original charter in 1873, until authorized by the local council to resume their operation. Justice Minister Alexander Campbell recommended against disallowance. Prime Minister Macdonald agreed, but recognized that his acquiescence in this unilateral termination of private rights might appear inconsistent with his insistence on the disallowance of the Rivers and Streams Act. He suggested that the dominion should simply allow the deadline for disallowing the so-called Gravel Road Act to expire, rather than explicitly endorsing Campbell's favourable report with an order in council.[67]

Even where political interests were more clearly involved, Macdonald was generally cautious about using the power of disallowance. In 1883 certain American lumbermen attempted by corrupt means to secure the defeat of Liberal candidates in the Ontario election. When this failed they attempted to bribe Liberal members to cross the floor, thus hoping to bring down Mowat's government, which had only a narrow majority.[68] The plot apparently involved some Canadian Conservatives as well as the Americans. Mowat established a royal commission and adopted a statute, the Election Law Amendment Act, which gave the commission unusually broad powers to investigate such matters, even in the event that the matters in question were simultaneously before the courts. A Conservative senator, J.B. Plumb, and a Conservative MP, Hector Cameron, wrote separately to Macdonald requesting the disallowance of the act. Macdonald replied to Plumb that disallowance would be "impolitic," presumably because it would be interpreted as an effort to shield the guilty persons, although he conceded that the act itself was "outrageous." Writing to Alexander Campbell, the prime minister suggested that he might change his mind, for "it behooves the Federal Gov't. to protect the Constitution from invasion." Campbell replied that he could see no legal grounds for disallowance and that the federal jurisdiction over criminal law was not really affected.[69] The act was not disallowed, and the royal commission proceeded as planned.

An instance of the federal government's reluctance to intervene in a private controversy having little constitutional or political significance was a Manitoba act of 1888 which unilaterally terminated a contract between a printing firm and the provincial government. The printing firm petitioned for its disallowance. Thompson described it as "a shocking piece of legislation," but recommended to Macdonald that it not be disallowed, since it affected only one company and since disallowance was already a controversial issue in Manitoba. The prime minister agreed, and no disallowance took place.[70]

At about the same time a British Columbia statute imposing higher assessments and taxes on land owned by businesses in the province inspired vigorous protests and requests for disallowance from no less an enterprise than the Canadian Pacific Railway, which then as now was one of the largest landowners in the province. The solicitor of the railway company wrote to both Thompson and Macdonald, describing the statute overdramatically as "the small edge of a wedge with which the provinces acting together may yet split the CPR into useless fragments." He also reminded the prime minister that "Mr. Laurier told Mr. Van Horne" that the Liberal opposition would not publicly criticize the disallowance if it took place.[71] However, Macdonald was having some difficulties in dealing with the CPR management at this point and he may have felt that he had risked his popularity often enough on the railway company's behalf, particularly by using the power of disallowance. He did not take any action.

One type of controversy in which the dominion government consistently refused to intervene by using its power of disallowance was controversy involving religion. This was shown not only by its refusal to disallow the acts that ended the support of Catholic schools in New Brunswick, Prince Edward Island, and Manitoba but in other episodes as well. All of the above acts, and the related statutes concerning taxation for educational purposes, were petitioned against by the Catholic clergy and laity, but to no avail. Similarly, a New Brunswick statute of 1870 to divide an Anglican parish into two parts, and an Ontario statute of 1875 attempting to regulate a dispute between Presbyterian churches, were not disallowed, although both were the subject of petitions for disallowance.[72] In 1873 some of Quebec's Protestant elites protested against municipal support for Curé Labelle's Colonization Railway, as noted above, and four years later the dominion Board of Trade petitioned for the disallowance of a Quebec act that authorized an order of nuns to engage in manufacturing and wholesale trade. The businessmen alleged that this measure was unfair since the nuns paid no taxes, that ordinary wage labour would be unable to compete, and that the act would interfere with trade and commerce.[73] No action was taken. A dozen years later, when the Jesuit Estates Act caused nationwide agitation among disgruntled Protestants, Macdonald firmly refused to disallow it before the one-year time limit expired and he tried to place the onus for his inaction on the law officers of the imperial government.

One of the few instances in which a petition for disallowance may have had a decisive impact concerned a Manitoba statute of 1889 requiring property owners whose municipal taxes were in arrears to pay interest on the balance. The Manitoba branch of the Knights of Labor petitioned for disallowance. Macdonald's son Hugh John, a partner in the Winnipeg law firm that represented some of the property owners, advised the prime minister to take the petition seriously because Frank Linn, the author of the petition, "is the leading light in the Knights of Labour here, and is a strong Conservative and a bitter opponent of the Greenway-Martin government. He is an awful bore but really has influence so it is as well to humour him as much as possible." Justice Minister Thompson doubted that the act was really *ultra vires*, but it was disallowed on the ostensible grounds that it dealt with "interest."[74]

By and large, the evidence does not suggest that the power of disallowance was used excessively, arbitrarily, or unfairly. The vast majority of the disallowed statutes were *ultra vires*, or at least appeared to be so at the time. Liberals were just as likely to disallow provincial acts as Conservatives; Mackenzie's government disallowed eighteen in five years, compared to forty-six in nineteen years for Macdonald (and thirty in fifteen years for Laurier after 1896). Business interests did not automatically, or even usually, get their way when they requested the disallowance of a statute, and Protestants were no more likely than Catholics to have the power used on behalf of their religious convictions. Admittedly the western provinces suffered more disallowances than the others, which continued to be the case in the twentieth century, but most of those disallowances were probably deserved.

The main difficulties with disallowance were that it involved the federal government in an excessive number of controversies, thus risking its popularity, and that it could not prevent a province, or different provinces, from repeatedly re-enacting measures that had already been disallowed. Reliance on the courts to deal with provincial legislation had neither of these disadvantages, and thus gradually became the normal procedure. In the second half of the twentieth century the use of disallowance was entirely abandoned.

10 The Imperial Connection

In a recent book Douglas Verney has argued that the regime established in Canada in 1867 should be described as "imperial federalism" since it cannot be fully understood or appreciated without reference to the ties between Canada and the United Kingdom. The executive powers of the queen and the governor general, the legislative power exercised by Westminster over Canada's constitution, and the judicial power of the Judicial Committee of the Privy Council were integral parts of a constitutional system of checks and balances, according to Verney, and their disappearance has left Canadian federalism incomplete and in some ways defective.[1]

Verney's argument that the imperial connection served to protect provincial interests, particularly those of Quebec, against centralization is not really supported by the evidence, apart from the decentralizing impact of Lord Watson's and Viscount Haldane's interpretations of the British North America Act. However, Verney is right to remind us that the theory and practice of Canadian federalism, in its early phase at least, cannot be fully understood without reference to the imperial connection. For better or for worse the imperial connection was a real fact in nineteenth-century Canada, not just a ceremonial vestige, and it did have some impact on how the system operated.

Present-day Canadians often appear to assume that Confederation was an abrupt transition from colonialism to nationhood, a myth perhaps unconsciously influenced by the proximity on the calendar between Dominion Day (now known as Canada Day) and the

American Fourth of July. In one sense, the myth is accurate: the expansion of "Canada" from the Quebec-Ontario core to a federation of transcontinental dimensions did facilitate Canada's development into a virtually sovereign state. Furthermore, the British authorities were aware in 1867 that a larger "Canada" would probably be more self-reliant than the old Province of Canada. Donald Creighton's comment that "the Statute of Westminster of 1931 is the logical outcome of the British North America Act of 1867" is correct as a statement of a broad historical tendency.[2]

At the same time it must be emphasized that the process was gradual and incremental. Formally, the Dominion of Canada in July 1867 was no more independent of the empire than the Province of Canada or the provinces of Nova Scotia and New Brunswick had been in June. The BNA Act provided that the queen, acting on the advice of her United Kingdom ministers, could disallow the acts of the Canadian Parliament and that the governor general could reserve bills "for the Signification of the Queen's Pleasure." Both powers were occasionally exercised until the 1880s. The governor general was selected by the United Kingdom government and reported to it through the Colonial Office at frequent and fairly regular intervals. He received frequent letters and dispatches from the colonial secretary, not all of which he shared with his Canadian ministers. Communication between the Canadian government and the United Kingdom government was almost totally confined to these official channels. (Communication between the provinces and the United Kingdom government was supposed to follow them as well, although there were occasional exceptions in practice.) Canada lacked any power to conduct its own foreign policy, a situation that lasted well into the twentieth century. Even its domestic legislative capacity was limited in regard to certain sensitive topics, such as shipping and copyright. The Colonial Laws Validity Act, adopted only two years before Confederation, gave the self-governing colonies more freedom of action by providing that their domestic legislation need not necessarily be identical with that which prevailed in the British Isles, but it also clearly stated that the colonies were subordinate and that the Parliament at Westminster could legislate for them as it saw fit, with or without their permission.

The United Kingdom in the second half of Queen Victoria's reign was a liberal but not really democratic polity. The suffrage, although enlarged significantly in 1867 and again in 1885, was still very limited; in fact, the percentage of the population who could vote was significantly lower in the United Kingdom than in Canada. The House of Lords shared power on a virtually equal basis with the House of

Commons, and important ministers, including the prime minister, were often selected from that house. In terms of direct intervention into the economy and society of the British Isles the British state of the Victorian era had very limited functions: more limited than those of most European states or even the Canadian state. It neither owned railways nor imposed tariffs, nor did it take more than a slight interest in the health, welfare, and education of the people. What it did, with apparent success, was to maintain the necessary conditions for the expansion of industrial and financial capitalism at home and for an active foreign and (at least after 1874) colonial policy overseas.

The government that presided over Canada's Confederation was a Conservative one, headed by the fourteenth earl of Derby. In February 1868 the earl was replaced as head of the government by Benjamin Disraeli, who resigned after an electoral defeat later in the year. The Liberals then governed under Gladstone until February 1874, when the Conservatives returned under Disraeli and remained in office for more than six years. Gladstone was prime minister again from April 1880 until July 1886, apart from a seven-month interlude in 1885–6 when the Conservatives took the helm under the third marquess of Salisbury. Salisbury formed another government in July 1886, which lasted until August 1892. The Liberals then returned under Gladstone, who retired in March 1894 in favour of the fifth earl of Rosebery. A year later Rosebery's government resigned and Salisbury returned to office as the last prime minister to sit in the House of Lords.[3]

There were thus ten changes of prime minister and eight changes in the incumbent political party in less than thirty years, only five of them as the result of a general election (1868, 1874, 1880, 1886, and 1892). This superficial instability masked a considerable continuity based on the essential cohesion of the governing class, at least until 1886. Gladstone's espousal of Irish Home Rule in that year, contrasted with the increasing chauvinism and imperialism of the Conservatives, added an ideological element to British politics which had not previously been as pronounced, but which has continued up to the present.

Although the social basis of political alignment in the two countries was actually quite different, there were vague sentimental affinities between the two Canadian political parties and their British namesakes. The fact that a Conservative government at Westminster had secured the passage of the BNA Act, largely at the behest of Canadian Conservatives, contributed to this affinity on the Conservative side, although it would probably have existed in any event. The similarity in personality, political views, and even physical appearance between Disraeli and Macdonald was remarked upon during their lifetime. Disraeli was impressed by Macdonald when they met.[4] Macdonald seems to have consciously copied some of Disraeli's policies, such as the legalization of trade unions, and he had a low opinion of Gladstone. More often than not, however, the two countries were governed by "opposite" parties. Gladstone's first government coincided roughly with Macdonald's first government, while Disraeli's second government coincided roughly with the Mackenzie government in Canada. The long period of Canadian Conservative rule from 1878 until 1896 was about evenly divided between Liberal and Conservative governments in the United Kingdom. Contrasting political affiliations might have seriously complicated relations, in the same way that they complicated relations between the federal government and the provinces, had not British governments tended to restrain themselves from active intervention in Canadian affairs. Arguably they still had some impact on a few occasions.

Canadian (and other colonial) governments had very few direct dealings with the British prime minister. For most practical purposes of Canadian concern, the imperial government meant the Colonial Office and the colonial secretary, whose correct but rarely used title was secretary of state for the colonies. Except in the most unusual circumstances, any decision of a British government on a Canadian matter would be based on the advice of the colonial secretary and his department.

According to David Farr, the Colonial Office was considered one of the less important departments in the United Kingdom government.[5] It had a staff of only sixty-seven persons in 1870, a number that had declined to sixty-five by 1880, a level at which it remained in 1890. By the latter half of Victoria's reign the self-governing settler colonies, in North America and elsewhere, were deemed to require only sporadic attention, while the tropical empire was only in the process of being assembled. India was handled by a separate department, not by the Colonial Office. The secretary of state for the colonies was almost always selected from the House of Lords, possibly because the work of his department had little direct impact on the electorate represented in the House of Commons.

Between 1867 and 1896 the colonial portfolio changed hands twelve times, although it was held by only nine individuals in total. Apart from Joseph Chamberlain, who assumed the portfolio in 1895, none of the nine had a major impact on the history of the United Kingdom. From a Canadian perspective the most important was the earl of Carnarvon, who piloted the British North America bill through the House of Lords in 1867 but resigned shortly afterwards because he disagreed with Disraeli's bill to extend the franchise. Despite this difference of opinion, Carnarvon was colonial secretary again in Disraeli's second government, from 1874 until 1878, and played a significant role during those years in the federal government's relations with British Columbia (see chapter 6). Carnarvon's personal correspondence with Governor General Lord Dufferin, a personal friend although a political opponent, helped him to keep in touch with Canadian affairs, and is a unique resource for students of Canadian history.[6] Presumably Carnarvon took a special interest in the dominion because he had presided over its creation. His eloquent speech on second reading of the British North America bill, quoted in chapter 1, suggests that he rightly regarded Confederation as an important event in history. None of his successors appears to have had this emotional interest in Canada, and most were probably guided by the advice of their officials insofar as they involved themselves in Canadian affairs. At any rate, sharp discontinuities of policy between different colonial secretaries, even when they belonged to different parties, are not apparent from the record. It is possible, however, that a Liberal colonial secretary would have been less inclined to acquiesce in the dismissal of lieutenant-governor Letellier than was Sir Michael Hicks-Beach, the Conservative who succeeded Carnarvon in 1878.

A far more visible actor in Canadian affairs than the colonial secretary was the governor general. He was both the ceremonial representative of the crown and, particularly before 1878, the guardian of imperial interests as interpreted by the United Kingdom government of the day. He was also the official channel for all communication between the two governments. In addition to the many dispatches he sent on the advice of his Canadian prime minister, he produced a smaller but significant number of dispatches which he drafted without Canadian advice, in his capacity as an imperial officer. Similarly the dispatches received by him were in most cases meant to be shared with his Canadian advisers, but in some cases were intended for his eyes alone.

Between 1867 and 1896 Canada had seven governors general, including Viscount Monck, a holdover from the pre-Confederation regime, who had arrived in 1861. Monck remained in office for more than a year after Confederation. He was followed by Sir John Young (subsequently known as Lord Lisgar) in 1868, the earl of Dufferin in 1872, the marquess of Lorne in 1878, the marquess of Lansdowne in 1883, Lord Stanley in 1888, and the earl of Aberdeen in 1893.

Apart from Young, who was given his title midway through his term of office, all of these men belonged to the hereditary British aristocracy. Lorne was married to the queen's daughter, Princess Louise. Stanley was the younger son of the earl of Derby who had been prime minister in 1867, and eventually succeeded to the title on his older brother's death. Aberdeen was the grandson of an earlier prime minister. Young, Dufferin, Lansdowne, and Stanley had held ministerial office before coming to Canada. Young had also been governor of New South Wales. Both Dufferin and Lansdowne were subsequently viceroy of India, the only colonial posting that outranked the governor generalship of Canada in prestige and importance.

In terms of party politics, Monck, Dufferin, Lansdowne, and Aberdeen were Liberals while Young, Lorne, and Stanley were Conservatives, and all were appointed by governments of their own party. The Canadian government played no part in the process of appointment.

Four of the seven governors-general – Monck, Young, Dufferin, and Lansdowne – were Irish Protestants, including three of the four appointed by Liberal governments. Lorne and Aberdeen were Scottish. Only Stanley was an Englishman. The penchant for Irish appointments appears to be more than coincidence, but the reason for it is not known. Possibly the experience of living as part of a Protestant elite in a Catholic country was considered good training for Canada, the only part of the overseas empire where the Catholic church enjoyed widespread support and quasi-official status. Possibly Englishmen simply preferred to be sent to warmer climates. Protestant Irish governors general were potential targets for Fenian terrorism, a fact that caused some anxiety, but in other respects they seem to have been appropriate choices. Farr argues that Monck, Dufferin, and Lansdowne were the ablest and most successful of the seven governors general under consideration.[7] Carman Miller makes a similar claim on behalf of Young.[8]

Governors general tended to be substantial landholders, and Dufferin's instinctive antipathy to land reform in Prince Edward Island illustrates one consequence of this fact. Actually Dufferin's estates, which amounted to 8000 acres in 1897, were modest in relation to some of the others. At the same date Monck's heir and successor owned 14,200 acres. (Monck himself had died in 1894.) Aberdeen, then the incumbent governor general, owned 63,000, and his immediate predecessor, Stanley, owned 69,000. Lansdowne owned a total of 143,000 acres, ten times as much as Dufferin and an area larger than the Island of Montreal. Lorne's father, the duke of Argyll, owned 170,000 acres, to which Lorne himself eventually succeeded along with the title.[9] Altogether, these six men owned a total of 467,000 acres, or 730 square miles, which is equivalent to one-third of Prince Edward Island. Young (Lisgar) is once again the odd man out; no information is available about his landholdings, but they were almost certainly modest.

The British North America Act established the governor general's salary, to be paid by the dominion, at an annual rate of £10,000 sterling, or almost $50,000. (By way of contrast, most deputy ministers in the public service of Canada earned only $2600.) This provision in the act was not entrenched but could be altered by the Parliament of Canada. Less than a year after Confederation Parliament voted to reduce the salary to $32,000, even though the bill, introduced by two Grits from Oxford County, Ontario, was opposed by John A. Macdonald and all his cabinet colleagues.[10] Viscount Monck reserved the bill, probably on Macdonald's advice, and the imperial government refused to grant assent. Although the status quo was thus maintained, this episode apparently made members of the British aristocracy reluctant to accept the position. As a result the Disraeli government had to appoint Young, an elderly untitled former politician and colonial governor who was close to retirement.

The year 1878 is something of a watershed in the history of the governor general's office. Prior to that date the governor general's instructions required him to preside over formal meetings of the Executive Council and also to reserve certain categories of bills, including those affecting imperial interests, those making a gift of any kind to the governor general himself, and those granting a divorce under unusual circumstances. Nineteen bills, including ten divorce bills, were actually reserved in eleven years.[11] It was also during this period that the Colonial Office alleged that the power of disallowance could be exercised without ministerial advice (see chapter 9).

At the insistence of Edward Blake, a convinced anti-imperialist, these instructions were drastically revised. Taking effect at the end of Lord Dufferin's term (which happened almost to coincide with the end of the Mackenzie government), the new instructions dropped the grounds for reservation and specified that practically all the governor general's powers would be exercised on the advice of the Canadian government. After this there was only one more reservatiion, a bill affecting foreign fishing vessels in 1886.

A more intangible reason for the lesser importance of the office after 1878 was the fact that the four governors general who followed Dufferin were all born in the 1840s, and were thus a generation younger than Macdonald and the other Fathers of Confederation.

Macdonald was the Old Chieftain, the acknowledged master of the country and a statesman of international renown. In contrast to Monck, who had exercised some discretion in selecting Macdonald as the first prime minister, and Dufferin, who had forced Macdonald to resign over the Pacific Scandal, the post-Dufferin governors general tended to defer to the old prime minister. Stanley even apologized to him, in 1889, for making a slight change in a minute of council, an event that would have been inconceivable twenty years earlier.[12]

In considering the impact of the Colonial Office and the governor general on federal-provincial relations, it is appropriate to classify instances of their involvement in terms of the source of the initiative which led them to become involved. There were five ways in which federal-provincial disputes attracted their involvement: at the initiative of the provincial government concerned, at the initiative of the dominion government, at the initiative of the governor general, at the initative of the imperial government, and at the initiative of private interests.

Confederation had, in theory, ended the direct relationship between each province and the imperial government. All communication between London and the provincial capitals, in either direction, was supposed to be by way of the federal government in Ottawa and the governor general. In practice the provinces that had enjoyed a separate existence as British colonies prior to Confederation (New Brunswick, Nova Scotia, British Columbia, and Prince Edward Island) did not take kindly to this rule. Furthermore, Macdonald allowed an exception for his "spoilt child," British Columbia, as early as 1871, when he suggested to Lieutenant-Governor Trutch that the province correspond directly with the imperial government regarding a boundary dispute with the Americans in Juan de Fuca Strait.[13] Direct contacts between provinces and the imperial government cannot reasonably be attributed to this suggestion, particularly since some of them preceded it, but the suggestion may have helped to legitimize the practice. Six years later the Mackenzie government formally reminded all provinces that they must communicate with London only by way of the governor general, but this reminder appears to have had no effect whatsoever.[14]

For whatever reason, certain provinces indulged in the practice of taking their grievances "to the foot of the throne," exactly as they might have done had Confederation not taken place. The pioneer in this regard was Nova Scotia, which did indeed wish that Confederation had not taken place. In February 1868, when the Nova Scotia legislature adopted the resolutions calling for the repeal of the

BNA Act, the resolutions were immediately sent directly from the lieutenant-governor's office to London. At the same time another copy of the resolutions was sent to the governor general. In forwarding the resolutions a week later to the colonial secretary, Monck explained that he realized General Doyle had already sent them directly. He added that he believed Doyle had acted appropriately in doing so, "rather than delaying your receipt of them by using the normal channels."[15]

Soon afterwards, the Nova Scotia delegation headed by Joseph Howe was sent to London, where its efforts met with little success. In retrospect it appears incredible that the Nova Scotians could have expected the imperial government to repudiate such an important measure as the BNA Act, only a year after its adoption by Parliament, in the certain knowledge that repeal would throw the northern half of North America into disarray at a time when relations between the empire and the United States were even more hostile than usual. Although Howe suggested that the machinations of "the Railway and Financial interests to be effected (sic) by this measure" might have brought about the failure of his mission, no such conspiratorial explanation seems to be necessary.[16]

In any event the colonial secretary, the duke of Buckingham, clearly stated the Disraeli government's opposition to repeal, and support for Confederation, in a detailed policy statement dated 4 June 1868, a statement to which Macdonald referred in his efforts to persuade Howe that further resistance would be futile. The Nova Scotia government attempted to rebut some of the arguments in the Buckingham statement, but to no avail. In December, just before the Disraeli government resigned, the duke issued another policy statement to supplement the first one, indicating that the imperial government's views had not changed.[17]

Nova Scotians' hopes rose, and federalists experienced some anxiety, when Gladstone replaced Disraeli in December 1868. The BNA Act had been carried by a Conservative government, and some British Liberals were perceived to be sceptical about Confederation and prepared to sacrifice Canada for the sake of good relations with the United States.[18] This perception ignored the fact that British support for the Confederation movement had commenced in 1864, when the Liberals had been in office. A month after taking office, the new colonial secretary, Lord Granville, issued a statement indicating that the Gladstone government would continue its predecessor's commitment to making Confederation work.[19] Although a later, secret and confidential dispatch warned that British troops must not be used to keep Nova Scotia in Confederation by force,[20] the public statement was more significant, since there was no real prospect that force would be required.

The secessionists were not entirely prepared to give up, however. In April 1870 the Nova Scotia legislature again appealed to the queen to intervene in their conflict with the dominion, although this time the address was sent through the proper channels by way of Ottawa. Granville had moved to the Foreign Office by this time, but the new colonial secretary, Lord Kimberley, indicated that imperial support for Confederation remained firm. His reply stated that "it is not within the legal power of the Sovereign to dismember the dominion of Canada" and that "Her Majesty would view with great regret" any effort to do so. Furthermore, Kimberley expressed the hope that Nova Scotians would become reconciled to Confederation, which had "laid the foundation of a great and prosperous Community" in which Nova Scotia would exercise the influence to which it was entitled.[21]

Nova Scotia's disappointing experience with imperial intervention did not deter another province, British Columbia, from carrying its own grievances to the foot of the throne a few years later. Macdonald's resignation over the Pacific Scandal caused consternation in British Columbia, partly because the revelation of the scandal was a major setback for the Pacific railway project and partly because the Liberals were known to consider the terms of union with British Columbia excessively generous. After the change of government the British Columbians wasted little time in seeking to enlist British support for their two major uncompleted projects: the Esquimalt graving dock and the railway. With the federal government's acquiescence, Amor de Cosmos was sent to London to seek financial aid for the graving dock. A few months later Premier George Walkem travelled to London on another mission: to persuade the imperial government to put pressure on Mackenzie to accelerate construction of the railway.

Both initiatives achieved some success (see chapter 6). The Admiralty recommended a subsidy for the graving dock as early as January 1874, and the Disraeli government that took office a month later agreed to make a financial commitment to the project, even before deteriorating relations with Russia increased its strategic significance. The Walkem mission also had an immediate impact and significantly exacerbated the worst political problem faced by the Mackenzie government during its five years in office: British Columbia's unhappiness with the slow rate of progress on the CPR.

Strictly speaking, imperial involvement in the dispute over the railway predated Walkem's visit, since the governor general, Lord

Dufferin, had sent Kimberley a copy of a memorandum outlining British Columbia's grievances in December 1873.[22] How Kimberley would have handled the matter is difficult to say, but in February 1874 the change of government brought Canada's godfather, Lord Carnarvon, back to the Colonial Office. In June, when Walkem decided to undertake his mission to London, his government sent a protest directly to Carnarvon, bypassing the governor general and the federal government and complaining of Mackenzie's failure to begin construction of the railway.[23] Carnarvon decided almost immediately to offer his services as a mediator between the dominion and British Columbia. After some pressure from Lord Dufferin, the Mackenzie government reluctantly accepted this offer in July. In August Carnarvon met Walkem, who had finally arrived in London, and issued the celebrated "Carnarvon terms." Walkem remained in London until the end of the year, and was still there when the revised version of the terms, incorporating some of Mackenzie's objections but essentially similar to the first version, was issued in November.

The Carnarvon terms were not really carried out (see chapter 6). Neither Carnarvon, Dufferin, Walkem, nor Mackenzie could prevent the Senate from defeating the bill to build the Esquimalt and Nanaimo railway, which Walkem and his colleagues considered to be the most important part of the terms. Nonetheless, significant progress was made on surveying the mainland portions of the transcontinental railway under Mackenzie's direction as minister of public works. At the same time the Mackenzie government suffered significant political damage, including the temporary departure of Blake from the cabinet in 1874–75, a deterioration in its relations with both the imperial government and the governor general, and a pronounced reinforcement of British Columbia's hostility towards the Liberal party, not to mention its disaffection with Canada itself.

The defeat of the Esquimalt and Nanaimo Railway bill in the Senate caused the British Columbia legislature to address another petition to the queen early in 1876. This was sent directly to the Colonial Office, although a copy was sent to Ottawa at the same time. The imperial government did not respond and the Mackenzie government's response, insisting that the island railway had not been part of the original terms of union, added fuel to the flames.[24] It was at this point that Lord Dufferin decided to undertake his visit to British Columbia later in the year. In 1878, still dissatisfied with Mackenzie's efforts regarding the transcontinental railway, the legislature adopted a resolution that the queen be asked to bring about British Columbia's separation from Canada if construction of the

CPR did not begin within a year. This resolution was sent to London by way of Ottawa, and Premier Walkem complained to prime minister Macdonald in January 1879 that British Columbians were hurt because the imperial government had not responded. Apparently neither man knew that the document was still in Ottawa, having been mislaid either accidentally or deliberately before the change of government.[25] It did not reach London until March. Macdonald's return and the signing of the CPR contract mollified the British Columbians only slightly, and in 1881 the legislature sent another address to the queen, demanding that the imperial government force the dominion to implement the original Carnarvon terms, including the island railway.[26]

Despite its disappointments, British Columbia clearly received more sympathy from the imperial authorities than did Nova Scotia. The main reason relates to the objectives of the two provinces. Nova Scotia's objective was secession and the undoing of Confederation, an objective that was contrary to British interests as interpreted by both British political parties. British Columbia, despite the threat of secession in the legislature's resolution of 1878, was really interested in strengthening the dominion, not in weakening or dissolving it. Although the Esquimalt and Nanaimo was arguably of little importance, the Canadian Pacific was in fact essential, as Macdonald succinctly observed, to make the dominion more than "a geographical expression." However self-interested and unrealistic the demands of the British Columbia politicians may have been, the achievement of their principal demand was actually beneficial to the interests of both Canada and the British Empire. It was Mackenzie and Blake, rather than the British Columbians, who could plausibly be accused of betraying the vision of 1867, and this fact was the most significant difference between British Columbia's situation and that of Nova Scotia a few years earlier. British Columbia's other objective, the graving dock, was less important and perhaps unnecessary, but it too could be plausibly related to the interests of both the empire and the dominion, particularly when war with Russia was a real possibility and relations with the United States remained cool.

British Columbia also benefited from a number of other circumstances that were not present in the Nova Scotian case. Lord Carnarvon's strong commitment to the survival of the Canadian federation motivated him to play a more active role in the controversy than a different colonial secretary would probably have done. Lord Dufferin's activist concept of the governor general's office, his friendship with Carnarvon, his lack of rapport with Mackenzie, and his suspicion of Blake all inclined him to play an active role as well, even though he was not favourably impressed by British Columbia's political elite when he met them on his visit to Victoria in 1876. Dufferin shared Carnarvon's commitment to the survival of a united Canada, an idea that clearly captured his imagination. He believed, perhaps correctly, that the indifference of some Canadian Liberals to British Columbia and its complaints was the greatest threat to the survival of the dominion. Dufferin's efforts in Ottawa supplemented Carnarvon's in London, and ensured that the Mackenzie government would face continuous pressure to compromise with British Columbia's views. The successful resolution of the issue, however, was only made possible by the Mackenzie government's defeat, caused by the depressed state of the economy and by Macdonald's discovery that tariff protection was a politically popular issue.

Another instance of a province seeking imperial support for its grievances against the dominion government was Prince Edward Island's discontent with the Northumberland Strait ferry service in the 1880s. After making unsuccessful representations to Macdonald's government in 1882, 1883, and 1884, the Conservative government of W.W. Sullivan finally appealed to the imperial government for help in 1885, using the standard device of a legislative resolution addressed to the queen.[27] Although the issue was just as important to Prince Edward Island as the CPR was to British Columbia, there was obviously less at stake in this instance; Prince Edward Island was the one province that was clearly not essential to the viability of the dominion. Nonetheless, the British government was concerned enough to encourage Macdonald and Tupper to discuss the issue with the islanders. These discussions led to a serious exploration of the feasibility of a "subway," a project that was still not realized a century later.

The fourth province to seek imperial support for its grievances, Manitoba, was also concerned with problems of transportation. Unlike the other three, Manitoba had never been a British colony under the direct supervision of the Colonial Office, so its action is perhaps somewhat surprising. Probably it was an act of desperation by the moribund Norquay/Harrison government, which succumbed to Thomas Greenway's Liberals a few days after its "memorial" protesting against the disallowance of its railway legislation reached the Colonial Office. It may be noted that Manitoba followed the correct procedure of sending its complaint by way of the governor general, which gave the Macdonald government the opportunity to send its own response simultaneously with the memorial.[28] The colonial secretary was apparently not reassured; less than three years had passed since the Riel Rebellion, and warnings of Manitoba's resentment against the CPR had already been sent to him by Lord Lansdowne. Only a few months previously, a false rumour had reached London to the effect that Macdonald had threatened to use imperial troops to enforce the CPR monopoly.[29] In the circumstances it is perhaps not surprising that Sir Henry Holland (who became Lord Knutsford while this episode was in progress) suggested referring Manitoba's grievance to the Judicial Committee of the Privy Council. The Macdonald government strongly opposed this course of action, which Lansdowne warned Holland would "lead to a serious weakening of the Federal Government and to the multiplication of similar attempts to limit its prerogatives."[30] In an unusually blunt order in council, drafted by Thompson, the federal government warned that imperial intervention would be "dangerous interference" and would be "regarded with feelings of alarm" by all loyal Canadians.[31] Nonetheless, Macdonald began to negotiate a compromise with the new Greenway government and with the CPR, a fact that Lansdowne used to dissuade the colonial secretary from any further action.[32] The monopoly clause was soon terminated.

In common with certain of the provinces, the dominion government itself was not adverse to involving the imperial government in domestic controversies when it perceived some political advantage in doing so. John A. Macdonald in particular had a penchant for seeking legal rulings from the law officers of the United Kingdom government, sometimes because he genuinely needed advice on the legality of a course of action, but sometimes because he anticipated that the law officers would endorse a course of action on which he had already decided. The fact that the BNA Act was an imperial statute provided some justification for this procedure; the law officers were perhaps better qualified to provide expert advice on a constitutional matter than anyone in Canada's Department of Justice, and recourse to their advice was of course less time consuming than referring a matter to the courts or to the Judicial Committee of the Privy Council. In any event the law officers were useful to place the imperial stamp of approval on a decision that might be politically controversial. For example, Macdonald consulted the law officers before disallowing the Ontario and Quebec statutes of 1868 defining the privileges of the provincial legislatures, statutes he strongly suspected were *ultra vires*.

Another early instance of Macdonald deliberately involving the imperial government in a federal-provincial dispute concerned the interpretation of a section of the terms of union with British Columbia, terms that obliged the federal government to provide pensions for certain provincial officials whose positions and salaries would be adversely affected by changes resulting from British Columbia's admission to the dominion. This provision had apparently been framed in deliberately vague terms, and the ink was hardly dry on the terms of union before the question arose of exactly which officials were entitled to the pensions. Macdonald's government submitted the question to the colonial secretary, who arrived at a decision promptly and so informed both the Canadian and British Columbian governments.[33] The matter was settled in time for British Columbia's formal commencement as a province on 1 July 1871.

A far more contentious matter that came before the imperial government the following year was the controversy over the termination of the privileges previously enjoyed by separate schools in New Brunswick. Macdonald did not wish to intervene in this matter, but there was strong sentiment among Catholics, including certain members of Parliament, to do so through disallowance, use of the remedial powers in Section 93, or even amendment of the BNA Act in the event that Section 93 was not applicable to New Brunswick. Although the supporters of such actions lacked the votes to secure the endorsement of Parliament, a resolution saying that the New Brunswick school law was harmless and should be left alone could not be carried either, until the operative clause was replaced by one expressing regret at New Brunswick's action. On the following day Mackenzie and Blake moved that the New Brunswick school act should be referred to the law officers of the crown, and if possible to the Judicial Committee of the Privy Council; their motion was adopted without a recorded vote.[34] Macdonald's government then submitted the question to the law officers, who reported there were no legal grounds for federal intervention since Section 93 did not apply to New Brunswick. This opinion disappointed the Catholics but relieved the pressure on the dominion government only slightly, particularly since New Brunswick showed no signs of modifying its policy. The law officers repeated their opinion in a second report in February 1873, and the colonial secretary informed Lord Dufferin a few days later that the matter was not one that could appropriately be submitted to the Judicial Committee.[35] Although the Commons adopted a resolution in May calling for disallowance, Macdonald ignored it, in part because the deadline for disallowance had passed. The government's policy of inaction, while not universally popular, appeared to be legally correct as well as politically expedient, and had gained some legitimacy from the imperial stamp of approval.

Efforts to keep the issue alive, and to involve the imperial government in it, continued in the next Parliament. The leading parliamentary spokesman of the New Brunswick Catholics, John

Costigan, introduced a resolution in 1875 which would have requested the queen to secure the amendment of the BNA Act so that Section 93 would apply to New Brunswick.[36] It was now the Mackenzie government's turn to be embarrassed by the issue, a development that presumably did not disturb the Conservative Costigan. Like his predecessor, Mackenzie relied on the imperial government to rescue him from his dilemma. The day after the debate on the Costigan resolution ended, he suggested to Lord Dufferin that "the whole controversy would be killed" if the colonial secretary were to formally state that Westminster would never legislate away any provincial rights without the consent of the province concerned.[37] Dufferin promptly relayed the suggestion to Lord Carnarvon, who produced the required statement later in the year. At the same time Carnarvon expressed the hope that New Brunswick would consider the sentiments of its Catholic minority. The colonial secretary also delivered a gentle rebuke to Costigan by suggesting that since education was a provincial matter it was probably unwise to discuss it in the federal Parliament, where it was likely to "engender much heat and irritation."[38]

The imperial government rescued the dominion government from embarrassment again a few years later when the Quebec wing of the Conservative party demanded the dismissal of Lieutenant-Governor Letellier. John A. Macdonald knew that failure to comply with this group's wishes might destroy his party and his government. Still, although Letellier had displayed poor judgment and outrageous partisanship, these were not legal grounds for his dismissal, and the governor general quite properly reminded Macdonald of this fact. Macdonald's solution – an appeal to the imperial government to resolve the issue – was hardly in keeping with the notion of Canada as a virtually independent "kingdom" that Creighton and others have attributed to him. It was also risky, although possibly less so with Disraeli's Conservatives in office than it would have been had Gladstone's Liberals been the government. Significantly, Gladstone, as leader of the opposition, did grant a sympathetic audience to Premier Joly of Quebec, who was in London to present the Liberal side of the controversy.[39] However, it was Sir Michael Hicks-Beach, the Conservative colonial secretary, who had the last word, and he agreed that the dismissal of Letellier was justified.

The last major instance in which Macdonald deliberately sought imperial intervention in a Canadian dispute arose from the Debt Conversion Act that the Quebec legislature adopted in 1888. Macdonald viewed the measure as "simply confiscation" and was determined to teach the Mercier government a lesson (see chapter 4). At the same time, he knew that low interest rates were popular with provincial governments and their electorates. He hoped to bring about the disallowance of the act in a way that could be attributed to the imperial government, or at least to pressure from British investors, rather than to himself. Not only did he direct Tupper, as Canada's high commissioner in London, to stir up the British financial community against the measure, but he also attempted to revive the long-discredited notion, which was contrary to his own view of Canadian federalism, that provincial legislation could be disallowed by the imperial government. The financiers did respond to Tupper's efforts but the imperial government, although Conservative, refused to play Macdonald's game and reminded him that disallowance was his own responsibility. In the end he decided that the political risks of disallowance were too great, and the Mercier government brought the episode to a close by amending the act at the next session of the legislature.

Yet another way in which federal-provincial controversies could involve the imperial government was at the initiative of the governor general. The extent to which this occurred is really a matter of definition; one of the governor general's duties was to keep the imperial government informed of developments in Canada, and the line between informing them and soliciting their intervention is not always easy to define. The subject cannot easily be explored without considering another question: To what extent did governors general act at their own discretion and on their own authority in relation to federal-provincial disputes, independently of the advice of the Canadian government or prime minister? Insofar as they did so, seeking imperial intervention was of course only one of the possibilities open to them; they could also seek to influence the outcome through their own independent efforts. In his three roles as the agent of the imperial government, the formal embodiment of the dominion government, and the guardian of constitutional propriety on behalf of the crown, a governor general had many pretexts and opportunities to become involved. However, the holders of the office generally displayed considerable caution and self-restraint by becoming involved only rarely.

Of all the post-Confederation governors general, the most inclined to play an active role was the earl of Dufferin. Dufferin seems to have genuinely enjoyed being governor general and to have had a considerable aptitude for political leadership. One suspects that if he had been born in Canada he would have wanted to be prime minister. The fact that prime minister Mackenzie, who held office for most of the Dufferin years, lacked either the political skills or the personal magnetism of Macdonald also gave Dufferin opportunities for leadership that were not available to other occupants of Rideau Hall. His friendship with Carnarvon was also an asset when the latter was colonial secretary.

The imperial government's involvement in the Mackenzie government's dispute with British Columbia over the terms of union was not Dufferin's doing, but he did play a decisive part in persuading the reluctant Mackenzie that it would be discourteous to refuse Carnarvon's offer of mediation. Subsequently he persuaded Mackenzie to agree to a slightly modified version of the original "Carnarvon terms," a feat that was facilitated although not guaranteed by the fact that Blake was temporarily out of the government.

Dufferin's most personal contribution, however, was his visit to British Columbia in 1876, which was entirely his own initiative. Both Mackenzie and Carnarvon accepted the idea. Dufferin suggested to Carnarvon that he should travel to British Columbia "in the double capacity of your delegate and also the representative of the dominion," but did not explain how anyone could simultaneously represent two governments whose views on the British Columbia situation were more conflicting than harmonious.[40] In his public address at Victoria, however, Dufferin emphasized that he was "not here to defend Mr. Mackenzie, his policy, his proceedings, or his utterances. I hope this will be clearly understood."[41] This assurance did not prevent Premier Walkem from describing the mission a few years later as the governor general's "unconstitutional tour as agent for Mr. McKenzie (sic)."[42] Walkem's credentials as an authority on the theory and practice of responsible government need not be taken too seriously. A viceregal visit to a remote and recently annexed province was an excellent idea in principle, and Dufferin neither said nor did anything improper while he was there. His defence of federalism, his pleas for patience regarding the CPR, and his much-needed advice to respect the rights of the native people were all constructive and useful. Macdonald, to whom Walkem's complaint about Dufferin was addressed, thought highly enough of Dufferin to hope that he would be appointed to a second term in office.

Dufferin also involved himself, somewhat less constructively, in the controversy over Prince Edward Island's land reform, but he was not responsible for bringing that matter to the attention of the imperial government. Carnarvon had sent him a secret dispatch on the question in May 1874, which was apparently before Dufferin informed Mackenzie of his own objections to the treatment of the proprietors.

Another subject that engaged Dufferin's attention was the ill-defined responsibilities of the two levels of government in Canada for protecting law and order through the deployment of military force.[43] In the year 1878 the province of Quebec, already disturbed by the Letellier affair, faced two other unrelated situations that threatened civil violence. Poorly paid labourers in Quebec City went out on strike, an event attributed by prime minister Mackenzie to "a portion of the communistic element from the United States."[44] Simultaneously, the Orange Order threatened to parade through the streets of Montreal on July 12th. The simultaneous crises revealed the inadequacy of the Canadian militia. Letellier and Joly insisted that the dominion send militia units from Montreal to reinforce those in Quebec City, but this left Montreal with no protection against the threat of violence between Catholics and Orangemen.[45] The problem was compounded by the fact that the mayor of Montreal refused to ask for military assistance, while the dominion apparently lacked the legal authority to intervene without an invitation.[46]

Even before the strike in Quebec City began, Dufferin warned Sir Michael Hicks-Beach about the threat of religious violence in Montreal. He reported that the Orangemen, in a breathtaking analogy, had compared their planned march through the metropolis with "the entry of our Saviour into Jerusalem." Although Dufferin thought the use of imperial troops from the Halifax garrison would be an unfortunate precedent, he feared it might become necessary and asked the colonial secretary for instructions whether it would be permitted.[47] Less than two weeks after this dispatch the militia battery from Montreal opened fire on the strikers in Quebec City, killing one man, and the provincial government requested imperial troops from Halifax to deal with the strike, a request that was refused by prime minister Mackenzie. Dufferin, who had suggested to Hicks-Beach that Canada needed a national police force (the Mounted Police at that time had jurisdiction only in the territories), now suggested to Mackenzie that Canada needed a permanent professional army.[48] As if to reinforce this argument, Hicks-Beach telegraphed the governor general that the use of imperial troops to prevent or control domestic violence was open to grave objections and could not be authorized in advance.[49]

Dufferin, who had sensibly attributed the strike to inadequate wages rather than communism, continued to worry about the threat of the Orange parade. Being from Northern Ireland himself, he was not inclined to minimize the seriousness of such a situation. He pressed Mackenzie to activate the Montreal militia, with or without the mayor's approval. Mackenzie was reluctant to act unilaterally, citing an opinion from the Department of Justice that it was *ultra vires*, but Dufferin countered that according to a recent letter from Hicks-Beach the Colonial Office believed that the dominion government had the legal authority to do so.[50] In the end Mackenzie found a loophole that enabled the militia to be called out at the request of any two magistrates. Three thousand troops were deployed in Montreal, and July 12th passed without violence. Four days later the colonial secretary sent another dispatch to the governor general. He had consulted the law officers of the crown, who had concluded that Mackenzie was right: the dominion had no power to intervene unilaterally.[51] Hicks-Beach suggested that perhaps the law should be changed, and Dufferin raised the matter with Mackenzie, but nothing came of the suggestion.

The viceregal office assumed a somewhat lower profile after Dufferin's return to the British Isles. Nonetheless, governors general continued to play a part from time to time in federal-provincial relations. Lorne followed his predecessor's example by travelling to British Columbia to smooth troubled waters in 1882, and took a general interest in relations with the Pacific province. Lansdowne took a great interest in the Ontario boundary dispute, conducting both correspondence and private conversations with Premier Mowat. Lansdowne also urged Macdonald to take the unrest in Manitoba seriously and to appease the province's discontent by terminating the CPR monopoly clause. In all these cases the occupant of Rideau Hall helped to soften Macdonald's increasing rigidity and impatience in dealing with provincial governments during the last decade of his life.

A more unusual and less successful intervention by a governor general in a federal-provincial dispute was Lord Aberdeen's effort to resolve the conflict over Catholic education in Manitoba. In January 1896, soon after the cabinet revolt against prime minister Bowell's lack of leadership on the issue, Aberdeen discussed the Manitoba question with Sir Donald Smith, better known to history as Lord Strathcona. Smith had spent a good part of his life in Manitoba before driving the last spike on the CPR main line at Craigellachie. Since 1887 he had been the Conservative MP for Montreal West, the riding that contained the CPR head office. In his conversation with Aberdeen he expressed his willingness to travel to Winnipeg and confer privately with both the provincial government and the Catholic archbishop. According to Aberdeen's account, Smith made the trip in February "without the official knowledge and sanction of the cabinet," and returned with some hope that a compromise might be possible. In a secret dispatch to the colonial secretary, Aberdeen strongly suggested that the government had fumbled this opportunity by instead persisting with a remedial bill they were unable to pass before Parliament's term expired.[52]

There were relatively few occasions on which the imperial government took the initiative to involve itself in a Canadian matter without having been asked by a provincial government, the dominion government, or the governor general to do so. However, the practice was not totally unknown. A few instances of this kind were matters carried over from before Confederation. These included a New Brunswick statute concerning trade marks, adopted at the last session of the colonial legislature in 1867, and a dispute between the imperial government and British Columbia over the shared cost of building certain lighthouses.[53]

A more serious issue that provoked imperial expressions of concern was the British Columbia government's penchant for anti-Chinese legislation. In November 1878 the head of the Chinese diplomatic mission in London complained to the Foreign Office about a recently enacted provincial statute imposing a tax of $40 per annum on each adult male Chinese in the province. The complaint was forwarded to the Colonial Office, which noted that the offending statute had already been declared *ultra vires* by the Supreme Court of British Columbia, and then to the governor general.[54] The dominion government referred it to the minister of justice, on whose recommendation it was disallowed nine months later, in August 1879. The minister's report cited the Supreme Court decision as the sole grounds for disallowance.

British Columbia's second attempt to impose discriminatory taxation on the Chinese was enacted in 1884 and described as "an act to regulate the Chinese population of British Columbia" (see chapter 6). The Chinese diplomatic representative again protested, although belatedly; his complaint was presented to the Foreign Office during the brief Gladstone ministry of 1886, and forwarded to Ottawa later that year after the Conservatives had returned under Lord Salisbury.[55] This time the federal government did not disallow the act, although it did disallow an act restricting Chinese immigration that was adopted simultaneously. The "act to regulate the Chinese population," like its predecessor, was struck down by the Supreme Court of British Columbia in 1887, and the provincial government decided not to appeal the decision. However, as Lord Lansdowne warned the colonial secretary, the issue was not dead. British Columbia's racism continued to complicate relations between the province, the dominion, and the empire until well into the twentieth century.

The controversy over land reform in Prince Edward Island is possibly one of the few cases in which private interests provoked the imperial government's intervention in a Canadian issue. Alternatively, the imperial government's involvement may be attributed to the initiative of Lord Carnarvon, or even to that of Lord Dufferin, who made no secret of his antipathy to the Land Purchase Act of 1874. Since some of the documents are missing, the facts are obscure. Carnarvon sent a secret dispatch on the subject to Dufferin as early as 7 May 1874, not long after the bill was reserved by acting Lieutenant-Governor Sir Robert Hodgson.[56] Hodgson, who had first been elected to the island legislature half a century earlier, apparently acted at his own discretion. The contents of Carnarvon's dispatch, and the documents he enclosed with it, are not known but probably owed something to representations from the proprietors, who continued to lobby the Colonial Office over the next few years. Either before or after receiving this dispatch, Dufferin told Mackenie that he would not give assent to the reserved bill. He reported this conversation in a private letter to Carnarvon on 29 May, more than a week before his formal acknowledgement of the secret dispatch.[57]

The Mackenzie government took no action through the summer. Although a reserved bill would lapse if not explicitly approved by the governor general in council, neither Carnarvon nor the proprietors were satisfied. The colonial secretary sent a secret dispatch to Dufferin on 2 November, referring to a petition he had received from the proprietors. Dufferin chided Mackenzie for not informing the provincial government that the bill was unacceptable. A second dispatch from Carnarvon, which Dufferin described as "disagreeable," followed in December, complaining of the delay, but the government had already withheld assent from the bill a few days before it was received.[58]

A less ambiguous example of private interests involving the imperial government in a federal-provincial controversy is the matter of the Jesuit Estates Act, adopted by Quebec under Mercier's leadership in 1888. Like the much earlier affair of the New Brunswick School Act, the episode illustrates John A. Macdonald's adroit use of the imperial connection to avoid intervening in a religious controversy. It also makes an interesting contrast with Macdonald's response to another of Mercier's measures, the Debt Conversion Act. In one case Macdonald wanted to leave the act in force while in the other he wanted to disallow it, but in both he attempted to transfer the responsibility for his preferred course of action to the imperial government.

The Jesuit Estates Act attracted widespread interest on both sides of the Atlantic. In December 1888 the duke of Norfolk, the highest ranking Catholic among the British aristocracy, asked Canada's high commissioner, Sir Charles Tupper, for an assurance that the act would not be disallowed.[59] A month later the Macdonald government decided not to disallow it, a decision that soon became public knowledge. The Protestant Alliance, a British evangelical group, responded with a petition to the colonial secretary protesting against the decision and demanding that "measures be taken by Her Majesty's Government, on behalf of the crown, to prevent any such Act being carried into effect."[60] This document was forwarded by the colonial secretary to the governor general, without comment, a few days before the issue was debated in the Canadian House of Commons.

The debate was marked by one of Macdonald's last great speeches, an eloquent plea for religious tolerance and a recapitulation of his lifelong effort to ensure that anglophone and francophone Canadians could coexist in harmony.[61] The overwhelming majority by which the government won the vote, however, did not reflect the sentiment in the country, particularly in Ontario. In April Macdonald advised the governor general, Lord Stanley, that no further action by the imperial government was necessary since the colonial secretary had already informed the Protestant Alliance that disallowance was the dominion's responsibility. By the middle of May Macdonald had changed his mind, apparently because the Evangelical Alliance of Canada, the proprietor of the Montreal *Star*, and other Protestant Canadians continued to bombard his government with abuse. The prime minister now asked Justice Minister John Thompson to prepare a memorandum explaining why the act should not be disallowed. At the same time he suggested to Lord Stanley one of his favourite tactics on such occasions: a request for a ruling from the law officers of the crown. Doubtless recalling his successful management of the controversy over New Brunswick schools, Macdonald suggested that the law officers be asked to state that the act was *intra vires*, that the dominion could not disallow it having already assured Mercier that it would not, and that there were no grounds for a reference to the Judicial Committee of the Privy Council. He also informed Stanley that the cabinet had decided to forward to the imperial government a petition addressed to the queen from the Evangelical Alliance of Canada.[62]

Stanley agreed with this strategy, although he suggested that the law officers' opinion should be formally communicated to the imperial Parliament to have the maximum effect. He also doubted whether the law officers would go so far as to say that there were no grounds for a reference to the Judicial Committee.[63] In July the law officers issued a brief statement expressing agreement with Thompson's memorandum but, as Stanley had predicted, they did not mention the Judicial Committee. After further representations from the dominion government, via the colonial secretary, they obligingly produced a second statement three weeks later to the effect that there were no grounds for reference to the Judicial Committee.[64] Macdonald wanted the opinion by the law officers to be published as soon as the one-year deadline for disallowance had passed. If it was published before the deadline the agitation for disallowance would continue, and if publication was delayed too long the dominion government would be accused of deliberately wasting time. Knutsford had no objection to the substance of the opinion being made known, but he at first objected to *verbatim* publication, which was not customary procedure. However, Macdonald and Stanley persisted and, late in August, about three weeks after the deadline, the colonial secretary agreed to publication of the opinions *verbatim*.[65]

Meanwhile the Evangelical Alliance continued to campaign for imperial, as opposed to federal, disallowance, a practice that had been extinct since Confederation. Knutsford had already stated in the House of Lords that this was impossible, and stated it again in June when he informed Stanley that the Evangelical petition had been forwarded to the queen. He stated it for the third time in August when he forwarded two more petitions to the queen, whom he again advised to take no action since it was the dominion's responsibility to do so.[66]

A few general conclusions are suggested by this survey of imperial involvement in Canadian federal-provincial relations. First, there were few cases in which the imperial government deliberately sought to become involved and in virtually all of those instances it was merely reacting to demands and representations of one kind or another. Far more typically, it was Canadian governments, either federal or provincial, that sought imperial intervention because they expected it to promote their own objectives. Few if any Canadian politicians seemed to object to imperial intervention on principle; most found it convenient and tried to use it to their advantage.

Second, there is no evidence that imperial intervention systematically favoured the provinces as opposed to the federal government. Neither in the positive sense suggested by Verney nor in the more destructive sense of "divide and rule" was this ever the case. Generally, imperial interventions were fair-minded, restrained, and dedicated to promoting harmony between the two levels of government; the Carnarvon terms are perhaps the best example. Insofar as there was a bias, it was pro-federal, not pro-provincial. This was shown most dramatically, and most significantly, in the response of both the Disraeli and Gladstone governments to the separatist movement in Nova Scotia. It was also shown by the willingness of the imperial authorities to endorse federal actions, such as the dismissal of Letellier, or federal inaction, as in the case of New Brunswick schools or the Jesuit estates. Even Dufferin's and Carnarvon's intervention in the conflict over British Columbia's terms of union, although resented by the Mackenzie government, was motivated by the desire to maintain a strong united Canada as a viable entity.

Third, the two British political parties do not seem to have differed substantially in their approaches to Canadian matters, nor do they seem to have displayed much partisan bias towards or against Canadian governments, either federal or provincial. Carnarvon's impatience with Mackenzie and Blake may partly refute the latter half of this observation but it must be remembered that Dufferin, who was a Liberal, shared much of the impatience and that Blake had something of a chip on his shoulder as regards the imperial government. Conversely, it is undeniable that John A. Macdonald usually got what he wanted from the imperial authorities, but this was more the result of his charm, tact, and effusive expressions of imperial loyalty than of his party label.

Finally, imperial influence should not be overrated. It was probably decisive in nipping Nova Scotia separatism in the bud at a time when the new dominion's existence was still precarious. In other cases it helped to make federal-provincial relations more harmonious and rescued federal governments from various embarrassments, but the course of Canadian history and the development of Canadian federalism in particular would perhaps not have been radically different in its absence. Perhaps for that reason there was little or no anti-imperial sentiment in nineteenth-century Canada, even among francophones. Canadians could take a vicarious pride in the empire and could use it as a psychological rampart against the United States, while knowing that their freedom, prosperity, and security were never adversely affected by its existence.

11 The Judicial Committee and the British North America Act

Students of Canadian government have for a long time attributed to the Judicial Committee of the Privy Council a significant, and perhaps decisive, impact on Canadian federalism. More often than not, evaluations of the Judicial Committee's influence on Canada have been unfavourable. In 1939 a report by the legal counsel to the Senate of Canada accused the Judicial Committee of systematically and deliberately distorting both the intentions of the Fathers of Confederation and the clear meaning of the British North America Act in a series of decisions extending over more than half a century.[1] The author of the report, W.F. O'Connor, specifically accused the Judicial Committee of wilfully ignoring the relationship between the dominion Parliament's general power to make laws for the "Peace, Order and Good Government of Canada" and the list of specific subjects entrusted to its jurisdiction. Scholars such as F.R. Scott, later dean of law at McGill University, and Bora Laskin, later chief justice of Canada, were less dogmatic about the textual inadequacies of the Judicial Committee's interpretations but blamed the committee for failing to adapt the constitution in a flexible and creative manner to the needs of the twentieth century.[2] As a result, they claimed that artificial constraints had been imposed on the central government while the provinces had been granted theoretical powers they were practically unable to exercise. J.R. Mallory attributed the Judicial Committee's curtailment of federal powers to a distrust of interventionist government and collectivism.[3] Other scholars blamed it on institutional self-interest (favouring the provinces so as to enlist provincial support for the retention of appeals), on the Scottish background of Lords Watson and Haldane (which allegedly predisposed them to sympathize with provincial demands for greater autonomy), and even on the forensic skills of Judah P. Benjamin, the former attorney general of the Confederate States of America.[4] (Benjamin was a London barrister after the Civil War who argued several Canadian cases before the Judicial Committee. He did not always take the provincial side, however, and he was not particularly successful. His clients lost eight of the ten cases in which he was involved.)

More recent writers on the Judicial Committee have taken a more favourable view of its activities, although many of them concede that it was biased in favour of the provinces. G.P. Browne challenged the claims of the O'Connor report and arguing that the Judicial Committee's "three compartment" approach (subordinating the general power to the enumerated powers) was a correct and logical reading of the BNA Act.[5] Pierre Elliott Trudeau (in his academic and anticentralist manifestation) suggested that the Judicial Committee's modification of an excessively centralized formal constitution had been necessary to reconcile Quebec to Canadian federalism.[6] Alan Cairns attacked both the "fundamentalists" (O'Connor) and the "constitutionalists" (Laskin and Scott) in an article that has been called the definitive study of the Judicial Committee's Canadian jurisprudence.[7] Gil Rémillard, subsequently Quebec's minister of justice and intergovernmental affairs, praised the Judicial Committee in his book on the constitutional law of Canadian federalism.[8]

In view of all this literature the subject of the Judicial Committee, and of judicial review more generally, cannot be ignored in a book on Canadian federalism, even one whose chronological boundaries exclude the twentieth century, when most of the great cases were decided. What expectations did nineteenth-century Canadians have about judicial review? What was the Judicial Committee and what role did it play during the first thirty years after Confederation? What were the political and legal consequences for Canada of its decisions?

It has become customary in the English-speaking world, following A.V. Dicey, to regard judicial review as being almost by definition a necessary and significant attribute of federalism. Scholars such as Barry Strayer have traced its origins, so far as Canada is concerned, back into colonial times.[9] Nonetheless, the Fathers of Confederation apparently devoted little attention to the subject. There are only a few scattered references to it in the proceedings of the Quebec Conference and in the Confederation Debates. The fact that the BNA Act did not provide for a Supreme Court (although Parliament was given the authority to establish "a General Court of Appeal" at some future date) suggests that judicial review was not a high priority.

Insofar as judicial review was wanted or anticipated, it was apparently viewed more as a means of controlling the provinces than as an impartial mechanism for balancing the two levels of government. The idea that a court could strike down the enactments of the national legislature was not widely popular at the time of Confederation. Even in the United States, where Chief Justice John Marshall has asserted the existence of such a power in 1803, the power was exercised only twice prior to the end of the Civil War. The first such instance, Marbury *vs* Madison, was ancient history by the time of the Quebec Conference, while the second, in the notorious affair of Dred Scott, was hardly a precedent that deserved or attracted imitation.

Moreover, judicial review was contrary to the British notion of the supremacy of Parliament. Jonathan McCully noted this fact at the Quebec Conference when R.B. Dickey and George Brown raised the subject. McCully described judicial review as an American notion and praised the constitution of New Zealand, which did not permit the supremacy of the central Parliament to be questioned. John A. Macdonald, whose private views were probably not much different from McCully's and whose constitutional ideas had certainly been influenced by New Zealand, pointed out, in deference to his Québécois colleagues, that Canada anticipated a federal constitution while New Zealand was a unitary state. He did not follow this *pro forma* observation with an eloquent endorsement of judicial review. Instead, he took the opportunity to repeat one of his favourite themes: that the United States Constitution gave too much power to the states and that the unhappy consequences foreseen by de Tocqueville had indeed come to pass in the Civil War.[10]

If judicial review was seen essentially as a method of curtailing the powers of the provinces, the lack of attention to it is understandable, for other and possibly more convenient methods were available. The power of disallowance would enable the federal government to strike down any provincial statute without the necessity of demonstrating it was *ultra vires*. The existence of a federally appointed lieutenant-governor in each provincial capital, exercising real and not merely formal powers over the provincial government and legislature, would be an additional safeguard for federal interests. In addition, the dominion government, and not the provinces, would have direct links of communication with the imperial government.

This advantage enabled Macdonald repeatedly to seek authoritative legal rulings from the law officers of the crown.

Strayer is right in attributing the origins of Canadian judicial review to colonialism rather than federalism. The Judicial Committee of the Privy Council had existed informally since the early days of the British overseas empire and had been explicitly provided for by statute since 1833. It was based on the historic notion that British subjects, even if they happened to live outside the British Isles, had the right to appeal for justice "to the foot of the throne." The Judicial Committee advised the crown on how to respond to these appeals. Like any British tribunal, it could recognize no law higher than an act of the imperial Parliament at Westminster, but since colonial constitutions were acts of Parliament the Judicial Committee could declare that colonial legislatures were exceeding the authority granted to them by Westminster. The Colonial Laws Validity Act, adopted not long before Confederation, narrowed the grounds on which such a ruling could be made but reminded colonial politicians that limits still existed and might be enforced.

Although the possibility of judicial review existed even before Confederation, there were few instances, if any, when a British North American colonial statute was struck down.[11] The powers of colonial governors, and the power of disallowance exercised by the imperial government itself, were more significant limitations on colonial autonomy. It was perhaps reasonable to anticipate that this would continue to be the case after Confederation. In fact, five dominion statutes fell victim to the imperial powers of disallowance and reservation between 1867 and 1896, while only one was declared *ultra vires* by the Judicial Committee.[12] In the same period the Judicial Committee struck down four provincial statutes, all from Quebec. Compared with the numerous provincial statutes disallowed by the dominion or reserved by lieutenant-governors and not subsequently given assent, this was an insignificant number.

The peculiar characteristics of the Judicial Committee have been noted by Browne, Cairns, and other writers on the subject and need not be discussed at great length. The most significant were its practice of consensual decision making, so that there were no minority opinions or dissents, its heterogeneous and frequently changing membership, and the fact that cases were heard by small panels of judges apparently selected at random from those eligible to participate. The thirty Canadian constitutional cases that the Judicial Committee dealt with in the thirty years after Confederation were heard by panels ranging in size from four to seven. Twenty-two individual

members of the Judicial Committee participated in at least one Canadian case, but six of them made notably frequent appearances and
accounted for about half the total work load. Sir Richard Couch participated in nineteen cases, Sir Barnes Peacock in seventeen, Sir
Montague Smith in sixteen, Sir Richard Collier in fifteen, and Sir
Arthur Hobhouse and Lord Watson each in fourteen. As a writer of
judgments, Lord Watson was by far the most prolific member of the
Judicial Committee, with nine to his credit. Lord Selborne and Sir
Montague Smith each wrote four. Ironically, Sir Richard Couch did
not write the judgment in any of the cases he participated in. All
members of the Judicial Committee in these years were residents of
the United Kingdom, although, in 1895, at the end of the period under consideration, the imperial Parliament authorized the appointment of up to five judges from the overseas empire.[13]

The question of abolishing Canadian appeals to the Judicial Committee arose as early as 1875, when the Mackenzie government's bill
to establish a Supreme Court of Canada was introduced in the dominion Parliament. Télesphore Fournier, the minister of justice, indicated that he favoured the abolition of appeals from the Supreme
Court, particularly in view of an imperial statute, adopted in 1873,
which envisaged replacing both the Judicial Committee and the ap-
pellate jurisdiction of the House of Lords with a new supreme court
for the entire empire.[14]Fournier's bill did not provide for abolition,
despite his personal views, but an amendment by a Liberal back-
bencher on third reading prohibited appeals from the Supreme
Court of Canada to any court established by the imperial Parliament
"saving any right which Her Majesty may be graciously pleased to
exercise by virtue of her royal prerogative." Despite the protests of
Sir John A. Macdonald, the amendment was adopted by an overwhelming majority and became Section 47 of the Supreme Court
Act.[15]

As Macdonald had predicted, the imperial government was highly
displeased with Section 47 and threatened to disallow the entire Act.
Edward Blake, who had succeeded Fournier in the Justice portfolio
soon after the act was adopted, persuaded the imperial government
not to disallow it and not to insist on the repeal of Section 47, but on
the tacit understanding that appeals would in fact be allowed to continue. The qualification regarding "prerogative" appeals provided
the rationale for this characteristically Canadian compromise, even
though the distinction between "prerogative" and statutory rights of
appeal had in fact been legally meaningless since at least 1844, if not
1833.[16]

The establishment of the Supreme Court of Canada in no way lessened the importance of the Judicial Committee of the Privy Council. Most of the Supreme Court's decisions on constitutional matters were appealed to the Judicial Committee, which overturned many of them. The few that were not appealed, such as Severn *vs* The Queen, Lenoir *vs* Ritchie, and Fredericton *vs* The Queen, were superseded by subsequent decisions of the Judicial Committee in similar cases. Many constitutional cases also went directly from Provincial courts to the Judicial Committee. Although the Supreme Court initially tended to interpret the BNA Act in a manner that favoured the dominion vis-à-vis the provinces, the gradual accumulation of Judicial Committee decisions, by which it was bound under the rule of *stare decisis*, increasingly restricted its ability to do so.[17] The Supreme Court had little real impact on the development of Canada's constitution in the early years, and it is appropriate to direct attention almost exclusively to the Judicial Committee.

Most of the Judicial Committee's early constitutional interpretations, including the first sixteen, arose out of litigation involving private individuals or corporations. The first reference case, regarding the validity of the McCarthy (liquor licensing) Act, was decided by the Judicial Committee in 1885. Following the example of the Supreme Court, to which the matter had originally been referred, the Judicial Committee gave no reasons for its decision. The next reference, submitted jointly by the dominion and British Columbia, concerned the dispute over ownership of precious metals in the railway belt, and was decided in 1889. This time, as on all subsequent occasions, the Judicial Committee gave reasons. Amendments to the Supreme Court Act soon after John A. Macdonald's death obliged the court to hear references submitted by the cabinet, allowed provincial governments to intervene in such cases, and provided for the appeal of judgments in reference cases to the Judicial Committee.[18] As a result, reference cases effectively replaced Macdonald's old practice of referring legal questions to the law officers of the crown. Between 1894 and 1897 the Judicial Committee delivered judgments on four references, two submitted by the dominion and two by Ontario.

About half the cases in which the Judicial Committee interpreted the BNA Act in the first three decades after Confederation involved the powers of provincial legislatures. Quebec and Ontario accounted for most of these cases, and Quebec accounted for all the cases in which provincial statutes were declared *ultra vires*. There was one case from each of New Brunswick, Manitoba, and Nova Scotia.

Federal legislation did not escape constitutional challenges either, and accounted for seven cases or about a quarter of the total. In only one case was it found to be *ultra vires*. In addition to the seven cases involving federal statutes, one case involved the power of the dominion government to issue remedial orders on behalf of Manitoba Roman Catholics deprived of their separate schools. For convenience this case may be placed in the same category, since a remedial order was in substance a form of legislation.

Another category of cases, particularly important in the development of Canadian federalism, involved the executive powers or property of the two levels of government. These cases were all provincial victories. Apart from the considerable importance of the land and other property that was immediately at issue, they were important because the Judicial Committee used them to expound the notion that the two levels of government were equal in status. Whatever its political or sociological merits, this notion fundamentally altered Canada's original constitution.

The first case necessitating an interpretation of the BNA Act, and also the first involving a provincial statute, was l'Union St. Jacques de Montréal *vs* Bélisle, decided in 1874.[19] The union was a mutual benefit society, of a type common before the rise of the welfare state, whose members contributed to pension plans payable to their survivors after death. In 1870 the union was apparently unable to pay benefits at the level originally promised, and the Quebec legislature authorized it to reduce the level of benefits. Madame Bélisle, beneficiary of a widow's pension, objected that this was legislation concerning "bankruptcy and insolvency," a matter confided to the dominion's exclusive jurisdiction. Her argument was upheld by the Court of Queen's Bench. The union appealed to the Judicial Committee, which reversed the lower court's decision. Lord Selborne, who delivered the judgment, noted that the union was neither bankrupt nor insolvent and that the relevant provision of the BNA Act was Section 92(16) ("Matters of a merely local or private Nature in the Province") rather than 91(21).

Dow *vs* Black, decided in 1875, upheld a New Brunswick act authorizing a municipality to subsidize construction of a railway and to finance the subsidy by issuing debentures.[20] William Black and other ratepayers objected to the fact that their property was taxed to pay the interest on the debentures and argued that because the railway in question was planned to extend beyond the limits of the province, the legislation trespassed on the dominion's jurisdiction and was *ultra vires*. Like Madame Bélisle, they were successful in the provincial court, an outcome that suggests the very centralist views of

Canadian judges in the early years after Confederation. The municipal tax assessor, Dow, appealed to the Judicial Committee. Sir James Colville's judgment declared that the scope of the railway's activities was not the relevant consideration, since the statute was essentially about direct taxation and municipal affairs rather than about railways. The railway had been authorized by an earlier statute, which was not at issue.

Provincial taxing powers were limited for the first time in 1878 with the judgment in Attorney General of Quebec *vs* Queen Insurance.[21] A Quebec statute of 1876 had required insurance companies to pay for a licence with a fee that was calculated as a percentage of the premiums paid to each company. Queen Insurance, a British firm that already held a licence from the dominion, argued that it had no obligation to pay the provincial fee, and its argument was accepted by the Court of Queen's Bench. The Judicial Committee, to which the province appealed, upheld this decision on the grounds that the provincial licensing fee, begin payable only after premiums were collected, was not really a licence fee but a tax. Furthermore, it was an indirect tax, since, being in proportion to the amount of premiums, it was presumably passed on to the policy holders.

The election of 1878, which brought the Macdonald Conservatives back to power in Ottawa, was the occasion for the first constitutional test of a federal statue, Valin *vs* Langlois.[22] The Mackenzie government had adopted legislation providing for controverted elections to be decided by the courts, instead of by the House of Commons itself. Valin, a Quebec Conservative elected in 1878, fell victim to the new procedure and claimed that the act was *ultra vires*, since it allegedly dealt with the administration of justice in the province. The Supreme Court upheld the statute, and the Judicial Committee, after the unusually short interval of six weeks, did likewise.

A considerably more complex matter was Bourgoin *vs* Quebec, Montreal, Ottawa and Occidental Railway, in which for the second time the Judicial Committee struck down a Quebec statute.[23] The dispute involved some land, including a quarry, that the railway had expropriated in 1873 when it was still a private corporation chartered by the province. Three years later a Quebec statute confirmed an agreement that forced the company to surrender all its lands and other property to the province, ignoring the fact that Parliament had already declared the projected railway to be a connecting link in the proposed transcontinental line and thus a work "for the general Advantage of Canada." Bourgoin and some other businessmen, who had leased the quarry from its original owner before the expropriation, were awarded compensation by arbitrators appointed under the terms of the Railway Act, a dominion statute. The railway company, supported by the attorney general of Quebec after the province took over the railway's assets, challenged the validity of the award. Both the Court of Queen's Bench and the Judicial Committee ruled that the arbitrators had exceeded their powers by awarding Bourgoin both a lump sum and an additional monthly payment until such time as the railway constructed works to drain the quarry.

Although this part of the dispute did not involve any constitutional issue, the case acquired a new dimension following the dismissal of the de Boucherville Government by Letellier in March 1878. The new Joly government disapproved of its predecessor's railway projects, which had at least ostensibly been the grounds for the dismissal, and it did not want the province to be liable in the event that the Judicial Committee upheld the arbitrators' award. Its attorney general, David Ross, therefore launched a new appeal arguing that the takeover of the railway's assets had been invalid since the railway already was under federal jurisdiction.[24] This issue was dealt with by the Judicial Committee in a second judgment, even though Joly and Ross were back on the opposition benches by the time it was handed down. Sir James Colville's judgment declared that since Parliament had already used its declaratory power to bring the railway under the dominion's jurisdiction, the province could not compel the railway to surrender its land and property without authorization by the dominion Parliament. The takeover and the provincial statute that ratified it were both invalid. In response to this decision, the Macdonald government caused Parliament in 1882 to adopt a statute that retroactively confirmed the province's action.[25]

Cushing *vs* Dupuy, a dispute over the property of an insolvent brewery in Montreal, led one litigant to challenge a dominion statute, the Canadian Insolvent Act.[26] Although Cushing's counsel made reference to "Property and Civil Rights," this argument could hardly hold water in view of the dominion's jurisdiction over "Bankruptcy and Insolvency." A more plausible argument was that a provision making the Court of Appeal's judgment "final" in insolvency cases interfered with the royal prerogative. The Judicial Committee decided it did not do so by reading the statute as a denial of an *automatic* right to an appeal. By this interpretation it could not have been intended to preclude the queen from allowing an appeal to the foot of the throne at her own discretion.

Citizens Insurance *vs* Parsons, decided in 1881, is generally considered the first really important case involving the distribution of legislative powers.[27] As most students of Canadian government and politics know, the Judicial Committee's decision in this case produced a restrictive definition of the dominion's power to regulate "Trade and Commerce" that was still being cited more than a century later. One of the great ironies of Canadian history is that Oliver Mowat, for whose Ontario government this was the first in a long list of favourable judgments from the Judicial Committee, had moved a resolution at the Quebec Conference in 1864 that would have placed insurance explicitly under federal jurisdiction. Although this motion was apparently adopted, second thoughts caused its deletion from the final draft of the Quebec Resolutions. Nine years after Confederation, Mowat's government caused the Ontario legislature to adopt the Insurance Act.[28] It provided a set of standard conditions for insurance policies. Insurance companies were free to vary the conditions, but only if the policy clearly indicated the variations in ink of a different colour from that used on the rest of the policy. The federal minister of justice, Edward Blake, noted in his report on provincial legislation that doubts had been expressed about the constitutionality of the Insurance Act. He recommended that the matter be left for decision by the courts.[29]

William Parsons owned a hardware store in Orangeville, a village northwest of Toronto. He seems to have been a firm believer in fire insurance, for he took out a policy with the Citizens Insurance Company in May 1877, even though the store was already insured by the Western Assurance Company. In August he took out a third policy, with Queen Insurance, and on the same day the hardware store was destroyed by fire.

Both Citizens Insurance and Queen Insurance refused to pay. Parsons had violated at least two of the statutory conditions, since he had informed neither company of insurance already in force and had stored more than twenty-five pounds of gunpowder in the store without their permission. Neither company had chosen to follow the statutory conditions precisely, however, and neither had printed their own conditions, which included requirements that other policies be disclosed to the insurer, in the precise way required by the statute. The trial judge ruled that both companies had to compensate Parsons for the fire. The companies argued that the Insurance Act was *ultra vires*, but the Court of Queen's Bench, the Court of Appeal, and the Supreme Court of Canada all upheld the original verdict.

The companies carried their case to the Judicial Committee, where their distinguished legal counsel included Judah P. Benjamin, the former attorney general of the Confederate States, and Sir Frederick Herschell, the actual solicitor general of the United Kingdom. (The law officers of the crown were at that time allowed to engage in private practice.) Benjamin and Herschell argued for a broad reading of the "Trade and Commerce" power, and also for a narrow reading of the provincial jurisdiction over "Property and Civil Rights," which they claimed was only intended to protect Quebec's distinctive system of civil law. However, Sir Montague Smith's judgment rejected these arguments and upheld the Insurance Act. Regulation of trade and commerce, according to Smith, did not include the regulation of particular trades such as insurance. The federal charters held by both companies were not based on the trade and commerce power, but on Parliament's general power, and did not prevent the provinces from validly regulating the companies. "Property and Civil Rights" included rights arising from private contracts, and not merely those conferred by law. In the absence of this broad interpretation, Quebec's right to its own civil law would be meaningless.

Although this interpretation was an important victory for Ontario, and for decentralized federalism, Parsons himself derived no satisfaction from it. While the Judicial Committee agreed with him that the Insurance Act was valid legislation, it rejected his claim that the act should be interpreted so as to exempt him from the statutory conditions. Instead, the statutory conditions were held to apply to the Citizens' policy, since its own conditions were not stated in the appropriate form. The contract of insurance with Queen had not yet been embodied in a policy when the store burned down, but the interim receipt given by that company to Parsons included conditions and those conditions would be upheld, in the absence of a policy document, provided they were just and reasonable. Thus, neither company had to pay.

Dobie *vs* The Board for the Management of the Temporalities Fund of the Presbyterian Church of Canada, decided in 1882, was the first Canadian case in which Lord Watson was involved.[30] The relatively junior Watson was selected to write and deliver the judgment, probably because he was a Presbyterian himself. Ironically, the first judgment by the man who is remembered as the leading champion of provincial rights declared a provincial statute to be *ultra vires*. The dispute was a financial one arising from the union of the various Presbyterian churches in Canada soon after Confederation. Dobie, a clergyman who opposed the union, argued that a Quebec statute providing for the administration of church property was *ultra vires*. Watson agreed that the statute could not be supported under any of the enumerated provincial powers in Section 92, although "Property and Civil Rights" was "the most plausible argument." The Temporalities Fund was not "in the Province," so only the dominion Parliament could transfer it to the newly united church. In other words, the dominion had residual power.

The dominion's residual power was again upheld in the better-known case of Russell *vs* The Queen.[31] Fredericton, New Brunswick, had been one of the first cities whose ratepayers voted for prohibition under the terms of the Canada Temperance Act. The municipality itself objected to the measure, presumably because of the loss of revenue involved, but the Supreme Court of Canada upheld the act as a regulation of trade and commerce. Meanwhile Charles Russell, a Fredericton tavern-keeper, had launched another challenge to the act. When the Supreme Court of New Brunswick ruled against him on grounds of *stare decisis*, Russell bypassed the Supreme Court of Canada and took his case directly to the foot of the throne. On behalf of the Judicial Committee, Sir Montague Smith affirmed that the subject of the Canada Temperance Act did not fall within any of the provincial fields of jurisdiction enumerated in Section 92, since it was primarily a matter of public order and safety. Although not necessarily rejecting the view that the act could be upheld under the trade and commerce power, the Judicial Committee preferred to regard it as an exercise of the general power to legislate for the "Peace, Order and good Government of Canada." Its incidental effect on the property and civil rights of Mr Russell did not render it invalid.

On hearing of this decision, Sir John A. Macdonald wrote to his minister of justice: "This decision will be a great protection to the central authority. A contrary one would have greatly distorted the integrity of the dominion."[32] Within a year, his government had caused Parliament to adopt a Liquor Licence Act, better known as the McCarthy Act, in an effort to drive the provinces out of the field.[33] However, even before the McCarthy Act was scheduled to take effect, the Judicial Committee upheld the liquor licensing power of the provinces in Hodge *vs* The Queen.[34] Archibald Hodge, the proprietor of a Toronto tavern known as the St James Hotel, had been fined twenty dollars and costs by a magistrate for allowing billiards to be played on Saturday night, contrary to the terms of his liquor licence. The conviction was overturned by the Court of Queen's Bench but then reinstated by the Court of Appeal. Hodge's appeal of the latter decision to the Judicial Committee suggests remarkable persistence if only twenty dollars was at stake, and it seems probable that he received encouragement, financial or otherwise, from the dominion government. His counsel argued that, in the light of Russell *vs* The Queen, the provincial licensing power must be considered only a power to raise revenue and not to regulate the beverage industry, an argument given credence by the wording of Section 92(9). They also cited federal powers over criminal law and the regulation of trade and commerce, even though Russell *vs* The Queen had not been decided on those grounds. Furthermore, they alleged that a provincial legislature could not delegate its powers to local boards, since it was itself a subordinate body.

The judgment by Sir Barnes Peacock rejected all these arguments. It found no conflict between the Canada Temperance Act and the Ontario statute, and it made the celebrated assertion that a subject such as liquor might fall under federal authority in one aspect and under provincial authority in another. Provincial powers over municipal institutions, punishment for infraction of provincial laws, and "Matters of a merely local or private Nature" were all explicitly provided in Section 92. Furthermore, the judgment disposed of the argument against delegation by declaring that the Ontario legislature was "supreme" within the limits of its jurisdiction, and thus had the same ability to delegate its own powers as did the imperial Parliament or the Parliament of the dominion.

Ridiculing Macdonald for failing to predict the outcome of this case, the *Globe* aptly observed in an editorial that "his meddlesome and mischievous Act of last session was introduced and pushed through Parliament under false pretences."[35] Macdonald reluctantly agreed to postpone the operation of the McCarthy Act until its constitutionality had been determined. Both the Supreme Court and the Judicial Committee found it *ultra vires*. It was the only dominion statute to suffer this fate in Macdonald's lifetime.

Meanwhile the Judicial Committee had continued to deal with other Canadian controversies. The dominion's incoherent policies regarding the railways of western Nova Scotia led to litigation between the two railway companies that had been granted rights to the Windsor branch (see chapter 5). The Windsor and Annapolis, which had been deprived by Mackenzie's government of the rights given it by Macdonald's in 1873, claimed that the statute of 1874 was *ultra vires*, a claim upheld by the Supreme Court of Nova Scotia. The Western Counties Railway appealed to the Judicial Committee. As it had done in Cushing *vs* Dupuy, the Judicial Committee chose to assume that Parliament had not intended the consequence complained of, and thus avoided ruling on the issue.[36]

In Colonial Building and Investment Association *vs* Attorney General of Quebec the attorney general, L.O. Loranger, initiated proceedings by claiming the right to prevent a federally incorporated building society from operating within the province.[37] Since the company operated nowhere else, he argued that Section 92(16) was applicable, an argument upheld by the Court of Queen's Bench. Sir Montague Smith, however, declared that the incorporation was an exercise of Parliament's general power (as in the case of Citizens Insurance *vs* Parsons) and that the geographical scope of the company's operations was irrelevant.

Two Quebec cases involving taxation led to contrasting outcomes. In Attorney General of Quebec *vs* Reed the Judicial Committee declared that a tax of ten cents imposed on every exhibit filed in a court of law was "indirect" and thus *ultra vires*, on the questionable argument that it could allegedly not be predicted who would ultimately bear the burden of the tax.[38] Just three years later, a completely different panel of Judicial Committee members considered Quebec's tax on commercial corporations in Bank of Toronto et al. *vs* Lambe.[39] This tax had been the object of a petition for disallowance and was challenged in court by three chartered banks and thirty-eight insurance companies.[40] Counsel for the banks, including Edward Blake, argued that the tax trespassed on federal jurisdiction over banking and that it was neither "direct" nor "within the Province," since it was imposed on the capital of firms domiciled outside the province. The Judicial Committee ruled, however, that the tax was direct and valid. Lord Hobhouse cited the same definition of direct and indirect taxation by John Stuart Mill that had been cited by Lord Selborne in the Reed case.

The controversy over denominational schools in Manitoba came before the Judicial Committee in City of Winnipeg *vs* Barrett and City of Winnipeg *vs* Logan, decided in 1892.[41] Barrett and Logan were a Roman Catholic and an Anglican ratepayer, respectively, who refused to pay taxes for the non-denominational public school system imposed by the province in 1890, arguing that it violated both their religious beliefs and the guarantees in the Manitoba Act. Lord McNaghten, better remembered for the narrow definition of insanity that is still used in American and British criminal law, ruled that the law was valid because religious minorities were not compelled to use the public schools, only to support them. No privilege that existed before Manitoba became a province had been violated, because the system of tax-supported denominational schools had been established one year *after* it became a province.

In 1895 a panel of four, three of whom had also been present for the Barrett and Logan cases, considered the different but related question of whether Manitoba Catholics could appeal to the dominion government for redress of their grievance and whether the dominion could issue a remedial order on their behalf.[42] Lord Chancellor Herschell, who had represented the dominion government in three earlier cases, not to mention the insurance companies in their dispute with Parsons, delivered the judgment. The remedial power would be superfluous if it applied only to provincial actions forbidden by the Manitoba Act, so it must have been intended to have a broader significance. The act of 1890 had certainly deprived Catholics of privileges they previously enjoyed, and the fact they had not enjoyed them before 1871 was irrelevant. Provincial powers over education were not as absolute as provincial powers over the matters listed in Section 92. Thus the appear was valid and a remedial order would be possible.

Tennant *vs* Union Bank of Canada was a complex dispute over insolvency, somewhat reminiscent of Cushing *vs* Dupuy.[43] The insolvent firm, a sawmill in Simcoe County, had issued warehouse receipts for logs as a form of currency, a practice allowed by a provision of the Bank Act that had already been repealed when the case reached the Judicial Committee. The Union Bank, which held some of these receipts, used them to take timber belonging to the company. The company's trustee went to court, arguing that this provision of the Bank Act trespassed on provincial jurisdiction over property and civil rights. D'Alton McCarthy, a former Macdonald Conservative who now marched to a different drummer, represented Tennant, the trustee. Lord Watson delivered the judgment. While agreeing that property and civil rights were affected, he declared that the enumerated powers in Section 91 must be considered paramount over those in Section 92 and that the use of warehouse receipts as currency clearly fell under the rubric of banking.

The subject of insolvency appeared again in a reference case initiated by Ontario and decided soon after the Tennant case, in 1894.[44] Although bankruptcy and insolvency fell under federal jurisdiction, the dominion's Insolvency Act was unpopular outside Ontario, and was repealed by the Macdonald government in 1880. Only Ontario seemed to want an Insolvency Act, so Oliver Mowat adopted one, even though he doubted that it fell under provincial jurisdiction.[45] At issue in the reference was a section of the act stating that an assignment of an insolvent person's assets for the general benefit of creditors would take preference over all other judgments. The Judicial Committee ruled that in the absence of federal legislation on the subject the provincial legislation was valid.

Lord Watson's most celebrated judgment came in another reference case, usually called the Local Prohibition reference (see chapter 3).[46] In upholding an Ontario statute somewhat similar to the Canada Temperance Act, Watson was careful not to repudiate Russell *vs* The Queen. Nonetheless, his interpretation of Parliament's power to make laws for the peace, order, and good government of Canada was significantly narrower (and, as it turned out, more influential) than Sir Montague Smith's interpretation in the earlier judgment. Watson stated that Parliament's general power, unlike its enumerated powers to which he had referred in the Tennant case, could not be used to "trench" on the enumerated powers of the provincial legislatures. Later critics would call this the "three compartment" view of the distribution of powers, since it divided Section 91 into two distinct parts, the general and the particular, rather than treating the latter as examples of the former. Watson conceded that a problem originally under provincial jurisdiction might over time acquire such dimensions as to bring it under the scope of the general power, but he asserted that "great caution must be observed" in applying this notion. His disciple Richard Haldane, who was acting as counsel for Ontario in the case, certainly took this warning to heart, with consequences that would shape Canada's constitutional history for a century to come.

Even before this decision was handed down, Ontario had submitted a reference to its Court of Appeal on the related question of whether the province could impose a licence fee on distillers and brewers as a condition for them to sell their products at wholesale in Ontario. The Judicial Committee's judgment on appeal was not handed down until 1897, placing it outside the chronological boundaries of this book.[47] It rejected Edward Blake's argument on behalf of the brewing industry that the licence was an indirect tax. Thus ended the long series of beverage-related cases that had done so much to shape the interpretation of the BNA Act in its first thirty years.

The only other interpretation of Section 92 that remains to be noted was Fielding *vs* Thomas, decided in 1896.[48] The Judicial Committee ruled that the Nova Scotia Legislative Assembly could punish breaches of privilege and contempt as part of its jurisdiction over the constitution of the province. Such action did not trespass on the dominion's jurisdiction over criminal law.

Although the constitutional judgments concerning the distribution of legislative powers have preoccupied twentieth-century students of Canadian federalism to the exclusion of most others, a number of decisions related to public property and the prerogatives of the crown attracted at least as much attention during the period under consideration. Their long-term impact on Canadian federalism may also have been as great, if not more so.

The BNA Act had stated in two places that the dominion Parliament included the queen, and had elsewhere stated that the executive government of Canada should be carried on in her name and on her behalf. It nowhere mentioned the queen in connection with the governments or legislatures of the provinces, despite many opportunities to do so. Nonetheless, Ontario and Quebec had from the outset adopted their statutes in the queen's name, and Oliver Mowat rarely missed an opportunity to argue that the lieutenant-governor was the queen's representative and that the royal prerogatives had been inherited in part by the provincial level of government.

In 1879 the Supreme Court administered a setback to this campaign in Lenoir *vs* Ritchie (see chapter 3). Mowat had lost only a battle, however, not the war. Among the traditional prerogatives of the crown was the possession of escheated property. In 1878 Mowat, as attorney general, filed suit on behalf of the province of Ontario or, as he put it, the crown to recover the land of Andrew Mercer, a Toronto resident who had died intestate in 1871. When the Court of Appeal upheld the province's claim, the dominion government appealed to the Supreme Court of Canada. Both governments agreed that the appeal should be limited to the question of which level of government was entitled to escheated property, and the Supreme Court upheld the dominion's claim. It was now Mowat's turn to appeal, and to argue Ontario's case in person before the Judicial Committee of the Privy Council. There he argued that the province shared in the prerogatives of the crown, and furthermore that escheated lands were among the "royalties" granted to the provinces by Section 109 of the BNA Act. Solicitor General Herschell and Zebulon A. Lash for the dominion countered that escheats were essentially a form of revenue and thus fell under Section 102, which gave the dominion all "Duties and Revenues" not specifically assigned to the provinces. Lord Selborne's judgment agreed with the province that Section 109 rather than Section 102 was the relevant provision, but did not emphasize the argument concerning the prerogative.[49] A few months later the judgment in Hodge *vs* The Queen suggested that the Judicial Committee inclined towards the view that the two levels of government were equal in status, but again the question of the prerogative was not directly addressed.

The Judicial Committee's decision on the Ontario boundary in 1884, although it marked another important round in the long struggle between Mowat and Macdonald, did not require any interpretation of the BNA Act. Macdonald's reluctance to admit defeat, however, led to a sequel that did raise important constitutional issues. The disputed territory that the Judicial Committee awarded to Ontario had been the subject of Treaty 3, which the dominion negotiated with the Ojibwa Indians in 1873. Macdonald argued, and apparently believed, that its public lands and resources belonged to the dominion, even if it was in other respects a part of Ontario. The idea of the dominion owning public lands and resources within a province was not without precedent; the dominion had withheld the public lands and resources from Manitoba when that province was created, and continued to do so until 1930. Macdonald's argument was nonetheless based on a very questionable interpretation of Section 91(24), which gave the dominion jurisdiction over "Indians, and lands reserved for the Indians." Alexander Campbell correctly predicted in October 1885 that the dominion would lose if it took its case to the Judicial Committee.[50] However, Campbell's influence in the government was declining and he had been demoted from the Department of Justice to the Post Office in September. Macdonald would not give up so easily.

Macdonald's government had issued licences to cut timber in the disputed territory prior to the Judicial Committee's decision on the boundary (see chapter 3). One holder of a licence, the St Catharines' Milling and Lumber Company, was sued by Ontario after the boundary award for continuing to cut timber without authorization by the province. The High Court of Ontario found in favour of the province in 1885, as did the Supreme Court of Canada in 1887. The cost of the appeal from the original judgment was paid to the company by the dominion government.[51] When the issue went to the Judicial Committee, the dominion was granted special leave to intervene. Oliver Mowat personally presented Ontario's case before the Judicial Committee, assisted by Edward Blake who had recently resigned as leader of the Liberal party.

The judgment by Lord Watson accepted Ontario's basic argument that the Indians had not really been the owners of the land prior to the treaty and thus could not assign it to the dominion.[52] The land had always belonged to the crown and "the tenure of the Indians was a personal and usufructary right, dependent upon the good will of the Sovereign." While this assertion might not sound like an argument for provincial ownership, Watson argued that it was because Section 109 of the BNA Act had assigned the crown's rights to lands and resources to the provinces. Section 91(24), in contrast, conferred no property rights on the dominion. It merely conferred legislative authority over land reserved for Indians. In the case of land surrendered by Indians, it conferred no authority at all. This was the clearest expression yet by the Judicial Committee of the notion that the crown and its prerogatives were divisible between the dominion and the provinces, with the unspoken corollary that the two levels of government were equal in status.

Meanwhile, the dominion and British Columbia had jointly referred to the Exchequer Court their dispute over the ownership of precious metals in the railway belt. The province based its case on the common law doctrine that precious metals were retained by the crown, even when the crown transferred ownership of land to another party. The dominion, significantly, accepted the province's claim to a share in the crown's prerogatives, but argued that the railway belt had been transferred from the crown in its provincial capacity to the crown in its federal capacity. Because the crown was the recipient as well as the grantor, it argued that the precious metals had been transferred along with the land.

The Exchequer Court judge who heard the case agreed with the dominion, as did the Supreme Court in a judgment that followed six months after its judgment in the St Catharines' case. The Judicial Committee, however, disagreed.[53] Lord Watson's judgment made the reasonable assertion that Section 109 must now be read to include British Columbia, as well as the original provinces. However, he ventured onto more questionable ground by asserting that the "royalties" mentioned in Section 109, unlike the other rights enumerated there, had not been included in the transfer of the railway belt because they were not specifically mentioned in the Terms of Union. The Terms of Union, Watson said, were more like a "commercial contract" than a treaty. This comment was apparently based on the irrelevant observation that the dominion intended to sell the land to private owners in due course. Once it did so, the land would no longer be public, but the precious metals, according to the law of England, would remain with the crown. In a bewildering *non sequitur*, Watson derived from this scenario the assertion that they must remain with the crown in its provincial manifestation.

Watson's most explicit statement on the nature of Canadian federalism, as he understood it, came three years later in Liquidators of the Maritime Bank of Canada *vs* Receiver General of New Brunswick.[54] The case concerned a bank that had collapsed in 1887, and the immediate issue was whether the province of New Brunswick, which had deposited a considerable sum, could exercise the crown's prerogative right of precedence over other creditors. Both the Supreme Court of New Brunswick and the Supreme Court of Canada said that it could, but the liquidators appealed to the Judicial Committee. In the light of previous judgments going back to Hodge *vs* The Queen, the result was almost a foregone conclusion. Watson asserted that Confederation has not severed the direct link between the crown and the individual provinces and that the lieutenant-governor was just as much a representative of the crown as was the governor general. The Hodge case was cited as demonstrating that the provinces were sovereign within their own fields of jurisdiction, while the Mercer and St Catharines Milling and Lumber decisions, as well as that in the railway belt reference, had indicated they could exercise prerogative powers. Rewriting history, Watson asserted that Confederation had not been intended to subordinate the provinces to the dominion, but to create a dual federalism on the American model, as described by Dicey in his *Introduction to the Study of the Law of the Constitution*.[55] The original theory of Canada's constitution was thus formally interred along with its principal architect, Sir John A. Macdonald, who had died just a year before.

Since the Judicial Committee played so large a part in undermining Macdonald's concept of Confederation, it seems ironic that Macdonald was the leading opponent of the effort to abolish appeals from the Supreme Court to the Judicial Committee in 1875. It is doubly ironic that Aemilius Irving, the MP who moved the amendment that became Section 47 of the Supreme Court Act, later represented Ontario in proceedings before the Judicial Committee.[56]

Whatever his private thoughts might have been, Macdonald seems never to have explicitly repudiated his early enthusiasm for appeals to the foot of the throne. His record indicates, however, that he preferred to refer legal questions to the law officers of the crown, and his government refused to submit its dispute with Manitoba over railway policy to the Judicial Committee. Some of Macdonald's associates were more openly critical of the Judicial Committee than he was. D'Alton McCarthy, who represented Peter McLaren before the Judicial Committee in the rivers and streams litigation, complained to Macdonald that most members of the Judicial Committee lacked ability and were ignorant of Canadian realities.[57] McCarthy's comments, however, were mild compared to those which John Thompson made to Lord Lansdowne regarding the Judicial Committee in 1886:

In many respects it is the most unsatisfactory tribunal in the Empire. It has displayed such ignorance of our geography and our constitution that many of the sayings of its Judges, and even many passages from its judgments, are treasured in the different Provinces as affording a fund of professional humour which time will make incredibly valuable ... When a constitutional question comes up they regard the Provincial authority as the weaker vessel – entitled to a decision on grounds of chivalry and generosity – while the fact is that the great danger of Canada is the weakness of the Federal authority, beset as it is on every side by the Provinces seeking to enlarge their powers at its expense and seeking to make it carry all their burthens.[58]

Thompson's harsh judgment has been repeated by many critics over the years, while his assertion that the Judicial Committee deliberately favoured the provinces out of "chivalry and generosity" has been at least implicitly conceded by many of the Judicial Committee's defenders.

It is doubtful that any consensus will ever be achieved on the impact of the Judicial Committee on Canadian federalism. A few observations can be made, however, based on the judgments rendered up to and including 1896.

In fairness to the Judicial Committee, it must be conceded that it did not always favour the provinces in its judgments. Four provincial statutes or portions of statutes were struck down and in at least one case, Attorney General of Quebec *vs* Reed, the Judicial Committee erred on the side of narrowness in defining provincial powers. The one federal statute struck down, the McCarthy Act, probably deserved its fate, although one might wish the Judicial Committee had given reasons for its judgment. Federal powers over the electoral process, railways, banking, insolvency, the incorporation of companies, and even the promotion of public order and safety through temperance were upheld in various judgments.

On the other hand the provincial victories were more numerous and more significant. Citizens' Insurance *vs* Parsons and Bank of Toronto *vs* Lambe gave the provincial level of government a significant share of the regulating and taxing powers of the modern state. The three judgments involving the interpretation of Section 109 reinforced provincial control over Canada's natural resources, a fact that would have important consequences in the twentieth century as Canada evolved from an agricultural British colony into a resource frontier of industrial America. Hodge *vs* The Queen and the Maritime Bank judgment effectively gave Canada a new formal constitution by conferring the imperial stamp of legitimacy on the notion that the two levels of government were equal in status. Watson's reasoning in the Local Prohibition reference judgment of 1896 paved the way for a significant erosion of the dominion's powers in a series of judgments between 1912 and 1949.

It is difficult to state conclusively whether D'Alton McCarthy and John Thompson were justified in their unflattering evaluations of the Judicial Committee's personnel. So many individuals participated in the committee's work, and so little is known of how it actually operated, that a general evaluation is not possible. The central role of Lord Watson is generally conceded, but it is not known to what extent he influenced, or was influenced by, his colleagues. In any event, he participated in only about half the judgments. The merits of the "three compartment" view of Section 91 will doubtless be debated for as long as there is a Canadian state. G.P. Browne's arguments on behalf of the three compartment interpretation have considerable merit, but doubts persist.

Consistency was not the Judicial Committee's greatest virtue, a fact that was perhaps inevitable given the diversity of its personnel and the practice of selecting a small panel of judges from the large number available at any one time. It is difficult to understand how a provincial tax on assets held outside the province by federally chartered banks could be upheld in Bank of Toronto *vs* Lambe when the same province had been denied the right to impose a trivial tax on the exhibits presented in its own courts only three years previously. It is equally difficult to see any consistency between Russell *vs* The Queen and the judgment in the Local Prohibition reference. Although the work "exclusive" or "exclusively" appeared in both Section 91 and Section 92, and although agriculture and immigration were stated to be the only concurrent fields of jurisdiction, the Judicial Committee upheld two almost identical statutes dealing with local prohibition, one adopted by the dominion Parliament and one by a provincial legislature. Neither logically nor pragmatically does the outcome seem to make any sense.

It is entirely possible that Lord Watson considered the BNA Act too centralized and deliberately set out to strengthen the provinces, although his reasons for doing so have not been identified. There was clearly no generalized imperial conspiracy, on the bench or elsewhere, to divide or weaken the dominion. Indeed, the imperial government quite consistently favoured a strong central government for Canada (see chapter 10). At least two of the law officers of the crown helped to defend the "centralist" position in cases that came before the Judicial Committee. Solicitor General Herschell, who would later be lord chancellor in Gladstone's last government, did so in the cases of Citizens Insurance *vs* Parsons, Attorney General of Ontario *vs* Mercer, and the McCarthy Act reference. Attorney General Webster argued for the dominion in St Catharines Milling and Lumber *vs* The Queen, and for the liquidators of the Maritime Bank in their dispute with New Brunswick.

Finally, J.R. Mallory's assertion that the Judicial Committee was motivated by a distaste for "collectivism" and state intervention may well be valid for the twentieth century, as he asserts, but there is little evidence for it in the nineteenth. The only judgments up to 1896 that might lend support to this interpretation were Attorney General of Quebec *vs* Queen Insurance and Colonial Building and Investment Association *vs* Attorney General of Quebec. Judgments giving governments, especially provincial governments, opportunities to tax and regulate business were far more frequent, and more important.

The Judicial Committee's judgments are probably the best remembered aspect of Canadian federalism in its first thirty years. While perhaps not quite as important, relative to other aspects, as the legal literature might suggest, they nonetheless cast considerable light on the issues and controversies of the time. The broad themes of money and land, railways and religion, which we have identified as central to the early development of Canadian federalism, appear in many of the judgments. The Macdonald-Mowat rivalry is clearly visible behind many of them. Insurance, always a high priority with cautious Canadians, was the occasion for several of the judgments. Intoxicating beverages, symbolizing the tension between the Protestant ethic and the rough conditions of a frontier society, were the occasion for even more.

Federalism, as Dicey observed, tends to magnify the influence of judges and lawyers.[59] Canada's experience with federalism, like that of Australia and the United States, illustrates the truth of this generalization. Intergovernmental disputes frequently ended up in the courtroom, and private litigation helped to define the relationship between the two levels of government. Canada was unique in the predominant role played by an external tribunal, the Judicial Committee, in interpreting its constitution. Had this not been the case it is probable that the dominion's powers would have been interpreted more broadly, and those of the provinces more narrowly. Perhaps learning from Canada's experience, Australia insisted when it became a federation that its own High Court have the last word on questions defining the jurisdictional boundaries between the two levels of government.[60] Those who remember the past can sometimes, although not always, avoid reliving it.

12 The Origins of Cooperative Federalism

The expression "cooperative federalism" arose in the United States in the 1930s and spread to Canada after the Second World War, attaining the peak of its popularity in the 1960s. The concept of cooperative federalism emphasizes the growing prominence of intergovernmental relations as a result of the expanding role of the state and the resulting difficulty of maintaining a rigid distinction between the two levels of government. Implicit in the concept is the assumption that prior to the New Deal in the United States, and to the postwar development of the Keynesian welfare state in Canada, the two levels of government in both federations had pursued their respective tasks in virtual isolation from one another. With little overlap between the responsibilities of the two levels of government, there was little need for intergovernmental relations involving either politicians or administrators. All that was needed was for the Supreme Court, or in Canada's case the Judicial Committee of the Privy Council, to maintain the jurisdictional boundary between the two levels by periodically striking down statutes that exceeded the constitutional powers of the legislature that enacted them.

Some time after the term cooperative federalism had become popular, Daniel Elazar's research demonstrated that the supposedly classic variety of "dual federalism" had not corresponded closely with reality, even at the time when its virtues were being extolled in numerous decisions of the Supreme Court of the United States. Instead, Elazar showed that the federal government and the states began to collaborate in performing a variety of shared or overlapping functions almost as soon as the constitution came into effect, and that such supposedly modern phenomena as conditional grants and jointly administered programs had emerged even before the Civil War, let alone the New Deal.[1]

In Canada the accepted orthodoxy regarding the early history of federalism is somewhat different from the orthodoxy Elazar refuted in the United States, though the two are parallel in certain respects. All students of Canadian federalism know that John A. Macdonald deliberately rejected many features of an American model which he believed had contributed to the breakdown that led to the Civil War. Instead, Macdonald designed a more hierarchical kind of federalism, largely based on the ideas of Alexander Hamilton, which was intended to subordinate the provinces to the central government by such means as the declaratory power of Parliament, the disallowance of provincial legislation, and the extensive powers of the federally appointed lieutenant-governor. In addition, the provinces were made dependent on federal subsidies, which the British North America Act optimistically assumed could be fixed forever at the level specified in Section 118. This model of "quasi-federalism," as K. C. Wheare later called it, implied intergovernmental relations of a kind. However, the Macdonaldian concept of intergovernmental relations seemed to make the provinces passive recipients of decisions made unilaterally in Ottawa. Such a model has little in common with the complex pattern of intergovernmental collaboration that have characterized both North American federations in recent decades.[2]

Intergovernmental relations in the modern sense would thus appear to have been no more necessary in Macdonaldian federalism than in the federalism of the nineteenth-century United States as it was understood prior to Elazar's revisionist interpretation. Macdonald's Canada appears to have shared with the nineteenth-century United States the essential conditions for the practice of "dual federalism": a constitutionally entrenched division of legislative powers, a relatively limited role for the state, and a judiciary willing and able to prevent either level of government from trespassing on the other's field of jurisdiction. In fact the distribution of legislative powers in the BNA Act was more detailed and apparently more rigid than that provided for in the United States Constitution, so the need for intergovernmental collaboration was perhaps even less in Canada.

There is, however, a provision of the BNA Act that has attracted little attention and that is an exception to the general rule that powers are exclusively assigned to either Parliament or the provincial legislatures. This exception is Section 95, which provides that either the provincial legislatures or Parliament may legislate in relation to agriculture and to immigration, but that provincial laws shall have effect only insofar as they are not "repugnant" to the terms of any act of Parliament. Why were these two subjects, and only these two, concurrent fields of jurisdiction in a constitution that carefully enumerated forty-six other fields of jurisdiction it assigned exclusively to either Parliament or the legislatures? What were the intergovernmental relations to which Section 95 gave rise during the early years of Canadian federalism?[3]

To the modern mind, agriculture and immigration may seem like a random juxtaposition of two unrelated subjects, both of which, for mysterious reasons, could not be exclusively assigned to either level of government. This is an understandable error now that more than half of the foreign-born population resides in the three largest metropolitan areas of Canada. In 1867, by contrast, agriculture and immigration were closely subjects. The circumstance that made British North America attractive to immigrants was its supply of unoccupied land that could be used for agriculture. Land was a means of absorbing immigrants, and immigrants were a means of occupying land and developing the country. Although manufacturing was beginning to develop, and although the older staples of fur, fish and timber were still significant, Canada was primarily an agricultural country in 1867. Confederation, followed by expansion to the west, was expected to make the country larger, in area, population, and what we could call GNP, but not to cause a qualitative change in the character of its economy. Canada wanted immigrants, and the most desirable immigrants were thought to be farmers, who would increase the cultivated acreage of the country, produce exportable commodities, and provide traffic for the railways and markets for indigenous secondary industries.

Both agriculture and immigration were subjects of great importance, a fact that seemed to argue for placing them under the jurisdiction of Parliament. At the same time, the original provinces retained (or in the case of Ontario and Quebec were given) ownership of crown land, which was the principal instrument of policy in relation to both agriculture and immigration. Section 95 must be read in conjunction with Section 92(5) ("The Management and Sale of Public Lands Belonging to the Province") and Section 109, which confers ownership of "All Lands, Mines, Minerals and Royalties." These provisions unavoidably gave the provinces primary responsibility for both agriculture and immigration. In contrast to mining and forestry, agriculture and immigration were too important to be left exclusively to the provinces. There had to be a federal role, but it could not be as exclusive as the federal role in relation to banking, interprovincial transport, or fisheries. Section 95 was the response to this set of circumstances.

Section 95 must also be read in the light of Canadian experience with immigration before 1867, as well as the experience of the United States. Public policy towards immigration can have two objectives: to attract immigrants or to exclude them. The two objectives are not mutually exclusive, since there may be a desire to attract some kinds of immigrants and to exclude others, or to attract them at some times and to exclude them at others, or to attract them to certain parts of the country and to exclude them from others. In the United States, as of 1867, there was hardly any explicit policy regarding immigration. The country had an abundance of land and resources, as well as political freedom and social mobility, and little effort was needed to attract immigrants from Europe. Whatever effort there was tended to be provided by private enterprise, particularly the transatlantic shipping companies. At the same time, there was little support for excluding immigrants from the United States until late in the nineteenth century. Congress seldom took any interest in the subject and did not legislate on immigration until 1882, when a measure restricting the immigration of Chinese was adopted.[4] Before that time anyone, at least in theory, could enter the United States. The reception of immigrants and their absorption into the community was left to state, local, and private initiatives, particularly in the Atlantic seaports where most immigrants then arrived. Perhaps because of this localized administration, immigrants tended to remain in the rapidly industrializing northeastern states, where they filled the needs of the manufacturing industries for cheap labour.[5] The task of populating the western frontier was largely left to native-born Americans, mainly of Anglo-Celtic ancestry and Protestant religion. This pattern of settlement, including the way immigrants avoided the South (where industrialization was limited and African-Americans provided the cheap labour), is still reflected in the ethnic and religious composition, as well as the political culture, of the different states.

In all these respects Canada's experience, before and after Confederation, was very different. The laissez-faire approach of the United States was inappropriate to Canada's needs, a fact recognized long before Confederation. Canada could not assume that immigrants would be attracted to its shores, because it had to compete with a generally more attractive destination: the United States. The United States had more land and resources, a higher standard of living, more political democracy and social mobility, and a better climate. Some immigrants came to Canada initially because it was slightly closer to northwestern Europe, making the ocean passage cheaper and less perilous, but most of those attracted for this reason soon moved on to the United States. Canada had to abandon laissez-faire in immigration policy to maintain, and still more to improve upon, its proportionate share of the North American population. As early as 1841, before responsible government was achieved and four decades before the United States Congress took any action on immigration, the United Province of Canada adopted legislation to create a fund for defraying the cost o f moving indigent immigrants from the port of entry to their destinations, and of supporting them until they found employment.[6]

Canada also had incentives to adopt exclusionary policies. Canada was a part of the British Empire, and in relation to other colonies it was not far from the British Isles. For both of these reasons there was a well-founded suspicion that Canada was used by the United Kingdom as an outlet for unwanted elements of that country's population, without regard for the interests of Canada or those of the immigrants themselves. The struggle for responsible government was in part a struggle for the right to control entry into Canada. The imperial government did not acknowledge that right until 1848, after the influx of Irish famine victims had persuaded most Canadians as well as the governor general (Lord Elgin) that controls were essential.[7] The first of several statutes imposing restrictions on entry was adopted in that year. Five years later the government of the United Province took over control of the immigration agencies in Quebec City, Montreal, Ottawa, Kingston, Toronto, and Hamilton. These offices had previously been operated by the imperial government. Significantly, after 1853 they reported to the minister of agriculture.[8]

Apart from measures to support immigrants and measures to exclude them, there was a third strand of pre-Confederation policy that gives some credence to the "merchants against industry" interpretation of Canada's development. A statute adopted in 1850 was designed to encourage immigrants bound from Europe to the United States to use the St Lawrence route as a means of getting there[9] – the converse of the traditional goal of directing American exports of agricultural produce through the St Lawrence system. The same boats that carried produce downstream could carry immigrants upstream. At the time of Confederation about four out of every five immigrants recorded as arriving in Canada continued on, within the same calendar year, into the United States.[10] Despite this fact, about one-sixth of Canada's population was foreign-born at the time of the first dominion census, almost exactly the same proportion as today.[11]

Confederation, from a central Canadian perspective, had the practical consequence that the existing functions of the colonial state had to be distributed between two levels of government, federal and provincial. The United Province of Canada had had a department and a minister of agriculture, and the successor governments of Quebec, Ontario, and the dominion all established such departments immediately. Like their predecessor in the United Province, all of these departments had responsibility for immigration as well. The appropriate division of responsibilities between the two levels of government would have to be discovered through trial and error. Common sense suggested, however, that the control of entry into Canada would be a responsibility of the dominion, particularly since it was closely associated with Section 91, subsection 11, "Quarantine and the Establishment and Maintenance of Marine Hospitals." Canada had already experienced epidemics of infectious disease caused by immigrants arriving from the British Isles, and this was one reason why the United Province had demanded the right to control entry in 1848. Virtually all immigrants arrived at Quebec City, Montreal, or Niagara Falls, and control of entry at these points was not difficult, but there was no feasible way to control the movement of persons between Quebec and Ontario.

The provinces would play a significant role in efforts to attract immigrants and in assisting them after they arrived, particularly if the immigrants were farmers and intended to settle on public lands. Prior to Confederation, according to Hodgetts, Canada had seemed resigned to a situation in which most "immigrants" continued on to permanent homes in the United States.[12] After Confederation this situation was frequently deplored and efforts were made, with some success, to correct it. The more optimistic mentality created by Confederation itself, as well as the anti-American sentiments stimulated by the Fenian raids and the termination of reciprocity, probably contributed to this change, at the same time as the resumption of railway building on a large scale increased the demand for labour.

The desire to attract immigrants was shared by the federal and provincial authorities after 1867. Ontario, then as now, attracted the largest share of the immigrants who remained in Canada; in 1871 it accounted for 75 per cent of the foreign-born persons enumerated by the census. Quebec and New Brunswick apparently wished to increase their share of immigration, and both had large areas of unoccupied land they considered suitable for agriculture, some of which would be made more accessible by the building of the Intercolonial Railway. Nova Scotia, which had the smallest foreign-born population of the four provinces, appeared relatively uninterested in immigration, perhaps because of its relatively high (by North American standards) density of population. At the federal level, interest in immigration is suggested by the fact that the House of Commons established a Standing Committee on Immigration and Colonization at its first session.

Logically enough, and in characteristically Canadian fashion, the first question with which this committee concerned itself was the appropriate division of responsibilities between the dominion and the provinces. In its first report the committee expressed the view that the word "colonization" in its title was not appropriate, since the subject fell under provincial jurisdiction. The committee dispatched letters to Sir John A. Macdonald and the premiers of the four provinces, requesting clarification of the meaning of Section 95 as it applied to immigration. Neither Macdonald nor the premiers of Quebec and New Brunswick bothered to reply, while the premier of Ontario replied that the question had not been discussed by his government. The only substantive reply, oddly enough, came from the attorney general of Nova Scotia, who was trying to extricate his province from Confederation, but his reply was no more than an elementary explanation of the meaning of the repugnancy clause. In its report the standing committee referred to Sections 92(5) and 109 of the BNA Act and concluded: "The clauses seem to place every interest in connection with the public lands and their settlement beyond the purview of this Committee, and to limit their inquiries and supervision of immigration matters simply to the sanitary arrangements for the reception of immigrants, the management of the existing agencies, and the transit of immigrants within the dominion."[13] Despite this conclusion, it continued to be known as the Standing (or Select) Committee on Immigration and Colonization for many years thereafter.

Even before this report, in November 1867, a question was asked in the House of Commons regarding the government's plans, if any, to encourage immigration. Sir George-Étienne Cartier replied that the government favoured immigration but would require cooperation from the provinces.[14] Two weeks later Charles Tupper (who did not enter the cabinet until 1870) introduced a motion requesting the correspondence between the dominion and provincial governments on the subject of immigration. Macdonald replied that he thought the only correspondence to date was of a purely formal character.[15] A motion similar to Tupper's was moved in the Senate the following year, and led to a somewhat longer debate than had taken place in the Commons. Most of the senators who participated lamented the fact that Canada was less attractive to immigrants than the United States. Senator David Macpherson, who later served in the second Macdonald government as minister of the interior, blamed this fact on the provinces, since it was they who controlled the public lands. The dominion government could do nothing to compete with the free land that was available in the United States. In reply, Senator Wark of New Brunswick noted that his province had adopted a statute making land available to settlers at a price of twenty cents an acre.[16]

A few months afterward, in September 1868, Premier Chauveau of Quebec proposed that a federal-provincial conference be held to clarify the responsibilities of the two levels of government regarding immigration.[17] No federal-provincial conference, on any subject, had yet taken place, but the idea may have been suggested by the conferences at Charlottetown, Quebec, and London that had led to Confederation. Chauveau's suggestion was accepted by the federal government in an order in council, which also appointed the minister of agriculture, J.-C. Chapais, as the "delegate" of the dominion. Chapais selected 29 October 1868 as the date for the opening of the conference, and invitations were sent to the four provinces.

The conference took place in Ottawa and lasted for two days. Since the prime minister of Canada and the premiers of Quebec and New Brunswick attended, as well as an additional minister from each, it was effectively a "first ministers" conference, an indication of the importance attached to the subject. Ontario, however, was represented only by the minister and the deputy minister of agriculture. Nova Scotia, not much interested in immigration and still attempting to withdraw from Confederation, was not represented at all. Despite Nova Scotia's absence, the conference was more fruitful than most of those that have occurred in Ottawa in more recent years. The delegates were able to agree on eleven recommendations regarding the allocation of responsibilities between the two levels of government, as follows:

• The dominion, described in the conference minutes as "the General Government," would establish and maintain an immigration office in London, and possibly other offices in the British Isles.
• The dominion would also establish and maintain at least one immigration office in continental Europe.
• The dominion would defray the expenses of quarantine stations at Quebec City, Halifax, and Saint John. (No mention was made of

Niagara Falls, which had been an important port of entry for immigrants since the completion of the international railway bridge more than a decade before the conference. Presumably the delegates had confidence in the quarantine arrangements at the port of New York.)

- The dominion at its own expense would maintain immigration offices at the eight principal cities of Canada: Halifax, Saint John, Quebec, Montreal, Ottawa, Kingston, Toronto, and Hamilton. These offices, except for the two in the Maritimes, had been taken over by the United Province of Canada from the imperial government in 1853.
- The dominion government would request funds from Parliament each year to cover its expenses on immigration.
- The provinces agreed to establish an efficient system of offices for the reception of immigrants within their borders, and as much as possible to pursue liberal policies regarding the settlement of their uncultivated lands.
- Each province could, if it so desired, appoint its own immigration agents in Europe and elsewhere, and the dominion promised that all such agents "shall be duly accredited by the General Government."
- Each province agreed to keep the dominion government and the dominion's immigration agents overseas informed of the province's policies regarding colonization and settlement.
- To avoid disappointing would-be immigrants, no province would alter its colonization policies without "due and reasonable" notice. If possible, any changes in policy should be made during the winter (which was when legislative sessions usually took place) and should remain in effect throughout the following summer (which was when most immigrants arrived.)
- Dominion-provincial conferences on immigration would take place four times each year.   *
- Each of the governments agreed to introduce whatever legislation would be required to carry out its commitments.

The dominion government embodied these terms in an order in council, and copies were sent to all provinces, including Nova Scotia, with the request that the provincial governments indicate in writing their formal acceptance of the agreements. All four replied, although Nova Scotia, which was in the process of negotiating "better terms," indicated via the lieutenant-governor that for financial reasons it was not in a position to cooperate. New Brunswick expressed second thoughts about the feasibility of sending a delegate to Ottawa every three months (the Intercolonial Railway was not completed until 1876) and stated it would not require any legislation to carry out its commitments, but it accepted the other terms. Quebec and Ontario accepted the agreements without reservation.[18]

Undeterred by New Brunswick's reservations, the dominion summoned another conference to be held in March 1869, at which it was hoped the provinces would supply information regarding their efforts to attract immigrants. Although all four provinces agreed to supply the information, only Ontario was willing to attend a conference at this time. Nova Scotia again pleaded financial stringency, Quebec excused itself on the grounds that its legislature would be in session at the time of the conference, and New Brunswick simply replied that attendance would not be convenient.[19] The conference nonetheless took place, with only Ontario and the dominion in attendance. Ontario was represented by its provincial secretary, while Chapais again represented the dominion. At this conference Ontario agreed to supply the dominion with any information about the province it would like prospective immigrants to have, and also agreed to pay the transportation costs for indigent immigrants from the port of entry to the place in Ontario where they wished to settle. A report of this conference was sent to the other three provinces in the hope they would agree to do likewise.[20] By the time the St Lawrence opened for navigation in 1869, the dominion had appointed immigration agents in London and Antwerp. It also had established immigration offices at Halifax, Saint John, and Miramichi (New Brunswick) in addition to the six existing offices in central Canada. All immigration agents, both at home and abroad, were instructed to cooperate with the provinces in distributing information supplied by the provincial governments and in directing immigrants towards the places where the provincial governments wished them to settle.[21] Ontario had its own immigration agent in London and had printed posters and leaflets, in German as well as in English, to direct prospective immigrants towards the province. Quebec reported that it was considering the appointment of immigration agents in Britain and Europe and that the legislature had voted a sum of $12,000 for the support of immigration over a period of eighteen months. New Brunswick reported that it had no department of agriculture and "as yet" no agents overseas, but that it had immigration agents at Saint John and other locations in the province. Nova Scotia did not submit a report on its immigration efforts, such as they were, although it had promised to do so.[22]

The dominion government carried out one of its pledges by introducing the Immigration Act, which received royal assent on 22 June

1869.[23] The preamble to the act referred to the concurrent jurisdiction conferred on the two levels of government by Section 95, and also to the dominion-provincial agreements of October 1868, which were summarized. The act itself stipulated that the dominion would maintain immigration agents and offices in London and in the eight major cities of Canada. Additional offices in Canada, the British Isles, and Europe could be opened "if the government so decides." The immigration agents were empowered to spend funds granted to them by a "Local Government" for the purpose of assisting immigrants who intended to settle in the province concerned. The remaining provisions of the act resembled those previously in effect, which the dominion had inherited from the old Province of Canada, and which were now repealed. They included the imposition of a tax on ships carrying immigrants, based on the number of persons landed, provisions to protect the passengers from various kinds of exploitation and inconvenience that might be imposed on them by ships' captains and others, and the imposition of fines on captains whose ships were overcrowded or who picked up additional passengers after leaving the original port of embarkation. There were also provisions empowering the government to control the entry of "paupers" or of the mentally and physically handicapped.

Not long after the adoption of this legislation a Canadian immigration office was opened in Dublin. The provincial governments were officially informed of this fact, and were invited to supply any information that might be of particular interest to prospective Irish immigrants.[24] In response, Ontario inquired whether agents had also been appointed in Northern Ireland, Scotland, and continental Europe. The dominion supplied the name and address of its agent at Antwerp, but indicated that there were none in Northern Ireland or Scotland.[25] An agent in Belfast was appointed shortly afterwards, probably as a result of this exchange.[26]

A third federal-provincial conference on immigration took place in October 1869. John A. Macdonald and J.-C. Chapais again represented the dominion, Premier Pierre Chauveau represented Quebec, and Ontario sent its minister of agriculture, John Carling, and his deputy. Neither Nova Scotia nor New Brunswick sent delegates to this conference, although Nova Scotia for the first time provided a report of its activities in the field of immigration. Despite the presence of two first ministers, the conference seems to have been a somewhat perfunctory ritual. The most interesting item of business considered was a proposal from a Mr Brown of Scotland, who offered to write a pamphlet extolling Canada's virtues for Scottish emigrants in return for a grant of a thousand acres of good agricultural land. Since the dominion had no land to grant, the proposal was referred to the provinces, but none expressed any interest.[27]

The reports by the provinces on their activities indicated that Ontario was continuing its active publicity campaign, and had produced a second edition of its pamphlet describing the opportunities for immigrants in the province. Counting both editions, 100,000 copies of the pamphlet had now been printed. Ontario had also produced posters in English, French, and German. Copies of the poster (presumably the English edition) were said to have been displayed, with the permission of the imperial government, in every post office in England. Nova Scotia had entered the field, on a much more modest scale, by producing its own pamphlet, of which 200 copies were given to the dominion authorities for distribution. Quebec was said to be contemplating posters and pamphlets of its own, and also to be still considering whether it should appoint its own immigration agents in Europe. New Brunswick apparently submitted no report.[28] Ontario's efforts seemed to be productive, since it attracted 92 per cent of all the immigrants who settled in Canada during 1869. However, three out of every four immigrants who passed through Canadian ports in that year were bound for the United States.[29]

Another federal-provincial conference on immigration took place in October 1870 and lasted for three days.[30] No fewer than eight members of the dominion cabinet attended, including Sir John A. Macdonald. Christopher Dunkin, who had replaced Chapais as minister of agriculture (and who had attended the first immigration conference in his previous capacity as provincial treasurer of Quebec), was the only federal minister present on the final day. Chauveau and Carling again represented Quebec and Ontario, respectively, and New Brunswick sent a minister as well, although Nova Scotia was not represented. The conference heard speeches by Canada's immigration agent in London and by several British visitors with an interest in promoting emigration, including an Anglican vicar and a Catholic priest. Premier Chauveau described Quebec's efforts to promote immigration, including a pamphlet of which it had produced 50,000 copies in English and 30,000 in French. He denied allegations that the small number of immigrants settling in Quebec (there had been only 503 in 1869) reflected a lack of enthusiasm on the part of the province. Chauveau urged greater efforts to attract immigrants from continental Europe, saying that Belgians in particular were good settlers who "would assimilate well with the people of Quebec." Earlier in the day Thomas White, who had served briefly as the Ontario immigration agent in London, had described the dominion agency in Antwerp as a waste of money.

Chauveau's government was apparently sincere in its support for immigration, for it had recently appointed provincial immigration agents at Quebec City and Montreal to assist new arrivals and to encourage them to remain in Quebec rather than continuing onwards to Ontario or the United States.[31] Soon after the conference, Quebec appointed its own immigration agent for continental Europe, based in Paris. The Colonial Office provided the Quebec agent with letters of introduction to the British ambassadors in various European capitals. However, the colonial secretary subsequently complained to the governor general that the order in council appointing the Quebec agent should have been transmitted by way of Ottawa, rather than being carried to London by the agent himself.[32]

The next federal-provincial conference, in September 1871, was the first at which the new provinces of Manitoba and British Columbia were represented, in addition to all four of the original provinces. At Dunkin's suggestion the agenda was not confined to immigration; the conference also considered the necessity of harmonizing provincial laws in relation to statistics, another subject that fell under his jurisdiction as minister of agriculture. Dunkin was apparently the only federal minister who attended this conference. Chauveau again represented Quebec, accompanied by three of his cabinet colleagues, and the premiers of New Brunswick and Manitoba were also present. British Columbia was unable to send a minister, perhaps because none was willing to make the long and difficult journey, but the cabinet delegated a private citizen who "was about to visit Canada on private business" to act on its behalf. This delegate was instructed by the provincial secretary to attend regularly, provide information, participate in the discussion, but not make any commitments on behalf of the province.[33]

This conference reaffirmed, in a somewhat revised form, the understandings regarding the division of responsibilities between dominion and provinces that had been arrived at in 1868. Having acquired the former territories of the Hudson's Bay Company, including Manitoba, the dominion now had public lands of its own. It committed itself to pursue a liberal policy of colonization in Manitoba and the Northwest Territories, and also to disseminate information regarding those areas for the benefit of would-be immigrants. The unrealistic and unnecessary commitment to hold conferences four times a year was abandoned, having been honoured more in the breach than in the observance. Instead, the delegates agreed that conferences would be convened from time to time if requested by one or more provinces or without such request, on the understanding that there would be at least one conference during each session of Parliament.[34]

Apparently no federal-provincial conferences took place during the remaining two years of the first Macdonald government. However, this period saw two significant innovations in the practice of co-operative federalism, both related to the subject of immigration.

The first of these concerned responsibility for the costs of transporting immigrants from the port of entry to their ultimate destination. The practice of subsidizing transportation from Quebec City to points west actually predated Confederation. Partly because many of the persons subsidized appeared to be bound for the United States, the dominion government restricted the practice in 1868 but did not abandon it entirely. Railway fares at that time were considerably higher, in relation to prices and other incomes, than they are now, so immigrants who were clearly without funds, and who gave some evidence that they intended to stay in Canada, might still expect to have their fares paid by the dominion government.[35]

Since most of these assisted immigrants went to Ontario, and since the province shared in the constitutional responsibility for immigration, the federal government began to suggest that Ontario should bear some or all of the cost. Ontario agreed to this proposition in March 1869 when it was governed by John Sandfield Macdonald, a political ally of Sir John A. Subsequently Sandfield Macdonald may have had second thoughts, for a year later his government agreed to a British-inspired scheme for exporting teenaged boys to Ontario only reluctantly and on condition that the overland transportation costs be fully covered by the dominion.[36] There was logic in Ontario's reservations, because the province did not particularly want immigrants who were unable to support themselves. In any event, the federal government had a more obvious interest in preventing the accumulation of indigent immigrants in Quebec City, a place not noted for its friendliness to immigrants of any description.

In 1872, however, Edward Blake's Ontario government agreed with the federal government on a compromise that was, in effect, a shared-cost program. The dominion would pay the railway fares initially for immigrants travelling between Quebec and Ontario, but at the end of the year it would bill Ontario for two-thirds of the costs it had incurred in doing so. This arrangement covered railway fares between the port of entry and any of the major cities of Ontario where there was a dominion immigration agent. Transportation costs from that point to the ultimate destination, which would probably be less than a hundred miles away, were exclusively a provincial responsibility.[37] In July 1873 Ontario paid the dominion the sum of $18,160.53, representing its two-thirds share of subsidized fares for the first year the program was in operation.[38] Quebec signed a similar agreement for the sharing of transportation costs between Quebec City and Montreal.

The second innovation in 1872 was possibly a *quid pro quo* for the first, although there is no direct evidence of this link. For the fiscal year 1872–73 Parliament voted a sun of $70,000 to assist the provinces in their efforts to encourage immigration. The original intention was for only the four original provinces to receive a share of this grant, but subsequently the cabinet diverted $5000 out of the original appropriation to British Columbia, which also (unlike Manitoba) controlled its own public lands.[39] In the following year another $70,000 was voted for the same purpose. In each year Ontario received $25,000, Quebec $20,000, Nova Scotia and New Brunswick each received $10,000, and British Columbia was given $5,000.[40] Using the term loosely, this might be considered the first conditional grant in Canadian history, although the conditions were certainly not rigorous. The deputy minister of agriculture admitted to the Select Committee on Immigration and Colonization in 1873 that "We do not receive regular reports of the operations of the Provincial Governments. Their jurisdiction in immigration matters is by law perfectly independent."[41] Nonetheless, if it was not quite a conditional grant, it was certainly a shared-cost program, as was the arrangement for covering immigrants' railway fares.

The House of Commons was apparently not satisfied with the deputy minister's interpretation of the constitution, for in April 1873 it passed a motion requesting information on how the provinces had spent the money granted to them for immigration purposes. Letters were dispatched to the five provinces concerned requesting the information, and replies were received from British Columbia, Nova Scotia, and Quebec. Only British Columbia's reply is still in the archives. It shows that the province spent its $5,000 on salaries for immigration agents at London and San Francisco, renting offices at both locations, and publishing a "prize essay," which presumably extolled the virtues of the province and was used as publicity material.[42] San Francisco may seem an odd choice of location, but the normal way of reaching British Columbia in those days was to cross the United States by rail and then travel by ship from San Francisco to Victoria.

In November 1873 Sir John A. Macdonald resigned as a result of the Pacific Scandal and the governor general called upon Alexander Mackenzie to form a Liberal government. These events coincided with the beginning of an economic recession in Canada and the world. From 1866 through 1873 the number of immigrants who settled in Canada had increased substantially from year to year, but in

1874 it declined by 20 per cent, the first such decline since Confederation.[43] The Mackenzie government's response to the economic crisis was to reduce expenditures wherever possible, and the immigration program was an early victim o f this strategy. No funds were voted by Parliament to assist the provinces with immigration in 1874, or thereafter.

While testifying before the House of Commons Committee on Immigration and Colonization in 1874, the deputy minister of agriculture was asked to explain the respective duties of dominion and provincial immigration agents, and replied as follows: "The dominion special agents have no connection with the provincial agents, and I cannot tell the Committee what are the duties of the latter. The Local Governments have independent jurisdiction on the subject of immigration under the Union Act. But it is also to some extent joint; and as a matter of fact the permanent agents of the dominion at every point aid the Provinces in as far as they can, the interests being common."[44]

The discontinuance of the federal grant, and the decline in the number of immigrants, seems to have caused provincial governments to question whether they should continue to spend as much on promoting immigration, or whether more economical arrangements were possible. At Ontario's suggestion a federal-provincial conference to consider this question was summoned in November 1874, apparently for the first time in three years.[45] It was presided over by the federal minister of agriculture, Luc Letellier de St-Just. Prime Minister Mackenzie and two other members of his cabinet also attended the immigration conference, as did representatives of Ontario, Quebec, Nova Scotia, and New Brunswick. Even the governor general, Lord Dufferin, made a brief appearance. The Nova Scotia delegation was headed for the first time by the premier, William Annand.

The conference was called at the suggestion of Ontario and generally agreed, according to Letellier's subsequent report, "that separate and individual action of the provinces in promoting immigration, by means of agents in the United Kingdom and the European continent, led not only to waste of strength and expense and divided counsels, but in some cases to actual conflicts, which had an injuriously prejudicial effect on the minds of intending emigrants." It also unanimously adopted a fourteen-point memorandum, which may be summarized as follows:

• The federal minister of agriculture would control and direct promotion of emigration from the United Kingdom and Europe to Canada.

- Independent provincial agencies would be discontinued.
- Each province could appoint a subagent who would be accommodated in the Canadian government's offices in London.
- Provinces could employ special agents "or other means" to encourage emigration.
- All provincial subagents or special agents would be under the direction of the agent-general of Canada, who would receive instructions from the minister of agriculture.
- Provinces would pay the salaries or any subagents or special agents whom they appointed.
- The dominion undertook to encourage immigration in any possible way, including the subsidization of ocean transport.
- The dominion would use its London office to disseminate information about the provinces and their resources.
- Each province would supply the London office with copies of its statutes and of all public documents and maps printed since Confederation.
- The London office should be accessible to persons from any province, as a source of information.
- The provinces would contribute as follows to the cost of maintaining the London office: $5,500 per annum from Ontario, $2,000 from Quebec, and $1,000 from each of New Brunswick and Nova Scotia. If British Columbia and Prince Edward Island decided to adhere to the agreement, they would contribute amounts to be agreed upon. (No mention was made of Manitoba.)
- The dominion would pursue a liberal policy regarding the settlement of the crown lands in Manitoba and the Northwest.
- These arrangements would last for five years, and for a further five if no notice was given to discontinue them.
- The proposals would be binding on any provincial government that subsequently confirmed acceptance of them.

By February 1875 all four of the original provinces had confirmed their acceptance of these arrangements, which were embodied in a dominion order in council. The House of Commons Select Committee on Immigration, in its annual report, welcomed the new arrangements. It also reported the following exchange between a member of the committee and the deputy minister of agriculture:

Question: Were not the provincial governments always adverse to yielding up their privileges on the subject of immigration?

Answer: Yes, they always showed the greatest reluctance to give up any of the concurrent powers conferred on them by the Act of Confederation, but it was seen during the last year that the employment of Provincial and Dominion agents in the same places, not only led to waste of strength, but in some cases to actual conflict of opinion, which was bewildering to intending immigrants, and therefore injurious. It was the perception of this fact that led to the memorandum of agreement to which I have referred, at the Conference in November last.[46]

Another question concerned the agents who would continue to be paid by Ontario, although ostensibly subordinate to the authority of the dominion:

Question: But don't you suppose that they will recognize in their masters those who pay them, and is there not danger of conflict of authority?

Answer: They will, of course, look to the Ontario Government, which employs and pays them, but if that Government places them under the direction of the Dominion authorities, there will be that much centralization.[47]

Ontario's initiative that led to the acceptance of these arrangements was doubtless a consequence of the close alliance between the Mowat and Mackenzie governments. Premier Annand of Nova Scotia may have had an additional motive for agreeing. In May 1875, six months after the conference, the Mackenzie government appointed him as Canada's agent-general in London, an office whose authority was increased by the new arrangements.

By 1875 provincial interest and involvement in immigration policy was declining, but this was true of the federal government as well. John Lowe, the deputy minister in the federal Department of Agriculture, informed a British MP with whom he corresponded that the public pressure to reduce spending on immigration was being felt by both levels of government. "The Ontario Government has felt its effect and it has literally swept away its Immigration Department at Toronto," he reported. Because of the economic crisis, he added, "mechanics" (or in other words the working class) were "crying out to stop immigration." Either in response to this sentiment or simply to save money, Lowe said he had been ordered (presumably by his minister, Letellier) to stop advertising for immigrants at once.[48] Immigration continued to decline from the peak it had reached in 1873. By 1881 there were actually fewer foreign-born persons in Quebec, Ontario, and the Maritime provinces than there had been a decade earlier.[49]

Although the provinces no longer received grants for their immigration programs from the dominion, and although their immigration offices outside Canada had been absorbed into those of the dominion, they continued to be involved in this field of concurrent jurisdiction. As David Spence, the official who administered Ontario's immigration program, told the House of Commons Committee on Immigration and Colonization in 1877: "the Ontario government leaves the general question of immigration to the Dominion Government, and ... confines its efforts to bringing out such immigrants as are in special demand in Ontario."[50]

Furthermore, the provinces still contributed financially to two aspects of the dominion's immigration efforts: the upkeep of the London office (in accordance with the decision of the 1874 conference) and the transportation costs of immigrants after they arrived at the port of entry. In the case of Ontario and Quebec, the latter item was governed by the agreements both provinces had signed in 1872, providing for reimbursement of two-thirds of the costs incurred initially by the dominion. The Maritime provinces had never signed such agreements, although New Brunswick paid the local transportation costs of immigrants after they left the main line of the federally owned Intercolonial Railway. Payments from the provinces covered about a quarter of the dominion's total expenditures on immigration in 1877, and the provinces' expenditures on their own immigration and colonization programs were in addition to this amount.[51]

These early experiments in cooperative federalism ended after Macdonald returned to office in October 1878. Annand, the Liberal and former Nova Scotia separatist, was promptly dismissed as Canada's agent-general in London, to be replaced by Sir Alexander T. Galt with the new title of high commissioner. Apparently in retaliation for this change, Nova Scotia terminated its financial contribution to the dominion office.[52] Instead, it appointed Annand himself as its own agent-general in London, a position he occupied until his death in 1887. The agreement to share the costs of the London office with the provinces expired in 1880 and was not renewed by the Macdonald government.

Meanwhile the Joly government in Quebec, which had been imposed on the province by Letellier in his bizarre coup a year earlier, gave notice in 1879 that it would no longer contribute to the overland transportation costs of immigrants.[53] Ontario continued to do so for certain classes of immigrants (agricultural labourers, their families, and female domestic servants), but in 1882 it also discontinued its contributions.[54] The provinces still pursued policies of colonization, particularly in Quebec where the subject had strong ideological overtones and where there was a minister of colonization until as late as 1962, but immigration was increasingly perceived as a federal responsibility, regardless of what the constitution might say on the subject.

Macdonald's National Policy lessened the provincial role in immigration in two ways. First, by industrializing the two central provinces, it ensured that most immigrants who settled in those provinces after 1878 would live in the cities, and thus the link between immigration and colonization was broken. Second, and far more significantly, the construction of the Canadian Pacific Railway opened a vast new field for agricultural immigrants on the northwestern prairies. Federal immigration policy adopted as its first priority the need to populate the Northwest. Since the federal government controlled the public lands in that region until the closing of the agricultural frontier was officially recognized in 1930, there was no reason for provincial involvement, even if provincial governments had existed, which they did not in Saskatchewan and Alberta until 1905.

Although there had been six federal-provincial conferences between 1868 and 1874, there were no more until 1906, when Sir Wilfrid Laurier summoned one to consider the revision of statutory subsidies. Similarly, shared-cost programs, which Macdonald's first government had pioneered in 1872, were not proposed again until 1912, when the Borden government attempted to provide financial aid for provincial highways. The real origins of cooperative federalism, as well as the significant role that the provinces once played in immigration policy, have been almost forgotten.

13 Intrastate Federalism: Myth or Reality?

Twentieth-century Canadians have usually thought of federalism in the terms employed by A.V. Dicey and K.C. Wheare: a regime of exclusive powers distributed between two distinct, autonomous, and competitive levels of government.[1] Sections 91 and 92, which allocate legislative powers between Parliament and the provincial assemblies, are viewed as the heart of the federal constitution, and federalism is considered almost synonymous with federal-provincial relations, particularly the relations between the prime minister of Canada and the premiers of the provinces. Indeed, the personal rivalries between particular heads of government seem to define whole eras of Canadian federalism: Macdonald and Mowat, King and Hepburn, St Laurent and Duplessis, or Trudeau and Lévesque.

As preceding chapters have shown, this is a fairly convincing view of Canadian federalism in the nineteenth century, not to mention the twentieth. It should be noted, however, that some writers on federalism, although not many Canadians, have questioned whether jurisdictional boundaries and intergovernmental competition are really the essence of the concept. Morton Grodzins, in a pioneering reinterpretation of American federalism, suggested that the metaphor of the marble cake be substituted for the "layer cake" of the traditional view.[2] He noted that there are few exclusively state or exclusively federal fields of jurisdiction, and that efforts to identify fields that the federal government should leave to the exclusive control of the states have been largely futile. Even more significantly, Grodzins suggested that the continuing viability of the individual states is the result not of jurisdictional boundaries but of the state and local orientation of national legislators. Congress could theoretically occupy almost any field of jurisdiction to the exclusion of the states, but it has made no effort to do so because individual senators and congressmen are elected by state-based party organizations and are sensitive to state interests. National programs and statutes are accordingly designed to strengthen the states rather than to weaken them.

A more recent book on the theory of federalism by Preston King, an expatriate American living in Australia, also rejects the Dicey-Wheare interpretation.[3] King sees no merit in the familiar notion that federalism is midway on a continuum of centralization between a unitary state and a voluntary alliance. In fact, he does not think that centralization can really be measured. He defines a federal regime as one that entrenches the representation of certain territorial units in the central government, thus guaranteeing that the units, or at least their representatives, will be involved in certain kinds of decisions.

Since the publication of King's book, the Supreme Court of the United States has expounded a similar understanding of federalism in one of its more celebrated decisions. Noting the role played by the states in selecting both the executive and legislative branches of the federal government, and particularly the constitutionally entrenched equal representation of each state in the Senate, the only constitutional right of which no state can be deprived without its consent, Justice Blackmun concluded: "In short, the Framers chose to rely on a federal system in which special restraints on federal power over the States inhered principally in the workings of the National Government itself, rather than in discrete limitations on the objects of federal authority. State sovereign interests, then, are more properly protected by procedural safeguards inherent in the structure of the federal system than by judicially created limitations on federal power."[4]

This aspect of federalism has recently come to be known as "intrastate federalism," to distinguish it from the "interstate federalism" of intergovernmental relations and jurisdictional disputes.[5] The subject, and the word, became fashionable in Canada around 1980 because of the perceived inadequacy of hinterland representation in a federal government apparently dominated by the concerns of Quebec and Ontario. The Royal Commission on the Economic Union and Development Prospects for Canada commissioned Donald Smiley and Ronald Watts to prepare a monograph on the subject.[6] More recently, concern over the inadequacy of intrastate federalism has been an explicit motivation behind the growing demand for an elected Senate.

While the word may be new, the concept of intrastate federalism is not without antecedents in Canadian history. As Smiley and Watts, among others, have noted, the Quebec Conference devoted very serious attention to the Senate, which was apparently expected to be the principal means of representing provincial interests within the central government. Not only was the Senate the first item of substantive business to be considered, but it occupied no fewer than six of the fourteen days of discussions.[7] By contrast, only three days were devoted to the distribution of legislative powers between the two levels of government. Possibly the fact that all four of what eventually became the Atlantic provinces were represented at this conference explains the preoccupation with intrastate federalism. The more frequently cited Confederation debates in the Canadian legislature, where of course only central Canadian concerns were expressed, contain relatively few references to intrastate federalism or to the Senate.

One possible indication of the importance attached to intrastate federalism is the subsequent careers of the Fathers of Confederation. Of the twenty-seven delegates from the four original provinces who attended either the Quebec or London conferences, or both, twenty-six were still living in July 1867. Fourteen of these were elected to the first House of Commons, and seven were appointed to the Senate in 1867. One more received a Senate appointment in 1868. William Henry of Nova Scotia ran unsuccessfully for the House of Commons; he was appointed to the Supreme Court of Canada when it was established eight years later. George Brown returned to his newspaper. Only E.B. Chandler of New Brunswick and Oliver Mowat pursued a subsequent political career at the provincial level. Assuming that the Fathers of Confederation were dedicated to promoting the interests of their provinces, it appears significant that they overwhelmingly chose to do so through national institutions, rather than remaining in the provincial capitals. Even the most prominent opponents of Confederation, A.-A. Dorion, Christopher Dunkin, Timothy Anglin, and Joseph Howe, soon found their way to Ottawa.

Be that as it may, John A. Macdonald expressed an intrastate view of federalism more than twenty years later in his instructions to Lieutenant-Governor Richey of Nova Scotia, who anticipated that his advisers would request a dissolution in order to campaign on the issue of secession. According to Macdonald this would be improper, because "the representatives of Nova Scotia as to all questions respecting the relations between the Dominion and Province sit in the Dominion Parliament, and are the constitutional exponents of the wishes of the people with regard to such relations."[8]

Macdonald may or may not have believed that Nova Scotia's representatives in Parliament (most of whom at the time of this letter were supporters of his own government) accurately represented the views of Nova Scotians on federalism, but his comment at least raises interesting questions. To what extent and in what way did the institutions of the central government in Macdonald's time represent the diversity of provincial interests and preferences? How effectively, if at all, did they protect provincial interests? Did their presence in Ottawa, and their representations, prevent the emergence of any federal-provincial conflicts that would otherwise have taken place? Did they help to resolve any of the conflicts that did emerge in ways that were at least partially satisfactory to the provinces concerned? How, if at all, was intrastate federalism related to the gradual emergence of a more decentralized federal regime than the one preferred, and apparently anticipated, by Macdonald himself? Did intrastate devices help to make Canadian federalism stable and successful?

These questions can probably not be answered conclusively, but it seems appropriate to examine whatever evidence is available concerning intrastate federalism in the first three decades after Confederation, in the hope that at least some suggestive inferences can be drawn. This chapter will do so by considering separately the three major representative institutions at the federal level: the Senate, the House of Commons, and the cabinet. In view of the weak and dependent nature of the public service at this time and the subordination of the Supreme Court to the Judicial Committee of the Privy Council, it does not seem necessary to consider either the public service or the Supreme Court as significant institutions of intrastate federalism in the nineteenth century.

The Senate is the appropriate starting point for this investigation for several reasons. It was the only institution that was explicitly designed to represent the provinces as such, even if it was not appointed by them. Its "intrastate" function was extensively discussed at the conferences that preceded Confederation, and to a lesser extent in the Confederation debates. Expectations regarding its representative role were apparently high, particularly in the Maritime provinces. Whatever its failings, it was a more important institution in the nineteenth century than it became subsequently. Every cabinet contained at least three senators, or about a quarter of the total number of ministers, and every portfolio except Finance was held by a senator on at least one occasion. Even two prime ministers were senators: John J. Abbott and Mackenzie Bowell.

Equal representation for Quebec and Ontario in the Senate, perpetuating the twenty-four seats that each had enjoyed in the old Legislative Council of the United Province, compensated Quebec for the concession of "rep by pop" in the House of Commons. Twenty-four seats for the Maritime provinces, whose combined population was considerably less than that of Quebec, was an additional counterweight to "rep by pop," even if it fell short of the American provision whereby each state received the same number of senators as the largest. Although four of these seats had been intended for Prince Edward Island, the twenty-four were divided equally between New Brunswick and Nova Scotia when the Island failed to enter the dominion in 1867. Six years later Prince Edward Island received its four seats, and by August 1874 deaths had reduced the representation of the other Maritime provinces to ten seats each, where it remained. Manitoba was given two seats in 1871, a third seat in 1882, and a fourth in 1892. British Columbia received three seats when it entered the dominion, and two were given to the North-West Territories in 1888. Thus there were eighty-one Senate seats by 1896, distributed among the provinces and territories in a way that was more pragmatic than logical.

The decision to have an appointed upper house, while consistent with the desire for a constitution on the British model, was somewhat controversial in central Canada, where the Legislative Council had been elected since 1856. Alexander Campbell defended the change during the Confederation debates on the grounds that if the upper house in the dominion were elected, Upper Canadians would eventually begin to agitate for "rep by pop" in that house as well as in the Commons. This would be unacceptable to the Maritimes, for whom the security of fixed representation was "essential."[9] There was perhaps another sense in which the Senate's two roles, as a "sober second thought" on behalf of propertied interests and as a bastion of the smaller provinces, were linked. Ontario was not only the largest province, but the most liberal. Both the method of selection and the allocation of seats made the Senate a counterweight to Ontario's democratic tendencies. The property qualification of $4000 was far from trivial, for real estate values were unbelievably low by modern standards. As late as 1896 the substantial Halifax home of Sir John Thompson, including a four-acre lot, was sold for $2000. Thirty-six other lots in Halifax that had also belonged to Thompson were sold for a total of $2000, suggesting that the late prime minister would barely have qualified for a Senate seat.[10]

Even before it commenced operations the Senate was a target of criticism, particularly on the part of Reformers from Canada West. Alexander Mackenzie admitted during the Confederation Debates that he would have preferred a unicameral Parliament, but he recognized that this would be unacceptable to the other provinces.[11] George Brown chimed in to suggest that an appointed, and presumably weak, Senate was a fair compromise between a powerful elected Senate and no Senate at all.[12] David Reesor, a legislative councillor who opposed the Quebec Resolutions, predicted correctly that the Senate would be insignificant when it was controlled by the same party that controlled the government, and a source of deadlock when it was not.[13] At the London Conference William Howland suggested that senators serve for limited terms and that they be chosen by the provincial legislatures, like their American counterparts, so as to give the dominion "a true Federal Parliament." He described a Senate appointed by the central government as "an anomaly."[14]

The senators initially appointed from Ontario and Quebec were all former members of the old Legislative Council of the Province of Canada, which ceased to exist on the day of Confederation. This produced a bipartisan, and quite representative, group of senators, including several who had opposed Confederation. To fill the Maritime seats, Macdonald consulted with the pro-Confederation governments in New Brunswick and Nova Scotia. The latter procedure had less fortunate results, even though all of those appointed had been members of the provincial legislatures. Joseph Howe was exaggerating only slightly when he called Nova Scotia's twelve senators "the most unpopular men in the province."[15]

Turnover of senators was surprisingly rapid and only half the original seventy-two appointees still held their seats at the end of 1878. By 1896 only six originals were left, including, ironically, David Reesor, whose disapproval of the institution had not prevented him from accepting a seat. Despite the indefinite term of office, death was not the only reason for departure from the Senate. Several senators resigned to accept judicial or other appointments. Edward Kenny of Nova Scotia, who had served briefly in the first dominion cabinet, lost his Senate seat in 1876 because he failed to attend for two consecutive sessions.[16] Possibly if the Intercolonial Railway had been completed more promptly he would have found senatorial service more convenient.

Although there were a number of Liberals among the original appointees, the Conservative majority in the Senate was never in question and lasted well into the twentieth century. In 1878, after five years of Liberal government, there were thirty Liberals in the Senate. As there were no more Liberal appointments for the next eighteen years, the number of Liberals had fallen to nine (including David Reesor) when the Conservative dynasty finally collapsed in 1896.

In the early years, a few senators were simultaneously members of the appointed Legislative Council in Quebec. Manitoba's first two senators, M.-A. Girard and John Sutherland, both retained their seats in the Legislative Assembly after their appointments. Quebec allowed J.-H. Bellerose to retain his seat in the Legislative Assembly until the 1875 election, although he had been appointed to the Senate in 1873. Two of the first four senators from Prince Edward Island also held provincial seats for a short time after their appointment.[17] Altogether eight senators benefited from the "double mandate" in 1873, but only two retained their provincial seats by 1878. They were joined in 1887 by former Quebec premier J.J. Ross, who kept his seat in the Legislative Council after Macdonald appointed him to the Senate, and even after John Abbott made him Speaker. More extensive use of the "double mandate" might have made the Senate a more effective vehicle of intrastate federalism, or even a federal council on the German model, but the practice was never widespread or popular enough to have much impact.

Although party discipline in the Senate was not rigid, instances of senators defying the party whips to support clearly provincial interests are not particularly numerous. In 1870 David Macpherson, an Ontario Conservative who was later minister of the interior, led a revolt against the government's tariff policy, which he claimed would "promote sectionalism and disunion." Eight other Conservatives and most of the Liberals supported him, so that his motion failed to carry by only four votes.[18] However, the dissidents included nine senators from Ontario, eight from Quebec, four from New Brunswick, and three from Nova Scotia, so the division was not really along regional lines.

In the following year twenty-one senators, including six Conservatives, voted against admitting British Columbia as a province.[19] This revolt was somewhat more regionally focused than the previous one, since three of the defecting Conservatives were from New Brunswick and that province was the only one whose senators cast more votes against admitting British Columbia than in favour. Presumably New Brunswickers feared that their own Intercolonial Railway would be sidetracked if the government agreed to build a Pacific railway as well.

The more celebrated episode in 1875, when the Senate embarrassed Prime Minister Mackenzie by rejecting his Esquimalt and Nanaimo Railway Bill, was essentially a vote along party lines.[20] It is worth noting, however, that John A. Macdonald had publicly supported the bill in the House of Commons. Allegations that Macdonald was playing a double game – publicly supporting the bill while privately working to secure its defeat in the Senate – have never been confirmed. In any event the three British Columbia senators – all appointed by Macdonald – defended their province's interests by voting for the Mackenzie bill.

British Columbia's efforts to reform its judicial institutions led to the defeat of a government measure in the Senate shortly after Macdonald returned to office (see chapter 9). The three British Columbia senators were supporters of the judges who had been lobbying against court reform ever since British Columbia became a province. To their disappointment, Macdonald's government not only refused to disallow the Administration of Justice Act but introduced its own measure to provide for the salaries of the two additional judges required to implement the provincial act. When this measure was introduced in the Senate, two of the British Columbians moved that it be given the six months' hoist. Supported by their British Columbia colleague, eight other Conservatives, and the entire Liberal opposition, the motion carried by a vote of 36–25.[21]

The government bill was introduced again at the following session. Senators Clement Cornwall and William Macdonald, who had moved and seconded the six months' hoist the year before, indicated that they had not changed their views but would defer to the wishes of the dominion and provincial governments, which were apparently supported by the people of British Columbia and by their representatives in the House of Commons. As Cornwall also noted, the third British Columbia senator, Robert Carrall, had died in September 1879 and his replacement, Hugh Nelson, was a supporter of judicial reform. The measure thus passed smoothly on the second attempt.[22]

Thomas McInnes, appointed to fill Cornwall's Senate seat after Cornwall became lieutenant-governor of British Columbia in 1881, was one senator who had no apparent loyalty to his party. In 1885 he moved an amendment to a government measure concerning the Canadian Pacific Railway in an effort to ensure that the railway's terminus would remain permanently at Port Moody.[23] Two years later he moved the three months' hoist for the government's Chinese immigration bill, which had been introduced at the behest of his own province.[24] In 1890 McInnes, whose eccentricity seemed to increase with age, sponsored a bill "to provide for the use of the Gaelic language in official proceedings."[25] None of these initiatives received more than a handful of votes.

A more serious assertion of senatorial independence occurred in 1889 when Senator Lawrence Power of Nova Scotia, a Liberal, introduced a bill "to revive certain Regulations respecting Fisheries in Nova Scotia." Five Nova Scotians, including three Conservatives, voted for the measure, and only two, both Conservatives, opposed it. Although the government also opposed it, the bill passed by a vote of 20–18 on second reading. This regional triumph was of short duration. Two days later Senator John Abbott moved the six months' hoist and his motion carried by 32–12. Two of the Nova Scotia Conservatives who had supported the Power bill on second reading voted for Abbott's motion.[26]

In summary, it is difficult to see any real substance in the Senate's alleged role as a defender of regional or provincial interests. Certainly it played no significant part in resolving any of the issues that arose between the provinces and the dominion government. Criticism of the Senate's inadequacies soon became, as it has remained, a recurring theme of Canadian political discourse. The Nova Scotia House of Assembly in May 1869 demanded, among other constitutional changes, that senators be chosen by the provinces. Senate reform was a major theme of Edward Blake's famous Aurora speech in October 1875. Lord Dufferin, although disagreeing with most of the speech, informed the colonial secretary that he entirely agreed with Blake regarding the Senate. "It is an absurdly effete body, and has given no sign of life since I have been in the country."[27] John A. Macdonald admitted in 1880 that "active and young politicians won't go into the Senate nor is it very desirable they should."[28] The Interprovincial Conference of 1887 made the moderate suggestion that half of the senators should be chosen by the provinces and that all senators should serve for a limited term. (Exactly the same proposal would be reintroduced by Prime Minister Pierre Trudeau almost a century later.) No action followed, and the Senate continued on its irrelevant course.

The House of Commons, unlike the Senate, was designed to represent Canadians in proportion to their numbers. It did so more accurately in 1867 than it does today, since the disparities in size between the ridings were not particularly great. The notorious Section 51A of the British North America Act, which guarantees the Atlantic provinces as many seats in the lower house as they have in the upper, was not added to the act until almost half a century later. Manitoba and British Columbia were somewhat overrepresented when they entered the dominion, but the bias was not great enough to alter significantly the composition of the house.

Anyone eligible to vote could be a candidate. Members received a stipend of $600 each session, raised to $1000 in 1873. Although

Norman Ward described these stipends as "hardly enough to live on," they were more than most Canadians earned for working three hundred or more days a year.[29] Sessions of Parliament usually began in February and hardly ever continued past May, the month when crops were planted in most parts of Canada.

Until 1878, the first general election at which the secret ballot was used, about a quarter of the members won their seats by acclamation. From 1878 onwards there were never more than a dozen acclamations, except in 1882 when there were twenty-five. Acclamations were particularly common in Quebec. A large proportion of the contested elections were subsequently controverted because of some alleged irregularity, both before and after the Mackenzie government's legislation that gave the courts the responsibility for settling such disputes. Among other innovations, 1878 saw the commencement of the practice of simultaneous voting in all ridings. Earlier elections, by contrast, were spread over several weeks, with incumbent governments arranging that their more reliable ridings would vote first so as to create a bandwagon effect.

The double mandate had a greater impact on the House of Commons than on the Senate, although both New Brunswick and Nova Scotia prohibited the practice from the outset. In central Canada, where incumbent politicians would otherwise have faced a difficult choice between retaining their seats in Ottawa or withdrawing to the new provincial capitals, the double mandate was initially popular. The first House of Commons included fifteen members from Quebec and four from Ontario who simultaneously held provincial seats.[30] These nineteen included the first two premiers of Ontario, Sandfield Macdonald and Edward Blake, the first premier of Quebec, Pierre Chauveau, and three members of the first Macdonald government: George-Étienne Cartier, Christopher Dunkin, and Hector Langevin. British Columbia's second premier, Amor de Cosmos, combined his office with a seat in the House of Commons. Two Manitoba members of Parliament, Donald Smith (later Lord Strathcona) and Pierre Delorme, were simultaneously members of the province's first legislature.[31] In the circumstances it is not surprising that federal-provincial relations were fairly intimate and that there were no serious conflicts between the dominion and the provinces where the double mandate was permitted. A reaction soon set in, however, as Liberals and Maritimers concluded that the double mandate violated federal principles by enabling John A. Macdonald to dominate the provincial governments. The practice was soon prohibited everywhere and by 1874 the double mandate was extinct, apart from a few Quebec legislative councillors who also sat in the Senate.

Responsible government did not yet seem to necessitate the extreme rigidity of party discipline that characterizes the Canadian House of Commons today. Practically all members acknowledged a party label, judging by their biographies in the *Parliamentary Companion*, but party labels were ambiguous, had different meanings in different parts of the country, and were not always accurate guides in predicting parliamentary behaviour. Unpredictable members known as "loose fish" were a common and generally accepted phenomenon. Although sometimes attributed to Macdonald, the expression "loose fish" is of Maritime origin, as might be expected, and was used by Joseph Howe long before Confederation.[32] The phenomenon, if not the word, was also common in British politics, where until 1868 no government apparently defeated in an election ever resigned before meeting the new Parliament. Soon after the Canadian general election of 1872 Macdonald estimated that he had a comfortable majority, but added that "with a new House, containing a great many new members, one cannot be at all certain until each man has shaken down into his place and defined his position."[33] The caveat was well advised in this case, because Macdonald's majority in the second Parliament turned out to be substantially less than he had estimated.

Who were the loose fish? A reasonable hypothesis might be that they were politicians with independent standing in their local communities, little or no ambition for ministerial office, and a strong attachment to local interests. Unfortunately the hypothesis is difficult to test after the lapse of more than a century. Members who won their seats by acclamation, and those who simultaneously sat in provincial legislatures, were apparently no more likely to be loose fish than those who did not have these characteristics, but these facts do not necessarily undermine the hypothesis.

Macdonald's majority in the first two parliaments seems to have included at least three distinct groups of loose fish. The first consisted of the British Columbians, who formed a marriage of convenience with Macdonald because of his determination to build the Pacific railway but who did not always support him on other issues. (Amor de Cosmos, the most prominent of them, was actually a radical liberal by the standards of his time.) The second group included a number of Quebec nationalists like G.-I. Barthe of Richelieu, J.-D. Brousseau of Portneuf, S.-X. Cimon of Charlevoix, L.-H. Masson of Soulanges, and C.-H. Pozer of Beauce. The third and largest group consisted of about eighteen Ontario members mainly from Irish Protestant ridings where the Orange lodges enjoyed great political influence. The contiguous counties of Hastings and Peterborough seem to have been particularly strong centres of independent political thought. All five of their representatives in the first Parliament, including future Prime Minister Mackenzie Bowell, could be classified as loose fish. Other prominent members of the group included Samuel Ault of Stormont, Francis Jones of Leeds and Grenville, and John Ross of Dundas.

On the other side of the House, the Nova Scotians elected to oppose Confederation in 1867 made a distinct group who only gradually melted into the two-party system. Most eventually joined with Ontario Reformers and Quebec Rouges to form a more or less coherent Liberal party. A few, like Joseph Howe, joined Macdonald's party. Macdonald's decision to negotiate "better terms" with Howe rather than with the provincial government, incidentally, is an interesting indication that he practised what he preached in the letter to Lieutenant-Governor Richey, quoted earlier in this chapter. The skill with which Howe extracted concessions on behalf of his province is also a classic instance of intrastate federalism contributing to the resolution of a serious intergovernmental problem. By 1872 four of the former secessionists indicated in their biographies in the *Parliamentary Companion* that they supported the Macdonald government, and two others specified that they were reconciled to Confederation, although not necessarily to Macdonald. Howe, who had become a minister but did not attempt to label himself, must be added to this group. Only two Nova Scotian members in 1872 still explicitly proclaimed themselves opponents of Confederation. Both of these, oddly enough, called themselves Conservatives although one of them, Alfred Jones, later became a minister in Mackenzie's Liberal government.

Macdonald's loose fish from Quebec and Ontario sometimes opposed his government on important issues. Three Conservatives from central Canada opposed acquisition of the Hudson's Bay Company territories in December 1867; seven Ontario Tories joined eighteen Ontario Reformers in March 1872 to vote that the decision of the arbitrators regarding the allocation of the Province of Canada debt should be accepted; and eleven Conservatives, seven from Ontario and four from Quebec, voted for a motion to postpone the admission of British Columbia into the dominion.[34] None of these votes was lost by the government, but in April 1870 an amendment opposed by the government carried by two votes, with nine Ontario Conservatives and five Quebec Conservatives voting in favour.[35] The amendment reduced the total appropriation for public service salaries in Nova Scotia to the same level as in the smaller province of New Brunswick, and apparently expressed a lingering resentment over the cost of the concessions made to Howe. The government chose not to regard this as a question of confidence.

A bill introduced by David Mills and A.-A. Dorion, making members of provincial legislatures ineligible to sit in the House of Commons, was adopted in 1873 over the objections of the prime minister. Quebec Conservatives attempted to amend the bill, with Macdonald's approval, so as to maintain the double mandate in provinces wishing to do so, but the amendments were overwhelmingly lost with even the four Maritime members of the cabinet voting against them.[36]

The Mackenzie government enjoyed a strong majority in the House of Commons after the 1874 election, but defections from the ranks on particular measures occurred from time to time. The Esquimalt and Nanaimo bill, whose defeat in the Senate has already been referred to, received only ninety-one votes in the Commons, or about two-thirds of the government's nominal supporters. Twenty-one Liberals voted against it, including Edward Blake, who would rejoin the cabinet less than two months later, and David Mills, who became a minister in October 1876.[37] There were also several defections over the Supreme Court bill, particularly on the part of Quebec members who were disturbed by the prospect of common law judges from other provinces deciding questions of civil law. The Conservatives, who supported the bill in principle, had similar problems with some of their Quebec members.[38]

After 1878 party politics in the House of Commons began to assume a more modern appearance. Both parties now contested almost every riding, and almost all ridings voted simultaneously. The double mandate was a thing of the past. Macdonald's commitment to a National Policy of tariff protection sharpened the philosophical difference between the parties and gave the labels "Conservative" and "Liberal" distinct meanings that transcended cultural and historical differences between the provinces. Henceforth it was almost unthinkable for a government to lose on a roll-call vote, and a government that did so was likely to ask for a dissolution. Most of the former "loose fish" had left the House. Those who survived, like Mackenzie Bowell, became more orthodox in their voting behaviour.

Some members continued to vote against their parties from time to time on issues of provincial concern. A private member's bill to abolish the Supreme Court received twenty-nine votes, of which twenty were from Quebec, in 1880.[39] In 1886 a Quebec Conservative, A.-C. Landry, moved that the House express regret at the execution of Louis Riel. Sixteen Quebec Conservatives and all the

Quebec Liberals present voted in favour, along with about half the English-speaking Liberals.[40] Also in 1886, two Nova Scotia Conservatives moved that the House reopen the question of "better terms" by repealing the provision in the act of 1869 that declared the financial arrangements negotiated with Joseph Howe to be a final settlement of Nova Scotia's claims. Ten Nova Scotians, including seven Conservatives, voted for the motion and only four, including the two cabinet ministers, against. However the motion attracted only six votes from outside of Nova Scotia, all of whom were opposition members and three of whom were from New Brunswick.[41]

Some other expressions of provincial grievances in the House were even more futile. Amor de Cosmos failed to find a seconder for a motion, in April 1879, that British Columbia secede from the dominion.[42] In 1884 two British Columbians moved the six months' hoist for the government's bill accepting lands from British Columbia in lieu of the original railway belt and subsidizing construction of the Esquimalt and Nanaimo. The motion received twenty-nine votes, including three from British Columbia and five other Conservatives. However, the two members from the city of Victoria, which looked forward to its long-awaited railway, opposed the motion.[43]

More serious divisions in the governing party concerned questions of language and religion. In 1889 eight Ontario Conservatives, four Ontario Liberals, and an anglophone Liberal from Quebec, subsequently enshrined in Protestant hagiography as "the Noble Thirteen," supported a motion calling for disallowance of the Jesuit Estates Act.[44] In the following year fifty-one Quebec members from both parties, and a scattering of members from other provinces including four francophones, supported a subamendment saying that bilingualism should be permanently entrenched in the North-West Territories. Even two ministers, John Costigan and Hector Langevin, supported the subamendment, but they were not asked to resign.[45] The Conservatives divided again over the government's remedial bill in 1896, with nineteen of their Ontario members and one from New Brunswick voting against. Surprisingly, the four Manitoba Conservatives all voted in favour.[46]

The role of the House of Commons in federal-provincial relations, however, is not adequately comprehended by these public expressions of dissent. Three episodes mentioned in previous chapters, all in the year 1881, illustrate ways in which individual members or groups of members might become involved in dominion-provincial relations. The first was when William McDougall, writing privately to Macdonald, threatened that he and other Ontario supporters of the government might defect if the government did not recognize Ontario's claim to the disputed territory west of Lake Superior. The second was when Prince Edward Island's five Conservative members of parliament, as well as its four senators, petitioned the government regarding the inadequacy of the ferry service. The third episode occurred when the British Columbia government appointed Amor de Cosmos, who was still a member of parliament although he no longer held any provincial office, as a special envoy to help resolve the federal-provincial dispute over the Terms of Union.

In 1883 Premier Smithe of British Columbia sent telegrams to two members of parliament from his province asking them to urge Macdonald to expedite the introduction of the government bill resolving British Columbia's grievances regarding the Esquimalt and Nanaimo Railway, the graving dock, and the railway lands.[47] Although the members promptly contacted the prime minister, the bill was not actually adopted until the following year. Lacking representation in the cabinet, British Columbia apparently relied more than other provinces on its backbench members in the House of Commons.

Far more significant than any of these events was the role played by Macdonald's Quebec caucus in relation to both the Letellier affair and the province's railway problems. Although Macdonald was not initially inclined to dismiss Letellier, the clear expression of sentiment by his Quebec supporters was decisive in changing his mind. Even had the prime minister not been a believer in intrastate federalism, newly elected members of parliament had at least as good a claim to represent public opinion on this issue as did the Joly government, given the peculiar circumstances of its installation in office. In the second case the financial problems of the Canadian Pacific Railway, and Macdonald's strong commitment to that project, gave Quebec members of parliament considerable leverage to demand that their province receive financial compensation for building the railway lines from Montreal to Ottawa and Quebec City. This advantage was exploited effectively and with success.

Parliament, however, was in session only a few months of the year, its members were divided in their views and interests, it was heavily influenced by the government, and its own influence on public policy could only be indirect. Any discussion of intrastate federalism must also consider the representation of provincial interests in the cabinet, where policy was actually made. While the way in which the cabinet operated can only be inferred from government documents and correspondence, since no minutes of its meetings were kept, it seems reasonable to assume that in a system of responsible government it was the most effective institution of intrastate federalism.

Christopher Dunkin, who was perhaps the most intelligent of Confederation's opponents, anticipated this fact in his lengthy critique of the Quebec Resolutions. Since the centrally appointed upper house would not really represent the provinces, and would not have the American Senate's powers over treaties and appointments, Dunkin realized that the task of representing provincial interests within the central government would inevitably fall upon the cabinet. He feared, however, that a cabinet of provincial spokesmen would lack the cohesion and solidarity that responsible government on the British model required. As Dunkin put it, "The British Cabinet is no Cabinet of sections, but a unit." A secondary concern for Dunkin was that if the cabinet gave adequate representation to every province, as well as the Protestant and Irish Catholic minorities within Quebec, it would be too large to function effectively.[48]

Some of these difficulties became apparent as early as the spring of 1867, when Macdonald selected the personnel of the first dominion cabinet. The main problem was that the Canada West Reformers insisted on only five seats for Ontario (so that the three Reformers would outnumber the two Tories), but also insisted that Ontario must have one more seat than Quebec. At the same time, Cartier insisted on three francophones from Quebec, and if Quebec had only four seats it would be impossible to include both a Protestant and an Irish Catholic from that province. The bizarre solution was to omit both Charles Tupper, the premier of Nova Scotia, and Thomas D'Arcy McGee, the acknowledged leader of the Quebec Irish, in favour of the obscure and unqualified Edward Kenny, "who happened to be both a Nova Scotian and a Roman Catholic."[49] This was the same Kenny who would subsequently lose his Senate seat for failing to attend. His inclusion forced Tupper to wait until 1870 for a ministerial post. McGee, tragically, was never appointed at all, since he was assassinated less than a year after Confederation.

Table 13.1 shows the evolution of cabinet representation for the different provinces from 1867 to 1896. Ontario's margin of one over Quebec, which even the francophobic Donald Creighton called "a somewhat perverted application of Rep by Pop," was normally but not invariably maintained. Nova Scotia and New Brunswick were rigidly allocated two members each, although their disparity in size was almost as great as that between the two central provinces. No Irish Catholic in Quebec emerged to fill the shoes of the fallen McGee, and the idea of representing that minority was soon aban-

Table 13.1
Representation in the Cabinet, by Province

Government	Ont.	Que.	NS	NB	Man.	BC	PEI	NWT
1867 (Macdonald)	5	3	2	2	na	na	na	na
1873 (Mackenzie)	4	3	2	2	—	—	1	—
1878 (Macdonald)	5	4	2	2	—	—	1	—
1891 (Abbott)	4	4	2	2	—	—	—	1
1892 (Thompson)	5	4	2	2	—	—	—	—
1894 (Bowell)	5	3	2	2	—	—	—	—
1896 (Tupper)	4	4	2	2	1	1	1	—

doned. Except between 1887 and 1891 there was never more than one Quebec anglophone in the cabinet, and he was always a Protestant.

The newer provinces, let alone the territories, did not receive automatic representation. Prince Edward Island was without a minister from 1882 until 1895. No Manitoban joined the ministry until Thomas Daly in 1892, and no British Columbian until Edward Prior in 1895, unless one counts Edgar Dewdney who lived in British Columbia for much of his life but was appointed in 1888 to represent the North-West Territories. Both Francis Hincks and John A. Macdonald represented British Columbia ridings for a short time while serving in the dominion cabinet, but their relationship with the Pacific province was tenuous to say the least. Cartier ostensibly represented the Manitoba riding of Provencher in the last months of his life, but he sailed to England to die soon after his acclamation and never saw either the riding or Ottawa again.[50]

Raw numbers of course give little indication of how much influence particular provinces enjoyed in cabinet. The ability of a minister, his standing in his province and in Ottawa, and the portfolio he held were all more important than his mere presence. Generally speaking the governments headed by John A. Macdonald had reasonably able and effective representatives from Quebec, Nova Scotia, and New Brunswick. Their Ontario representation was weaker, apart from the prime minister himself. The longest-serving Ontario ministers, Campbell and Bowell, were both from eastern Ontario, like Macdonald himself, and Campbell was also a senator in a province where the appointed upper house was not viewed with much enthusiasm. (Bowell did not become a senator until 1892.)

Alexander Mackenzie had the opposite problem. He and his most able and prominent ministers – Cartweight, Blake, and Mills – were all from Ontario and his cabinet had weak and ineffective representation everywhere else. A.-A. Dorion was certainly prominent, but he escaped to the bench after less than seven months. David Laird from Prince Edward Island was a good minister of the interior for three years, until he too departed. The other Quebec and Maritime ministers were nonentities.

Certain patterns emerge from an examination of provincial representation in the main portfolios. The prime ministership, of course, was always an Ontario preserve, apart from the brief regimes of Abbott, Thompson, and Tupper. Leonard Tilley served in Finance for almost a year before the Pacific Scandal, returned to it in 1878, and established a tradition of Maritime ministers of finance that lasted without interruption until 1911. Justice was held by three Quebec ministers (in addition to Edward Blake) during the Mackenzie interlude, establishing something of a Liberal party tradition, but when the Conservatives were in office it was held by Ontarians or Nova Scotians, more usually the latter. Public Works was almost always headed by a Quebec minister, except when Mackenzie held the portfolio while prime minister. After 1879 it was a relatively minor department, since its most important functions were transferred to the new Department of Railways and Canals. The latter department was held successively by Tupper, the Quebec anglophone J.H. Pope, John A. Macdonald, and finally J.G. Haggart from the Ottawa Valley. Agriculture usually went to a Quebec minister, often an anglophone, while Marine and Fisheries was reserved for Maritimers. Militia and Defence, held by Cartier in the first government, was usually given to a Quebec minister. The secretary of state for the provinces, while the title existed, was always a Nova Scotian. Dewdney's appointment to Interior in 1888 began a tradition of westerners in that portfolio that lasted until it was abolished.[51]

Cabinet's two committees, the Railway Committee and the Treasury Board, were less visible than the cabinet itself and were not subject to rigid rules of provincial representation. Quebec was usually overrepresented on the Railway Committee, perhaps because both the Canadian Pacific and the Grand Trunk had their headquarters there, but was sometimes omitted from the Treasury Board. Ontario seems to have been always represented on both committees.[52] The prime minister did not sit on either, unless he happened to hold the portfolio responsible for railways, as Mackenzie did throughout his government.

Interprovincial jealousies continued to complicate the task of cabinet making long after Confederation. J.-A. Chapleau complained to Macdonald in 1888 that Quebec should have more representation.

Macdonald replied that more portfolios were currently held by Quebec than by Ontario ministers, that Ontario was complaining because Maritimers held too many senior portfolios, and that the West also demanded representation. With heroic optimism the prime minister concluded, "The time has come, I think, when we must choose men for their qualifications rather than for their locality."[53] Six years later, C.H. Tupper, sone of Sir Charles, complained to Prime Minister Mackenzie Bowell because his fellow Nova Scotian, A.R. Dickey, had been offered a more junior portfolio than John Costigan of New Brunswick. Tupper neglected to add that he had himself been offered the Justice portfolio. Bowell wearily replied that the arrangement seemed reasonable because Dickey was the youngest member of the government and Costigan the oldest. He was sure that Nova Scotia would still be adequately represented.[54]

How effective was the dominion cabinet as a mechanism of intrastate federalism? In some ways the circumstances were conducive to its success. Although two committees had already emerged to perform specialized tasks, most government business was still transacted in meetings of the full cabinet, and the cabinet was small enough to function as a deliberative body in which each member had frequent opportunities to participate.[55] Ministers still enjoyed great influence over their departments, including the selection of personnel. Since departments were very small, all of the personnel at departmental headquarters, and even some of those in the field, would be personally known to the minister. Finally, public policy was still mainly of the kind described by Theodore Lowi as "distributive," in the sense that it involved allocating concrete and divisible benefits of patronage, public expenditure, and private legislation between provinces and constituencies.[56] Since the dominion's revenues were in a reasonably healthy state, relative to its needs, and since neither Parliament nor the cabinet was overburdened with work, it was relatively easy to avoid disappointing any province or region. A favour to one could be counterbalanced with a favour to another.

Another advantage was the fact that party organizations were integrated, in the sense that the same machinery functioned at both the federal and provincial levels. This fact facilitated the efficient distribution of patronage in a way that maximized its impact on the provinces and also contributed to close and harmonious ties between politicians at the two levels, unless they happened to be on opposing sides of the increasingly polarized two-party system. Many federal ministers had provincial experience and retained provincial contacts. In the early years after Confederation this was true almost by definition, but it was even true of some of the younger men who appeared after 1878, men like Thompson, Chapleau, J.C. Pope of Prince Edward Island, and A.R. Angers.

Unfortunately, however, integrated party organizations were only an asset in intergovernmental relations when the two governments were already friendly. They could be a serious liability when the prime minister and a premier were partisan opponents. Relations between the dominion and Nova Scotia before 1873 and after 1882, between the dominion and Quebec from November 1873 until 1878, and between the dominion and Ontario after Macdonald returned to power all testify to this unhappy fact. Although Alexander Campbell, and to some extent John Thompson, managed to maintain fairly correct if not cordial relations with political opponents in the provinces, not all federal politicians had this ability or inclination. John A. Macdonald's extreme partisanship, and that of practically all politicians in Quebec, may have been the legacy of central Canada's bitter history in the first half of the nineteenth century, as Gordon Stewart has suggested.[57] Whatever its cause, it was not conducive to the harmonious operation of a federal constitution.

Generally speaking, it appears that the effectiveness of the cabinet in terms of intrastate federalism varied from one region of Canada to another. In the Maritimes, which initially presented the most serious problems of dominion-provincial relations, a tradition of strong regional cabinet representation was established at the outset. Tilley's appointment as minister of customs in 1867 reassured a region fearful of high Canadian tariffs, and the invention of the secretary of state for the provinces was obviously designed to reassure Nova Scotia. After 1878 the predominance of Maritimers in both Justice and Finance, the two most significant portfolios in terms of intergovernmental relations, helped to reconcile the region to Confederation. Tilley was an effective minister of finance whose experience as a provincial premier and lieutenant-governor made him sensitive to the financial needs of the provinces. His two adjustments of debt allowances, in 1873 and 1884, considerably improved the climate of dominion-provincial relations, not least in his own region.

In Quebec the record was more mixed. No subsequent "Quebec lieutenant" enjoyed Cartier's influence, although admittedly even Cartier would have found his task more difficult had he lived to see the abolition of the double mandate. Subsequent Quebec ministers were of uneven quality, and they rarely held the portfolios that had the greatest impact on federal-provincial relations. Quebec was usually governed by the same party as the dominion, however, and the same byzantine factional intrigues took place within the Bleu organization at both levels. While the nature of the party made it difficult for one individual to represent all of it in Ottawa, Langevin, Chapleau, Mousseau, and other Quebec ministers tried with some success to represent their province's interests and to remind Macdonald that his government could not survive without Quebec support. Given the cultural and ideological barriers between Quebec and the rest of the country, the reasonably harmonious relations between the Conservative governments in Ottawa and Quebec City were a considerable achievement and the Quebec ministers deserve a large part of the credit for it. Their only real failure, as defenders of their province's interests and aspirations, was the failure to prevent the execution of Louis Riel.

Ontario's representation in the cabinet, as mentioned above, was almost excessive during the Mackenzie interlude but less satisfactory at other times. John A. Macdonald had no particular loyalty to the province in which he spent most of his life, and could just as easily have been a Quebec anglophone. He once privately described the area southwest of Toronto, where most Ontarians lived, as "occupied by Yankees and Covenanters – in fact the most yeasty and unsafe of populations."[58] His animosity towards Mowat has already been sufficiently emphasized. Macdonald's national vision and his freedom from partiality towards his own province were appropriate in a prime minister, and Canadians rightly remember him as one of the great nation-builders of the nineteenth century, but they did not make the task of smoothing relations with Ontario any easier.

At the same time, Ontario had little cause to complain. About a third of the cabinet were always drawn from that province, and it cannot be said that it suffered from federal policies. In fact its economy and finances were so healthy and its infrastructure so developed that it really needed little help from the central government. Much of the conflict between the two governments after 1878 was really partisan in character and probably unavoidable. Insofar as it was not, Alexander Campbell made valiant although not always successful efforts to find common ground between the dominion and the largest province.

As for the West, since the region had no cabinet representation at all until 1888, and minimal representation in both houses of Parliament, it is not surprising that intrastate federalism was a failure. If the proof of the pudding is in the eating, the fact that two provinces whose combined population was less than that of New Brunswick accounted for well over a third, and probably almost half, of federal-provincial conflicts and controversies really speaks for itself. Obviously the lack of western representation in the cabinet was not the only reason for these problems, but it was certainly a contributing factor, and one whose importance should not be overlooked. Partisanship was not a problem, since British Columbia really lacked a party system and Manitoba developed one only towards the end of the period under consideration. Dewdney's appointment as the first western minister came at a time when the dominion's relations with Manitoba could not have been worse and when its relations with British Columbia were only slightly better. Predictably it seems to have been followed by at least some improvement.

Intrastate federalism was thus not a completely negligible factor in nineteenth-century Canada, and its importance has perhaps not been given adequate recognition. At the same time, it could not be a panacea. Responsible government was conducive to concentration and centralization of political power at both levels, in contrast to the more polycentric and competitive American system from which the concept of federalism was borrowed. The broadening of the electorate and the polarization of the party system around the issue of tariff protection, as well as the declining (and never very great) legitimacy of the Senate probably reinforced this tendency. The disappearance of the double mandate was probably regrettable as well from a standpoint of intrastate federalism. Intrastate federalism was better suited to making policy choices of a distributive nature, especially those involving federal-provincial finance, than it was to dealing with the increasingly serious ethnic and religious controversies (Riel, the Jesuit estates, separate schools, and bilingualism) that divided Canadians in the last years of the Macdonald era.

14 Conclusion: From Gristle into Bone

By 1896 the Canadian federal state had lasted almost thirty years. It had been founded at a time when Laura Secord still lived in her house by the Niagara River, when sailing ships and pine timber rafts filled the busy harbour of Quebec, and when the great herds of buffalo still roamed across the unfenced prairies of North America. All those things were distant memories by 1896, and as the old century drew to a close the first signs of a new world were emerging. Henry Ford built his first car in 1896, a hydroelectric power station opened at Niagara Falls, and Henri Becquerel discovered radioactivity. In the same year the first modern Olympic Games were held at Athens, Theodor Herzl published his book advocating a Jewish nation-state, and Vladimir Ulianov, subsequently known as Lenin, began to write his first book in a St Petersburg jail. The winds of change had even blown through the University of Toronto a year earlier, when the students in the political economy department went out on strike. In the summer of 1896 the student who had led the strike cast his first vote, for Laurier's Liberals, and left his native land to pursue graduate studies at the University of Chicago. He would be back in time for the new century, and Canadians would hear more about William Lyon Mackenzie King.

Thirty years is not a long time in the history of a country or a state, despite the dramatic nature of these developments. In that relatively short time the Canadian federal state had come of age, absorbing a vast northern and western hinterland, adding three new provinces to the original four, and building railways from the Atlantic to the Pacific. A certain amount of intercultural, interregional, and intergovernmental conflict had accompanied these achievements, including a brief but tragic outbreak of military violence in 1885. Nonetheless, these unhappy byproducts of state-building were probably no more than might have been expected. The United States in the three decades after 1787 had experienced the Whiskey Rebellion, the Alien and Sedition acts, the Virginia and Kentucky resolutions, and the virtual abstention of Federalist New England from the War of 1812. Thirty-two years after Australia became a federation the people of Western Australia voted overwhelmingly in favour of secession, although in the end it did not take place. India's first thirty years as a federal republic were marked by the ongoing problems of Kashmir and Punjab, sporadic outbreaks of violence in the northeastern frontier regions, a wholesale reorganization of state boundaries along linguistic lines, the imposition of emergency rule at the state level on forty different occasions, and the temporary suspension of democratic government at the national level between 1975 and 1977.[1] Nigeria's first three decades of independence saw an effort to secede by one state that culminated in a bloody civil war, followed by a long period of military dictatorship. Mention of these other events may help to place the problems of late nineteenth-century Canada in their proper perspective.

"Confederation is only yet in the gristle," wrote John A. Macdonald to his friend John Rose in 1872, "and it will require five years more before it hardens into bone."[2] Maccdonald was right in predicting that the next five years would be decisive, but wrong in the direction he expected the evolution of the new dominion to take. The centralized quasi-federal regime on the New Zealand pattern he had planned and hoped for was not destined to last. The crumbling of Cartier's political machine and the death of Cartier himself, the resurgence of Ontario Liberalism under the capable leadership of Oliver Mowat, the abolition of the double mandate, and Macdonald's own temporary eclipse after the Pacific Scandal all helped to seal its fate, although there were more fundamental causes as well. Contrary to Macdonald's hopes, the "bone" into which Confederation had hardened by 1877 was a regime in which strong autonomous provincial governments competed on fairly equal terms with the central government for political authority, legitimacy, and power. For most Canadians, provincial government was just as important and influential as federal government, and the power of one level counterbalanced the power of the other. This was not yet true of the small western provinces, let alone the territories, but the overwhelming majority of Canadians (88 per cent as late as the turn of the century) still lived in Ontario, Quebec, or the Maritimes.

This fact has been obscured by the widespread belief that the highly centralized regime preferred by Macdonald lasted until his death, or even until the defeat of his party in 1896. Alan Cairns has expressed this erroneous view in the statement, "Laurier assumed power and commenced to wield federal authority with much looser reins than had his Conservative predecessors."[3] While the Laurier government falls outside the scope of the present work, it was in fact surprisingly similar to Macdonald's government, in this and other respects. Laurier, for example, continued to use the power of disallowance as frequently as Macdonald had done. Like Macdonald, he used it mainly against the western provinces. Laurier also retained control of prairie lands and the British Columbia railway belt, as did every government until 1930. He asserted federal authority in the Yukon gold rush as firmly as Macdonald had done in sending the Mounted Police to the prairies a quarter century earlier. Like Macdonald, he pursued a policy of transcontinental railway building and western settlement. Like Macdonald, he opposed Ontario's province-building when the Tory Whitney attempted to follow in the footsteps of the Liberal Mowat. Like Macdonald, he based his government on a solid bedrock of Quebec support while resisting the more extreme manifestations of French-Canadian nationalism. Party labels changed in 1896 but not the fundamental characteristics of Canadian federalism and intergovernmental relations. Those characteristics had in fact been established more than twenty years earlier.

Macdonaldian quasi-federalism lasted longest in the West, where public lands and natural resources remained in federal hands until 1930, where the power of disallowance was used forty-one times in the half century that followed the formation of Laurier's government, and where lieutenant-governors occasionally wielded their reserve powers.[4] As some westerners ruefully observed in the 1930s, they were a colony of a colony. The realization that the substitution of Liberals for Conservatives in Ottawa did not alter these facts contributed to the rise of new political parties in western Canada, and even to demands for abolition of Westminster-style responsible government.[5]

Nonetheless, the slow progress of the West towards constitutional equality was only the exception that proved the rule. By 1878 it was obvious that Canadian provinces, unlike their counterparts in New Zealand, would survive as functioning entities for as long as Canada itself lasted. Furthermore, provincial governments were almost always at least partially successful in their conflicts with the federal government or in the demands they made upon it. Policies that provinces were determined to pursue, like Ontario's Rivers and

Streams acts and regulation of liquor or Manitoba's railway projects, were delayed but not really prevented by the federal government. Demands for financial concessions, or "better terms," were almost invariably successful, sooner or later. Only when provinces were deeply divided (as Quebec was on the Letellier affair) or when their demands threatened the very survival of the dominion (Nova Scotia's efforts to secede) or when they were opposed by other provinces (Manitoba's loss of the disputed territory to Ontario) did they really suffer defeat.

Yet the federal government did not fare badly either. As fragile and artificial as it appeared at the outset, the dominion survived and even prospered. Provincial triumphs, while sometimes disappointing to federal politicians, did not prevent the achievement of such major initiatives as the settlement of outstanding disputes with the United States, the absorption of the prairies, British Columbia, and Prince Edward Island, the building of the Intercolonial and Canadian Pacific railways, or the National Policy tariff.

Both sides had significant assets that contributed to these successful outcomes, and thus to the maintenance of an equilibrium between the two levels of government. The provinces benefited from the decision to establish or maintain responsible government at that level, rather than the municipal-type institutions many Ontarians favoured at the outset. This decision helped to concentrate power at the provincial level in strong leaders like Mowat and Fielding. They also benefited from the association of the ceremonies and symbols of monarchy with the provincial governments, even before the Maritime Bank decision.[6] History and tradition gave the provinces, or at least the central and eastern provinces, popular support and legitimacy, as did their responsibility for most of the subjects that affected people's lives in a direct and obvious way. Geography made centralized rule of half a continent from Ottawa almost impossible, and increased the tendency of Canadians to identify their interests with the particular province in which they lived. The cultural and religious cleavage between Quebec and Ontario strengthened the governments of both provinces by making the residents of each reluctant to concentrate power in a central government that might be unduly influenced by the other. The very large size of the two central provinces in relation to the dominion as a whole also inhibited centralization. The decisions of the Judicial Committee of the Privy Council reinforced these tendencies towards provincial autonomy, as did the fact that the British North America Act specifically enumerated some fields of provincial jurisdiction.

As for the federal government, what K. C. Wheare called its quasi-federal powers to disallow provincial acts, declare works for the general advantage of Canada, and appoint judges and lieutenant-governors proved to be of some value. Far more important, however, were its monopoly over customs and excise revenue and its control of public lands in the West. These assets enabled it to meet its own financial needs, to pay political debts to the provinces, to influence provincial budgets, and to shape the development of the Canadian economy. Also important were the dominion's virtual monopoly of communications with the imperial government and the imperial government's fairly consistent support for the federal side in federal-provincial conflicts. Finally, the National Policy, controversial though it was, captured the imagination of some Canadians and created a clientele, particularly among businessmen, that was favourable to centralization.

Confederation was thus on the whole a success, and in retrospect it appears as the only possible solution to the problems faced by the British North American colonies in the middle of Queen Victoria's long reign. A unitary state had proved unpopular and difficult to operate even when confined to central Canada, and would surely have been unworkable for a Canada extending from coast to coast. At the same time, had the provinces continued as separate entities with no central government it seems reasonable to conclude that they would have remained dependent on the United Kingdom (as Newfoundland in fact did) or drifted inexorably into the United States. The prairies would surely have become American had there not been a Dominion of Canada to annex them, for so vast a tract of rich agricultural land could not have been held by a handful of Indians and Métis against the expanding population to the south.

As the events described in this book suggest, Canada's combination of responsible government at both levels with federalism was not without its problems. It made effective brokerage of regional interests in the central institutions of government more difficult than in the United States. It promoted in the nineteenth century, as it still does, the exacerbation of intergovernmental disputes and their entanglement with personal and partisan rivalries. Nonetheless, it was successful enough to be imitated in the twentieth century by Australia, India, and other successor states of the British Empire. The alternative American model of federalism with a separation of powers, although seemingly more logical, has not been successfully imitated anywhere, even though it remains appealing to some Canadians.[7]

Although much, inevitably, has changed, the pattern of federal-provincial relations described in this book would prove, like the dominion itself, to be surprisingly durable. Canada's formal constitution, although recently supplemented by a Charter of Rights and Freedoms, is essentially still that of 1867; even the appointed Senate and the non-resident monarchy have survived, for lack of more acceptable alternatives. Only four changes to the distribution of legislative powers were made in 125 years after Confederation, and the courts are still grappling with peace, order and good government, the regulation of trade and commerce, and property and civil rights. Prime ministers and provincial premiers still devote much of their attention to intergovernmental relations, and the rhetoric they direct at one another often echoes that of Macdonald, Mowat, and Mercier.

Despite these continuities, history, whose ultimate end remains beyond our understanding, does not stand still. The Canada of today is several times as large in population as that which Macdonald and Mowat knew, and incomparably more wealthy and productive. Technology has revolutionized everyday life. Easy credit and continuous inflation encourage Canadians to buy goods they don't need with money they don't have, a process euphemistically described as stimulating the economy. The influence of the state over civil society has increased to a level that no one in the nineteenth century could have imagined. Fewer and fewer Canadians live on farms. Toronto, Montreal, and Vancouver are as large today as London, Paris, and New York were in 1867. Aboriginal peoples claim a fairer share of Canada's resources and a constitutionally entrenched right to self-government. Women demand equality with men, in the political realm and elsewhere. A bewildering variety of special interest groups press their claims on the state by invoking their individual and collective "rights." Quebec has emerged as a viable nation, with as credible a claim to be ready for complete independence as most of those that have already achieved it. The United Kingdom has long since disappeared as an effective counterweight to the United States.[8]

As Canada approaches the centennial of Laurier's rise to power, Canadian federalism faces a crisis of exceptional severity. Laurier's boast that the twentieth century would belong to Canada rings hollow, as Canadians ask themselves whether a recognizable entity known as Canada will even survive until the century's end. Three decades of efforts to overhaul the constitution have accomplished little more than to undermine its legitimacy while drawing attention to the fundamentally different objectives of francophone Quebec and the anglophone majority. Recent efforts to democratize the process of constitutional revision, while well-intentioned, have apparently only added to the confusion.

Che sarà, sarà is perhaps the only certain answer that the historian or social scientist can provide to the questions posed by these developments. Nonetheless, it may be instructive or even encouraging to recall that Canadians in the 1860s also saw their constitutional order collapsing in the midst of a rapidly changing domestic and international environment. They rose to the challenge by creating a new constitutional order that, with all its faults, lasted for well over a century. Perhaps their successors can at least hope to do as well.

Notes

CHAPTER 1

1 Donald Creighton, *The Road to Confederation: The Emergence of Canada, 1863–1867* (Toronto: Macmillan, 1964); W.L. Morton, *The Critical Years: The Union of British North America, 1857–1873* (Toronto: McClelland and Stewart, 1964); P.B. Waite, *The Life and Times of Confederation, 1864–1867: Politics, Newspapers, and the Union of British North America,* 2nd ed. (Toronto: University of Toronto Press, 1962).
2 This is emphasized by W.L. White et al., *Canadian Confederation: A Decision-Making Analysis* (Toronto: Macmillan, 1979).
3 Donald Creighton, *Towards the Discovery of Canada* (Toronto: Macmillan, 1972), 160.
4 Donald Creighton, *John A. Macdonald: The Young Politician* (Toronto: Macmillan, 1952), 1.
5 Donald Creighton, *John A. Macdonald: The Old Chieftain* (Toronto: Macmillan, 1955), 578.
6 Frank H. Underhill, "The Conception of a National Interest," *Canadian Journal of Economics and Political Science* 1 (1935): 400.
7 Stanley B. Ryerson, *Unequal Union: Confederation and the Roots of Conflict in the Canadas, 1815–1873* (Toronto: Progress Books, 1968), 309.
8 R.T. Naylor, "The Rise and Fall of the Third Commercial Empire of the St. Lawrence," in Gary Teeple, ed., *Capitalism and the National Question in Canada* (Toronto: University of Toronto Press, 1968), 1–41.
9 Canada, *Parliamentary Debates on the Subject of the Confederation of the British North American Provinces* (Quebec, 1865), 25–45 (Macdonald) and 53–62 (Cartier).

10 National Archives of Canada (NA), John A. Macdonald Papers, vol. 13, Macdonald to Howland, 3 February 1870.

11 Arend Lijphart, *The Politics of Accommodation: Pluralism and Democracy in the Netherlands* (Berkeley and Los Angeles: University of California Press, 1968).

12 Ibid., 122–38.

13 S.J.R. Noel, *Patrons, Clients, Brokers: Ontario Society and Politics, 1791–1896* (Toronto: University of Toronto Press, 1990), 174–5.

14 NA, Joseph Howe Papers, vol. 4, Macdonald to Howe, 26 September 1868.

15 Macdonald Papers, vol. 79, Macdonald to Northcote, 1 May 1878.

16 Ibid., vol. 54, Mitchell to Macdonald, 27 May 1867.

17 Waite, *The Life and Times of Confederation*, 235.

18 Ibid., 200.

19 Chester Martin, "British Policy in Canadian Confederation," *Canadian Historical Review* 13 (1932): 3–19.

20 Goldwin Smith, *Reminiscences* (New York: Macmillan, 1911), 194–5.

21 William G. Ormsby, *The Emergence of the Federal Concept in Canada* (Toronto: University of Toronto Press, 1969).

22 William Bennett Munro, *American Influences on Canadian Government* (Toronto: Macmillan, 1929), 14–20.

23 W.P. Morrell, *The Provincial System in New Zealand*, 2nd ed. (Christchurch: Whitcombe and Tombs, 1964).

24 Joseph Pope, ed., *Confederation: Being a Series of Hitherto Unpublished Documents Bearing on the British North America Act* (Toronto: Carswell, 1895), 1–38.

25 The concept of intrastate federalism is discussed in chapter 13 of this book. See also Donald V. Smiley and Ronald L. Watts, *Intrastate Federalism in Canada* (Toronto: University of Toronto Press, 1985).

26 Waite, *The Life and Times of Confederation*, 110, 202–6, 237–8.

27 Pope, ed., *Confederation Documents*, 81–2.

28 Canada, *Parliamentary Debates*, 31.

29 NA, RG6, vol. 320, file 150, lieutenant-governor of New Brunswick to secretary of state for the provinces, 24 March 1870.

30 Ramsay Cook, *Provincial Autonomy, Minority Rights, and the Compact Theory, 1867–1921* (Ottawa: Queen's Printer, 1969), 51–63.

31 Pope, ed., *Confederation Documents*, 79–80.

32 Canada, *Parliamentary Debates*, 250–1.

33 *Ibid.*, 482–544.

34 Creighton, *The Road to Confederation*, 410–12.

35 F.R. Scott, "The Development of Canadian Federalism," in his *Essays on the Constitution: Aspects of Canadian Law and Politics* (Toronto: University of Toronto Press, 1977), 35–48.

36 *The Times*, 20 February 1867.
37 *Hansard's Parliamentary Debates* (London, 1867), third series, vol. 185, 576-b.

CHAPTER 2

1 For example, W.J. Easterbrook and Hugh Aitken, *Canadian Economic History* (Toronto: Macmillan, 1956), 400, announces Laurier's arrival with the heading, "The Dawn of Prosperity."
2 L.E. Truesdell, *The Canadian-Born in the United States* (New Haven: Yale University Press, 1943).
3 Richard Pomfret, *The Economic Development of Canada* (Toronto: Methuen, 1981), 55.
4 Ibid., 179–82.
5 Canada, *Statistical Yearbook, 1900*, 195–6.
6 Pomfret, *Economic Development*, 61.
7 Ibid., 180.
8 Canada, *Statistical Yearbook, 1900*, 284.
9 Ibid., 206–7.
10 Ibid., 259.
11 Canada, *Census*, 1870–1, vol. 3, table 54; 1880–1, vol. 3, table 55; 1891, vol. 3, table 2.
12 Ibid., 1870–1, vol. 3, table 15; 1880–1, vol. 3, table 16; 1891, vol. 3, table 1.
13 Ibid., 1870–1, vol. 3, table 54; 1880–1, vol. 3, table 15; 1891, vol. 3, table 2.
14 Donald Creighton, "George Brown, Sir John Macdonald, and the Workingman," in his *Towards the Discovery of Canada* (Toronto: Macmillan, 1972), 174–93.
15 Gregory S. Kealey, *Toronto Workers Respond to Industrial Capitalism, 1867–1892* (Toronto: University of Toronto Press, 1980), 200–12.
16 National Archives of Canada (NA), John Thompson Papers, vol. 44: Macdonald to Thompson, 3 September 1886.
17 A useful description of the various French minorities at the time of Confederation is in A.I. Silver, *The French-Canadian Idea of Confederation, 1864–1900* (Toronto: University of Toronto Press, 1982), 3–32.
18 On the Irish Canadians see Donald Harman Akenson, *Small Differences: Irish Catholics and Irish Protestants, 1815–1922: An International Perspective* (Kingston and Montreal: McGill-Queen's University Press, 1988), 87–99.
19 A. Gordon Darroch and Michael D. Ornstein, "Ethnicity and Occupational Structure in Canada in 1871: The Vertical Mosaic in Historical Perspective," *Canadian Historical Review*, 61 (1980): 305–33.

20 Canada, *Sessional Papers*, vol. 5 (1872), no. 38.

21 S.D. Clark, "Religious Organization and the Rise of the Canadian Nation, 1850–85," in his *The Developing Canadian Community*, 2nd edition (Toronto: University of Toronto Press, 1962), 115–30.

22 Akenson, *Small Differences*, 98.

23 Hereward Senior, *Orangeism: The Canadian Phase* (Toronto: McGraw-Hill Ryerson, 1972), 12, 96.

24 Gordon Stewart, *The Origins of Canadian Politics: A Comparative Approach* (Vancouver: University of British Columbia Press, 1986), 5–6.

25 Ibid., 29, 43, 92.

26 NA, Richard Cartwright Papers, Macdonald to Cartwright, 17 November 1869; Cartwright to Macdonald, 22 November 1869.

27 Electoral data are from J. Murray Beck, *Pendulum of Power: Canada's Federal Elections* (Scarborough: Prentice-Hall, 1968).

28 C.B. Macpherson, *Democracy in Alberta: Social Credit and the Party System*, 2nd edition (Toronto: University of Toronto Press, 1962).

29 William H., Riker, *The Theory of Political Coalitions* (New Haven and London: Yale University Press, 1962).

30 Escott M. Reid, "The Rise of National Parties in Canada," in Hugh G. Thorborn, ed., *Party Politics in Canada*, 6th edition (Scarborough: Prentice-Hall, 1991), 11–18.

31 Terence H. Qualter, *The Election Process in Canada* (Toronto: McGraw-Hill, 1970), 4–12.

32 Data on the number of persons eligible to vote are found in *The Canadian Parliamentary Companion*, various years.

33 Canada, Statutes, 48–49 Victoria, ch. 40.

34 Data from Beck, *Pendulum of Power*.

35 Robert C. Vipond, *Liberty and Community: Canadian Federalism and the Failure of the Constitution* (Albany: State University of New York Press, 1991).

36 Canada, *Statistical Yearbook, 1900*, 458, 463, 469–70.

37 Ibid., 483.

38 James A. Maxwell, *Federal Subsidies to the Provincial Governments in Canada* (Cambridge: Harvard University Press, 1937).

CHAPTER 3

1 A good account of Sandfield's career by Bruce W. Hodgins may be found in J.M.S. Careless, ed., *The Pre-Confederation Premiers: Ontario Government Leaders, 1841–1867* (Toronto: University of Toronto Press, 1980), 246–314.

2 Donald Creighton, *John A. Macdonald: The Young Politician* (Toronto: Macmillan, 1952), 310.

3 Sir John Willison, *Reminiscences Political and Personal* (Toronto: McClelland and Stewart, 1919), 233–4.

4 C.R.W. Biggar, *Sir Oliver Mowat*, vol. 2 (Toronto: Warwick and Rutter, 1905), 601–2.

5 Bruce W. Hodgins, "Disagreement at the Commencement: Divergent Ontarian Views of Federalism, 1867–1871," in Donald Swainson, ed., *Oliver Mowat's Ontario* (Toronto: Macmillan, 1972), 52–68.

6 J.K. Johnson, "John A. Macdonald," in Careless, ed., *The Pre-Confederation Premiers*, 236.

7 The quality of Ontario land and the importance of agriculture are emphasized by S.J.R. Noel, *Patrons, Clients, Brokers: Ontario Society and Politics, 1791–1896* (Toronto: University of Toronto Press, 1990).

8 National Archives of Canada (NA), John A. Macdonald Papers, vol. 527, Macdonald to Campbell, 27 January 1888.

9 Bruce W. Hodgins and Robert C. Edwards, "Federalism and the Politics of Ontario: 1867–1880," in Bruce W. Hodgins, ed., *Federalism in Canada and Australia: The Early Years* (Waterloo: Wilfrid Laurier University Press, 1978), 96.

10 Macdonald Papers, vol. 513, John A. Macdonald to Sandfield Macdonald, 9 August 1867.

11 Ibid., vol. 514, John A. Macdonald to Sandfield Macdonald, 10 October 1867.

12 Ibid., vol. 514, John A. Macdonald to Sandfield Macdonald, 29 November 1867.

13 Ibid., vol. 518, John A. Macdonald to Sandfield Macdonald, 23 January 1871.

14 Ontario, Statutes, 32 Victoria, ch. 4.

15 Macdonald Papers, vol. 515, John A. Macdonald to Sandfield Macdonald, 20 November 1868.

16 Ibid., vol. 516, John A. Macdonald to Sandfield Macdonald, 6 and 27 December 1869.

17 Ontario, Statutes, 35 Victoria, ch. 4.

18 Macdonald Papers, vol. 119, Scott to Macdonald, 20 December 1871.

19 Ibid., Macdonald to Scott, 21 December 1871.

20 Ibid., Macdonald to Scott, 13 July 1872; Scott to Macdonald, 19 July 1872; Macdonald to Scott, 20 July 1872.

21 Ibid., vol. 522, Macdonald to Mowat, 25 October 1872.

22 Ibid., vol. 253, Mowat to Macdonald, 29 October 1872.

23 Archives of Ontario (AO), Edward Blake Papers, Mowat to Blake, 6 July 1875 (microfilm in NA, reel M-242).

24 Queen's University Archives (QUA), Alexander Mackenzie Papers, Mowat to Mackenzie, 12 August 1876 and 18 June 1877 (microfilm in NA, reel M-198).

25 Ibid., Mowat to Mackenzie, 24 July 1877.
26 Macdonald Papers, vol. 517, John A. Macdonald to Sandfield Macdonald, 29 November 1870; Canada, Statutes, 34 Vic., c. 26.
27 Blake Papers, Mowat to Blake, 31 August 1875 (microfilm in NA, reel
M-242); NA, Alexander Mackenzie Papers, vol. 14, Mowat to
Mackenzie, 20 November 1875, Mackenzie to Mowat, 23 November
1875.
28 Canada, Statutes, 40 Victoria, ch. 38.
29 QUA, Mackenzie Papers, Mowat to Mackenzie, 4 October 1878 (microfilm in NA, reel M-199).
30 NA, RG6, vol. 38, file 1043.
31 A useful recent account is in Paul Romney, *Mr. Attorney: The Attorney
General for Ontario in Court, Cabinet, and Legislature, 1791–1899*
(Toronto: University of Toronto Press, 1986), 240–81.
32 NA, RG 6, vols. 352 (1871) and 354 (1872), contain letters sent from the
secretary of state for the Provinces to Ontario concerning this matter. Ontario's decision to cease efforts at a solution was acknowledged
in a letter from Howe to the lieutenant-governor, 5 April 1872.
33 NA, RG6, vol 335, file 1350, Report of Committee of the Privy Council,
approved 2 October 1872.
34 Ibid., vol. 68, file 4909, Report of Committee of the Privy Council, approved 3 June 1874. The provisional boundary line and other aspects of the dispute are illustrated in *Economic Atlas of Ontario* (Toronto:
University of Toronto Press, 1969), plate 97.
35 QUA, Mackenzie Papers, Mowat to Mackenzie, 24 June 1874 (microfilm
in NA, reel M-197). Copies of the correspondence involving the Hudson's Bay Company may be found in the Macdonald Papers, vol. 34.
36 Canada, *Sessional Papers*, vol. 14 (1881), no. 37, 23–5.
37 Ontario, Statutes, 42 Victoria, ch. 19.
38 NA, Macdonald Papers, vol. 35, McDougall to Macdonald, 11 April 1881.
39 NA, Alexander Campbell Papers, microfilm reel M-23, Macdonald to
Campbell, 20 May 1881.
40 Canada, Statutes, 44 Victoria, ch. 14.
41 Campbell Papers, microfilm reel M-23, Mowat to Campbell, 31 October
1881, Macdonald to Campbell, 3 November 1881, Mowat to Campbell, 4 November 1881.
42 Canada, House of Commons, *Journals*, vol. 16 (1882), 253–4.
43 NA, RG6, vol. 55, files 699–701, Report of the Committee of the Privy
Council, approved 12 March 1884.
44 Macdonald Papers, vol. 35, Lansdowne to Macdonald, 29 August 1885.
45 NA, RG6, vol. 335, file 1373, Report of the Committee of the Privy Council, approved 2 October 1872.
46 Ibid., copy of the minute of council approved by the lieutenant-governor,

23 October 1872. This was two days before Mowat took over the government.

47 Ibid., Report of the Committee of the Privy Council approved 13 December 1872; Ontario Statutes, 36 Vic., ch. 3.

48 Blake Papers, Blake to Mowat, 3 September 1875, Mowat to Blake, 6 September 1875 (microfilm in NA, reels M-248 and M-242).

49 Ontario, Statutes, 37 Victoria, ch. 8.

50 NA, RG6, vol. 15, file 408.

51 Blake Papers, Blake to Mowat, 27 September and 4 October 1876 (microfilm in NA, reel M-257).

52 NA, John Thompson Papers, vol. 17, Mowat to Thompson, 5 and 26 November 1880.

53 NA, RG6, vol. 81, file 6231. The printed statement of Ontario's case, presented to the Court of Appeal in 1892, includes the full text of Mowat's memorandum.

54 NA, marquess of Lansdowne Papers, MG 27 IB4, microfilm reel A-623, Lansdowne to Thompson, 17 July 1886; microfilm reel A-627, Thompson to Lansdowne, 28 July 1886.

55 Thompson Papers, vol. 96, Mowat to Thompson, 25 November 1889.

56 Willison, *Reminiscences Political and Personal*, 93–4.

57 Ontario, Statutes, 32 Victoria, ch. 32.

58 W.E. Hodgins, *Correspondence, Reports of the Ministers of Justice and Orders in Council upon the Subject of Dominion and Provincial Legislation 1867–1895* (Ottawa: Government Printing Bureau, 1896), 102.

59 Ontario, Statutes, 36 Victoria, ch. 34.

60 Ibid., 37 Victoria, ch. 32.

61 NA, RG6, vol. 15, file 408, report by H. Bernard, 18 November 1874.

62 Ibid., vol. 356, Howe to lieutenant-governor of Ontario, 18 April 1873; vol. 16, file 441, lieutenant-governor to secretary of state, 7 April 1874; vol. 20, file 1548, lieutenant-governor to secretary of state, 12 December 1874.

63 Ontario, Statutes, 39 Victoria, ch. 26.

64 Blake Papers, Mowat to Blake, 30 December 1876 and 17 January 1877 (microfilm in NA, reel M-242).

65 Ibid., Mowat to Blake, 26 January 1877 (microfilm in NA, reel M-242).

66 Canada, Statutes, 41 Victoria, ch. 16.

67 Biggar, *Sir Oliver Mowat*, vol. 1, 359–61.

68 Canada, Statutes, 46 Victoria, ch. 30.

69 Ontario, Statutes, 47 Victoria, ch. 35.

70 Canada, *Sessional Papers*, vol. 28 (1895), no. 11, appendix 50.

71 Ontario, Statutes, 53 Victoria, ch. 56.

72 Thompson Papers, vol. 185, Mowat to Thompson, 11 Sept. 1893; vol. 187, Mowat to Thompson, 10 October 1893.

73 NA, RG6, vol. 160, files 2200–6.
74 Ontario, Statutes, 44 Victoria, ch. 11, subsequently re-enacted as 45 Victoria, ch. 14, and again as 46 Victoria, ch. 10.
75 NA, RG6, vol. 160, files 2200–6, McLaren to Mousseau, 22 March 1882.
76 Macdonald Papers, vol. 199, Campbell to Macdonald, 10 November 1881; vol. 229, Meredith to Macdonald, 26 December 1881; vol. 228, McCarthy to Macdonald, 29 January 1883.
77 Ontario, Statutes, 47 Victoria, ch. 17.
78 Macdonald Papers, vol. 482, McLaren to Macdonald, 25 February 1890; NA, Peter McLaren Papers, Macdonald to Mrs McLaren, 6 November 1889.
79 Macdonald Papers, vol. 35, Mowat to Macdonald, 17 January 1889.
80 Campbell Papers, microfilm reel M-22, Mowat to Campbell, 20 October 1879; Macdonald Papers, vol. 35, Campbell to Macdonald, 14 January 1882; Campbell Papers, microfilm reel M-24, Mowat to Campbell, 4 and 9 June, and 15 November 1883.
81 Thompson Papers, vol. 226, Thompson to Mowat, 17 March 1886. The act was Canada Statutes, 49 Vic., ch. 49.
82 Thompson Papers, vol. 249, Thompson to Mowat, 13 May 1891.
83 Macdonald Papers, vol. 527, Macdonald to Campbell, 3 December 1887.

CHAPTER 4

1 A.I. Silver, *The French-Canadian Idea of Confederation* (Toronto: University of Toronto Press, 1982), 33–50.
2 John McCallum, *Unequal Beginnings: Agriculture and Economic Development in Quebec and Ontario* (Toronto: University of Toronto Press, 1980).
3 Calculated from data in Canada, *Census*, 1870–1, vol. 3, table 54.
4 Brian Young, *Promoters and Politicians: The North Shore Railways in the History of Quebec* (Toronto: University of Toronto Press, 1978).
5 Brian Young, *George-Étienne Cartier: Montreal Bourgeois* (Kingston and Montreal: McGill-Queen's University Press, 1981), 120.
6 P.B. Waite, *Canada 1874–1896: Arduous Destiny* (Toronto: McClelland and Stewart, 1971), 46–7.
7 Ronald Rudin, *The Forgotten Quebecers: A History of English-Speaking Quebec* (Montreal: Institut québécois de recherche sur la culture, 1985), 97.
8 National Archives of Canada (NA), Alexander Campbell Papers, Abbott to Campbell, 20 January 1880.
9 Young, *George-Étienne Cartier*, 90.
10 Andrée Désilets, *Hector Louis Langevin, un père de la confédération canadienne* (Québec: Presses de l'université Laval, 1969), is a comprehensive account of his career.

11 Marcel Hamelin, *Les premieres années du parlementarisme québécois* (Québec: Presses de l'université Laval, 1974), 12–13.
12 Ibid., 137.
13 NA, John A. Macdonald Papers, vol. 253, Mousseau to Macdonald, 11 August 1882.
14 Robert Rumilly, *Honoré Mercier et son temps* (Montreal: Fides, 1975), vol. 1, 51–9.
15 Macdonald Papers, vol. 345, Chauveau to Macdonald, 8 January 1873.
16 NA, RG2, series 1, vol. 22, "Memo of informal Conference this 24th July 1869."
17 Canada, *Sessional Papers*, vol. 4 (1871), no. 21, 9–13.
18 J.A. Maxwell, *Federal Subsidies to the Provincial Governments in Canada* (Cambridge, Mass.: Harvard University Press, 1937), 52–3.
19 Canada, *Sessional Papers*, vol. 4 (1871), no. 21, 1–2.
20 Ibid., vol. 17 (1884), no. 56, 9–10.
21 Canada, Statutes, 36 Victoria, ch. 30.
22 NA, RG6, vol. 338, file 160, lieutenant-governor of Ontario to secretary of state for the provinces, 5 May 1873, enclosing Treasury memorandum and order in council.
23 NA, RG13 C1, vol. 977, item 1A includes a chronology of events up to 1888.
24 NA, Alexander Mackenzie Papers, microfilm reel M-199, Letellier to Mackenzie, 11 March 1878.
25 Ibid., Letellier to Mackenzie, 19 March 1878.
26 NA, Marquess of Dufferin and Ava Papers, microfilm reel A-411, Mackenzie to Dufferin, 26 March 1878.
27 He had said so at the Quebec Conference on 20 October 1864. See Joseph Pope, ed., *Confederation: Being a Series of Hitherto Unpublished Documents Bearing on the British North America Act* (Toronto: Carswell, 1895), 79.
28 NA, RG6, vol. 34, file 1200.
29 Macdonald Papers, vol. 95, Mousseau to Macdonald, 15 November 1878.
30 Ibid., Chapleau to Macdonald, 2 December 1878.
31 NA, RG6, vol. 34, file 1200, Letellier to secretary of state, 9 December 1878.
32 NA, Marquess of Lorne Papers, vol. 4, item 2, Todd to Lorne, 10 December 1878.
33 Macdonald Papers, vol. 95, Lorne to Macdonald, 30 December 1878; RG7, G12, vol. 77, Lorne to Hicks-Beach, 1 January 1879.
34 Ibid., Lorne to Hicks-Beach, 9 April 1879.
35 NA, RG6, vol. 34, file 1200: Quebec Minutes of Council, 8 April 1879; Report of Committee of the Privy Council, approved 11 April 1879.

36 NA, Henri-Gustave Joly de Lotbinière Papers, microfilm reel M-795, 8619–23, undated account of Joly's mission.
37 NA, RG6, vol. 34, file 1200, Hicks-Beach to Lorne, 3 July 1879.
38 H. Blair Neatby and John T. Saywell, "Chapleau and the Conservative Party in Quebec," *Canadian Historical Review*, 37, 1 (1956): 1–22.
39 Young, *Promoters and Politicians*, 87.
40 Joly Papers, microfilm reel M-790, Courtney to Joly, 24 September 1878; Joly to Mackenzie, 30 September 1878; Courtney to Joly, 2 October 1878.
41 NA, RG6, vol. 39, file 1934, Report of Committee of the Privy Council, 8 December 1879; vol. 40, file 1424, Report of Committee of the Privy Council, 1 April 1880.
42 Macdonald Papers, vol. 204, Chapleau to Macdonald, 15 October 1880.
43 Ibid., Chapleau to Macdonald, 31 October 1880.
44 Ibid., Macdonald to Chapleau, 19 January 1881; Chapleau to Macdonald, 26 January 1881.
45 Young, *Promoters and Politicians*, 129–34.
46 Macdonald Papers, vol. 204, Chapleau to Macdonald, 6 January 1881; Campbell to Macdonald, 12 January 1881; Chapleau to Campbell, 21 April 1881; Macdonald to Chapleau, 30 April 1881; Chapleau to Jules Ferry, 30 August 1881; vol. 524, Macdonald to Chapleau, 8 November 1881.
47 Ibid., vol. 524, Macdonald to Chapleau, 8 November 1881; vol. 204, Chapleau to Macdonald, 6 and 16 January 1882.
48 NA, RG6, vol. 55, files 727–9; Macdonald Papers, vol. 329, lieutenant-governor to secretary of state, 7 April 1883, Mousseau to Macdonald, 24 April 1883; vol. 525, Macdonald to Masson, 21 December 1883 and 3 January 1884.
49 Macdonald Papers, vol. 329, Ross to Macdonald, 12 February 1884; vol. 400, Ross to Macdonald, 11 February 1884.
50 Canada, Statutes, 47 Victoria, ch. 4 and ch. 8.
51 Macdonald Papers, vol. 119, Ross to Macdonald, 5 April 1884; Robertson to Macdonald, 21 April 1884; Tilley to Macdonald, 25 April 1884.
52 Ibid., Ross to Macdonald, 21 March and 21 May 1885.
53 Ibid., vol. 253, Mousseau to Macdonald, 1 and 3 February, 3 April 1883.
54 Macdonald Papers, vol. 119, Robertson to Hall, 30 January 1884.
55 Ibid., vol. 329, Mercier to Macdonald, 4 April 1887; Macdonald to Mercier, 6 April 1887; vol. 119, Mercier to Macdonald, 7 May 1887.
56 Ibid., vol. 119, Mercier to Macdonald, 24 September 1887.
57 Quebec, Statutes, 51–52 Victoria, ch. 9.
58 Macdonald Papers, vol. 284, Tupper to Macdonald, 9 August 1888; Vol. 528, Macdonald to Tupper, 21 July and 22 October 1888.
59 Quebec, Statutes, 51–52 Victoria, ch. 20.

60 Macdonald Papers, vol. 273, Thompson to Macdonald, 19 July 1888; vol. 528, Macdonald to Thompson, 21 July 1888.

61 Ibid., vol. 186; Angers to Macdonald, 19 September 1888; vol. 528, Macdonald to Angers, 22 and 27 September, 4 October 1888.

62 Ibid., vol. 186, Thompson to Macdonald, 2 February 1889; vol. 528, Macdonald to Angers, 20 February 1889.

63 Quebec, Statutes, 51–52 Victoria, ch. 13.

64 Canada, House of Commons, Journals, vol. 23 (1889), 205–7.

65 NA, Lord Stanley of Preston Papers, microfilm reel A-446, Macdonald to Stanley, 5 April and 16 May 1889.

66 Ibid., Macdonald to Stanley, 12 and 17 July, 3 August 1889; Stanley to Macdonald, 19 August 1889; Macdonald to Stanley, 21, 24, and 27 August 1889; Stanley to Macdonald, 21 January 1890.

67 NA, John Thompson Papers, vol. 127, Macdonald to Thompson, 24 April 1891; Macdonald Papers, vol. 275, Thompson to Macdonald, 25 April 1891.

68 NA, Marquess of Lansdowne Papers, microfilm reel A-624, Lansdowne to Mercier, 24 September 1887.

69 Campbell Papers, microfilm reel M-25, Macdonald to Campbell, 3 December 1887.

70 NA, A.R. Angers Papers, vol. 1, Angers to Macdonald, 6 December 1889; Macdonald to Angers, 10 December 1889.

71 NA, RG6, vol. 87, file 6569, lieutenant-governor to secretary of state, 6 December 1894; Canada, Statutes, 61 Victoria, ch. 3.

72 Canada, Statutes, 54–55 Victoria, ch. 6; Ontario, Statutes, 54 Victoria, ch. 2; Quebec, Statutes, 54 Victoria, ch. 4.

73 NA, RG13 C1, volumes 977–80; RG6, vol. 90, file 7193.

CHAPTER 5

1 John Bartlet Brebner, *North Atlantic Triangle: The Interplay of Canada, the United States, and Great Britain* (Toronto: McClelland and Stewart, 1966), 55–8.

2 Calculated from data in Canada, *Census*, 1870–1, vol. 1, table 13.

3 J. Murray Beck, *Politics of Nova Scotia*, vol. 1 (Tantallon, NS: Four East Publications, 1985), 157–86.

4 Electoral data, unless otherwise identified, are from J. Murray Beck, *Pendulum of Power* (Scarborough: Prentice-Hall, 1968).

5 National Archives of Canada (NA), RG7, G12, vol. 73, Monck to Buckingham, 24 October 1867; Young to Granville, 27 April 1869.

6 Ibid., Monck to Buckingham, 13 February 1868.

7 NA, John A. Macdonald Papers, vol. 282, Tupper to Macdonald, 9 April 1868.

8 NA, RG6, vol. 309, file 268, Buckingham to Monck, 4 June 1868.

9 Macdonald Papers, vol. 75, Monck to Macdonald, 28 July 1868.

10 Ibid., vol. 115, Macdonald to Monck, 4 September 1868.

11 NA, Joseph Howe Papers, vol. 9, Howe to Macdonald, 15 September 1868.

12 Ibid., vol. 4, Macdonald to Howe, 26 September and 6 October 1868; vol. 9, Howe to Rose, 19 October 1868, Howe to Macdonald, 21 October 1868.

13 Ibid., vol. 9, Macdonald to Howe, 11 November 1868, Howe to Macdonald, 16 November 1868, Howe to Rose, 4 December 1868; vol. 4, Macdonald to Howe, 24 November 1868.

14 Ibid., vol. 9, Howe to Macdonald, 4 January 1869; NA, RG7 G12, vol. 73, Young to Granville, 7 January 1869; RG6, vol. 6, file 231, Granville to Young, 13 January 1869; Macdonald Papers, vol. 515, Macdonald to Doyle, 1 February 1869.

15 Canada, Statutes, 32–33 Victoria, ch. 2.

16 NA, RG7 G3, vol. 3, Granville to Young, 29 March 1869.

17 NA, RG6, vol. 323, file 374, Edward Kenny (administrator of Nova Scotia) to secretary of state for the provinces, 25 August 1870, enclosing resolution and address to the queen.

18 Ibid., vol. 313, file 687, report by the minister of justice, 11 August 1869.

19 Public Archives of Nova Scotia (PANS), MG1, vol. 871, no. 69, Hill to Mackenzie, 24 December 1877; NA, RG6, vol. 27, file 171, Hill to Cartwright, 22 January 1877; Report of Committee of the Privy Council, 13 February 1877.

20 RG6, vol. 37, files 935–6, Holmes to Macdonald, 2 January 1879.

21 Canada, Statutes, 37 Victoria, ch. 17.

22 PANS, RG2, vol. 9, no. 1690, "Further Memorandum on the Affairs of the Province of Nova Scotia, 7 January 1880."

23 PANS, Simon Holmes Papers, MG2, vol. 557, folders 24, 25, and, 26 contain numerous documents pertaining to Nova Scotia's railway problems. See also NA, RG6, vol. 60, file 1181, memorandum by J.H. Pope re: Windsor Branch Railway, 23 September 1885.

24 Canada, Statutes, 40 Victoria, ch. 46.

25 Ibid., 42 Victoria, ch. 12.

26 Nova Scotia, Statutes, 43 Victoria, ch. 20.

27 Macdonald Papers, vol. 524, Macdonald to Holmes, 31 March 1881.

28 Holmes Papers, vol. 557, folder 25, indenture between the government of Nova Scotia and E.W. Plunkett, 6 September 1881.

29 Nova Scotia, Statutes, 44 Victoria, ch. 16.

30 NA, RG6, vol. 159, files 4983–4, P. Innes to undersecretary of state, 1 August 1881; vol. 160, file 532, Report of the Committee of the Privy Council approved 6 March 1882.

31 Nova Scotia, Statutes, 45 Victoria, ch. 20.

32 Canada, Statutes, 45 Victoria, ch. 16.

33 Holmes Papers, vol. 557, folder 24, Thompson to Holmes (no date), Thompson to Holmes, 1 November 1881.

34 Canada, Statutes, 47 Victoria, ch. 5.

35 NA, RG6, vol. 60, file 1181, report of the Committee of the Privy Council approved 15 January 1886.

36 Canada, Statutes, 50–51 Victoria, ch. 77.

37 NA, John Thompson Papers, vol. 56, Fielding to Thompson, 16 June 1887.

38 Holmes Papers, vol. 491, Fielding to Fraser, 2 May 1888.

39 The quotation is from a printed copy of the speech in the John A. Macdonald Papers, vol. 117.

40 This correspondence was printed by order of the Nova Scotia legislature and a copy may also be found in the Macdonald Papers, vol. 117.

41 NA, RG6, vol. 64, file 10981, Report of the Committee of the Privy Council approved 9 December 1885.

42 Ibid., vol. 60, file 1181, memorandum by J.M. Courtney, 21 December 1885; Report of the Committee of the Privy Council approved 17 February 1886.

43 NA, RG6, vol. 64, file 10981, lieutenant-governor of Nova Scotia to secretary of state, 22 April 1886, enclosing joint address of 21 April 1886.

44 NA, Marquess of Lansdowne Papers, microfilm reel A-625, Lansdowne to Macdonald, 25 June 1886; Macdonald to Lansdowne, 1 July 1886.

45 PANS, MG2, vol. 503, report to council by Fielding, 30 November 1888; Thompson Papers, vol. 98, Fielding to Thompson, 30 December 1889.

46 Holmes Papers, vol. 490, Fielding to A.S. Hardy, 19 August 1887.

47 Donald Creighton, *The Road to Confederation* (Toronto: Macmillan, 1964), maps on 261 and 387. Data on Acadian population by county based on Canada, Census, 1870–1, vol. 1, table 3.

48 NA, RG6, vol. 316, file 939.

49 Ibid., vol. 322, file 330, lieutenant-governor to secretary of state for the provinces, 13 July 1870; Beckwith to Howe, 12 July 1870; Langton to Meredith, 20 July 1870.

50 A printed copy of the resolutions is in the Macdonald Papers, vol. 301.

51 Canada, Statutes, 36 Victoria, ch. 41.

52 Peter M. Toner, "New Brunswick Schools and the Rise of Provincial Rights," in Bruce W. Hodgins et al., *Federalism in Canada and Australia: The Early Years* (Waterloo: Wilfrid Laurier University Press, 1978).

53 NA, RG6, vol. 157, file 1061, Report of the Committee of the Privy Council approved 22 January 1872.

54 Canada, House of Commons, *Journals*, 1872, 134, 153–5, 173–9.

55 NA, RG6, vol. 334, file 1252, lieutenant-governor to secretary of state for the provinces, 29 May 1872.

56 New Brunswick, Statutes, 36 Victoria, ch. 12.

57 House of Commons, *Journals*, 1873, 345–7.

58 Macdonald Papers, vol. 523, Macdonald to Dufferin, 10 July 1873; RG6, vol. 15, file 393, Anglin to Dorion, 31 March 1874.

59 House of Commons, *Journals*, 1874, 189, 268–9.

60 Ibid., 1875, 178–9, 197–203.

61 NA, Alexander Mackenzie Papers, microfilm reel M-197, Blake to Mackenzie, 12 March 1875; Marquess of Dufferin and Ava Papers, microfilm reel A-410, Mackenzie to Dufferin, 12 March 1875.

62 The text of Carnarvon's reply appears in Canada, House of Commons, *Journals*, 1876, 55–6.

63 NA, RG6, vol. 27, file 170; vol. 36, files 638, 758, 1693; vol. 41, file 3090.

64 Ibid., vol. 40, file 709, Report of the Committee of the Privy Council approved 18 February 1880.

65 Thompson Papers, vol. 102, Blair to Thompson, 25 February 1890; vol. 242, Thompson to Blair, 27 February 1890.

66 Macdonald Papers, vol. 328, Tilley to Macdonald, 15 February 1888.

67 Thompson Papers, vol. 102, Blair to Thompson, 25 February 1890; vol. 242, Thompson to Blair, 27 February 1890; vol. 103, Blair to Thompson, 10 March 1890.

68 NA, RG6, vol. 76, files 4412 and 4413; vol. 82, file 1059.

69 Canada, Department of Transport, *A Statutory History of the Steam and Electric Railways of Canada: 1836–1937* (Ottawa: King's Printer, 1938), 192.

70 NA, RG6, vol. 76, file 4414; vol. 83, file 3668.

71 Frank Mackinnon, *The Government of Prince Edward Island* (Toronto: University of Toronto Press, 1951), 139.

72 Ibid., 187.

73 NA, RG6, vol. 41, files 4021 and 4022, Donald Ferguson, commissioner of public lands to lieutenant-governor of PEI, 4 November 1880.

74 Ibid., vol. 17, file 712, Hodgson to secretary of state, 30 April 1874.

75 NA, RG7 G12, vol. 77, Dufferin to Carnarvon, 6 June 1874; Dufferin to Carnarvon, 31 December 1874.

76 Mackenzie Papers, microfilm reel M-197, Dufferin to Mackenzie, 19 November 1874.

77 NA, RG6, vol. 19, file 1255, memorandum by H. Bernard, 2 January 1875; Report of the Committee of the Privy Council approved 11 January 1875.

78 Prime Edward Island, Statutes, 38 Victoria, ch. 32.

79 Dufferin Papers, microfilm reel A-409, Dufferin to Mackenzie, 7 February 1875; NA, RG7 G12, vol. 77, Haly to Carnarvon, 6 September 1875.

80 Dufferin Papers, microfilm reel A-409, Dufferin to Mackenzie, 19 and 31 January, 2 February, and 11 April l876; reel A-410, Mackenzie to Dufferin, 19 June 1875, 2 February and 14 April 1876.
81 Prince Edward Island, Statutes, 39 Victoria, ch. 5.
82 Ibid., 58 Victoria, ch. 7.
83 Canada, Sessional Papers, vol. 15 (1882), no. 141A, 164–71.
84 Macdonald Papers, vol. 119, Sullivan to Macdonald, 29 April and 12 June 1879, 24 March and 14 December 1881.
85 Ibid., extract from minutes of the PEI Executive Council, 31 January 1883 (printed); clipping from Daily Examiner, 19 March l885.
86 Canada, House of Commons, Debates, 1891, 208.
87 Macdonald Papers, vol. 119, Sullivan to Macdonald, 19 March 1887.
88 Canada, Statutes, 50–51 Victoria, ch. 8; House of Commons, Debates, 1887, 814–15.

CHAPTER 6

1 Doug Owram, Promise of Eden: The Canadian Expansionist Movement and the Idea of the West, 1856–1900 (Toronto: University of Toronto Press, 1980).
2 The celebrated quotation is from a letter to the Marquess of Lorne. National Archives of Canada (NA), Marquess of Lorne Papers, vol. 1, Macdonald to Lorne, 11 July 1883.
3 W.L. Morton, Manitoba: A History (Toronto: University of Toronto Press, 1957), 145.
4 NA, John A. Macdonald Papers, vol. 517, Macdonald to Archibald, 1 November 1870.
5 Ibid., vol. 519, Macdonald to Archibald, 30 November 1871.
6 Ibid., Macdonald to Archibald, 12 July 1871; vol. 187, Archibald to Macdonald, 9 August 1871.
7 NA, RG6, vol. 333, file 1210, Archibald to secretary of state for the provinces, 14 April 1872; Report of Committee of the Privy Council approved 30 September 1872.
8 Ibid., vol. 337, file 131, Morris to secretary of state for the provinces, 15 March 1873; Morris to secretary of state, 29 November 1873.
9 Macdonald Papers, vol. 524, Macdonald to Norquay, 22 October 1881; vol. 378, Norquay to Macdonald, 4 November 1881.
10 Canada, Statutes, 33 Victoria, ch. 3.
11 NA, RG6, vol. 354, item 157, Howe to lieutenant-governor, 9 March 1872.
12 Ibid., vol. 158, file 740, memorandum from Manitoba delegates, 24 April 1873; Report of Committee of the Privy Council approved 17 September 1873.
13 Manitoba, Statutes, 37 Victoria, ch. 2.

14   NA, RG6, vol. 158, file 740, memorandum of Manitoba delegation, 3 March 1874; Report of Committee of the Privy Council, 11 March 1874.

15   Ibid., file 209, lieutenant-governor of Manitoba to secretary of state, 12 February 1876.

16   Canada, Statutes, 40 Victoria, ch. 6.

17   Ibid., 41 Victoria, ch. 13.

18   NA, Macdonald Papers, vol. 352, Norquay to Macdonald, 31 October 1878.

19   Canada, Statutes, 42 Victoria, ch. 2; Macdonald Papers, vol. 312, extract from a Report of Select Committee of the Privy Council, 8 April 1880.

20   Canada, Statutes, 44 Victoria, ch. 14.

21   NA, RG6, vol. 45, file 2979, Report of Committee of the Privy Council approved 25 April 1881.

22   Canada, Statutes, 45 Victoria, ch. 5.

23   NA, Alexander Campbell Papers, microfilm reel M-24, Macdonald to Campbell, 15 June 1883.

24   NA, RG6, vol. 53, file 3094, Report of Committee of the Executive Council of Manitoba, 5 May 1883; vol. 54, files 8215–17, memorandum from A. Larivière, 26 November 1883; Report of Subcommittee of Council, 27 November 1883; Report of Committee of the Privy Council approved 13 December 1883; Macdonald Papers, vol. 186, Aikins to Macdonald, 30 November 1883; vol. 119, Aikins to Macdonald, 29 February 1884.

25   NA, RG7 G12, vol. 82, Lansdowne to Derby, 28 April 1884; Macdonald Papers, vol. 525, Macdonald to Aikins, 6 June 1884.

26   Macdonald Papers, vol. 249, Macpherson to Macdonald, 20 June and 9 July 1884; Canada, Statutes, 48–49 Victoria, ch. 50.

27   Macdonald Papers, vol. 156, Norquay to Macdonald, 11 June 1886; NA, Mackenzie Bowell Papers, vol. 15, Norquay to Tupper, 2 April 1887; Report to Council by Tupper, 4 April 1887; Report to Council by Bowell, 14 February 1888; Patterson to Bowell, 15 February 1896.

28   Canada, Statutes, 44 Victoria, ch. 1, Schedule, clause 15.

29   Bowell Papers, vol. 15, Report of Committee of the Privy Council approved 18 April 1879.

30   Gerald V. Laforest, *Disallowance and Reservation of Provincial Legislation* (Ottawa: Queen's Printer, 1955), appendix A, 83–101.

31   Lorne Papers, vol. 1, Macdonald to Lorne, 2 December 1882.

32   Canada, Department of Transport, *A Statutory History of the Steam and Electric Railways of Canada: 1836–1937* (Ottawa: King's Printer, 1938), 273.

33   Macdonald Papers, vol. 525, Macdonald to Norquay, 3 March 1884.

34 Morton, *Manitoba*, 217, 222, 229–32.
35 Macdonald Papers, vol. 527, Macdonald to Aikins, 26 June 1887.
36 Ibid., vol. 131, Daly to Macdonald, 17 August 1887; Marquess of Lansdowne Papers, microfilm reel A-624, Lansdowne to Macdonald, 8 July 1887.
37 Macdonald Papers, vol. 284, Tupper to Macdonald, 23, 25, and 26 August 1887; Macdonald to Tupper, 24 August 1887.
38 NA, RG7 G12, vol. 85, Lansdowne to Holland, 18 February 1888; Lansdowne to Knutsford, 13 March 1888; RG2, series 1, vol. 388, Report of Committee of the Privy Council approved 10 March 1888.
39 Macdonald Papers, vol. 119, Greenway to Macdonald, 30 March 1888; Canada, Statutes, 51 Victoria, ch. 32.
40 Macdonald Papers, vol. 131, Schultz to Macdonald, 20 August 1888; vol. 264, Greenway to Macdonald, 18 October 1888; vol. 528, Macdonald to Greenway, 18 October 1888; Macdonald to Schultz, 20 October 1888.
41 Ibid., vol. 264, Schultz to Macdonald, 3 August and 9 December 1889; vol. 529, Macdonald to Schultz, 8 January 1890.
42 Manitoba, Statutes, 53 Victoria, chs. 14, 37, 38.
43 NA, RG6, vol. 77, file 828, Archbishop Taché to secretary of state, 23 March 1891.
44 NA, RG2, series 1, vol. 475, Two reports by the minister of justice, both dated 21 March 1891.
45 NA, John Thompson Papers, vol. 171, Chapleau to Thompson, 29 December 1892. Chapleau stated in this letter, which announced his resignation, that Macdonald had allowed him to convey assurances to "certain parties."
46 Ibid.
47 Ibid., vol. 172, Schultz to Thompson, 7 January 1893; vol. 173, Schultz to Thompson, 13 January 1893; vol. 259, Thompson to Schultz, 26 January 1893.
48 Ibid., vol. 197, Schultz to Thompson, 19 January 1894; vol. 199, Schultz to Thompson, 21 January 1894; vol. 200, Schultz to Thompson, 17 February 1894; vol. 201, Schultz to Thompson, 21 February 1894.
49 Brophy *vs* A.G. Manitoba [1895] A.C. 202.
50 Bowell Papers, vol. 77, Bowell to Schultz, 7 March 1895.
51 NA, RG6, vol. 88, file 1640, memorial from W. Kennedy, mayor of Toronto, 12 March 1895.
52 Bowell Papers, vol. 14, C.H. Tupper to Bowell, 21 March 1895.
53 NA, RG6, vol. 88, file 1675, lieutenant-governor to secretary of state, 25 June 1895; extract from Report of Committee of the Privy Council approved 27 July 1895; lieutenant-governor to secretary of state, 21 December 1895.

54 Canada, House of Commons, *Journals*, 1896, 138–9.

55 Macdonald Papers, vol. 196, Campbell to Macdonald, 28 August 1883.

56 Pierre Berton, *The National Dream: The Great Railway, 1871–1881* (Toronto: McClelland and Stewart, 1970), 188, 194, 212.

57 Canada, *Census*, 1881, vol. 2, table 14.

58 These episodes are discussed in John Saywell, *The Office of lieutenant-governor* (Toronto: University of Toronto Press, 1957), 130–43.

59 Richard J. Cartwright, *Reminiscences* (Toronto: William Briggs, 1912), 93–7.

60 Order of Her Majesty in Council admitting British Columbia into the Union, reprinted in Maurice Oliver, ed., *British North America Acts and Selected Statutes* (Ottawa: Queen's Printer, 1962), 174–80.

61 Harold A. Innis, *A History of the Canadian Pacific Railway* (Toronto: University of Toronto Press, 1971), 84.

62 NA, RG7 G1, vol. 182, Carnarvon to Dufferin, 18 June 1874; Marquess of Dufferin and Ava Papers, microfilm reel A-411, Mackenzie to Dufferin, 2 July 1874, reel A-409, Dufferin to Mackenzie, 9 July 1874, reel A-411, Mackenzie to Dufferin, 16 July 1874.

63 NA, RG7 G3, vol. 5, Carnarvon to Dufferin, 16 August 1874.

64 The revised Carnarvon terms are in RG7 G2, vol. 11, Carnarvon to Dufferin, 17 November 1874. Mackenzie's response is in the Dufferin Papers, reel A-411, Mackenzie to Dufferin, 17 December 1874.

65 NA, RG7 G12, vol. 77, Dufferin to Carnarvon, 9 March 1876. In the same dispatch Dufferin explained to Carnarvon that "a clerk's oversight" had delayed the dominion government's offer by two months.

66 Ibid., G2, vol. 12, Report of Committee of the Privy Council approved 13 March 1876; Canada, House of Commons, *Journals*, 1876, 285.

67 *Address of His Excellency the Governor-General of Canada on the Subject of the Relations between the Dominion Government and British Columbia in Respect to the Canadian Pacific Railway* (Victoria: Government Printer, 1876), 27.

68 NA, Alexander Mackenzie Papers, microfilm reel M-198, Richards to Mackenzie, 30 September 1876; Dufferin Papers, microfilm reel A-409, Dufferin to Mackenzie, 9 October 1876.

69 Dufferin Papers, microfilm reel A-407, Dufferin to Hicks-Beach, 21 March 1878.

70 A printed copy is filed in the Macdonald Papers, vol. 305.

71 Ibid., vol. 79, Macdonald to Northcote, 1 May 1878.

72 Ibid., vol. 294, Walkem to Macdonald, 18 March 1879, 3 and 5 May 1879.

73 Ibid., Macdonald to Walkem, 25 October 1880, Walkem to Macdonald, 12 November 1880.

74 Campbell Papers, microfilm reel M-23, Macdonald to Campbell, 18 April 1881; Macdonald Papers, vol. 524, Macdonald to Walkem, 13 May 1881.

75 Macdonald Papers, vol. 524, Macdonald to Walkem, 3 February 1882; vol. 37, Walkem to Macdonald, 30 April 1882.

76 Ibid., vol. 525, Macdonald to Trutch, 3 May 1883, Macdonald to Cornwall, 11 June 1883; vol. 37, Campbell to Macdonald, 6 August 1883; vol. 196, Campbell to Macdonald, 28 August 1883.

77 NA, RG6, vol. 53, files 2457 and 3013–14; Macdonald Papers, vol. 83, Lorne to Macdonald, 5 May 1883; vol. 37, Campbell to Macdonald, 6 August 1883; Campbell Papers, microfilm reel M-24, Stephen to Campbell, 20 September 1883.

78 British Columbia, Statutes, 37 Victoria, ch. 1.

79 RG6, vol. 213, unnumbered file: "Drydock at Esquimalt, 1873–75"; Mackenzie to de Cosmos, 14 November 1873.

80 Ibid., Admiralty to Colonial Office, 17 January 1874.

81 Canada, Statutes, 37 Victoria, ch. 17.

82 NA, RG6, vol. 213, unnumbered file: "Drydock at Esquimalt, 1873–75"; Walkem to secretary of the Admiralty, 25 November 1874; Admiralty to Colonial Office, 17 January 1874; Carnarvon to provincial secretary of British Columbia, 29 April 1874.

83 Ibid., Trutch to secretary of state, 28 April 1875; Report of Committee of the Privy Council, 20 May 1875; Report of Committee of the British Columbia Executive Council, 22 June 1875.

84 Ibid., vol. 17, file 805, Report of Committee of the British Columbia Executive Council, 13 April 1876; Scott to Trutch, 5 May 1876; Trutch to Scott, 16 May 1876; Scott to Trutch, 18 May 1876; Report of Committee of the British Columbia Executive Council, 22 July 1876.

85 Ibid., Report of Committee of the British Columbia Executive Council (printed), 11 June 1877; Report of Committee of the Privy Council, 27 August 1877; Dufferin Papers, microfilm reel A-411, Mackenzie to Dufferin, 2 November 1877; Mackenzie Papers, microfilm reel M-199, Dufferin to Mackenzie, 5 November 1877.

86 Dufferin Papers, microfilm reel A-407, Dufferin to Hicks-Beach, 2 April, 23 May, 6 June, 28 August, and 4 September 1878.

87 Ibid., Dufferin to Hicks-Beach, 12 October 1878; reel A-409, Dufferin to Macdonald, 12 October 1878.

88 Macdonald Papers, vol. 294, Macdonald to Walkem, 13 November 1879; Walkem to Macdonald, 4 December 1879.

89 NA, RG6, vol. 17, file 805, memorandum by Tilley, 11 February 1880; Canada, Statutes, 43 Victoria, ch. 15.

90 Lorne Papers, vol. 1, Macdonald to Lorne, 2 December 1882; Canada, Statutes, 47 Victoria, ch. 6; Lansdowne Papers, microfilm reel A-623, letterbook, vol. 2, Lansdowne to Macdonald, 30 January 1885; reel A-626, Canadian correspondence, Langevin to Lansdowne, 9 December 1885.

91 British Columbia, Statutes, 43 Victoria, ch. 11.

92 Macdonald Papers, vol. 525, Macdonald to Campbell, 28 July 1883; vol. 196, Campbell to Macdonald, 30 October 1883.

93 Canada, Statutes, 47 Victoria, ch. 6; Macdonald Papers, vol. 38, Cornwall to Macdonald, 11 June 1884.

94 NA, RG6, vol. 59, file 5522, memorandum by Macpherson, 8 April 1885; memorandum by Campbell, 6 June 1885; Report of the Committee of the Privy Council, 1 December 1885. The disallowed statute was 48 Victoria, ch. 9, an act to amend the Sumas Diking Act of 1878.

95 Macdonald Papers, vol. 325, White to Macdonald, 3, 15, and 16 August 1887.

96 NA, RG6, vol. 71, file 3063, memorandum from the Department of the Interior, 16 December 1888; Report of Committee of the Privy Council, 16 December 1888; Report of Committee of the Privy Council, 17 August 1889.

97 A.G. British Columbia vs A.G. Canada [1889] A.C. 295.

98 NA, RG6, vol. 77, file 242, lieutenant-governor of British Columbia to secretary of state, 11 October 1889; Report of Committee of the Privy Council, 11 February 1890; Report of Committee of the Privy Council, 28 February 1890; Report of Committee of the British Columbia Executive Council, 13 March 1890.

99 Thompson Papers, vol. 165, Theodore Davie to Thompson, 28 and 29 October 1892; NA, RG6, vol. 88, file 2567, extract from a Report of Committee of the Privy Council, 29 March 1895; Canada, Statutes, 58–59 Victoria, ch. 4.

100 Dufferin to Carnarvon, 8 October 1876, in C.W. de Kiewiet and F.H. Underhill, eds., *The Dufferin-Carnarvon Correspondence, 1874–1878* (Toronto: Champlain Society, 1955), 264

101 NA, RG6, vol. 20, file 1456; vol. 15, file 350, Report of Committee of the Privy Council, 16 March 1875.

102 *Address of His Excellency the Governor-General of Canada*, 29.

103 NA, RG6, vol. 20, file 1456; RG2, series 1, vol. 138, Report of Committee of the Privy Council, 23 February 1877.

104 NA, RG6, vol. 56, files 960–1, lieutenant-governor of British Columbia to secretary of state, 31 January 1884; Report of Committee of the Privy Council approved 30 May 1884.

105 Ibid., vol. 75, file 1479; vol. 82, file 1196; vol. 88, file 1637.

106 Ibid., vol. 36, file 837, Hicks-Beach to Lorne, 29 November 1878.

107 Macdonald Papers, vol. 294, Macdonald to Walkem, 13 November 1879; vol. 321, Onderdonk to Macdonald, 14 June 1882.
108 NA, RG6, vol. 53, files 1740–1; Macdonald Papers, vol. 38, Smithe to Macdonald, 7 March 1884.
109 British Columbia, Statutes, 47 Victoria, ch. 3 and 4; NA, RG6, vol. 66, file 23759, Colonial Office to governor general, 5 August 1886; vol. 160, files 2458–9, Report of Committee of the Privy Council, 8 April 1884; Macdonald Papers, vol. 38, Macdonald to Smithe, 10 April 1884.
110 British Columbia, Statutes, 48 Victoria, ch. 13; NA, RG6, vol. 160, Report by Minister of Justice, 26 March 1885; Report of Committee of the Privy Council, 27 March 1885; RG7 G12, vol. 82, Lansdowne to Derby, 31 March 1885.
111 Canada, Statutes, 48–49 Victoria, ch. 71.
112 NA, RG6, vol. 60, file 2235, Report of Committee of the Executive Council of British Columbia, 21 November 1885; Report of Committee of the Privy Council, 19 February 1886.
113 Ibid., vol. 77, file 698, Report of Committee of the Executive Council of British Columbia, 3 March 1891.
114 Canada, Statutes, 55–56 Victoria, ch. 25.
115 NA, RG6, vol. 79, file 1313; vol. 82, file 1527.
116 Ibid., vol. 83, file 4905; vol. 88, file 1634.

CHAPTER 7

1 S.J.R. Noel, *Patrons, Clients, Brokers: Ontario Society and Politics, 1791–1896* (Toronto: University of Toronto Press, 1990).
2 J.A. Maxwell, "Better Terms," *Queen's Quarterly* 40 (1933): 125–39.
3 Data from Andrée Lajoie, *Le pouvoir déclaratoire du Parlement* (Montréal: Les Presses de l'Université de Montréal, 1969), 123–51.
4 National Archives of Canada (NA), Marquess of Dufferin and Ava Papers, microfilm reel A-410, Mackenzie to Dufferin 27 July 1874.
5 NA, John A. Macdonald Papers, vol. 87, Lansdowne to Macdonald, 19 November 1887.
6 Donald V. Smiley, *The Federal Condition in Canada* (Toronto: McGraw-Hill Ryerson, 1987), 103–4.
7 R. MacGregor Dawson, *The Government of Canada*, 4th edition (Toronto: University of Toronto Press, 1963), 528.
8 Macdonald Papers, vol. 294, Walkem to Macdonald, 24 April 1879; vol. 255, Pope to Macdonald, 26 April 1880; vol. 119, Norquay to Macdonald, 8 January 1884.
9 Ibid., vol. 121, Bell to Macdonald, 26 October 1883.
10 Ibid., vol. 151, Meredith to Macdonald, 14 February 1885.

11 Ibid., vol. 327, Hespeler to Macdonald, 28 February 1888; vol. 328, Harrison to Macdonald, 17 January 1888; vol. 457, Harrison to White, 16 April 1888.

12 NA, Charles Tupper Papers, vol. 9, Tupper to C.H. Tupper, 18 January 1890.

13 Macdonald Papers, vol. 285, Tupper to Macdonald, 13 August 1890.

14 NA, RG6, vol. 309, file 229, Vail to Archibald, 28 January 1868.

15 Ibid., vol. 329, file 892.

16 NA, Pierre-Joseph-Olivier Chauveau Papers, vol. 1, Chauveau to Connell, 3 December 1870.

17 NA, Henri-Gustave Joly de Lotbinière Papers, microfilm reel M-790, Mowat to Joly, 8 October 1878.

18 NA, John Thompson Papers, vol. 17, Mowat to Thompson, 5 and 26 November 1880.

19 Public Archives of Nova Scotia (PANS), Fielding Papers, vol. 503, Mowat to Fielding, 10 October 1884 and 20 February 1885.

20 Ibid., vol. 503, Mowat to Fielding, 22 June 1887, Hardy to Fielding, 16 August 1887; vol. 490, Fielding to Hardy, 30 June and 19 August 1887.

21 Macdonald Papers, vol. 38, Davie to Macdonald, 30 September 1887.

22 Fielding Papers, vol. 503, Blair to Fielding, 25 January 1888, Mowat to Fielding, 8 and 23 March, 10 April 1888; vol. 490, Fielding to Blair, 19 January and 21 March 1888; vol. 491, Fielding to Mowat, 21 April 1888; vol. 503, Mowat to Fielding, 20 January 1890.

23 K.C. Wheare, *Federal Government*, 4th edition (New York: Oxford University Press, 1964), 18–19.

24 Direct evidence of most of these visits may be found in the Macdonald or Mackenzie Papers, depending on who was prime minister at the time. Macdonald mentioned the Mowat visit in a letter to the governor general on the day it occurred: NA, Lord Stanley of Preston Papers, microfilm reel A-446, Macdonald to Stanley, 5 April 1889.

25 Macdonald Papers, vol. 196, Campbell to Macdonald, 28 August 1883.

26 C.W. de Kiewiet and F.H. Underhill, eds., *The Dufferin-Carnarvon Correspondence, 1874–1878* (Toronto: Champlain Society, 1955), 252.

27 Maurice Pope, ed., *Public Servant: The Memoirs of Sir Joseph Pope* (Toronto: Oxford University Press, 1960), 52–61.

28 Desmond Morton, "Aid to the Civil Power: The Canadian Militia in Support of Social Order, 1867–1914," *Canadian Historical Review* 51 (1970): 407–25.

29 W.L. Morton, *The Critical Years: The Union of British North America, 1857–1873* (Toronto: McClelland and Stewart, 1964), 239.

30 NA, RG6, vol. 307, file 8, 19 July 1867.

31 Ibid., vol. 311, file 467, return prepared for a commission of inquiry into the public service, no date.

32 David M.L. Farr, *The Colonial Office and Canada, 1867–1887* (Toronto: University of Toronto Press, 1955), 34.

33 Macdonald Papers, vol. 187, Archibald to Macdonald, 20 September 1867 and 14 March 1868.

34 Ibid., vol. 299, Meredith to Macdonald, 26 March 1868.

35 NA, RG6, vol. 311, file 467, return prepared for a commission of inquiry into the public service, no date.

36 All information regarding changes in the ministry is taken from Canada, Privy Council Office, *Guide to Canadian Ministries since Confederation, July 1, 1867–February 1, 1982* (Ottawa, 1982).

37 NA, RG6, vol. 307, file 8, 20 November 1869.

38 Ibid., file 8, Macdonald to Meredith, 28 December 1869.

39 Ibid., vol. 331, file 1054, Report of the Committee of the Privy Council approved 16 January 1872.

40 Canada, Senate, *Journals*, 1870, 76, 81, 86, and Canada, House of Commons, *Journals*, 1870, 137, 188–9.

41 Canada, Statutes, 36 Victoria, ch. 4.

42 Macdonald Papers, vol. 194, Campbell to Macdonald, 27 July 1873.

43 Sir Joseph Pope, ed., *Correspondence of Sir John Macdonald* (Toronto: Oxford University Press, 1921), 44, note.

44 Peter B. Waite, *The Man from Halifax: Sir John Thompson, Prime Minister* (Toronto: University of Toronto Press, 1985).

45 R.B. Bryce, *Maturing in Hard Times: Canada's Department of Finance through the Great Depression* (Montreal: McGill-Queen's University Press, 1986), 1–15.

46 Quoted in O.D. Skelton, *Life and Letters of Sir Wilfrid Laurier*, vol. 1 (Toronto: Oxford University Press, 1921), 417.

47 Maxwell, "Better Terms," 136.

48 Macdonald Papers, vol. 116, Wilkins to Macdonald, 18 April 1870.

49 Ibid., vol. 517, Macdonald to Doyle, 22 February 1870.

50 NA, Mackenzie Bowell Papers, vol. 77, Bowell to Tilley, 26 February 1895.

51 Macdonald Papers, vol. 521, Macdonald to Walkem, 4 October 1872.

52 Macdonald Papers, vol. 519, Macdonald to Archibald, 30 November 1871; vol. 522, Macdonald to Clarke, 29 October 1872.

53 A.V. Dicey, *Introduction to the Study of the Law of the Constitution*, 10th edition (London: Macmillan, 1961), 166.

CHAPTER 8

1 John T. Saywell, *The Office of Lieutenant-Governor* (Toronto: University Press, 1957), 3.

2 Joseph Pope, ed., *Confederation: Being a Series of Hitherto Unpublished Doc-*

uments Bearing on the British North America Act (Toronto: Carswell, 1895), 78.

3 Canada, Legislature, *Parliamentary Debates on the Subject of the Confederation of the British North American Provinces* (Quebec, 1865), 255–6, 361, 502, 504–5.

4 National Archives of Canada (NA), John Abbott Papers, vol. 4, Davie to Thompson, 15 July 1892; Davie to Abbott, 11 August 1892.

5 NA, Alexander Mackenzie Papers, microfilm reel M-198, Joly to Mackenzie, 6 December 1876.

6 NA, John A. Macdonald Papers, vol. 525, Macdonald to Masson, 21 December 1883, 3 January 1884.

7 Ibid., vol. 526, Macdonald to Wilmot, 26 October 1885.

8 Ibid., vol. 528, Macdonald to McLelan, 14 June 1888.

9 NA, A.-R. Angers Papers, vol. 1, Angers to Macdonald, 22 December 1890; Angers to Abbott, 2 January 1892.

10 NA, RG6, vol. 307, file 8, Crawford to Scott, 18 May 1874.

11 Ibid., Report of Committee of the Privy Council approved 14 May 1875.

12 Ibid., Report of Committee of the Privy Council approved 16 February 1880.

13 Ibid., vol. 318, file 51, Doyle to Young, 4 January 1870.

14 Macdonald Papers, vol. 515, Macdonald to Doyle, 16 June 1869.

15 H. Moody, "Political Experiences in Nova Scotia, 1867–1869," *Dalhousie Review* 14 (1934–5): 65–76.

16 Macdonald Papers, vol. 520, Macdonald to Doyle, 11 June 1872.

17 NA, Joseph Howe Papers, vol. 4, Doyle to Howe, 1 October 1867.

18 Public Archives of Nova Scotia (PANS), RG2, vol. 6, Doyle to Wilkins, 4 September 1868; Wilkins to Doyle, 5 September 1868.

19 Ibid., Doyle to Macdonald, 16 September 1868; Macdonald to Doyle, 17 September 1868; note by Doyle, 18 September 1868; memoranda by Wilkins, 18 and 19 September 1868; Doyle to secretary of state for the provinces, 22 September 1868.

20 Macdonald Papers, vol. 114, Doyle to Macdonald, 30 October 1868.

21 Ibid., vol. 515, Macdonald to Doyle, 16 June 1869; vol. 114, Doyle to Macdonald, 25 June 1869.

22 Ibid., vol. 516, Macdonald to Doyle, 28 September 1869; vol. 114, Doyle to Macdonald, 26 October 1869.

23 Ibid., vol. 516, Macdonald to Doyle, 10 November 1869; vol. 114, Doyle to Macdonald, 23 November 1869.

24 Ibid., vol. 114, Doyle to Macdonald, 29 January 1870.

25 Ibid., vol. 520, Macdonald to Doyle, 11 June 1872.

26 Saywell, *The Office of Lieutenant-Governor*, 61.

27 Macdonald Papers, vol. 517, Macdonald to Archibald, 1 November 1870.

28 Ibid., vol. 187, Archibald to Macdonald, 16 January 1871; vol. 518, Macdonald to Archibald, 25 January 1871.

29 Howe Papers, vol. 9, Howe to Archibald, 4 November 1871.

30 NA, RG2, series 1, vol. 59, Archibald to Lisgar, 25 November 1871; Macdonald Papers, vol. 187, Archibald to Macdonald, 31 December 1871.

31 NA, RG2, series 1, vol. 59, memorandum by Tupper, 9 April 1872; RG6, vol. 333, file 1183, House of Commons resolution, 16 April 1872.

32 Macdonald Papers, vol. 522, Macdonald to Morris, 8 November 1872.

33 Ibid., Macdonald to Morris, 9 December 1872.

34 Saywell, *The Office of Lieutenant-Governor*, 80.

35 Macdonald Papers, vol. 520, Macdonald to Trutch, 16 January and 16 April 1872.

36 Macdonald Papers, vol. 278, Trutch to Macdonald, 25 November 1872; vol. 522, Macdonald to Trutch, 4 January 1873.

37 See note 40, and for another reference to Bagehot in connection with a lieutenant-governor's powers, see NA, Alexander Campbell Papers, Macdonald to Campbell, 3 February 1888. For Macdonald's view that lieutenant-governors lacked prerogative powers see his memorandum on marriage licences in W.E. Hodgins, ed., *Correspondence, Reports of the Ministers of Justice and Orders in Council upon the Subject of Dominion and Provincial Legislation 1867–1895* (Ottawa: Government Printing Bureau, 1896), 655.

38 Macdonald Papers, vol. 525, Macdonald to Robinson, 18 August 1883.

39 Ibid., Macdonald to lieutenant-governors of Ontario, Quebec, Nova Scotia, and New Brunswick, 27 February 1884.

40 Ibid., vol. 526, Macdonald to Richey, 29 July and 18 August 1884.

41 Ibid., Macdonald to Richey, 14 May 1886.

42 Ibid., Macdonald to Richey, 3 June 1886.

43 Ibid., vol. 117, Richey to Macdonald, 17 June 1886.

44 Ibid., vol. 273, Thompson to Macdonald, 3 July 1886.

45 Ibid., vol. 527, Macdonald to Masson, 8 December 1886.

46 Ibid., Macdonald to Masson, 24 May 1887.

47 Ibid., Macdonald to Aikins, 15 September and 23 November 1887.

48 Ibid., vol. 119, Aikins to Macdonald, 30 May 1884.

49 Ibid., vol. 38, Cornwall to Macdonald, 11 June 1884.

50 Ibid., vol. 229, Masson to Macdonald, 7 April 1885.

51 Ibid., vol. 108, Masson to Macdonald, 13 November 1885.

52 Ibid., vol. 328, Tilley to Macdonald, 15 February 1888.

53 Angers Papers, vol. 1, Angers to Macdonald, 6 December 1889.

54 Macdonald Papers, vol. 335, Carvell to Macdonald, 22 March 1890.

55 NA, John Thompson Papers, vol. 259, Thompson to Schultz, 26 January 1893.

56 NA, Mackenzie Bowell Papers, vol. 15, Patterson to Bowell, 15 February 1896.

57 Macdonald Papers, vol. 299, undated draft by Macdonald.

58 Hodgins, *Dominion and Provincial Legislation*, 655.

59 NA, RG6, vol. 337, file 122, memorandum by Macdonald, 26 August 1873.

60 Ibid., vol. 38, file 1159, report by the deputy minister of justice, 14 June 1879.

61 Canada, *Sessional Papers*, vol. 10 (1877), no. 89, 64–8.

62 NA, RG2, series 1, vol. 241, memorandum to council by Macdonald, 28 November 1882. See also Macdonald Papers, vol. 196, Campbell to Macdonald, 25 and 27 November 1882.

63 A printed copy of the instructions is in the Macdonald Papers, vol. 322. See also NA, RG2, series 1, vol. 375, minute of council approved 8 October 1887.

64 Hodgins, *Dominion and Provincial Legislation*, 195.

65 Thompson Papers, vol. 255, Thompson to Carvell, 13 May 1892.

CHAPTER 9

1 J.R. Mallory, *Social Credit and the Federal Power in Canada* (Toronto: University of Toronto Press, 1954), 8–24.

2 Jean Yarbrough, "Madison and Modern Federalism," in Robert A. Goldwin and William A. Schambra, eds., *How Federal Is the Constitution?* (Washington: American Enterprise Institute, 1987), 84–108.

3 C.R.W. Biggar, *Sir Oliver Mowat*, vol. 1 (Toronto: Warwick Bros and Rutter, 1905), 132–3.

4 Joseph Pope, ed., *Confederation: Being a Series of Hitherto Unpublished Documents Bearing on the British North American Act* (Toronto: Carswell, 1895), 31.

5 David M.L. Farr, *The Colonial Office and Canada, 1867–1887* (Toronto: University of Toronto Press, 1955), 107–32.

6 Canada, *Sessional Papers*, vol. 3 (1870), no. 5, 4–5.

7 Original in National Archives of Canada (NA), RG6, vol. 310, file 455. Printed in Canada, *Sessional Papers*, vol. 2 (1869), no. 18.

8 P.B. Waite, *The Man from Halifax: Sir John Thompson, Prime Minister* (Toronto: University of Toronto Press, 1985), 229–44.

9 NA, John A. Macdonald Papers, vol. 528, Macdonald to Angers, 18, 22, and 27 September, and 4 October 1888.

10 Mallory, *Social Credit*, 13.

11 One student of comparative federalism has suggested that virtually every statute disallowed in Canada would have been declared unconstitutional by the courts if adopted in an American state. William

Bennett Munro, *American Influences on Canadian Government*
(Toronto: Macmillan, 1929), 37.

12 Manitoba, Statutes, 50 Victoria, ch. 28, disallowed by PC 1563, 18 July
1887.

13 Waite, *The Man from Halifax*, 189, notes Thompson's absence from Ottawa. Macdonald's report is printed in W.E. Hodgins, *Correspondence, Reports of the Ministers of Justice and Orders in Council upon the Subject of Dominion and Provincial Legislation 1867–1895* (Ottawa: Government Printing Bureau, 1896), 856–7.

14 Ontario, Statutes, 47 Victoria, ch. 35, disallowed by PC 953, 30 April
1884.

15 Hodgins, *Dominion and Provincial Legislation*, 804; Manitoba, Statutes,
38 Victoria, ch. 37, disallowed by PC 953, 7 October 1876.

16 Nova Scotia, Statutes, 31 Victoria, ch. 21, disallowed by PC 629, 20 August 1869.

17 NA, RG6, vol. 313, file 687.

18 Macdonald Papers, vol. 116, Wilkins to Macdonald, 5 October 1869;
Wilkins to Macdonald, 14 January 1870.

19 Ontario, Statutes, 32 Victoria, ch. 1, disallowed by PC 1081, 20 January
1870; Macdonald Papers, vol. 516, John A. Macdonald to Sandfield
Macdonald, 18 November 1869; vol. 230, Sandfield Macdonald to John
A. Macdonald, 22 December 1869.

20 Macdonald Papers, vol. 278, Trutch to Macdonald, 21 November 1871;
vol. 522, Macdonald to Trutch, 28 January 1873.

21 Ibid., vol. 520, Macdonald to Blake, 22 February 1872; vol. 188, Blake
to Macdonald, 4 March 1872.

22 NA, RG6, vol. 15, file 408; vol. 20, file 1541; vol. 19, file 1255.

23 Macdonald Papers, vol. 522, Macdonald to Trutch, 28 January 1873.

24 British Columbia, Statutes, 37 Victoria, ch. 9, disallowed by PC 233,
16 March 1875; NA, RG6, vol. 15, file 350, Pemberton to minister
of justice, 23 April 1874.

25 British Columbia Statutes, 38 Victoria, ch. 6, disallowed by PC 436,
5 May 1876; 40 Victoria, ch. 22, disallowed by PC 425, 16 May 1878.

26 NA, RG6, vol. 36, file 786; vol. 38, file 1169.

27 British Columbia, Statutes, 45 Victoria, ch. 8, disallowed by PC 1106,
12 May 1883.

28 British Columbia, Statutes, 50 Victoria, ch. 7, disallowed by PC 842,
19 April 1888.

29 Macdonald Papers, vol. 275, Thompson to Macdonald, 16 July 1889.

30 Manitoba, Statutes, 38 Victoria, ch. 12, disallowed by PC 756, 16 August
1876.

31 Ontario, Statutes, 42 Victoria, ch. 19, disallowed by PC 169, 12 February
1880.

32 NA, Alexander Campbell Papers, microfilm reel M-24, Macdonald to Campbell, 12 December 1882.

33 NA, John Thompson Papers, vol. 84, Schultz to Thompson, 1 April 1889.

34 Quebec, Statutes, 51–52 Victoria, ch. 20, disallowed by PC 1993, 7 September 1888; 52 Victoria, ch. 30, disallowed by PC 1508, 1 July 1889.

35 The preamble to the 1889 act mentioned this fact, and Macdonald had privately admitted it the year before. Macdonald Papers, vol. 528, Macdonald to Thompson, 21 July 1888.

36 Macdonald Papers, vol. 524, Macdonald to Chapleau, 20 April 1881.

37 NA, RG6, vol. 72, file 2258, Report of Committee of the Privy Council approved 13 November 1890.

38 Quebec, Statutes, 32 Victoria, ch. 4, disallowed by PC 891, 26 November 1869; Ontario, Statutes, 32 Victoria, ch. 3, disallowed by PC 892, 26 November 1869.

39 NA, Edward Blake Papers, microfilm reel M-242, Mowat to Blake, 7 December 1875; reel M-251, Blake to Mowat, 8 December 1875.

40 Manitoba, Statutes, 36 Victoria, ch. 2, disallowed by PC 1106, 7 September 1874; NA, RG6, vol. 158, file 1254.

41 Manitoba, Statutes, 48 Victoria, ch. 2, disallowed by PC 56, 13 January 1887; Quebec, Statutes, 49–50 Victoria, ch. 98, disallowed by PC 1583, 19 July 1887; Hodgins, *Dominion and Provincial Legislation*, 851, 313, 338.

42 Nova Scotia, Statutes, 34 Victoria, ch. 32, disallowed by PC 1631, 16 December 1871; Hodgins, *Dominion and Provincial Legislation*, 476.

43 Nova Scotia, Statutes, 37 Victoria, ch. 74, 82, 83, disallowed by PC 1492 and 1493, 12 December 1874, and PC 294, 31 March 1875; Hodgins, *Dominion and Provincial Legislation*, 479, 480, 488.

44 Quebec, Statutes, 38 Victoria, ch. 47, disallowed by PC 990, 25 October 1876; Manitoba, Statutes, 38 Victoria (1875), ch. 33, disallowed by PC 953, 7 October 1876.

45 New Brunswick, Statutes, 45 Victoria, ch. 69, disallowed by PC 1683, 24 July 1883.

46 British Columbia, Statutes, 40 Victoria, ch. 32, disallowed by PC 425, 16 May 1878.

47 Hodgins, *Dominion and Provincial Legislation*, 1045, 1057.

48 British Columbia, Statutes, 41–42 Victoria, ch. 37; 43 Victoria (1880), ch. 28 and 29, disallowed by PC 1362, 2 October 1879, and PC 1130, 29 July 1881. Hodgins, *Dominion and Provincial Legislation*, 1068, 1078; NA, RG6, vol. 41, files 3843–5, Walkem to Campbell, 10 August 1881.

49 Nova Scotia, Statutes, 49 Victoria, ch. 56, disallowed by PC 675, 11 April 1887.
50 Manitoba, Statutes, 45 Victoria, ch. 30; 50 Victoria, ch. 47 and 28, disallowed by PC 2151, 3 November 1882, PC 1413, 6 July 1887, and PC 1563, 18 July 1887; Hodgins, *Dominion and Provincial Legislation*, 828, 855–7.
51 Manitoba, Statutes, 36 Victoria, ch. 32, disallowed by PC 1107, 7 September 1874.
52 NA, RG 6, vol. 19, file 1253, Morris to secretary of state, 10 October 1874; memorandum by H. Bernard, 3 November 1874.
53 British Columbia, Statutes, 40 Victoria, ch. 33, disallowed by PC 425, 16 May 1878.
54 Manitoba, Statutes, 53 Victoria, ch. 23, disallowed by PC 605, 4 April 1891; 58 Victoria, ch. 4, disallowed by PC 1047, 25 March 1896; 60 Victoria, ch. 2, disallowed by PC 796, 2 April 1898.
55 British Columbia, Statutes, 37 Victoria, ch. 2, disallowed by PC 246, 16 March 1875.
56 Manitoba, Statutes, 38 Victoria, ch. 12, disallowed by PC 468D, 6 June 1876.
57 British Columbia, Statutes, 41–42 Victoria, ch. 25, disallowed by PC 1189, 22 August 1879.
58 Manitoba, Statutes, 47 Victoria, ch. 26, disallowed by PC 1601, 27 August 1885.
59 British Columbia, Statutes, 41 Victoria, ch. 6; 46 Victoria, ch. 10.
60 Macdonald Papers, vol. 321, Davie to Campbell, 14 June 1883.
61 British Columbia, Statutes, 48 Victoria, ch. 9, disallowed by PC 479, 16 March 1886.
62 Ibid., ch. 16, disallowed by PC 481, 16 March 1886.
63 NA, RG6, vol. 315, files 889–90.
64 Ibid., vol. 11, file 591.
65 Ibid., vol. 336, file 19.
66 Macdonald Papers, vol. 258, Rose to Macdonald, 2 April 1873.
67 Ontario, Statutes, 44 Victoria, ch. 57; Macdonald Papers, vol. 524, Macdonald to Campbell, 27 February 1882.
68 The "bribery plot" is described in S.J.R. Noel, *Patrons, Clients, Brokers: Ontario Society and Politics, 1791–1896* (Toronto: University of Toronto Press, 1990), 269–74.
69 Campbell Papers, Macdonald to Campbell, nd; Plumb to Macdonald, 18 June 1884; Cameron to Macdonald, 26 June 1884; Campbell to Macdonald, 12 July 1884.
70 Macdonald Papers, vol. 275, Thompson to Macdonald, 11 July 1889; Hodgins, *Dominion and Provincial Legislation*, 887–9.

71 Macdonald Papers, vol. 471, Clark to Macdonald, 16 and 19 March 1889.

72 NA, RG6, vol. 324, file 458; vol. 23, file 1281.

73 Ibid., vol. 27, file 77.

74 Manitoba, Statutes, 52 Victoria, ch. 45, disallowed by PC 664, 8 March 1890; Macdonald Papers, vol. 275, Hugh John Macdonald to John A. Macdonald, 21 August 1889; Thompson to John A. Macdonald, 12 September 1889.

CHAPTER 10

1 Douglas V. Verney, *Three Civilizations, Two Cultures, One State: Canada's Political Traditions* (Durham: Duke University Press, 1986), 146–8, 159–62, 301–10.

2 D.G. Creighton, "Canada in the English-speaking World," *Canadian Historical Review* 26 (1945): 123.

3 Data from Sir Ivor Jennings, *Cabinet Government*, 3rd edition (Cambridge: Cambridge University Press, 1969), 516–22.

4 George Earle Buckle, *The Life of Benjamin Disraeli*, vol. 6 (London: John Murray, 1920), 477.

5 David M.L. Farr, *The Colonial Office and Canada, 1867–1887* (Toronto: University of Toronto Press, 1955), 31.

6 C.W. de Kiewiet and F.H. Underhill, eds., *The Dufferin-Carnarvon Correspondence: 1874–1878* (Toronto: The Champlain Society, 1955).

7 Farr, *The Colonial Office and Canada*, 55–6.

8 Carman Miller, "Lisgar," in *The Canadian Encyclopedia*, 1st edition (Edmonton: Hurtig, 1985), 1011.

9 Data from *Who's Who*, 1897 edition (London: Adam and Charles Black, 1897).

10 Canada, House of Commons, *Journals*, 1867–8, 278, 341, 431.

11 W. E. Hodgins, *Correspondence, Reports of the Ministers of Justice, and Orders in Council upon the Subject of Dominion and Provincial Legislation 1867–1895* (Ottawa: Government Printing Bureau, 1896), 6–60.

12 National Archives of Canada (NA), John A. Macdonald Papers, vol. 89, Stanley to Macdonald, 21 January 1889.

13 Ibid., vol. 519, Macdonald to Trutch, 3 October 1871.

14 NA, RG2, series 1, vol. 139, minute of council approved 28 March 1877.

15 NA, RG7 G12, vol. 73, Monck to Buckingham, 21 February 1868.

16 NA, Joseph Howe Papers, vol. 9, Howe to Macdonald, 19 October 1868.

17 NA, RG6, vol. 309, file 268, Buckingham to Monck, 4 June 1868; vol. 312, file 643, Buckingham to Monck, 8 December 1868.

18 Donald Creighton, *John A. Macdonald: The Old Chieftain* (Toronto: Macmillan, 1955), 28.
19 NA, RG6, vol. 6, file 231, Granville to Young, 13 January 1869.
20 NA, RG7 G3, vol. 3, Granville to Young, 29 March 1869.
21 NA, RG6, vol. 323, file 374, Kimberley to Young, 8 October 1870.
22 NA, RG7 G2, vol. 11, Dufferin to Kimberley, 26 December 1873.
23 Carnarvon to Dufferin, 17 June 1874, in de Kiewiet and Underhill, eds., *The Dufferin-Carnarvon Correspondence*, 47–8.
24 NA, RG7 G2, vol. 12, Report of Committee of the Privy Council approved 13 March 1876; Dufferin to Carvarvon, 16 March 1876, in de Kiewiet and Underhill, eds., *The Dufferin-Carnarvon Correspondence*, 200–1.
25 Macdonald Papers, vol. 294, Walkem to Macdonald, 29 January 1879; Margaret Ormsby, *British Columbia: A History* (Toronto: Macmillan, 1958), 278.
26 NA, RG6, vol. 44, files 2720–2, lieutenant-governor of British Columbia to secretary of state, 30 March 1881.
27 Macdonald Papers, vol. 119, extract from Minutes of the PEI Executive Council (printed) 31 January 1883; clipping from *Daily Examiner*, 19 March 1885.
28 NA, RG7 G12, vol. 85, Lansdowne to Holland, 4 January 1888.
29 Macdonald Papers, vol. 284, Tupper to Macdonald, 23 August 1887.
30 NA, RG7 G12, vol. 85, Lansdowne to Holland, 18 February 1888.
31 NA, RG2, series 1, vol. 388, Report of Committee of the Privy Council approved 10 March 1888.
32 NA, marquess of Lansdowne Papers, microfilm reel A-624, letterbook, vol. 5, Lansdowne to Knutsford, 19 March 1888.
33 NA, Lord Lisgar Papers, Kimberley to Lisgar, 3 June 1871.
34 House of Commons, *Journals*, 1872, 179.
35 Canada, *Sessional Papers*, vol. 6 (1873), no. 44, 63–4.
36 House of Commons, *Journals*, 1875, 178–9.
37 NA, marquess of Dufferin and Ava Papers, microfilm reel A-410, Mackenzie to Dufferin, 12 March 1875.
38 House of Commons, *Journals*, 1876, 55–6.
39 Joly's account of the interview is in NA, Henri-Gustave Joly de Lotbinière Papers, microfilm reel M-795, 8532–43.
40 Dufferin to Carnarvon, 31 March 1876, in de Kiewiet and Underhill, eds., *The Dufferin-Carnarvon Correspondence*, 204–5.
41 *Address of His Excellency the Governor-General of Canada on the Subject of the Relations between the Dominion Government and British Columbia in Respect to the Canadian Pacific Railway* (Victoria: Government Printer, 1876), 18.

42 Macdonald Papers, vol. 294, Walkem to Macdonald, 28 November 1881.
43 For a general discussion of this topic see Desmond Morton, "Aid to the Civil Power: The Canadian Militia in Support of Social Order, 1867–1914," *Canadian Historical Review* 51 (1970), 407–25.
44 Dufferin Papers, microfilm reel A-411, Mackenzie to Dufferin, 14 June 1878.
45 Ibid., reel A-414, Letellier to Dufferin, 13 June 1878.
46 Ibid., reel A-411, Mackenzie to Dufferin, 3 and 6 July 1878.
47 NA, RG7 G12, vol. 77, Dufferin to Hicks-Beach, 3 June 1878.
48 Dufferin Papers, microfilm reel A-409, Dufferin to Mackenzie, 18 June 1878.
49 NA, RG7 G3, vol. 6, Hicks-Beach to Dufferin, 16 July 1878, referring to telegram of 27 June 1878.
50 Dufferin Papers, microfilm reel A-411, Mackenzie to Dufferin, 6 July 1878; reel A-409, Dufferin to Mackenzie, 7 July 1878.
51 NA, RG7 G3, vol. 6, Hicks-Beach to Dufferin, 16 July 1878.
52 Ibid., G12, vol. 85, Aberdeen to Chamberlain, 29 April 1896.
53 NA, RG6, vol. 66, file 23821; vol. 310, file 355.
54 Ibid., vol. 36, file 837, Hicks-Beach to Lorne, 29 November 1878.
55 Ibid., vol. 66, file 23759.
56 NA, RG7 G12, vol. 77, Dufferin to Carnarvon, 6 June 1874 (acknowledging dispatch of 7 May 1874).
57 Dufferin to Carnarvon, 29 May 1874, in de Kiewiet and Underhill, eds., *The Dufferin-Carnarvon Correspondence*, 44–6.
58 NA, RG7 G12, vol. 77, Dufferin to Carnarvon, 31 December 1874; Dufferin Papers, microfilm reel A-409, Dufferin to Mackenzie, 19 November and 28 December 1874.
59 Macdonald Papers, vol. 284, Tupper to Macdonald, 19 December 1888.
60 Canada, *Sessional Papers*, vol. 23 (1890), no. 70, 3.
61 House of Commons, *Debates*, 1889, 903–8.
62 Macdonald Papers, vol. 528, Macdonald to Stanley, 16 May 1889.
63 NA, Lord Stanley of Preston Papers, microfilm reel A-446, Stanley to Macdonald, 17 May 1889.
64 Canada, *Sessional Papers*, vol. 23 (1890), no. 70, 8–9.
65 Ibid., 7, 15.
66 Ibid., 15.

CHAPTER 11

1 Canada, Senate, 1939, *Report to the Honourable the Speaker by the Parliamentary Counsel Relating to the Enactment of the British North America Act, 1867, Any Lack of Consonance between Its Terms and Judicial Construction of Them and Cognate Matters* (Ottawa: Queen's Printer, 1961).

2 Bora Laskin, "Peace, Order and Good Government Re-examined," *Canadian Bar Review* 25 (1947): 1054–87; Frank R. Scott, *Essays on the Constitution: Aspects of Canadian Law and Politics* (Toronto: University of Toronto Press, 1977).

3 J.R. Mallory, *Social Credit and the Federal Power in Canada* (Toronto: University of Toronto Press, 1954), 47–56.

4 The Benjamin theory was apparently invented by Arthur R.M. Lower, who erroneously stated that Benjamin only once supported a centralist position. See A.R.M. Lower and F.R. Scott, eds., *Evolving Canadian Federalism* (Durham: Duke University Press, 1958), 29.

5 G.P. Browne, *The Judicial Committee and the British North America Act* (Toronto: University of Toronto Press, 1967).

6 Pierre E. Trudeau, "Federalism, Nationalism and Reason," in P.A. Crepeau and C.B. Macpherson, eds., *The Future of Canadian Federalism* (Toronto: University of Toronto Press, 1965), 30.

7 Alan C. Cairns, "The Judicial Committee and Its Critics," *Canadian Journal of Political Science* 4 (1971): 301–45.

8 Gil Rémillard, *Le fédéralisme canadien*, vol. 1: *La loi constitutionnelle de 1867* (Montreal: Editions Québec/Amérique, 1980), 162.

9 B.L. Strayer, *Judicial Review of Legislation in Canada* (Toronto: University of Toronto Press, 1968), 3. For a somewhat different view see Jennifer Smith, "The Origins of Judical Review in Canada," *Canadian Journal of Political Science* 16 (1983): 115–34.

10 Joseph Pope, ed., *Confederation: Being a Series of Hitherto Unpublished Documents Bearing on the British North America Act* (Toronto: Carswell, 1895), 84–6.

11 Strayer, *Judicial Review*, 9.

12 W.E. Hodgins, *Correspondence, Reports of the Ministers of Justice, and Orders in Council upon the Subject of Dominion and Provincial Legislation 1867–1895*, (Ottawa: Government Printing Bureau, 1896), 6–60.

13 United Kingdom, Statutes, 58–59 Victoria, ch. 44.

14 Canada, House of Commons, *Debates*, 1875, 286–9.

15 Ibid., 976–80.

16 David M.L. Farr, *The Colonial Office and Canada, 1867–1887:* (Toronto: University of Toronto Press, 1955), 133–65.

17 James G. Snell and Frederick Vaughan, *The Supreme Court of Canada: History of the Institution* (Toronto: University of Toronto Press, 1985), 42.

18 Canada, Statutes, 54–55 Victoria, ch. 25.

19 (1874) 6 A.C. 31. Also in Richard A. Olmsted, *Decisions of the Judicial Committee of the Privy Council Relating to the B.N.A. Act 1867 and the Canadian Constitution 1867–1954*, 3 volumes, (Ottawa: Queen's Printer, 1954), I, 11–18.

20 (1875), 6 A.C. 272; Olmsted, *Decisions*, I, 19–30.

21 (1875), 3 A.C. 1090; Olmsted, *Decisions*, I, 30–42.

22 (1879), 5 A.C. 115; Olmsted, *Decisions*, I, 42–50.

23 (1880), 5 A.C. 381; Olmsted, *Decisions*, I, 66–93.

24 In the report of this case, Ross was erroneously referred to as the attorney general of Canada.

25 Canada, Statutes, 45 Victoria, ch. 67.

26 (1880), 5 A.C. 409; Olmsted, *Decisions*, I, 50–65.

27 (1881), 7 A.C. 96; Olmsted, *Decisions*, I, 94–124.

28 Ontario Statutes, 39 Victoria, ch. 24. For Mowat's resolution on insurance see Pope, ed., *Confederation Documents*, 30–1, 88.

29 Hodgins *Dominion and Provincial Legislation*, 281.

30 (1881), 7 A.C. 136; Olmsted, *Decisions*, I, 125–44.

31 (1882), 7 A.C. 829; Olmsted, *Decisions*, I, 145–59.

32 National Archives of Canada (NA), Alexander Campbell Papers, microfilm reel M-24, Macdonald to Campbell, 28 August 1882.

33 Canada, Statutes, 46 Victoria, ch. 30.

34 (1883), 9 A.C. 117; Olmsted, *Decisions*, I, 184–202.

35 *The Globe*, 3 January 1884, clipping in Macdonald Papers, vol. 98.

36 Western Counties Ry. *vs* Windsor and Annapolis Ry. (1882), 7 A.C. 178; Olmsted, III, 847–859.

37 (1883), 9 A.C. 157; Olmsted, *Decisions*, I, 203–16.

38 (1884), 10 A.C. 141; Olmsted, *Decisions*, I, 216–21.

39 (1887), 12 A.C. 575: Olmsted, *Decisions*, I, 222–36.

40 The minister of justice noted the petition for disallowance in his report of 5 June 1883. Hodgins, *Dominion and Provincial Legislation*, 307.

41 (1892) A.C. 445; Olmsted, *Decisions*, I, 272–86.

42 Brophy *vs* Attorney General of Manitoba (1895), A.C. 202; Olmsted, *Decisions*, I, 316–43.

43 (1894) A.C. 31; Olmsted, *Decisions*, I, 287–303.

44 Attorney General of Ontario *vs* Attorney General of Canada (1894), A.C. 189; Olmsted, *Decisions*, I, 304–16.

45 Ontario, Statutes, 48 Victoria, ch. 26. Before adopting the measure, Mowat urged the federal government to do so instead. Campbell Papers, microfilm reel M-22, Mowat to Campbell, 20 October 1879.

46 Attorney General of Ontario *vs* Attorney General of Canada (1896), A.C. 348; Olmsted, *Decisions*, I, 343–66.

47 Brewers and Maltsters Assn. *vs* Attorney General of Ontario (1897) A.C. 231; Olmsted, *Decisions*, I, 402–8.

48 (1896), A.C. 600; Olmsted, *Decisions*, I, 378–86.

49 Attorney General of Ontario *vs* Mercer (1883), 8 A.C. 767; Olmsted, *Decisions*, I, 171–83.

50 NA, Macdonald Papers, vol. 197, Campbell to Macdonald, 23 October 1885.

51 NA, RG2, series 1 (Privy Council Minutes), vol. 361, Minute of Council approved 12 April 1887.

52 St. Catharines Milling and Lumber Co. *vs* The Queen (1889), 14 A.C. 46; Olmsted, *Decisions*, I, 236–51.

53 Attorney General of British Columbia *vs* Attorney General of Canada (1889), 14 A.C. 295; Olmsted, *Decisions*, I, 251–63.

54 (1892) A.C. 437; Olmsted, *Decisions*, I, 263–71.

55 See A.V. Dicey, *Introduction to the Study of the Law of the Constitution*, 10th edition (London: Macmillan, 1961), 138–80.

56 *The Canadian Directory of Parliament 1867–1967* (Ottawa: Public Archives of Canada, 1968), 287. Among the cases in which he represented Ontario was Hodge *vs* The Queen.

57 Macdonald Papers, vol. 228, McCarthy to Macdonald, 7 March 1884.

58 NA, marquess of Lansdowne Papers, microfilm reel A-627, Thompson to Lansdowne, 28 July 1886.

59 Dicey, *Introduction*, 175.

60 Constitution of the Commonwealth of Australia, Section 74.

CHAPTER 12

1 Daniel J. Elazar, *The American Partnership: Intergovernmental Cooperation in the Nineteenth-Century United States* (Chicago: University of Chicago Press, 1962).

2 For an example of the orthodox interpretation see Gérard Veilleux, *Les relations intergouvernementales au Canada 1867–1967* (Montreal: Les presses de l'Université du Québec, 1971), especially 17–25.

3 A partial exception is W.H. McConnell, *Commentary on the British North America Act* (Toronto: Macmillan, 1977), 304–5.

4 Loren Beth, *The Development of the American Constitution 1877–1917* (New York: Harper and Row, 1971), 28.

5 See the testimony of Peter O'Leary in Canada, House of Commons, *Journals*, vol. 12, appendix 2 (1878), 35.

6 Province of Canada, Statutes, 4–5 Victoria, ch. 13.

7 J.E. Hodgetts, *Pioneer Public Service: An Administrative History of the United Canadas, 1841–1867* (Toronto: University of Toronto Press, 1956), 240–6.

8 Ibid., 40.

9 Province of Canada, Statutes, 13–14 Victoria, ch. 4.

10 House of Commons, *Journals*, vol. 2, appendix 7 (1869), 11.

11 Canada, *Census* 1870–1, vol. 5, 28.

12 Hodgetts, *Pioneer Public Service*, 255–6.

13 House of Commons, *Journals*, vol. 1, appendix 8 (1867–8), 1.

14 House of Commons, *Debates*, 25 November, 1867, 131.

15 Ibid., 9 December, 1867, 221.

16 Canada, Senate, *Debates*, 7 May, 1868, 256–60.
17 National Archives of Canada (NA), RG6, vol. 312, file 573.
18 House of Commons, *Journals*, vol. 2, appendix 7 (1869), 1–5.
19 NA, RG6, vol. 312, file 640.
20 Ibid., vol. 313, file 723.
21 Ibid., vol. 313, file 768.
22 House of Commons, *Journals*, vol. 2, appendix 7 (1869), 6–10.
23 Statutes of Canada, 1868–9, ch. 10.
24 NA, RG6, vol. 315, file 932.
25 Ibid., vol. 315, file 938.
26 Ibid., vol. 318, file 34.
27 House of Commons, *Journals*, vol. 3, appendix 5 (1870), 12.
28 Ibid., 2, 13.
29 Ibid., 8–9.
30 NA, RG17, vol. 2395 (unnumbered file), contains a complete account of the proceedings.
31 NA, RG6, vol. 321, file 264, Belleau to Howe, 25 May 1870.
32 Ibid., vol. 327, file 704, Kimberley to Dufferin, 15 March 1871.
33 Ibid., vol. 329, file 866–7.
34 Ibid., vol. 330, file 927.
35 Canada, *Sessional Papers*, vol. 8, part 8, no. 40, appendix 1 (1875), 1–2.
36 NA, RG6, vol. 317, file 1016.
37 Canada, *Sessional Papers*, vol. 8, part 8, no. 40 (1875), xviii-xix.
38 NA, RG6, vol. 338, file 222.
39 Ibid., vol. 335, file 1359.
40 Canada, *Sessional Papers*, vol. 8, part 8, no. 40, appendix 1 (1875), 6.
41 House of Commons, *Journals*, vol. 6, appendix 7 (1873), 5.
42 NA, RG6, vol. 338, file 150.
43 Canada, *Sessional Papers*, vol. 8, part 8, no. 40 (1875), v.
44 House of Commons, *Journals*, vol. 6, appendix 7 (1873), 15–6.
45 Canada, *Sessional Papers*, Vol. 8, part 8, no. 40, appendix 1 (1875), contains a complete account of the proceedings.
46 House of Commons, *Journals*, vol. 9, appendix 4 (1875), 8.
47 Ibid., 6.
48 NA, RG7, vol. 1665, Lowe to Jenkins, 11 December 1875.
49 Canada, *Census*, 1881, vol. 4, 14–15.
50 House of Commons, *Journals*, vol. 11, appendix 6 (1877), 55.
51 Ibid., vol. 12, appendix 2 (1878), 14.
52 Ibid., vol. 13, appendix 1 (1879), 14.
53 Ibid., vol. 14, appendix 3 (1880), 7.
54 Ibid., vol. 17, appendix 6 (1883), 26.

CHAPTER 13

1 A.V. Dicey, *Introduction to the Study of the Law of the Constitution*, 10th edition (London: Macmillan, 1961), 138–80; K.C. Wheare, *Federal Government*, 4th edition (New York: Oxford University Press, 1964).
2 Morton Grodzins, *The American System* (Chicago: Rand McNally, 1966).
3 Preston King, *Federalism and Federation* (Baltimore: Johns Hopkins University Press, 1982).
4 Garcia *vs* San Antonio Metropolitan Transit Authority, 469 U.S. 528 (1985)
5 Karl Lowenstein, *Political Power and the Governmental Process* (Chicago: University of Chicago Press, 1965), 405.
6 Donald V. Smiley and Ronald L. Watts, *Intrastate Federalism in Canada* (Toronto: University of Toronto Press, 1985).
7 Joseph Pope, *Confederation: Being a Series of Hitherto Unpublished Documents Bearing on the British North America Act* (Toronto: Carswell, 1895).
8 National Archives of Canada (NA), John A. Macdonald Papers, vol. 526, Macdonald to Richey, 14 May 1886.
9 Canada, *Parliamentary Debates on the Subject of the Confederation of the British North American Provinces* (Quebec, 1865), 21–3.
10 P.B. Waite, *The Man from Halifax: Sir John Thompson, Prime Minister* (Toronto: University of Toronto Press, 1985), 441.
11 Pope, ed., *Confederation Debates*, 425.
12 Ibid., 427.
13 Ibid., 331.
14 Ibid., 119.
15 Macdonald Papers, vol. 115, Howe to Macdonald, 16 November 1868.
16 N. Omer Coté, ed., *Political Appointments, Parliaments and the Judicial Bench in the Dominion of Canada, 1867 to 1895* (Ottawa: Thoburn and Co., 1896), 172. A complete list of senators with dates of appointment, death, or resignation appears at 165–77.
17 *The Canadian Parliamentary Companion*, 7th edition (Montreal: John Lovell, 1874).
18 Canada, Senate, *Journals*, vol. 3 (1870), 175–7.
19 Ibid., vol. 4 (1871), 107–9.
20 Ibid., vol. 9 (1875), 282–3.
21 Ibid., vol. 13 (1879), 227.
22 Canada, Senate, *Debates*, 1880 session, 247 (5 April 1880).
23 Senate, *Journals*, vol. 19 (1885), 406–7.
24 Ibid., vol. 21 (1887), 237
25 Ibid., vol. 24 (1890), 132–3.

26 Ibid., vol. 23 (1889), 158–9, 170–1.

27 F.W. de Kiewiet and F.H. Underhill, eds., *The Dufferin-Carnarvon Correspondence* (Toronto: Champlain Society, 1955), 80–1.

28 NA, marquess of Lorne Papers, vol. 1, Macdonald to Lorne, 17 December 1880.

29 Norman Ward, *The Canadian House of Commons: Representation*, 2nd edition (Toronto: University of Toronto Press, 1963), 100.

30 *The Canadian Parliamentary Companion* (Ottawa: G.E. Desbarats, 1867).

31 Ibid., 5th edition (Montreal: John Lovell, 1872).

32 J. Murray Beck, *Politics of Nova Scotia*, vol. I (Tantallon: Four East Publications, 1985), 112.

33 Macdonald Papers, vol. 521, Macdonald to Trutch, 25 September 1872.

34 Canada, House of Commons, *Journals*, vol. 1 (1867–8), 65–6; vol. 4 (1871), 75 and 163–4.

35 Ibid., vol. 3 (1870), 211–12.

36 Ibid., vol. 6 (1873), 77–9.

37 Ibid., vol. 9 (1875), 299.

38 Ibid., 305–6, 313.

39 Ibid., vol. 14 (1880), 68.

40 Ibid., vol. 20 (1886), 73–4.

41 Ibid., 99.

42 Canada, House of Commons, *Debates*, 1879 session, 1079–80 (8 April 1879).

43 House of Commons, *Journals*, vol. 18 (1884), 306–7.

44 Ibid., vol. 23 (1889), 205–7.

45 Ibid., vol. 24 (1890), 101–2.

46 Ibid., vol. 30 (1896), 138–9.

47 Macdonald Papers, vol. 37, Baker and Shakespeare to Macdonald, 22 May 1883.

48 Pope, *Confederation Debates*, 497.

49 Donald Creighton, *John A. Macdonald: The Young Politician* (Toronto: Macmillan, 1952), 471–4.

50 Brian Young, *George-Étienne Cartier* (Kingston and Montreal: McGill-Queen's University Press, 1981), 124.

51 Data from Canada, Public Archives, *Guide to Canadian Ministries since Confederation* (Ottawa: Supply and Services, 1982).

52 The members of these committees were listed in *The Canadian Parliamentary Companion*, editions of 1871, 1874, 1879, 1883, and 1891.

53 Macdonald Papers, vol. 528, Macdonald to Chapleau, 6 June 1888.

54 NA, C.H. Tupper Papers, microfilm reel M-107, Tupper to Bowell, 19 December 1894; Bowell to Tupper, 19 December 1894.

55 The influence of cabinet structure on federal-provincial relations is discussed by J. Stefan Dupré, "Reflections on the Workability of Ex-

ecutive Federalism," in Richard Simeon, ed., *Intergovernmental Relations* (Toronto: University of Toronto Press, 1985), 1–32.

56 Theodore Lowi, "Four Systems of Policy, Politics and Choice," *Public Administration Review*, 32, 4 (July/August 1972): 298–310.

57 Gordon Stewart, *The Origins of Canadian Politics: A Comparative Approach* (Vancouver: University of British Columbia Press, 1986).

58 Quoted in Robert M. Hamilton, ed., *Canadian Quotations and Phrases* (Toronto: McClelland and Stewart, 1952), 154.

CHAPTER 14

1 On the number of instances of emergency rule at the state level see A.T. Philip and K.H. Shivaji Rao, *Indian Government and Politics* (New Delhi: Sterling Publishers, 1981), 104.

2 Macdonald to Rose, 5 March 1872, in Joseph Pope, ed., *Correspondence of Sir John Macdonald* (Toronto: Oxford University Press, 1921), 165.

3 Alan C. Cairns, "The Judicial Committee and Its Critics," *Canadian Journal of Political Science* 14 (1971): 323.

4 J.R. Mallory, *Social Credit and the Federal Power in Canada* (Toronto: University of Toronto Press, 1954; reprinted 1976).

5 The classic analysis of these developments is C.B. Macpherson, *Democracy in Alberta: Social Credit and the Party System*, 2nd edition (Toronto: University of Toronto Press, 1962).

6 David E. Smith, "Empire, Crown, and Canadian Federalism," *Canadian Journal of Political Science* 24 (1991): 451–73.

7 On the difficulties of exporting American-style government see Fred W. Riggs, "The Survival of Presidentialism in America: Para-constitutional Practices," *International Political Science Review* 9 (1988): 247–78.

8 The implications of these developments for federalism are explored in recent writings by Alan C. Cairns, particularly in his *Charter versus Federalism: The Dilemmas of Constitutional Reform* (Montreal and Kingston: McGill-Queen's University Press, 1992).

Index

THE ANGUS L. MacDONALD LIBRARY
ST. FRANCIS XAVIER UNIVERSITY
ANTIGONISH N S